OUR MOTHERS' WAR

American Women
at Home and at the Front
During World War II

EMILY YELLIN

FREE PRESS   New York London Toronto Sydney

FREE PRESS

A Division of Simon & Schuster, Inc.

1230 Avenue of the Americas

New York, NY 10020

Permission credits appear on p. 448

FREE PRESS and colophon are
trademarks of Simon & Schuster, Inc.

For information about special discounts for bulk purchases,
please contact Simon & Schuster Special Sales:
1-800-456-6798 or business@simonandschuster.com

Designed by Elliott Beard

Manufactured in the United States of America

1   3   5   7   9   10   8   6   4   2

Library of Congress Cataloging-in-Publication Data
Yellin, Emily.
Our mothers' war: American women at home and at the Front during
World War II / Emily Yellin.
p.   cm.
Includes bibliographical references and index.
1. World War, 1939–1945—Women—United States.   I. Title.
D810.W7 Y45   2004
940.53'082'0973—dc22   2004040496
ISBN 0-7432-4514-8

To
CHRISTIE WATTS KELLY
1969–2002

For her unconditional love, wry humor, and unwavering belief in me and this book. My dear friend and guiding light, I miss you every single day.

And to
ARABELLA KELLY
and my godson
GRAHAM KELLY

For showing me how devotion, attachment, and hope live on.

CONTENTS

For Carol Lynn

UNEARTHING OUR
MOTHERS' WAR YEARS

Aﬀ︎TER MY MOTHER DIED in 1999, I was going through some of the things from her life that had made their way into my attic, when I came upon an old manila envelope I had never seen before, neatly labeled in my mother's handwriting, "Saipan Diary and Pictures." I knew right away it was from the time my mother spent as a Red Cross worker in the Pacific during World War II. Carefully, I extracted a number of thin, yellowing pages with typewritten entries on both sides, and about thirty pictures, in black and white. As I read my mother's words, her familiar voice resonating once again, and as I saw my mother's youthful image, the cheerful smile she wore in every picture ever taken of her glowing still, I felt like an archaeologist, unearthing a precious past. And then, under another pile of papers, inside four shoeboxes labeled "1940s," I found hundreds of letters my mother had written home to her parents in Oklahoma during World War II. My grandmother had lovingly saved every one of them. I was becoming a prospector, discovering gold.

I already knew a lot of the details of her war years. In August 1942, eight months after the attack on Pearl Harbor and America's entry into World War II, my mother, Carol Lynn Gilmer, had married Tom Heggen, a promising writer and an editor at *Reader's Digest*. She had just finished her bachelor's degree in history and master's degree in journalism at Northwestern University. After he joined the Navy, my mother was one of a couple of women hired in editorial jobs at *Reader's Digest* in New York to replace the men, like her new husband, leaving for war. In 1945, the last year of the war, she quit her job, joined the Red Cross, and was sent to Saipan. Right around that time, Tom Heggen began sending chapters to her of a novel he was writing while serving aboard his Navy cargo ship in the Pacific. When the war ended, my mother did not go back to her editorial work right away, but instead tried unsuccessfully to devote herself to being a full-time wife. After only a few months, in spring of 1946, she and Tom Heggen were divorced. Months later, the novel he had written, *Mr. Roberts,* was published. It centered around the crew of a supply boat in the Pacific, like the one on which he served, and the book's dedication read, "For Carol Lynn."

It went on to become a best-seller. The stage version won the 1948 Tony Award for best play. In 1955, the film version of *Mr. Roberts,* starring Henry Fonda, James Cagney, and Jack Lemmon, was nominated for best picture and won a best supporting actor Academy Award for Jack Lemmon. But in 1949, Tom Heggen was found dead, drowned in the bathtub of the New York apartment he was sharing at the time with writer Dorothy Parker's ex-husband, Alan Campbell. He had taken an overdose of sleeping pills.

Mom had talked to me about the pain of that marriage and her divorce and his death. But the happy ending was always that she moved on, met and married David Yellin, my father, her true love, a few years later, gave birth to my three older brothers and me, and continued a long editorial career at *Reader's Digest.* I had not asked much else about her time during the war. It never came up. Like most of us, I had mostly known the war through my father's stories of serving in the Army in Burma, not my mother's story.

Suddenly, sitting there on the attic floor, I was beginning to realize there were more dimensions in my mother's wartime experience than I knew. I saw that it had been a transforming time for her, a time when she first came into her own, exerted her courage and took advantage of new opportunities for herself, as a woman. In these letters and pictures, and her diary, I began to see the war through a new lens, a female perspective. It was an unfamiliar but intriguing view.

I found it in letters like the one to her parents dated January 4, 1945, in which my mother, then twenty-three, tried to explain her decision to leave *Reader's Digest* and join the Red Cross.

> Hope you can see how the Digest life is almost too perfect, with the world in the sorry mess it's in. . . . I just have to get out and try to do something active and direct when so many other people are doing so

much. It's not enough for me to say that my husband is doing it—and
that's my part in the war. I want to do something myself. Do you see
what I mean?

My grandparents did understand and wrote back supporting her move. But in
her grappling with that decision, I was learning what a huge step joining the
Red Cross had been for her. In her next letter I also recognized a younger version of the woman I remember, who organized Equal Rights Amendment
rallies in the 1970s and 1980s. The letter, dated January 8, 1945, showed prevailing attitudes about women and being a wife that my mother and many
other women faced down during the war.

> You see, when I decided to do this, I anticipated that lots of people
> would think I was doing a pretty foolish thing. I'm finding that lots of
> people who don't know the facts of the case think just that. Julie's
> husband Ken for example, who's one of these people who think that
> the only reason any girl joins the WACs, WAVES or Red Cross or any
> other such thing is just to have a wonderful time and meet lots of
> men. He thinks that I must be a pretty unstable sort of war wife who
> doesn't keep the home fires burning.
>   . . . And I expect that many other people, when I announce the de-
> cision more publicly will have the same reaction. But . . . I'm pre-
> pared for it. I don't expect everyone to heartily approve of what I'm
> doing. But now that I know that the people who really matter—my
> parents and Tom's parents think I'm doing the right thing, I have
> the moral reinforcement that I really do need. And I'll be able to go
> ahead with it now with so much greater peace of mind, and really
> work for what I'm trying to accomplish—establish a better and
> broader basis of understanding between Tom and me, while at the
> same time doing something direct and satisfying in the war effort.

In her diary too, I saw for the first time what it must have been like for a
woman in the mostly male world of war. Her good humor about it all is evident in this early excerpt from 1945, when she arrived by boat in Hawaii from
Seattle, before being sent to Saipan.

> APRIL 19 (THURSDAY)
> Tonight we went to our first dance overseas—at an on-post Red
> Cross club. And we got our first taste of the uneven ratio of men to

women in these islands. At this point, the ratio is about 75 to 1—
not nearly as bad as it used to be when it was 250 to 1. But even so,
if you don't bear it constantly in mind you begin to think you're
pretty irresistible. The boys are so grateful for small favors that it
hurts—just the fact that you come to their club and dance with
them seems to be the finest thing in the world. . . . Many told us it
was the first time they'd danced with any girl for more than a year.

And from my mother's writings, I was understanding for the first time
what ultimate sacrifices women made for the war. While women were not
usually the ones killed in combat, they were the ones who bravely had to endure the news, and keep going after husbands, sons, and brothers were killed.

WEDNESDAY, MAY 2
Today I was with Jean Archer when she received a letter telling of
her older brother's death in Europe. We were on our way to the
hospital to get our yellow fever shots. Jean had just picked up her
mail at headquarters. The first letters she opened were from
neighbors back home—letters of sympathy. . . . He was more than
an ordinarily favorite brother. I'd heard her speak of him so often
and had read some of his letters approving of her joining Red
Cross. She was very composed about it—didn't even break down
and cry until she was going through the rest of her mail and found
a letter from her brother himself—written only a few days before he
was killed.

When I read another entry in my mother's diary from 1945, after she had
arrived in Saipan, I saw the modest, initial stirrings that led to her support of
the civil rights movement living in Memphis during the 1960s. Though Americans were fighting injustice abroad, segregation was encoded in the U.S.
Army in 1945, just as it was encoded in the Jim Crow laws of the American
South at that time. And its inextricable partner, racism, was prevalent among
many Americans then too.

THURSDAY, MAY 31
Today I went on my first clubmobile run. Taking coffee and
doughnuts to the ground crews as they serviced the B-29s. . . . We
then began stopping and serving various working groups, engineers
and warehouse workers, road construction gangs, etc. One
interesting experience was serving Negro soldiers. I'm sure that for

most of them it was the first time they'd been served by Red Cross girls. Most of them had to be invited several times before they realized we wanted to give them refreshments. One of them said, "The good Lord must have sent you, ma'am." Another group said "Well, that's the first time I ever believed it about Red Cross being at your side, yes sir." Both Jean Quirk, the other girl I was working with, and I were very glad we'd stopped. And we almost didn't because we had quite an argument with our driver (an Indian boy from Oklahoma, incidentally) before we convinced him that we wouldn't be raped or murdered on the spot if we stopped to serve Negroes.

Among her letters I also found a few that my mom's former mother-in-law, Mina Heggen, Tom's mother, had written to my grandmother. Particularly telling was one letter, written in April 1950, in which mom's former mother-in-law talked about Tom's death, his marriage to my mother, and the war. Reading it, I found not only more insight into my mother's life, but also the pain of another mother who, although belatedly, felt she somehow had lost her son to the war as well.

I remember him [Tom] calling up right after they had separated and saying how badly he felt about it all. He said it was all his fault, that he had writing on his mind always, and knew he could not make her happy. It was too bad that the war separated them all those years. I think if they could have lived together, they might have understood each other better.

Tom was so adolescent when they were first married. He knew very little about girls, and really had no responsibilities until he got in the war. The war made him rather sad, so many of his friends killed and then that long weary stretch in the Pacific. He never would tell very much about his experiences but I know he grieved about it a lot.

As I sat on the attic floor, rooting through these mementos, musty and fragile from years in the other family attics that had held them, I got a sense that my mother and grandmother had left this bounty behind, carrying it with them through their years, as a gift for me somehow, a scavenger hunt map that was to lead me on a quest back to the rare reward of knowing my mother's life during her first big adventure, in an earlier time and place, before she was my mother.

It was that quest which led to this book.

I had always visualized World War II in black and white, just like the movies and photos from it. But all of this mining through my mother's war years was giving me a more personal connection. World War II started to take on color and dimension like never before. And I began to see those four years of the war as a kind of inadvertent revolution in America, a time when, while men were not really watching, women all over this country from every walk of life learned they could accomplish things they had never been allowed or asked to try before.

As the daughter of a woman who lived through it, I wanted to know more about women in that war. And as a journalist, I wanted to open up this world of our mothers and grandmothers for others. I saw that my scavenger hunt would not really end with the story of how my mother lived through the war. In fact, that was only the beginning.

Like many women during the war, my mother had planted a Victory Garden, volunteered at a USO canteen, and coped with rationing. And my mother had played a number of the roles that women all over the country played during that time—war bride, military wife, career woman, Red Cross girl. But what about the millions of women who worked in defense plants to produce the weapons that helped the Allies win the war? And what about the women who joined the military in noncombat positions in the Army as WACs, the Navy as WAVES, as Army pilots called WASPs, or in any of the other branches of the military that opened to women for the first time during World War II? And what about all the lesser-known stories that my writer's instinct was telling me were just waiting to be told?

Through my mother's experiences I had found a window to that larger story of what might be called "the other American soldiers" of World War II, who, like the men, displayed courage, experienced sacrifice, and endured heartbreak.

So I set out. Armed with the guidance my own mother's letters provided me, I began to, in effect, riffle through the memories stored in the attics of other women's lives from World War II. And sure enough, I found gems waiting there just like the pearls of drama I had found in my mother's story, all manner of gems—some smooth, some rough, some sparkling, some worn down—but all precious gems that have hardly ever been appraised or even displayed before.

PART I

Chicago
Tuesday, Dec 9, 1941

DEAREST FAMILY

Everyone is more and more shocked with the war news. . . . No one can talk of anything else and War discussions seem to have broken down all social barriers in Chicago. Perfect strangers start discussing it on El platforms and street cars. People walk down the street carrying portable radios with the war news on full blast. In fact it is really amazing the way the entire atmosphere has changed since Sunday.

Out at Evanston none of the university students can get any studying done at all. All the 11:30 classes were dismissed yesterday so everyone could hear the President's message asking for the declaration of war. I talked to Gordon Johnson and he says that it is certainly interesting to be living around a fraternity house. All the boys who are eligible for the draft are just waiting to be called. . . .

As far as my feelings go, I just can't seem to realize that I'm really a part of it. I feel entirely objective about the whole thing. I see crowds of people gathered around a radio or talking about the war, and I feel as if I were watching a play or a movie of what went on way back in 1941 when the war between the US and Japan started.

> Lots of Love,
> CAROL LYNN

CHAPTER ONE

To Bring Him Home Safely

WIVES, MOTHERS, AND SISTERS OF SERVICEMEN

Hail to the women of America! You have taken up your heritage from the brave women of the past. Just as did the women of other wars, you have taken your positions as soldiers on the Home Front. ... The efforts and accomplishments of women today are boundless!

But whatever else you do—you are, first and foremost, homemakers—women with the welfare of your families deepest in your hearts. ... Never has there been such an opportunity, and a need, for what American women can contribute.

So to you women behind the men, behind the guns, we offer this little book, with its daily helps for wartime mealplanning and cooking.

And we salute you all!

BETTY CROCKER, 1943[1]

Courtesy of James B. and Jean Murray

Aﬁer Pearl Harbor was attacked in December 1941, and the United States officially joined the war already in progress against Japan, Germany, and Italy, the warnings to young women started coming with a fury. From parents, from the clergy, on the radio, in newspapers and magazines, and even from boyfriends, they went something like this: Be wary of wartime romance. Hasty war marriages are recipes for heartache, for failure. Don't tie your fate to an uncertain future. There will be plenty of time for emotion after the war. Real love can wait.

Apparently, not everyone listened. Because despite the naysaying, 1.8 million couples married in 1942, a huge increase from the year before.[2] One bride of a young draftee described her reasons in the June 1942 *Good Housekeeping*.

> "He may come back a cripple. . . . The separation will break you up. . . . You can't tell how you'll change or how he'll change." Maybe. But I married my soldier anyway.
> . . . The deciding factor was the realization that this topsy-turvy world might not right itself for years. Perhaps my reasoning is perverse. But it seems to me that the world's chaos and uncertainty are reasons for marriage, not for postponement.

When the writer's boyfriend, Danny, got his draft card during Christmas vacation, he would not consider getting married. Like many men at the time, he didn't feel it was fair to her. But he changed his mind when the couple visited a friend, Irita, the wife of an Air Corps lieutenant.

> "If you love a man," Irita said, "you are involved in his destiny whether you are married or not. Everyone, in peace or war, runs a risk when he falls in love. A husband or wife may be killed crossing a street. If you want to protect yourself emotionally, the to do is not to fall in love at all."

It was too late to stop that. The couple had already fallen in love. And Irita's words finally swayed Danny to consider marriage. As they discussed it in earnest, their concerns echoed those of most couples on the brink of war marriages. They talked about how Danny may come back wounded, or missing a leg or an arm. She assured him she would love him anyway. They talked, as best they could, about the possibility he might not come back at all. They agreed to delay children until after the war. And they decided she would finish college and then find a job to help build a financial foundation for their postwar life. A young wife working had not been the norm before the war, but as the writer said, "This was no time to bother with peacetime conventions about the husband's being the breadwinner."

Finally, they set about convincing their parents. Warnings and concerns about the dangers of wartime marriages surfaced again. But after many talks and many tears, their parents warmed to the idea. As the writer said, "Danny and I are making the best of a difficult situation. In war, love is a luxury. It comes at a high price. . . . This brand of marriage, I guess, takes steady nerves." They were married New Year's Day 1942. She was nineteen and he was twenty-two. They believed the sacrifices they were making were worth it.

> Both Danny and I feel that the democratic way of life is deeply a part of us. We want to defend it with all we have, with all our heart and soul. We're young, we've got a future to fight for, we wouldn't want to raise those babies we're going to have in a country that wasn't worth fighting for.[3]

WAR BRIDES

And so it was for younger women all across the country, as young men joined up or were drafted, and left home. A book published in 1943 called *Marriage Is a Serious Business* was meant to sober up couples caught in a fleeting wartime romance, as its cautionary title suggests. The author, the Reverend Dr. Randolph Ray, was rector of the Little Church Around the Corner at Madison Avenue and 23rd Street in New York City, a popular marriage spot. According to the church's history, 2,900 weddings took place during 1943 alone, most performed by Reverend Ray. In fact, just about every Saturday, a line of young couples would form in the nineteenth-century church's idyllic, ivy-covered courtyard, waiting for their turn to say their vows, quickly, and without much fanfare or family present, and often just before the groom was to be shipped off to war. Not wanting to condone easy wedlock, Reverend Ray spoke clearly in the book of the pressures he saw facing wartime marriages, and especially war brides.

Reverend Ray opposed war marriages because he felt they lacked the essentials of enduring marriage. Instead of time for adjustment, he said, there is separation. Instead of shared experience, each partner is having new and often overwhelming experiences alone. Thereby, a gulf is created instead of a bond. And he singled out women as the ones who had the greater responsibility and duty to shoulder the majority of the emotional burdens in any marriage, adding that in wartime a woman's obligation grew more acute and intense.

> The problems of marriage are preponderantly the problems of women. Now, in time of war, the future seems to depend on what the women do today. Everything depends on that. The future is based on women's preparation for it.[4]

Yet, no amount of preparation could have braced many newlywed couples, both the women and the men, for the challenging terrain they were to travel during the four years of war.

Genevieve Eppens grew up on her parents' farm in Nebraska and was seventeen years old when she married her sweetheart, Glen, on February 19, 1942. He was twenty-one. As she said, they were "very much in love and just wanted to be together." But looking back, she saw they had no idea how painful fulfilling that simple wish would be.

> Both of us were so young and naive, how could we have imagined that we would soon lose all control of our lives?
>
> . . . How could we have known the next three-and-a-half years would seem like a nightmare, that I would become a mother and be traveling thousands of miles alone with a little baby just to see my husband . . . ?
>
> The war had begun December 7, 1941, but I really hadn't comprehended how it could affect us. I thought wars were something you studied about in history books. World War I had been fought long before I was even born. So, we had five wonderful months, and then we had to grow up real fast. . . .
>
> As the war intensified, my daily trips to the mailbox became a real worry to us. We knew one day his draft notice would be delivered

and in the latter part of July it arrived. We had often seen the poster of Uncle Sam pointing his finger and the caption "I Want You," and we knew he meant it. . . .

The week before he had to report, we moved our things to the farm [her parents' home] where I expected to stay for the duration. I was two months' pregnant and needed my parents to help me.

. . . We didn't dare think about the future. Our main concern was for him to be accepted in the Coast Guard or Navy. . . . Glen thought he would rather be on a ship than end up in some dirty foxhole.[5]

Glen was accepted into the Coast Guard and had one last evening with his wife and her family before he had to report for duty in Omaha at eight the next morning.

There was so little anyone could say, and finally the folks went back to finish whatever they were doing, and we slowly headed for our bedroom to be alone.

I don't remember if I slept that night or not. We were up early and all sat down to one of Mother's big farm-style breakfasts of home-made sausage, hot biscuits with gravy, and fresh eggs. When [his ride] arrived, Glen kissed my baby sister Wanda, Dad and Mom, and then my younger brother Willis, who burst into tears and stomped from the house muttering, "Those damn Japs!" Glen hugged me close, we kissed each other and both said, "I love you," and he was gone.

I stood at the door with my mother and father, watching the car disappear over the hill. I had been raised around people who didn't show their emotions. I was a seventeen-year-old girl, two months' pregnant, and had just felt the collapse of my world, but I didn't know how to react. Finally, I burst into a torrent of tears and ran into my parents' bedroom, threw myself across the bed, and sobbed for hours.

. . . The days passed slowly, one by one. . . . I received long letters from Glen every day, repeating over and over how much he missed me, how much he loved me, and how he wished he could feel our baby kick and move inside me. I wrote him every day and walked to and from the mailbox about a mile, with his little dog beside me. . . . I read and reread his letters as Butch and I walked back to the house. Neither of us had much news to write, but we poured out our hearts to each other, longing for the day when we could be together again.[6]

WAR WIVES AND THEIR CHILDREN

It was not only young brides who had to endure this strange new loneliness. Women who had been married for a while, and had children, also began to see their husbands head off to war. At first, men with families were exempt from the draft. But as the war escalated through 1942 and 1943, most able-bodied men between eighteen and thirty-five were either called away or volunteered.

The mail became the lifeline for many relationships. Many women wrote to their husbands every day. But delivery of the mail to and from overseas military outposts was sporadic. Sometimes, both on the home front and overseas, weeks or months would go by without a letter, and then in one day five letters would arrive. At least one mail carrier could not take the pressure. Mabel Wiggins remembered noticing that the mailman who had delivered to her home in St. Paul, Minnesota, for several years suddenly stopped coming.

> I said to a neighbor, "Isn't that funny? I thought our mailman just had a vacation." And she said, "He couldn't stand all the women left behind who were always meeting him at the door and saying, 'You don't have a letter for me this morning?' He said he just couldn't stand all the worry, so he asked to be put in the office somewhere."[7]

Isabel Alden used her letters to her husband to share the intimate feelings of a wife and mother putting her married life on hold for the duration of the war. She had met and married Maurice Kidder in the mid-1930s while they were students at the University of New Hampshire at Durham. They then moved to Boston, where Maurice attended theological seminary. And they had two children, Joel and Phyllis, before the war. Maurice joined the Army in the summer of 1942, and was shipped to England in October as part of the Chaplain's Corps. Isabel moved back to New Hampshire to finish her schooling while Maurice was away. In an October 1942 letter to him just after he left the country, and at the beginning of what was to become a three-year separation, she expressed her already piercing longing for him. She talked of walking home in the afternoon just after a football game ended between New Hampshire and Maine and seeing a sailor and his girlfriend happily holding hands. She watched how happy they were, "And a lump as big as a cannon ball came up in my throat," Isabel wrote, "remembering homecoming games last year and how happy we were, and just wishing we were back in school again, anyway, and all was safe."

As the first year of their separation dragged on through the summer of 1943, Maurice continued to serve as an Army chaplain in England. The Germans had surrendered Stalingrad in February. The Allies had taken North Africa in May, and they were making headway into Italy, which surrendered in early September. But those victories seemed remote in Isabel's letters, as she kept on expressing a penetrating loneliness for her husband. And in an August 1943 letter, she didn't hold back from showing Maurice the kinds of heartbreaking feelings she also had to face every day in their children. She reported that before their son, Joel, went to sleep one night he told his mommy he would like life better if his daddy just went to work each morning and came home at night, the way it used to be. Isabel told Joel she would like that better too. But then she tried to explain to their little son that thousands of daddies had to go to war to fight for our country. To which Joel replied, "And thousands of them will get killed too."

In October 1943 Isabel wrote to her husband about the mounting insecurities and emptiness she was facing within herself. She talked of feeling "pretty low at times," when she thought about her wartime life. "There is no real test of courage . . . in it," she wrote. Letting her worry build, she wondered how she would compare to "the women you will meet who are really doing things." She told her husband that all this inadequacy made her feel "hopeless" and "left out." Then she wrote, "You and I have never had anything big like this which we did not share before. What will it do to us?"

Isabel told her husband how thoughts of him were with her constantly, even as she went about her daily routine, getting dressed, going to the hairdresser, cooking, and "nagging at the children." She ended the letter with her longing for connection to his everyday life, expressing her need in a way that was safe to do only with a most trusted partner. "I wish, if it doesn't ask too much, that you would put what you think and feel as you go along, down on paper for me. Try, even though it is hard for you. Hold me close."

It is unclear from her letters if Maurice was ever stationed anywhere but England. If he was, it was only briefly. And by early 1944 he was still serving in Britain as an Army chaplain. Like most wives, Isabel followed as much news of the war and its progress as she could take in, but sometimes even a seemingly happy newspaper clipping could set off her personal despair, as she expressed in a March 1944 letter. She told her husband that she had gone to pieces when his mother sent her a newspaper clipping about a wedding in England. She began to read it not sure why his mother had sent it until she got to the end and realized that he had been at the wedding and given the toast. "It hit me like a ton of bricks," wrote Isabel. "I feel exactly as they say Mrs. Eisenhower feels on going to the movies and seeing her husband in the news reels. They say she can't go to movies at all hardly, for that is the thing that cuts her up the most." Isabel said the clipping brought home to her again "how completely vast a gulf exists between our lives. And what a full life you lead in which I have no part, and of which I know nothing."

Later in that same letter the recurring needs of a woman who has not been touched by her beloved husband in almost two years rose to the surface. She told how she wished he could come home. She explained that the longing was often unbearable. "I wouldn't describe to you in this letter just how it affects me, but you know. I knew exactly how I wanted you, and it hasn't dulled at all, not one physical symptom of it."

By the end of 1944, the war appeared to be wrapping up in Europe. D-Day in June 1944 had been such an encouraging turning point for the Allies. Peace seemed possible. But for Isabel, even if the fighting stopped overseas the war would not truly be done. Her dreams of peace would be complete only when she once again felt the physical presence of her husband.

> Oh honey, Monday morning in Chaucer class I got to picturing your back, just after you had taken your shorts off, and I could see those two little dimpled places you have, clear as crystal, and I wanted to sneak up behind you and put both arms around you and press my face against them, and I couldn't pay any attention to Chaucer. . . . Every time my mind slipped away from the subject at hand it went right to your back, and a lump came to my throat, and I had to blink all the time. There have been tears crowding up in me for nearly a week now. . . . I want to hear your voice, see your eyes looking deeply into mine, feel your hands searching my body, and be at peace.

Maurice finally came home from England in the late summer of 1945, after three years of separation from Isabel and their children. She finished her degree, and he received a master's degree from Yale Divinity School in 1946. Their third child, Alden, was born in 1947. They stayed together and Maurice taught and served at a small Massachusetts parish before he died in 1975. Isabel received an MA in poetry in the mid-1960s, and taught English until she retired in 1986 at the age of seventy-three. Isabel died in 1989.[8]

So many women were facing the same kinds of emotional hurdles as Isabel Alden that magazine editors and book publishers began responding. While most of the women's magazines freely acknowledged even the most personal problems women faced, they mostly offered martyrlike stoicism and contributions to the war effort as the acceptable solutions. The March 1942 *Good Housekeeping* had an example of such advice in an article entitled "Women Without Men," written for the increased number of women coping with absent husbands and man shortages brought on by the war.

Maxine Davis, the writer, spoke of three general categories of "manless women"—single women who expect to be married someday, older single women who don't, and women who are separated from their husbands, either temporarily, or permanently by divorce or death. She went on to present a surprisingly frank acknowledgment of a central problem for many women as they "fear that they may not be able to live successfully without normal outlets for an indefinite period of time." Then she asked: "Is the danger of developing serious neuroses as the result of sex deprivation real or imaginary? If the menace is authentic . . . what are the remedies?"

Her answer was "sublimation," which she defined as "the transferring of energy originally designed to emerge in sexual channels into paths that are not sexual. . . . Some medical men say that sublimation is successful repression." She went on to point out that "society, by imposing stricter rules of conduct upon women, makes the solution for them more difficult. That is why nervous symptoms resulting from repression are more prevalent among women than among men." And then she suggested that "most women really can work out their own emotional salvation, can achieve a successful repression." And the main means she advised by which to do that was through war work, volunteer or paid, or through concentrating on raising children and keeping their houses in order.

The magazine's final words on the volatile subject reflected an underlying ambivalence and dismissive attitude toward women's serious issues that often permeated this kind of seemingly caring public discourse during the war years. In the end, the magazine told women who were not able to achieve "successful sublimation" to visit a family physician.

He will know when there is a special need to bring in a psychiatrist; and in everyday cases he will prescribe the proper sports, exercise and other activities. As likely as not, in most instances he will say: "Forget it. There's nothing wrong with you that a little sunshine won't cure . . . go and lead your normal life, normally."

And as likely as not, he will be right.[9]

In a bit more considered attempt to address the wartime needs of some women, Ethel Gorham, a military wife, mother of a small child, and a fashion writer at Bonwit Teller department store in New York, wrote a book in 1942, *So Your Husband's Gone to War!* In it she offered lively, girl-to-girl advice. The book's introduction said: "This witty, wise, and practical handbook is designed to aid the wartime wife in solving the perplexities and problems of her strange, new, and husbandless world. . . . Mrs. Gorham advises all classes of war wives—the moneyed and the budget-minded, the career woman and the housewife, the woman with children and the woman without. . . . Mrs. Gorham . . . combines a deep understanding of the feminine mind with an alert awareness of the exact quality of the adjustment which every wartime wife must make."[10]

Gorham started the book with a portrait of how women first face the idea of their husbands going to war, and then hinted at some of what the war years may have had in store for these wives.

Perhaps you are the wife whose husband just couldn't stand it after Pearl Harbor and woke you up one morning about five and said, "Listen, dear, I can't sleep; it's no use, I'm going to volunteer."

. . . So many wives lost their husbands that eventful Sunday. . . . A quiet Sunday it was, weather good, cool but lovely. There was your husband, ears glued to the radio. Suddenly he looked across at you and you at him and he was a disembodied stranger. Eyes turned on distant places. . . . You saw his spirit go off to war that day and it was only a matter of time before his body would follow.

Well, good-by. You come home from the station or airport or the little gray ferry and it seems like a farewell to everything about life you love.

The everybody's-home-now feeling of a man in the house. The solid companionship of two big bath towels in the bathroom, two pairs of slippers under the bed, two people talking in the privacy of their souls. The security of depending on somebody else, of having somebody depend on you.[11]

After further acknowledging and giving voice to the wave of grief that was almost sure to descend on war wives, Gorham then admonished them with the prevalent idea that their duty was to buck up, meet the challenges, and surprise everyone, including themselves.

> After all, you've never had such a chance before of proving what you could get used to if you had to. You've been going along depending on the world. Now the world, your world, the world you and your husband have lived in together, is going to depend on you. It won't even exist unless you make it.

> You're going to have to balance a budget like you've never balanced before.
> You're going to have to take care of the children, if you have any, and decide the vital problem of whether to have one or not while the war is on.
> . . . You're going to have to keep your own roof over your head or decide whether to settle under another roof—and whose.
> . . . You're going to be lonesome; you're going to be unhappy, and many is the time you're going to be mad.
> . . . You're going to have to look for kindling wood in the unlikeliest places to keep the home fires burning.
> . . . You're going to discover that spare time can be a frightening thing unless you make it something else.
> . . . You're going to be baffled by the discovery that leaves are not always periods of unalloyed happiness.
> . . . You're going to learn how to wait and wait and wait. Waiting for letters. Waiting for phone calls. Waiting for leaves to come, waiting for leaves to end. Waiting for this war to be over with, so you won't have to wait any more.[12]

There were very few guidelines on negotiating the practical issues these women had to deal with during the war. Many young wives turned to their own mothers for aid, some in closer quarters than they ever expected. With wartime housing shortages and a soldier's wartime base pay at $50 a month, many women could not afford their own homes or apartments. Typically they either doubled up with other women or moved in with family members.

Patricia Davidson Guinan wrote "Back Home to Mother" in *House Beautiful* in August 1943 about what that decision could mean in a woman's life. She spoke of the bravery and pride of supporting a husband going off to fight a noble war. But once he left, she said, a woman may be faced with "the impossibility of maintaining your home alone," and may decide there is wisdom in moving back home to the family, despite the shock she might feel at first.

> Back in the room that was yours before you were married, you're brought up short by the startling realization that you are not the same person whose room this used to be, and for that reason your status in your mother's household has changed. You are not a guest and you are no longer an intrinsic part of the family. You have an entirely new set of interests which basically are the same as your mother's and yet, strangely their very sameness can be the cause of friction. You've been used to planning your own meals, entertaining when and whom you chose, trying to keep your food bills down and basking in the independence of a young married woman. But now you find yourself transplanted to another woman's domain and you resent being neither fish nor fowl.

The article then made suggestions for adapting to this "man-sized problem." It advised women to be neat, help out around the house, and chip in on household expenses. But the most pressing advice in the article was a refrain heard throughout the war in the messages conveyed to most wartime women in magazines, books, songs, and movies: "Lastly," the article stressed, "and perhaps most important of all, *don't mope!*" It said, "standing up to heartache and loneliness is your contribution to righting a topsy-turvy world." [13]

Moving home to family clearly disrupted the adult lives of war wives without children in significant ways. But dependence on extended family increased even more when pregnancy and childbirth were involved. Jean Lechnir of Prairie du Chien, Wisconsin, married Ray Lechnir in 1940. They had two children and she was pregnant with their third when Ray was drafted in 1944 and sent to Europe. Jean, suddenly a single mother, with two children and another on the way, moved in with her grandparents.

> At first you feel abandoned and you feel angry because they took him when you needed him more at home. Then you turn around and you feel proud because he was not afraid to go. He was afraid—they were all afraid—but he went and he was doing his duty, and we fig-

ured that was part of our job . . . to give our husband to the war effort and do the best we could without him. . . . But then after a while
you have lonely times, and especially when I had my son and my husband wasn't with me, and the lady in the bed next to me . . . her husband was allowed to come home to be with her with his sailor suit
on, and I was alone and that was a very traumatic time. . . . This
other gal's husband came in and mine was down in Arkansas being
trained to go overseas.[14]

Another woman described childbirth after her husband was unexpectedly
sent away to military training in Kentucky during the ninth month of her first
pregnancy. Since there was no maternity facility in the town where her husband was to be stationed, she had to go live with her husband's brother and
sister-in-law, whom she said she didn't like very much:

That was a very big trauma in my life. . . . Waiting every day to have
the baby. . . . When I went into labor my sister and her husband
drove me to [the hospital]. The conditions were such that there were
a lot of women having babies and no husbands around. And so you
had to make reservations. I had no reservations, so they put me in a
corridor; as soon as a room was open, or part of a room, they put me
in there. And my husband wasn't there, my family wasn't there—my
sister drove me in and left me, they couldn't stay. So I actually had the
baby alone. When I woke up. I had a baby and nobody was there.[15]

CAMP FOLLOWERS

Many women rebelled against the idea that they had to accept such exile from
their husbands. Many decided they were going to have as much time together
as they could while their husbands were still in the United States. These
women were often called "camp followers," because they followed their husbands from military base to military base. In previous wars, the term camp
followers had referred to women who flocked around military camps. One
connotation of the term implied that many were prostitutes. But in World
War II, camp followers generally meant military wives. They found whatever
housing they could, as near to their husbands as they could be, and took
whatever time he had left over after the military got their allotment of him.
But these camp followers were often resented by other women and men on

the home front, seen as not making the same kinds of sacrifices as everyone else, not strong enough to take the real heat of wartime.

And their presence was often unwelcome on already overloaded trains, in strange towns, and even in long grocery lines when food rationing was implemented. Many thought that instead of traipsing across the country using up valuable space and resources, these women should instead stick close to home and do something more useful, less selfish, for the overall war effort.

The August 30, 1943, *Time* magazine described "a strange, unorganized home-front battle being fought all over the U.S. by a vast, unorganized army of women. They are the wives, mothers, sweethearts or fiancées of service men. Their only plan of campaign is to follow their men. The enemies these women must fight are the painfully crowded transportation system, soaring prices and low military pay, appalling housing shortages and brutal rent gouges, plus the thousand and one exasperating accidents of fortune—the missed connections, wrong addresses . . . the unpredictable changes in military orders which can cancel out months of planning and thousands of miles of travel."[16] But camp following was only allowed in the United States; once the men were shipped overseas, the women went home.

In *The New York Times* on October 3, 1943, Helen B. Sweedy, a camp follower herself, wrote "I'm Following You," in which she interviewed other wives about their reasons for camp following, and then gave some justification of her own:

> In answer to the question, "Why do you think it's worth while to follow your husband?" she said, "How do Tom and I know how long we can be together? He might be ordered overseas next week. So we figure that even a few hours are better than nothing. When he's sent over, I'll go back and get a job. But until that happens I'm going wherever he goes."
>
> . . . Our merit badge is a "Gee, I'm glad you're here darling!" As long as we get that response I'm afraid no amount of outside moaning about "selfishness" will hit us very hard. Of course, if Uncle Sam says, "No more," that will be different. Till then, boys, we're following you.[17]

There were few hard numbers on how many women became camp followers during the war, since, as *Time* magazine reported in 1943, no one agency had any coordinated information on them. Only when the women ran into some sort of trouble did agencies like Traveler's Aid, the USO, the Red Cross, or Army and Navy relief agencies come into contact with them. Traveler's Aid reported 885,000 cases in 1942, about six times the total for 1941. In the first six months of 1943 the total rose to 1,250,000. But there was no doubt that there were a great number of additional women who did not contact any agency in their travels after their husbands.[18]

Barbara Klaw's husband joined the Army before Pearl Harbor and was sent to training in Camp Crowder, Missouri. After America joined the war, she gave up her job in Washington, D.C., and followed him. In 1943, her book, *Camp Follower: The Story of a Soldier's Wife*, came out, chronicling her experiences. By then, her husband had been sent to England and she was working as a reporter at the *New York Post*. She described the status of camp followers when she told of her departure from a Kansas City train station on her way to be with her husband.

> I began to run into the society of wandering Army wives in whose company I was to spend the next few months. Lugging baggage, tired and lonely, but all excited, they were going to see their husbands, some for a visit, some for as long as possible. They were mostly young, mostly well dressed, mostly attractive. That morning there were hundreds of us congregated in the Kansas City station.
>
> We stood in front of the train gate, jockeying for position, waiting. It isn't only the men in the Army who get used to waiting—the Army wives get used to it, too. Waiting in train stations, waiting for husbands who might be scouring pots in the messhalls and can't let you know. In time I was to learn the art of waiting—of stretching out little tasks and insignificant thoughts.

Klaw commented on a sign in the station that said, "Servicemen will board all trains before civilians," and pointed out that while she supported the concept, after a few weeks of such deferring she began to "feel like an excessively useless object, or a member of a persecuted class." Once on the train, she met another wife who had just returned from visiting her husband who filled her in on one of the problems of camp following.

> "I stayed at the Guest House," she told me. "There isn't a town anywhere around. My God, you can't imagine that place. The men weren't allowed to come up to our rooms, and you had to hide in a

telephone booth to kiss your husband goodnight. I finally left before
I had to. My husband was getting frustrated."

Indeed, the Army and other services were not very accommodating to
these women. They kept no records of them and provided no financial or
practical support for them. It was the being with him that kept them going,
the shared experiences with their men they were after. But the first meeting
was sometimes jarring, as a friend had told Barbara Klaw it might be.

> "It's a shock when you first see your husband," she had said. "In
> strange clothes, and talking somehow differently. And the worst
> thing is that they even look different."

Klaw settled into a room in a boarding house in a town near her husband's
base and began her life as a camp follower, spending as many hours a night as
she could with her husband and seeing him off on a ten o'clock bus.

> I didn't even feel sad when I saw him take his place among the GIs to
> ride back to camp. I stood outside the window he was sitting by and
> chatted with him till the bus pulled out, feeling gay and permanent,
> and knowing he would be back the next evening, and that I would be
> there in our new room waiting for him. It isn't much to see your hus-
> band two hours a day, but after not seeing him at all, it seemed pretty
> wonderful.[19]

As *Time* magazine said in 1943, "When a service wife sets out to follow her
husband, nothing is sure to stop her except the man's departure overseas.
Thus it seems certain that as large bodies of troops are shifted around in the
U.S., the woman's army will move in their train."[20]

RATIONING

Rose Truckey was pregnant and newly married when her husband was
shipped overseas in 1944. So she moved back from Rockford, Illinois, to her
hometown of Racine, Wisconsin, where her parents lived. That is where she
began to learn about the effects of wartime shortages.

> You're starting to buy all these things for the baby. You're looking for diapers, and they didn't have diapers then. You had flannel.
>
> . . . But then you couldn't even buy flannel because it was the war. Well, the man next door to us worked at Penney's. He was the assistant manager, and so when flannel came in he brought me a bolt of flannel, so we cut that up and made diapers of that. It was terrible, really, when you stop and think of it. You just couldn't get anything. I had a highchair from when I was a very little girl. . . . But we bought a buggy. We found one of those collapsible buggies, so we were lucky.

Another effect of shortages was that women began to stick together more in the face of limited resources. Rose Truckey said:

> You could always make sure that somebody would be there if you needed them because you couldn't depend on a man, there weren't any around. So it was really what we could do for ourselves.[21]

Another expectant mother wrote her military husband in February 1943 about how the normal cravings of a pregnant woman were harder to satisfy in the face of civilian food shortages. Ships that once carried imports from South America were being diverted to wartime transport. So even a fruit that was taken for granted before the war became exotic.

> Last night . . . I dreamed was that I was eating banana splits one right after the other and were they good! When I awakened I thought to myself, "Boy, what I wouldn't give for a nice banana." But that is just wishful thinking. I don't think anyone in America has seen a banana for over six months.[22]

Indeed shortages and rationing altered the lifestyle of all American civilians during World War II, but the impact on the lives of the women in charge of running a home reached into most aspects of their daily routines. In a report to the National Academy of Sciences by the Committee on Food Habits, an advisory committee of social scientists headed by anthropologist Margaret Mead, women were pegged as the ones in the family through which the government could influence and alter civilian eating and shopping habits, as necessary, during wartime. The committee's report said, "In all daily matters of food choices and preparation, women, and particularly mothers and wives, play a leading role."[23]

Changing Americans' attitudes toward consumption was no small task. During World War I rationing had been voluntary, and many agreed it had not worked. But with World War II the United States had a bigger job on its hands. The U.S. was once again responsible for feeding and clothing its military. But the government had also taken on more responsibility in this war for stemming food shortages in Allied nations like Britain and Russia, as well as in newly liberated countries.[24]

In addition, there was a new psychological barrier to all this on the home front. During the Depression of the 1930s, goods were available but very few people had enough money to buy what they needed. In fact, people had seen the government pay farmers to destroy tons of surplus food that no one could afford and ask factories to slow down production because no one had enough money to buy much. Now the government was telling its citizens that the problem was the opposite. Because of the boom in production that the war brought on, America had recovered from the Depression, so people had money again. And the factories and farms were producing at a breakneck pace. But everything produced had to go toward the war effort first. So the newly flush civilians were seeing factories and farms buzzing with activity but still were being asked to cut back their consumption.[25]

Also, in the earliest part of the 1940s, as America's economy was recovering, the government set out to reeducate the public on the subject of nutrition, a concept that had gone by the wayside for many during leaner times. Then, after Pearl Harbor in late 1941, it became evident that some rationing might have to occur, since people began hoarding some items, and supplies from other countries were blocked, making production of certain items almost possible. For example, Japanese invasions of rubber-producing areas of the Pacific meant the United States's rubber supply was essentially cut off. Tires became precious. The solution, as the government saw it, was to ration not only rubber products but gasoline too. That way, people would not unnecessarily wear down the tires they already had.[26] Soon clothes and shoes were rationed as well. Even girdles were threatened with rationing for the rubber they contained, until women cried out so loudly against it that the government relented on that idea.[27]

The first food item to be rationed, in May of 1942, was sugar. Later that year coffee was rationed. And by the end of 1942, the government had rationed red meat. Though never rationed, butter, milk, and eggs were also scarce in some places. People were also encouraged to plant fruit and vegetables on any spare patch of land they had, to compensate for what American farmers were diverting from civilians to the military. These personal plots of produce were considered the patriotic thing to do, so they became known as Victory Gardens. And women were encouraged to can and preserve this home-grown food for the winter months.[28]

The Office of Price Administration oversaw rationing through a network of ration boards in every county in the nation. There were three types of rationing. First, there was a complex system of ration books with stamps for a weekly or monthly allotment of some items, such as sugar and coffee. Then, as items with varying grades of quality were rationed, a system of assigning points based on value was also implemented. So, better cuts of meat required more ration points from a weekly allotment of points. And a third factor was used in some rationing too—need. For gasoline, those who did the least driving were given an A stamp, allowing them four gallons of gas per week. Those who needed more, such as workers at war plants driving carpools to factories each day, were given B and C stamps, allowing them more gasoline.[29]

One wife wrote her husband in February 1943 about negotiating the shortages and rationing.

> Last week we didn't have a scratch of butter in the house from Monday until Friday—and how I hate dry bread! It's a lot worse on we people in the country than it is on the city folks. They can go out and get some kind of meat every day while we have plenty of meatless days here. They can also stand in line for 2 or 3 hours for a pound of butter, but up here there are no lines as there is no butter and when there is a little butter everyone gets a ¼ of a pound. So you can imagine how far a ¼ of a pound goes in this family of five adults. And that's supposed to last us for a week.[30]

Saidee Leach, a Rhode Island mother, responded to her son Douglas's letters from the Pacific, in which he mentioned the steak he was eating in the Navy. She, in turn, told him about the meat she was using in her kitchen. She seemed to have heeded the advice many magazines gave women to keep letters to soldiers cheerful and upbeat, as in this December 1944 letter to her son.

> No, I am not envious of your eating steak, for we want you men to have the best. . . . Last week I bought a piece of beef called Utility

Grade which is so far below Grade A that no points were required and by adding catsup to the kettle which helped to tenderize it, we had one of the nicest stews I ever made, but often we will get a pot roast that no amount of working can make tender.

In a January 1945 letter she told him more of their circumstances, still careful not to complain.

Possibly you have been reading of the severe cold and fuel shortage. We are very comfortable, have not had to shut off any rooms and Marilyn is still sleeping upstairs. We can only have a ton of coal at a time and ours had just been delivered and since then, the only way to get any is a bag at a time from the municipal coal yard and bag it yourself! I remember when Grandpa Raybold had to do that in the last war. It still is very cold. . . . But the weather should warm up in a week or two and that will ease the situation.[31]

Advertisers, magazines, newspapers, and food companies responded to the challenges women faced in negotiating the shortage and rationing situations by publishing articles, booklets, and cookbooks to help. One important source of information in that effort was one of the most trusted homemakers in America during World War II—Betty Crocker. However, she was not a real woman, but a creation of the makers of Gold Medal flour. After being flooded with baking questions from their customers, the Washburn Company of Minneapolis, which later became General Mills, had created the persona of Betty Crocker in 1921 to give a more personal touch to their answers. She had gotten her name by taking the last name of a retired company executive, and the first name Betty, because her creators thought it sounded warm and friendly. Her trademark autograph was the winning entry from a contest for the most distinctive signature among the company's pool of secretaries.

In 1936, Betty got a face when an artist came up with a composite of all the employees in General Mills Home Service Department, the area in charge of Betty's products and persona. Soon that face was everywhere, along with her signature. She put out cookbooks and appeared on the radio and in women's magazines. The idea that she was real, or at least a real presence, seemed to have penetrated the consciousness of the country, because in 1945, a *Fortune* magazine poll named Betty Crocker the second most famous woman in America, after First Lady Eleanor Roosevelt.[32]

In 1943, the Home Service Staff of General Mills published a Betty Crocker "cookbooklet" called *Your Share: How to Prepare Appetizing, Healthful Meals with Foods Available Today.* Its foreword, with a picture of the motherly-looking Betty Crocker and bearing her familiar signature at the end, said, in part:

> Now you face a new and more difficult problem in the management of your homes. You must make a little do where there was an abundance before. In spite of sectional problems and shortages, you must prepare satisfying meals out of *your share* of what there is. You must heed the government request to increase the use of available foods, and save those that are scarce—and, at the same time, safeguard your family's nutrition.[33]

One of the many recipes in *Your Share* was something called War-time Cake:

WAR-TIME CAKE . . . Eggless, Milkless, Butterless

Mix in a saucepan
    1 cup brown sugar
    1¼ cups water
    ⅓ cup lard or other shortening
    2 cups seeded raisins
    ½ tsp. nutmeg
    2 tsp. cinnamon
    ½ tsp. cloves

Boil for 3 min.

Cool.

Then add
    1 tsp. salt and 1 tsp. baking soda dissolved in 2 tsp. water

Blend in 2 cups *sifted* GOLD MEDAL Flour mixed with 1 tsp. baking powder

Pour into greased, floured 8-in. sq. pan. Bake *about 50 min.* in *slow mod. oven* (325°). Delicious uniced.[34]

Variations of that same war cake appeared in many wartime cookbooks. The famous food writer M. F. K. Fisher talked of one in her 1942 book, *How to Cook a Wolf:*

A surprisingly good cake, which I loved so much in the last war that I dreamed about it at night, and which I have tried on this war's children with practically the same results, can be whipped together and put in the oven with the ham and whatever else you are storing up for the week ahead. It is called War Cake, for want of a pleasanter name, and it is a rather crude moist dark loaf which keeps well and costs little.

. . . War cake can be made in muffin tins, and baked more quickly, but in a loaf it stays fresh longer. It is very good with a glass of milk, I remember.[35]

WOMEN'S MAGAZINES

Throughout the war, women's magazines played a pivotal role in both reflecting and influencing women's lives. As Nancy A. Walker pointed out in a study of women's magazines during the middle part of the twentieth century: "With the stresses and shortages of wartime, the advice-giving function of the women's magazines took on a particular sense of urgency. Both articles and advertisements offered information on product rationing, tips on keeping the family healthy, guidelines for thrifty shopping, counsel on parenting . . . and, of course, advice on how to look good through it all. The ideal middle-class homemaker that emerges cumulatively from the pages of the magazines is efficient, vigilant, self-reliant, and at the same time the emotional center of the home."[36]

Newspapers, radio, and posters in public places were the only other outlets besides magazines to reach wide audiences. But when the government needed to convey messages to American women, women's magazines were a prime place they turned. In fact, the government issued a monthly *Magazine War Guide* to hundreds of magazine editors detailing guidelines on how their content, focus of articles, and photographs could support the war effort. Women's magazine editors were encouraged to highlight women coping nobly, unselfishly, and efficiently with their sacrifices and pressures during wartime. If housewives were the specific target audience the government wanted to reach with a particular war-related advertisement or article, *Ladies' Home Journal* was considered one of the most trusted venues. Plus, it was the most read women's magazine during wartime, with a circulation of more than four million.[37]

In 1942, *Ladies' Home Journal* even started touting its own catch-all, volunteer coalition that it called WINS (Women in National Service), made up of its readers. Thirty-two governors' wives became state chairs of WINS. In the March 1943 magazine the WINS obligations were lauded mightily:

> You are in charge at home for the duration: twenty million of you, with no uniforms or titles; on twenty-four hour duty, with no days off, and no furloughs till it's over. There won't be any citations—and you won't expect one. Medals aren't awarded for taking care of the two and a half million babies born last year, for washing behind the ears of ten million children under five and getting another twenty-five million off to school every morning.[38]

Throughout the war, the magazine published WINS tips in its pages for housewives and even offered WINS booklets that women could order from the magazine for 25 cents, such as the *Wartime Homemaking Manual,* which promised "answers to hundreds of wartime housekeeping problems." One such tip from the manual was:

Bring Out the Soup Tureen

> Salvage in the soup pot every bit of flavor and good from foods that would otherwise be wasted. A little meat goes a long way. Rice, oatmeal, noodles, barley, etc. add backbone. Start a meal with soup, or let it be the main attraction.[39]

Another popular and telling *Ladies' Home Journal* feature, which began in 1940 and continued to run in every issue during the war and on into the 1960s, was called, "How America Lives." A number of different articles in an issue focused on one representative American family, to convey the way they lived at home in their everyday lives.

In May 1944, the series looked at the Faulds family, who lived on an orange grove in Clearwater, Florida. Ten articles and many photographs portrayed them as a wholesome, All-American family facing typical wartime issues. Almira and Norval Faulds had six children, three sons and three daughters. Their son Vincent, twenty-five, had become a prisoner of war when his plane was shot down over Italy in 1943. Another younger son, Stanley, was just about to enlist.

But it is the magazine's portrayal of the Faulds's women that gives the most insight into public expectations of the wives, mothers, and sisters of the approximately 12 million men who were in the armed services during World War II.

Almira, the mother, was a teacher of home economics at the local junior high, and her husband, Norval, was the school's principal. Almira was described admiringly in the series as "plump" and "peppy," and "the kind of cook whose cake people clamor for at church suppers." She radiated contentment in all the pictures of her. As she sat in the family living room with her children and grandchildren around her, she beamed. She glowed as she shared time reading with her husband in the new chairs in their bedroom, redecorated courtesy of *Ladies' Home Journal*. And she transmitted an air of pleasant assurance and efficiency as she was pictured teaching household management and canning to the girls in her junior high home economics classes. Even in the lead picture in the series, showing Almira and Norval reading Vincent's letter from the prisoner of war camp, Almira's face conveyed motherly concern, but a gentle and calm brand of it.

One of the articles in the series, written by a male psychiatrist and titled "What Makes a Good Wife," used Almira as a shining example of how women could find true and ultimate success through homemaking.

> So much recent popular literature has emphasized "the facts of life" as the basis for success in marriage that it is a delight to find a teacher of homemaking like Mrs. Norval Faulds, of Clearwater, Florida, who approaches the subject from the standpoint of daily living. Exceptionally successful herself as a mother of six and a homemaker extraordinary, she considers such practical aspects as household management and budgeting the main points because, she says, their tremendous importance for happy marriages has been all but forgotten today. . . . I can testify to the sound basis for Mrs. Faulds' idea. I am not denying the essentials of healthy physical and intellectual companionship between husbands and wives when I say it is simply slovenly housekeeping, bad management of money and bad cooking which are at the root of innumerable divorces.[40]

Looking back sixty years later, Almira's youngest daughter, Ruth, said of the way her mother was presented in the magazine, "I think she enjoyed the whole thing. But I don't think it portrayed her in any depth. It wasn't inaccurate, but I don't think a great deal of soul searching went into the reporting."[41]

The magazine called Ruth, then twenty-one, a "sedate senior at Florida State College for Women." Ruth said that while she too had fun working with the editors and going to New York for a makeover, she also felt she was cast in a role by the magazine that did not fit her reality. Ruth had majored in chemistry and already had a job lined up after graduation in a lab, a job that was available partly because the men who would have gotten those jobs were in the military. But she said she sensed that the magazine's editors would rather she had not been so career-minded. "I think," said Ruth, "that they were really disappointed in me that I wasn't going into a job that was more directly war-related—the shipyards or the services, the WACS. Here my brother was a prisoner of war and I certainly should have been going to do everything I could to get him home." [42]

In fact, an article about college women finding jobs never mentioned Ruth, even though an accompanying photo showed Ruth in a stylish white lab coat cinched at the waist. She was well coiffed and well manicured, with the liquid-filled glass tubes she might use in a chemistry lab surrounding her. Another photo for that article showed Ruth and a number of her classmates lying on a dorm room bed chatting. The photo's caption said, "Girl graduates are facing a topsy-turvy situation today. In typical 'huddles,' Ruth and her friends make future plans." Instead of focusing on Ruth, the article emphasized the obligation of young, unmarried women, many with brothers in the military, to contribute directly to the war effort.

> Your first duty is to see if you cannot be of value to your country in uniform. . . . The girl who qualifies for a uniform of navy, khaki or olive can well feel an inward glow; first, because she has proven, by being accepted, that she has a 1-A mentality and well co-ordinated body, and second, because there will never need be any doubt in her mind that she has given her best to the war effort. She can be proud all her life. She will share, as outsiders will never be able to do, in the richest memories of a generation of fighters. [43]

Ruth's oldest sister, Melisse Faulds Meeth, then thirty, also was mentioned in the lead article on the family. The caption below a photo of her, pictured with her two children arriving home from Alabama, contained a quotation from her mother: "We thought Melisse might be a career woman, with such a high I.Q. But she married at 18, proving she was smarter than we thought!" [44]

Ruth said that quotation did not ring true either. "I doubt my mother ever said that. There wasn't any emphasis in my family that we had to get married." In fact, with two teachers as parents, Ruth said, the idea of a college education was much more important in their family than any pressure on the women to marry.[45]

Many years later, after retiring from a teaching career that she had built after raising her kids, Melisse wrote a memoir called *How Dear to My Heart* for her grandchildren in which she described her war circumstances. It is perhaps a more genuine portrait than the depiction in the magazine of how a lot of American wives, mothers, and sisters lived during the war.

> Those of us who stayed home escaped the danger and discomforts which many of the men and women in the armed services experienced. But there were difficulties and hardships for us too, imposed by a nation at war. As America changed from a peacetime economy to full war production, thousands of people were uprooted and moved across the country to work in shipyards and factories. My husband, Lou, was working in the field of vocational education. He was in his 30s, the father of two children, and probably would not have been drafted. But like so many others at the that time, he was prompted by his patriotism to volunteer for officer candidate school in the Navy.
> . . . Months went by and we heard nothing.

In December 1942 Lou took a job as personnel training director at a shipbuilding company in Mobile, Alabama. Since he had not heard from the Navy and was so anxious to be a part of the war effort, he jumped at the civilian war job. Two weeks later, the Navy commissioned him. But by then his job was classified as essential war work and the company would not release him. Melisse began adjusting to life as the wife of a war worker.

> Living in a village and housing development owned by a large corporation, especially during the war years, was an experience very different from any I have encountered. . . .
> Some of the best friends of my life were made during those years. . . . We were all far from home and families then. We all had young children and we knew that these years would be a temporary interlude. We needed and depended on each other.
> We kept each other's children and shared the marketing which consumed so much of our time.

. . . The hardships were the very basic problems of finding enough food to nourish the children, and getting the laundry done. A number of foods, meat, sugar, coffee and fats among them, were rationed. But it was not there that the problem lay for us. With the influx of war workers to the shipyards, the population of the Mobile area had quadrupled in a few months time. Food allotments to the area were made on the basis of the last census. There was simply not enough food to go around and little in the stores to buy, whether one had rations stamps or not.

There was no meat. If you found any it looked so bad that its source was questionable and you were afraid to buy it. After some months, we found a farmer 30 miles up in the country who would sell us chickens and eggs. One of us women would drive up every couple of weeks and bring back a dozen chickens and a case of eggs to be shared among the four or five families. Those, with the fairly plentiful shrimp and fish, provided our protein for four years.

Lines were everywhere. I refused to stand in line for anything except the necessities but milk was a necessity for the children. If you were not in line when milk was delivered to the grocery you got none. Even if you were it might be gone before you reached it. This took an hour or more at least every other day. Usually, a bottle or two would be dropped and broken in the snatching and grabbing melee that ensued when the first cases were set down.

Even the youngsters joined the "seek and hide" game. . . . Rick [her son] and a couple of his cronies spent many hours hanging around the stores. If some scarce item, such as soap powder, was put on the shelves each boy would take one and hide it behind some other goods in the store. He then ran home to tell his mother where he had hidden it.[46]

The Faulds had learned to live with those kinds of restrictions, but also with the uncertainty of Vincent's fate. Vincent's mother, Almira, had said in the magazine, "I never dreamed I'd see the day I'd rejoice to hear my son was a prisoner of war, but for anguished weeks when he was missing, we thought we'd lost him."

Melisse also spoke of that uncertainty, fear, and anguish:

The greatest hardship, of course, for those who were left at home, was the secret and constant anxiety for those we loved. It was seldom

spoken but always there as we read and listened to the news, following the course of the war. . . .

Vincent was a flight leader with the 310th Bomb Group, stationed
near Tunis. By May 1943 he was flying B25s over Italy in preparation
for the first invasion of the mainland by ground forces.

The human animal is so constituted that no matter how grave our
fears there remains some remnant that refuses to believe that the
dreaded catastrophe will strike *us*. But the day came. I opened the
door to see the Western Union messenger standing on the porch. . . .

*"Vincent today reported missing in action over Italy July 20. Must trust
and believe he is prisoner and we shall hear more soon—all our love—Dad
and Mother"*

. . . Through the long, long weeks of the summer of '43 we hoped
and believed. By the calendar they measured only 63 days but they
seemed forever then. My parents' hope and courage never flagged.
I suspect mother may have had times in the dark hours of night
when her faith faltered. I did too. But if she did she did not let us
know. . . .

When the second yellow envelope came on September 20th it was
not quite as hard to open as the first had been. There was now an
equal chance that the news would be good rather than bad. It was
good, Vincent was alive.

*"Received word from the War Department that Vincent prisoner of war of
Italian government. No details yet. —Stanley"*[47]

Vincent was originally in Italian hands, but then ended up in the Stalag Luft
prison camp in Germany, the same prison camp on which the 1960s television
series *Hogan's Heroes* was based. Vincent was freed when the Allied forces entered Germany and liberated it in 1945.

THE WAR DEPARTMENT REGRETS
TO INFORM YOU

As with the Faulds, to have your soldier become a prisoner often felt like a
lucky break. And sometimes, other lucky breaks occurred for anxious families. Mary Devereux Crist's husband was a Marine Corps colonel. During his
twenty-nine months in the Pacific, he was part of a maneuver that went into

Guam. In July 1944, American troops had taken the strategic Marianas Islands in the South Pacific, which consisted of Saipan, Guam, and Tinian. This was considered a turning point in the Pacific war, since the islands' location gave the Allies closer air access to Japan. Sure enough, it was from Tinian, about a year later, that the U.S. launched the B-29 aircraft that dropped nuclear bombs on Hiroshima and Nagasaki and ended the war.[48]

But in 1944, Marines going into Guam like Crist's husband faced enemy fire all around. When he was sitting in what he thought to be a safe place, a deep cave, he took off his helmet. Just then, a piece of shrapnel exploded outside and flew past his head, grazing it, but not seriously wounding him. Crist was not given any of those details. She was informed only that her husband had been wounded and was mistakenly led to believe he might be dead.

> I received a telegram—the telegraph office got mixed up and put the four black stars, which meant death, on his telegram. I was hesitant, to say the least, about opening it, and then I found the message was, "Your husband has sustained a wound to the head."[49]

She was frantic at that message. She called the Marine headquarters in Washington trying to get more information. Days passed, and no word came. Finally, she heard the news that it was a superficial wound that had not even required any hospital time. It had all been a false alarm.[50]

But Mary King, a Rhode Island mother, was not so lucky. She got the worst news possible about her son in the last months of the war.

> I first got a telegram that he was missing in action. . . . And it came to me at a very bad time. My daughter was making her wedding gown to be married to a man in uniform, and here I was reading this, and it wasn't sinking in for a while.
>   He lost his life on March 19, 1945, on the USS Franklin, fifty miles off the coast of Japan. All the boys were ready for a takeoff when this lone Jap—how he got there nobody knows—a kamikaze, hit the ship, and all of them, there were four hundred and some, were lost.
>   . . . I have two other sons. They took it very hard. And of course, my daughter did too. She thought I was going to stop the wedding. I debated in my mind, should I, and I thought: No, if she had it all planned, then let her go through with it. But it wasn't an easy thing to do.[51]

Mary King joined an organization called Gold Star Mothers of America, and later went on to become its president. It was formed during World War I. The name came from the practice of hanging stars in the windows of families with men in the military. If you had a family member serving, you hung a blue star in your window. If he died, you hung a gold star. At the end of World War II, widows started their own organization called Gold Star Wives of America.

Natalie Mirenda married Frank Maddalena in 1940. They had two children when Frank was drafted in February 1944 at the age of twenty-nine. He was sent to Europe, where he replaced troops who had mounted the D-Day invasion in June 1944. He was killed in the Battle of the Huertgen Forest on November 22, 1944. On December 5, 1944, Natalie got word that her husband was missing. Before his death she sent many letters to him from her apartment in New York City, where she looked after their two children and her parents, who lived upstairs. In October 1944, she had just gotten a letter from him and it prompted her to tell him again how much she missed him.

> Oh God, I think I'll go nuts. I see you everywhere—in the chair, behind me, in the shadows of the rooms. Everyplace I go you are always with me in the back of my mind. I seem to have a continuous headache because I'm so worried about you.

She told him she had to stop reading the newspaper or listening to the radio because they made the war sound as if it would not end soon. And at the thought of that, she said, "I only eat my heart out, knowing that it will keep you away from me all the more."

By mid-November 1944, Frank's letters to Natalie had come far less frequently. In a November 19 letter she showed the strain that was causing her. She told him how the days were "endless" because she had no mail from him "since Monday." She wondered, "Frank my dearest, what is happening to us? We were going to grow old together. Enjoy and raise our children. The thought that you may be at this very moment fighting is maddening." She tried to guess where he was and what division of the Army he was with by the stamp of the censor. She decided he was in northern France and had read in the papers of lots of snow and sleet there. So she told her husband, "Oh Frank, take care of yourself. You know you catch cold easily. Take care of yourself also as we need you home so much."

On December 5, 1944, Natalie wrote her final letter to her husband. She was very worried by then because she had not gotten any mail for more than two weeks.

> Frank, when I walk alone, I seem to feel you sneaking up on me and putting your arms around me. I turn around and you're not there. I guess I'm just wishing in vain. Gee, soon it will be Xmas. Well, for me it's just another day, but for the kids I'll do my best to make it merry. If only I could hear that perhaps the war was soon over and then you were to come home.

Natalie learned Frank was missing just hours after writing that last letter. But it took a year before Frank was officially declared dead. Natalie never married again.[52]

Possibly the best-known grieving family during the war was the Sullivan family of Waterloo, Iowa. All five of Alleta Sullivan's sons were killed together in 1942 when the USS *Juneau,* the ship on which the brothers were all serving, was sunk in the Pacific just after the Battle of Guadalcanal. After that, Mrs. Sullivan, her husband, and her only daughter, Genevieve, were recruited by the Navy to visit defense plants and advocate for more war production. In addition, a feature film was made during the war about the family called *The Fighting Sullivans.* And in 1943 Genevieve joined the women's branch of the Army, the WAC.

In the March 1944 issue of *The American Magazine,* Alleta (Mrs. Thomas F. Sullivan) wrote a first-person account of her experiences called "I Lost Five Sons."

> The way the news first came to me was through a neighbor who had received a letter from her son in the Navy, saying, "Isn't it too bad about the Sullivan boys? I heard that their ship was sunk."

Mrs. Sullivan advised other mothers and wives not to listen to those kinds of rumors, because usually they were not true. The problem was, she said, they stick in your mind even if you know to discount them.

> When I went to bed that night I could hardly sleep. When I did fall asleep, I had terrible dreams in which my boys were in danger. I

wanted to help them and couldn't. In my nightmare I could even hear their voices calling, "Mother."

It was a week later that three Navy men knocked on the Sullivans' door at 7:00 A.M. Mrs. Sullivan's husband woke her up, along with their daughter, Genevieve, and Katherine Mary, the wife of the youngest brother, Albert. They all gathered in the living room in their bathrobes and slippers to hear the Navy commander clear his throat and deliver the official news.

> "The Navy Department deeply regrets to inform you that your sons, Albert, Francis, George, Joseph and Madison Sullivan are missing in action in the South Pacific."

They had all died. And it did not take long for that truth to sink in with the family. In the wake of the news, Mrs. Sullivan was particularly concerned with her only married son Albert's family, his wife Katherine and son Jimmy. Albert might not have had to go to war until later, because he had a young son. But, according to his mother, he didn't want to let his brothers enlist and not go with them. His mother said Katherine knew he had to do it. Alleta said Katherine "knew how it was with the Sullivan boys." Katherine understood that they stuck together. And she assured Albert that she and the baby would be okay, and they agreed Katherine and Jimmy would go to live with Mr. and Mrs. Sullivan.

When Alleta officially heard the news of her sons' deaths her world stood still. "In my first blind grief," she said, "it seemed as if almost everything I had lived for was gone. I couldn't eat or sleep, and I cried a lot." Her husband was worried about her health and said the boys wouldn't want her to let the news defeat her. He said they would want her to keep going.

> I felt that just keeping busy wasn't the whole answer for us. I knew that it had been God's will that my boys should die, and I felt that it must be His will that we should, in some way, carry on the work they had begun. If we could only do something that would help the war effort.

Very soon, that something came to Mrs. Sullivan in the form of a request from the Navy that she and her husband and daughter travel to shipyards and

armament factories and speak to the workers as part of a Navy effort to motivate defense plant employees to increase their production efficiency. The Sullivans accepted the offer and began touring around the country.[53]

During World War II, the American idea of home necessarily expanded
to mean more than the house or the town where a person lived or grew
up. Home became the whole country. And the neighborhood was a band of
allied nations fighting to defend themselves against Nazis, Fascists, and all
threats to a humane way of life. This suddenly smaller world forced Americans to adopt a broader worldview than they ever had before. In the process,
American women were called upon by their country to venture beyond the
safety, familiarity, and some may say confinement of what had always been
the most socially acceptable realm for them, their own families and houses.
And they were asked to send their husbands, sons, and brothers far away, into
a great unknown as well. All the while, American women also were under im-
mense pressure from their country to protect and defend steadfastly the very
idea of traditional home and family, and their central place in it, that was
transforming so quickly. It was comforting perhaps to believe that after the
war everything could go back to the way it always had been. Yet, trying to rec-
oncile such contradictory duties demanded sometimes impossible contor-
tions from women, calling upon all their powers of resourcefulness, sacrifice,
and bravery.

Thus, along with the idea of home, the connotation of the term *homemaker*—so often used to evoke a contrived, one-dimensional woman, like
Betty Crocker—could be said to have grown in scope and significance during
the war years too, whether anyone was aware of it or not. As American men
were marching into combat to change the balance of power throughout Europe and the East, the wives, mothers, and sisters of America found themselves thrust into a quieter revolution of their own. Without due recognition
or validation, and most often unwittingly, wartime women embarked on an
odyssey that would, for better or worse, begin to explode their time-honored
roles within their own families. And the four years of World War II would
also start to blow wide open previous notions of just how fully and adeptly
women were capable of contributing to and participating in American society as a whole.

CHAPTER TWO

Soldiers Without Guns

FEMALE DEFENSE
INDUSTRY WORKERS

The War Department must fully utilize, immediately and effectively, the largest and potentially the finest single source of labor available today—the vast reserve of woman power.

HENRY L. STIMSON, Secretary of War, 1943[1]

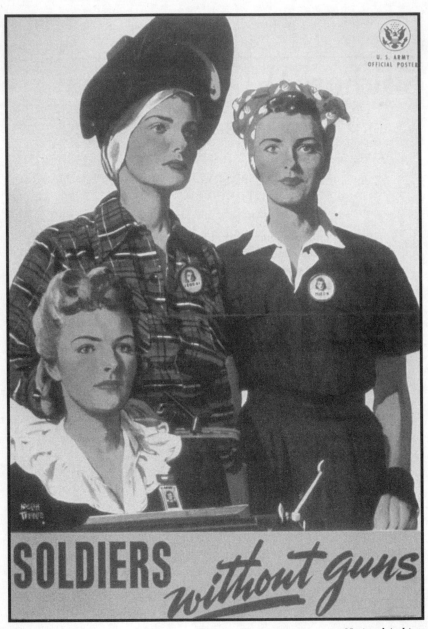

National Archives

SIMPLE NECESSITY PROPELLED more than six million women into America's workforce during the war years, opening job opportunities for women in many previously male bastions such as factories, shipyards, and steel mills. For employers, the main incentive was economics. Among the women workers, money was also one of the most compelling motivations. American men were heading off to war just as American industry was signing lucrative contracts with the government to produce massive numbers of bombs, guns, ships, and planes. Companies were losing the core of their labor pool at the very time they required more and more workers. The call the government put out urging any able-bodied person to fill the void came right when American families were watching their main breadwinners leave to join the military. Suddenly, the standard idea of seeing women as fragile creatures, ill-suited for work outside the home, much less for hard labor, seemed a peacetime luxury. Like never before, America asked women to take up the slack—to join in producing the vital machinery of war.

For America's women, becoming some of the most viable "manpower" available was a profound switch from what had come before. Women had never been very welcome in the lucrative parts of the American workplace. In fact, during the Depression years of the 1930s when jobs were so scarce, women had been openly discouraged from working outside the home. In 1936, one poll found that 82 percent of Americans believed wives should not work if their husbands had jobs.[2] Women were told they had no right to take jobs from the men who really needed them to support a family. World War II began to change that.

But some serious obstacles sprang up in the path of the female solution to wartime labor shortages. There were those entrenched attitudes of many employers, male workers, husbands, fathers, and women themselves against females working outside the home, particularly in industrial jobs. Somehow, that mind-set had to change. As President Roosevelt said in a Columbus Day Speech in 1942, "In some communities employers dislike to hire women. In others they are reluctant to hire Negroes. We can no longer afford to indulge such prejudice."[3] Then came the formidable task of convincing middle-class housewives that the coast was clear for them to head off to work without their family lives falling apart, or at least, their competence as wives and mothers coming into question. And great practical challenges existed in adapting the male strongholds of industry to female workers' needs. About the only way to surmount these hurdles quickly and effectively, and get on with the work at hand, was for everyone to agree in principle that women working was a temporary fix for wartime, not a permanent change in American society.

RECRUITING WOMEN TO WAR WORK

This push for female workers had its roots in the late 1930s. America was busy recovering from economic depression and was taking a hands-off approach to the growing war in Europe. At the same time, the Axis countries of Germany, Italy, and Japan were building an arsenal of planes, tanks, ships, and bombs that was to exceed the firepower of Britain, France, or the United States. Then as Germany advanced through Europe into France and toward Great Britain, President Roosevelt instituted America's first peacetime military draft in October 1940. But Roosevelt increasingly found himself caught between the isolationists here, who did not want to send American soldiers into the war abroad, and British Prime Minister Winston Churchill, who pleaded for help against Nazi aggression.[4]

So in December 1940, the president announced America's stepped-up nonmilitary commitment to the war effort abroad in his famous "Arsenal of Democracy" speech, delivered to the American people on the radio:

> Guns, planes, and ships have to be built in the factories and arsenals of America. . . . Manufacturers of watches, of farm implements, linotypes, cash registers, automobiles, sewing machines, lawn mowers, and locomotives are now making fuses, bomb-packing crates, telescope mounts, shells, pistols, and tanks. . . . But all our present efforts are not enough. We must have more ships, more guns, more planes—more of everything. This can only be accomplished if we discard the notion of "business as usual." . . . We must be the great arsenal of democracy. For us this is an emergency as serious as war itself. We must apply ourselves to our task with the same resolution, the same sense of urgency, the same spirit of patriotism and sacrifice,

as we would show were we at war. . . . We have furnished the British great material support and we will furnish far more in the future.[5]

America would take the middle ground, engaging in the battle by supplying Britain with the equipment of war, if not the soldiers. The plan was called Lend-Lease.[6]

By 1941, car factories, steel mills, and other industrial plants all over the country had begun signing contracts with the government to produce various types of war machinery, and they were converting their facilities to war production. Even then, some companies realized they were on the verge of a labor shortage and might need to hire women. So advertisements for women workers began to appear.

The first women to answer the call to the factories were blue-collar women who were already in the labor force in 1940. Many were married mothers who had always had to work to keep their families solvent. Most had been in traditionally lower-paying female positions, such as waitressing or cleaning work.[7] While a waitress averaged $14 a week, a woman working in a shipyard during the war took home an average of $37 a week. Many women were understandably happy for the opportunity to take industrial jobs. In fact, many laundries and restaurants closed during the war because their owners could not keep workers at the wages they paid.[8] The war also meant most white women and many black women left cleaning jobs for factory work.

Bessie Stokes came across the ad that changed her life when she was doing dishes one night in the spring of 1941 at her modest little house in McKeesport, Pennsylvania, just outside Pittsburgh. Her three-year-old son, Almie, was playing on the floor, and her husband, Spike, was sitting at the kitchen table reading the *McKeesport Daily News*. To Spike, the ad for women workers struck him as funny. So he showed it to Bessie. She remembered, "It said, 'Army ordnance, hiring inspectors, male or female. No high school education necessary.' " Bessie had dropped out of school in sixth grade to take care of her ailing mother and her younger siblings, and had only ever worked as a cleaning woman, making $2 a week. That night, Bessie started to see a new path for herself and her family through one of these war jobs. "But you had to take a Civil Service exam," Bessie recalled. "So my husband was laughing and he said, 'You could never pass the test.' Well, I didn't say too much but I was thinking a whole lot."

Bessie thought about her past and her present, and what she could do for the future. "I made up my mind I wasn't going to live like my mother," she said. "We never had a bathroom. We always had relatives staying with us. We had a big coal stove in the kitchen that we cooked on. My father had double pneumonia and I went around to the church and asked for donations of food during the Depression. My mother got a job making pies up at the Gaddis airport. We had it rough." Bessie knew Spike would probably be heading to war soon, and the money she would earn in this war job could ensure that she could pay their house note while he was away.

Bessie remembered that Spike had always kidded her, "You know, if I ever left you, you couldn't live on $2 a week." So when Spike showed her that ad she thought to herself, "Oh boy, I'm gonna fool you." The next day, while Spike was at work, Bessie walked downtown and applied to take the Civil Service exam. It was a brave move since she was not so sure she could pass it either. She did not tell anyone what she had done, until afterward. Spike was a little surprised that she took the test, but figured it was just a whim. Then, a few weeks later, Bessie learned she had passed.

In the fall of 1941, she started work at a steel mill inspecting bombshells. Her pay was around 75 cents an hour, more than ten times what she made cleaning houses. Bessie worked for the entire war, even after Spike was drafted in 1943. Through war work she found the power to take care of herself and her family.

In January 1946, when Spike returned home, as he sat at the same kitchen table where he had first jokingly showed her the ad for women war workers, Bessie made sure he understood one of the main things she had learned while he was away. "I kept every one of my pay stubs from all my work," said Bessie. "So when Spike came back from the war, the first day he was home, I put them in front of him. And I said, 'Don't you ever tell me I have to depend on you for a living.' " Spike looked at the pile of pay stubs, and then up at his wife proudly, laughed, and said, "Oh girl, you proved it."[9]

Women like Bessie, who had been in the workforce before the war, eventually made up half of all female defense workers. But America's industrial labor shortage remained, especially as more husbands like Spike were drafted, husbands who had originally been exempt from the war because they had children. It was quickly apparent to industry and government that women who were not currently in the workforce would have to be recruited too. That was a tricky proposition since the prospect of middle-class married women and those with children going to work threatened too many people.[10]

So, single women became the next logical group under pressure to go into factory work. Before the war, women who did not go to college often had jobs until they married. And those who went to college often did not take jobs. It was assumed in society that many in both of these groups of young women would prefer clerical jobs to factory work, even though it paid less, since those jobs were considered more respectable, less gritty. But in the face of wartime obligation, the hope was that young women, particularly those just graduating from high school, could be convinced to take factory jobs, even if it meant putting off college.[11]

In 1943, a fictional character emerged who embodied the ideal single woman war worker. Her name was Rosie the Riveter. She was everything the government wanted in a female war worker. She was loyal, efficient, patriotic, compliant, even pretty. Her myth started with a song by a male quartet called the Four Vagabonds:

> While other girls attend a favorite cocktail bar,
> Sipping dry martinis, munching caviar;
> There's a girl who's really putting them to shame—
> Rosie is her name.
>
> All day long, whether rain or shine,
> She's part of the assembly line,
> She's making history working for victory,
> Rosie, Rosie, Rosie, Rosie, Rosie, Rosie the Riveter.[12]

In the song, Rosie's boyfriend Charlie was off fighting the war, and she worked patriotically to bring him home so they could get married. Then, presumably, she was to quit working and go home to raise a family. The Rosie icon took off. After the song, Norman Rockwell's *Saturday Evening Post* cover illustration of Rosie appeared on May 29, 1943. His rugged and portly war worker sits wearing dark denim overalls and staring downward to one side with a resolute but slightly guarded look. Her beefy arm rests on a black lunchbox with "Rosie" written across the top. In her manly hand she holds a hearty sandwich, while a heavy, battered rivet gun rests across her lap. A powder puff sticks out of her pocket and her foot is stamping down on a copy of Adolf Hitler's *Mein Kampf.*

A few months later, a softer rendering of Rosie appeared, including plucked eyebrows, full makeup, and a red bandanna covering her dark, curly hair. In this government-commissioned poster, Rosie stares straight ahead with a pleasant but determined look, making one hand into a fist and using the other hand's polished fingernails to pull back the sleeve of her light, denim workshirt to show off a gently flexed arm muscle. Quoting her, the words above the image read, "We Can Do It!"

Lois Wolfe was a bit like Rosie herself. She and her boyfriend both graduated from high school in Chicago in 1942, and he was sent off to war almost immediately. She had planned to go to college, but instead responded to the push for single women to take up war jobs. She went straight to work at a Buick plant in Melrose Park, Illinois, that had a government contract to build airplane engines for the B-24 Liberator bomber. "The men were all being drafted," said Lois. "They were taking them right and left, and even those that had been exempt in the beginning were being called, and they desperately needed people to fill their jobs. That's what we girls did, we filled men's jobs.[13]

But these young, unmarried women were only one other part of the answer. In February 1943, a *Fortune* magazine article entitled "The Margin Now Is Womanpower" said that the war industry would be "unable to meet its schedules without a big army of new women workers."[14] An article in *Newsweek* on September 6, 1943, noted, "This week the call was clear—the nation wants still more women at work." The magazine reported that the government had looked at labor needs and had decided that "in the next two months alone, at least 3,200,000 new workers are vitally needed for industry—principally munitions work. And most of these will have to be women."[15]

The 1943 *Fortune* also reported, "There are virtually no unmarried women left to draw upon. . . . The four million or more women who have entered the working force in the past three years were much easier to recruit than the three or four million housewives about to be called upon."[16] The government could not require companies to hire women, though, partly at the urging of First Lady Eleanor Roosevelt, it did consider briefly drafting women into industry, as had been done successfully in Britain. Yet in the end, the government turned to using public relations to recruit more female labor.[17]

Among the many agencies President Roosevelt had created during the war was the War Manpower Commission, formed in April 1942 to oversee war labor issues in the military, industrial, and civilian sectors.[18] And in June 1942, the Office of War Information was formed to manage the flow of news and propaganda about the war to the public.[19] By 1943, when the labor shortage was most acute, the two agencies worked together in concerted campaigns, targeting employers to hire women and women to become "production soldiers."[20] As Paul McNutt, the director of the War Manpower Commission, said in 1943, "Getting these women to go into industry is a tremendous sales proposition."[21]

Recruiting housewives to war work was indeed a delicate prospect. Even women who might have wanted to work often had to contend with doubting husbands. In early 1943, a Gallup poll found only 30 percent of all husbands gave unqualified support to the idea of their wives working in industrial war jobs.[22] Although the idea persisted that the majority of wives who worked during the war were married to soldiers, in fact, only one in ten new women workers had husbands in the military. And only 8 percent of all women had husbands in the service.[23] The average wartime American family on the home front was still firmly composed of a housewife with a working husband.

These were the men who were called to task for their attitudes by the left-wing periodical *The Nation*, which published a revolutionary article entitled "America's Pampered Husbands" in July 1943:

> Husbandly pressure on housewives not to enlist for the war-production front takes much subtler terms than an overt "I object." Largely, it shapes up as men's time-hallowed, unspoken refusal to share in home responsibilities, an attitude that puts an intolerable double burden on the working wife. . . . When household equipment needs replacement, when the children's shoe size changes, when the toothpaste runs out, it is Mother not Father who scribbles memoranda on scraps of paper and squeezes in necessary shopping sometime, somewhere. . . . If a woman can learn to run a drill press, why can't a man learn to run a washing machine?[24]

But the more accepted idea was that men and their wives could be forgiven for believing that the only proper place for women was as homemakers. *Fortune* said, "The manpower shortage confronts us with unexpected political and social issues. We are a kindly, somewhat sentimental people, with strong, ingrained ideas about what women should or should not do."[25]

Despite the tide of public opinion against working wives, War Manpower Commission director Paul McNutt had a strategy for quelling opposition: "The money appeal will continue strong," he said in 1943, "but we'll concentrate on patriotism." Sure enough, all across the country, the public was bombarded with spirited print and radio ads, magazine articles, and posters with slogans like "Do the Job He Left Behind" or "Women in the War—We Can't Win Without Them" depicting noble, pretty but serious, female war workers on the job. Another poster showed three female war workers above the slogan "Soldiers Without Guns." The campaigns glamorized war work, always showing that women could maintain their femininity and still be useful. A telling poster aimed at housewives, created by the War Manpower Commission in 1944, depicted a woman worker in overalls with her husband behind her smiling and an American flag in the background. The caption read, "I'm proud . . . my husband wants me to do my part."

Eugenia Holman got a job making ammunition in Alabama and wrote a letter to a friend in 1943, explaining her reasons for taking up defense work.

> I wanted to win the war, naturally. Who didn't? . . . I thought of it in kind of an abstract way. Something that had to be done, but mostly by the boys at the front. You see, I hadn't learned then about the battles of production and assembly lines as I have now. I hadn't learned of the vital necessity of every able-bodied person doing their share no matter how small, and working! working! working! And when my husband and my brother and my cousins and all the other boys come back home, I want to be able to look them in the eye with a clear conscience and say, "I did all I could." [26]

While patriotism was certainly a part of what drew women in, it was still the economic incentives that hooked many housewives. Kay Wells took a job in 1942 making nuts and bolts for airplanes at an appliance manufacturing company in Pittsburgh.

> They started you out at $1.72 per hour. That was a lot of money. So many women were working. We learned how to do a lot of things. People were shocked. The women were not going to sit at home. Our boys were doing a job, and we were going to work. [27]

For many wives the work provided that first taste of financial latitude. Polly Crow took a job at Jefferson Boat and Machine Company in Anderson, Indiana. She wrote about her new job on June 12, 1944, in a letter to her husband, who was fighting overseas.

Darlin'

You are now the husband of a career woman—just call me your
little Ship Yard Babe! . . . I finally ended up with just what I wanted.
Comptometer job—4:00 'til midnite—70 cents an hour to start
which amounts to $36.40 a week, $145.60 per month, increase in
two months if I'm any good and I know I will be.

Women were able to make more money than they could have hoped to make
before the war, and it was their own, as Polly Crow expresses a few lines later
in the same letter to her husband: "Opened my first little checking account
too and it's a grand and glorious feeling to write a check all your own and not
have to ask for one."[28]

The women being lured into the workforce were many of the same
women who were seeing their husbands, sons, brothers, and boyfriends off to
war. But it is important to clarify more specifically which women made up
the wartime workforce. In 1940, before the war, more than 11.5 million
women worked. An additional 6.5 million, like Polly Crow, joined the workforce during the war. While those numbers are important, the lasting significance lies in the shifting nature of their jobs during the war and the briefly
altered attitude of society toward these pioneering women workers. Approximately four million of the women who were in the workforce before the war
took industrial war jobs. In addition, almost half of the new women workers,
or upward of 2.5 million, went into wartime industrial jobs. But many
women workers also took other traditionally male jobs during the war, in
agriculture, sales, and clerical work. These were jobs that opened up for
women as working men either went to war or took higher-paying industrial
war jobs themselves.

Almost 50 percent of all adult women were employed in this country at
some point during the height of war production in 1943 and early 1944, a
larger percentage than ever before.[29] And more women older than thirty-five
were working than ever before. Also for the first time, more married women
were working than single women. One third of those married female workers had been full-time housewives before the war. That meant the majority of
the married women in factories were blue-collar women who had to work for
economic reasons before the war and shifted to higher-paying jobs as a result
of the war.[30]

But there was always a caveat for any woman in these newfound jobs. At every turn, along with the urgings to go to work, there was a reminder that these jobs were given to women only temporarily. When the men came back home from war, Rosie would unfurl her fist, unflex her muscle, change back into her dress, and trade in her rivet gun for a mop and a spatula. In the meantime, there was work to be done.

THE AIRCRAFT INDUSTRY

Lee Turner Foringer, a tall, thin, stylish Texan, was twenty-two years old when she took her war job in the beginning of 1942. She had married just before the war started and moved with her husband from Texas to California. War work gave her a sense of purpose.

> My husband had wanted to start a family. But then, he wanted to join up, because of his brother, who was captured by the Japanese and was in Bataan, in the death march. That was his youngest brother. They were very close. So when his brother was captured, my husband volunteered for the Air Force.
>
> That's when I decided I wanted to do something, because I was lonesome. So when I saw the ad in the paper saying Douglas Aircraft was looking for women, I thought, "Gee, that's great. They need me."

Lee worked as a riveter at Douglas Aircraft in Long Beach, near Los Angeles, building B-17 bombers. She had never ridden in an airplane, since air travel was so new, but she was building them. "I worked on the jigs, the assembly line, where someone would weld the plane parts and then we would rivet the parts of the plane together. We would make the fuselage of the plane."

Lee's job was to take the rivet—a metal pin or bolt with a head at one end—and drive it with the rivet gun through pre-drilled holes in the airplane body. Then a bucker would use a metal bucking bar to bend the other end of the rivet into a second head that secured the plane parts together. "My friend Peggy and I worked in the same department, riveting and bucking. It was fun. We could laugh and do whatever we wanted to, but we had to make sure we were doing a good job."

The B-17 Flying Fortress was the workhorse on the European front, carrying ten-man crews and huge bomb loads into enemy territory as never before. It was the first bomber equipped with gunner turrets so its crews could fight off enemy defenses in the air, during such famous and strategic missions as the Eighth Air Force's daylight bombing raids over Germany. Like Lee, most of the women who built the planes understood that at the height of an air battle, the steel they riveted on American assembly lines might be the only barrier between death and their beloved husbands, sons, boyfriends, or brothers.

> When we were inside the cockpit I was thinking, "I don't want anything to be put in crooked where it will come out, because it could make the plane crash." You think about things like that all the time you're in there. I just wanted to make sure it was a good plane.[31]

During the war a new emphasis on aircraft building emerged. In 1940, the entire aircraft industry had produced a total of only 13,000 planes. In 1942, President Roosevelt requested 60,000 war planes be built. Douglas Aircraft was one of the largest aircraft plants in the U.S. throughout the early 1940s. It employed nearly 22,000 women during the war to help build many of the bombers and transport planes used in Europe and the Pacific. The eleven-building plant covered 1.4 million square feet.[32]

Lee worked there for almost two years. But her airplane-building life was cut short when family commitments took precedence over her newfound independence.

> I really looked forward to going to work every day. In October of 1943 my husband came back from El Paso on a three-day leave, and a few weeks later I found out I was pregnant. I stayed as long as I could. All the guys at the plant were so good to me. They took up a donation for a gift for me for the baby, and I got enough to buy a baby crib. And the girls had a shower for me.[33]

Some provisions were made for pregnant women working, because like Lee, some wanted to work as long as they could before quitting to have a child. Generally women could work up to the seventh month of pregnancy, and there were wide variations on postnatal leave.[34] Lee never worked again during the war.

LoRay Tewalt already had two children when she began working in 1942 at another Southern California Douglas Aircraft plant in El Segundo, California. Though her husband had a job and was too old to be drafted, LoRay still felt a need to join the workforce.

> I was in production control. I was out on the line a lot because when the parts came in we had to go inspect and check the parts. This was the first time I had ever worked. I had one year at the University in Indiana and got pregnant. Of course, that was the end of my college career. I married him and we had another child and moved to California when the war started.
>
> I was the third woman hired on the night shift. I worked 11:00 P.M. to 7:00 A.M. I thought that will be good because I can do that with the kids. After work, I would go home and sleep until about noon. Then I had to get up and fix the kids lunch and be with them in the afternoon. Then, I could go back to bed, after dinner, at about six and sleep until ten. So I got some sleep, except for the kids, who were always tiptoeing through the room looking for a toy or something. Oh, I was sleepy all the time. I never got enough sleep when I was working.

The shortages that produced rationing, in particular gas rationing, meant LoRay carpooled with other night shift workers, as did most war workers. But even the ride to work at night was tinged with danger. War workers in the United States were more insulated, by virtue of geography, from enemy bombing threats than were their counterparts in Germany, Japan, and even Britain. But the massive roofs of plants producing war planes on the West Coast, such as Boeing in Seattle or the Douglas plants in Southern California, were covered by camouflage netting with scenes painted on them to resemble a residential area. That way, any enemy planes flying overhead would not know for sure that these were actually prime targets, with thousands of war planes being produced inside. People living near the coast also had to keep lights off at home at night, and drivers were not allowed to have on headlights. So LoRay's carpool proved treacherous.

> It was three miles, and at night there would be no lights, you were allowed to use fog lights. They weren't very bright at all. I was in one dandy wreck. It was heavy fog, you just couldn't see. And we were going along and one car ran into the train. They didn't see it. And we were the second one, and there were seven cars before it ended, a chain reaction. It bashed the car I was in pretty good. One lady who

was sitting in the back, her glasses broke. I was in the front seat. We were going about 20. I knew I was hurt but nothing was broken, just black and blue. So we went on to work. There were a lot of accidents in the cars in the blackouts.

Even seemingly simple issues, such as work clothing, ended up changing LoRay's idea of what was possible.

I had never had a pair of slacks. In Indiana you didn't wear slacks. When I found out we had to wear slacks, I bought two outfits and alternated them. And I had always worn high heels because I'm short. The higher the better. So we had to wear flat shoes. But I didn't have a pair. And since I wore a size four, I had to go to the girls department. And I bought the flat Girl Scout shoes that buckled on the side. They were brown. But it was so comfortable that I took to it. I just about gave up dresses during the war.

LoRay's parents moved out to California soon after the war started as well, because it was the best place for her father to get work. Her mother did not work, and she provided some help with the kids. But LoRay was the one charged with managing the juggling of work and family. And she had to cope with an issue that dogged many female war workers: child care. Day care was a new concept—one that was not yet established in most places or trusted by many parents. LoRay said, "I would have trouble finding baby-sitters. Mother wasn't much of a baby-sitter. I had a day care center and then I had a neighbor and various others."[35]

During the war, women like Lee and LoRay made up about 40 percent of the workforce in the relatively new aircraft-building industry, a larger percentage of women than in almost any other single wartime industry.[36] And they were often accepted with little dissension by male coworkers.

But Lois Wolfe found a different reaction among her male coworkers. She worked in Chicago during the war, inspecting engines on the B-24 Liberator bombers. The B-24 was a bigger bomber than the B-17, which had been used primarily in Europe. Lois, a short, thin, perky woman, had planned to go to college when she finished high school, but instead went straight to work.

My job was as a tester of the B-24 engine. I would go in on Sunday night and start my 12:00 A.M. to 8:00 A.M. shift. It was six days a week.

It was such a confusing time . . . a grind. It was very depressing for
me because I was so young. To be so regimented when you're not
used to being that way. When you're flitting through high school
you're having all kinds of fun and then all of a sudden . . . it was so
heavy.

Lois's job testing B-24 engines opened up when the car plants were converted to war production after auto manufacturing was stopped in 1942.
Longtime male workers in the auto industry were not accustomed to working with women. So along with other women workers like her, Lois found a
rockier transition to the workplace at a converted Buick plant than did most
women in the newer, less-entrenched, aircraft plants.

I think the men resented us in some ways. Along with having to try
and figure out all of the other things, we had to put up with their
shenanigans. The men had all kinds of little tricks that they thought
were funny. When we would go up to take some of the readings and
change some of the oil they would pull the chair out from under-
neath us. Then they would catch us, and scare the life out of you.
And they used wet rags and set those on the seats so that when we sat
down our pants would get wet. And a lot of times they would just
drift off and leave us with all of that work, and go down and shoot
craps in the men's washroom.
    It became very frustrating, because you were trying to do your best
and you were getting nothing but teasing. . . . You were working
with the slide ruler, all the time calculating. There were a lot of us
girls out of school and good at math. We had to learn so much in
such a short time. Every step you did was vital because the engine
could be ruined if you did it in any other pattern.

Lois talked warmly of the role all women played in supporting each other.

At home, I said to my mother I don't want to go back. But she said
you have to. You're assigned to do this. . . . My mother felt as though
she was helping the war effort just getting me off and keeping me organized and giving me the courage, I guess, to say, "Yes Lois, you can
do it."

But along with that spirit, women like Lois also had to adopt an air of secrecy about their work. It meant that some of the pressures she faced she

could not share with anyone. The workers all took that charge seriously because they were schooled in it at work.

> There were big signs as we came into the factory that said, "Loose Lips Sink Ships" and "What You Know Here, Leave Here. What You See Here, Leave Here. Take Nothing from Here." And as we came in they checked us all over, and they checked our bag for our lunch or our purse, every day. And we had a big badge and we went through metal detectors or whatever they had. We walked through single file and then we punched our card.[37]

War work also changed the course of lives for women with professional ambitions, like Barbara Walls. She worked at a converted Chevrolet plant in Tarrytown, New York, building the Grumman Avenger torpedo bomber for the U.S. Navy in 1942. Barbara took the job to make the money she would save to pay for college. Her mother also worked at the plant and they carpooled together from their home twenty miles away.

One of the most vivid incidents of Barbara's work life shows the highly pronounced racial divide that existed in the war plants and factories. During the war, Jim Crow segregation laws were still very much in place in the American South. The military was also racially segregated. Racial segregation was a way of life, whether by law or custom, throughout the country.

> This was 1942, and everything was pretty frantic. I was the riveter. And on the other side of the A frame facing me was the bucker. This bucker was a very tall black man. The noise of the riveting going on deadened any conversation. But we worked great together. We just had it all figured out and we just went at it. And it was fine.
>
> But working near us were groups of men. I was the only woman in that section. And every time we had a break these white, former automakers who were not in the military, they would come over and hassle me.
>
> "You don't have to work with that nigger. We'll find you another place to work. Join the union and we'll take care of you."
>
> And they persisted and they persisted. And I told them, "Hey, leave me alone. I'm working fine with my partner. I don't have any gripes."
>
> They kept telling me they could get me a white man to work with. But I kept telling them that we were a good team, and I kept my partner.

After a year working, Barbara had saved up enough money for her first year at New York University. About that time the plant changed her mother and her to different shifts, so they could not carpool together, making it impossible for her mother to get to work. So both mother and daughter quit. But Barbara says that year of war work stuck with her, fostering a sense of new possibility, even after she earned her English degree at NYU.

> That job was just a reinforcement of the idea that I could do anything. I went and did something I never thought of. And I managed to graduate from college. That was important, that I had enough money to start and was able to finish college. The war job made that possible.[38]

But as was the norm in those days, any newfound independence or accomplishment was always tempered, if not curbed, by the idea that no matter what they did, women should maintain a feminine image doing it. Otherwise their gains, according to the prevailing notions of women's roles, came at too high a cost to the values of American society.

Even in the liberal tabloid PM, Max Lerner noted in 1943, "The traditional maidenly modesty is showing signs of cracking. A group of girls coming out of a war factory behaves very much like a gang of young fellows." As he went on about the new female war workers, he commented, "There is a new type of tough girl emerging, although still in a minority; she can outdrink, outswear, outswagger the men. Does this mean we must prepare for the new Amazons? Who knows? Certainly there are signs that the medieval court-of-love woman, whose type still is dominant in our day, is doomed." [39]

It was in that climate that perhaps the most glamorous female production soldier of all was originally spotted in the fall of 1944, by a photographer from the Army's First Motion Picture Unit. War worker Norma Jeane Dougherty would soon turn into the embodiment of a potent male ideal of womanliness. But when the Army photographer discovered her, she was just another war worker, packing parachutes at a war production plant in Burbank, California. The crew of Army photographers arrived under orders from their commanding officer, Captain Ronald Reagan, to document women's role in the war effort by photographing the prettiest women on the assembly line, patriotically working in their war jobs.

Norma Jeane Dougherty, then eighteen, stood out. She was a typical war wife, but with something a little extra, who had started working at the Radio-plane Company in April of 1944 after her husband, Jim Dougherty, joined the Merchant Marine and went to the Pacific. She was living with her husband's family in Southern California and had gotten a job in the same war plant as her mother-in-law, Ethel Dougherty. On June 15, 1944, she wrote to her friend Grace McKee about her new employment.

> I am working 10 hrs. a day at Radioplane Co., at Metropolitan Air-port. I am saving almost everything I earn (to help pay for our future home after the war). The work isn't easy at all for I am on my feet all day and walking quite a bit.[40]

The photographer, David Conover, reportedly said to Norma Jeane, "I'm going to take your picture for the boys in the Army, to keep their morale high."

Her June 4, 1945, letter to Grace, just after one of her husband's leaves, de-scribed that fateful time in the war plant—Norma Jeane's inauguration to ap-pearing before cameras. She said the plant supervisors and the photographers asked her to pose for a lot of pictures, and the photographers loved her.

> They all asked where in the h_____ I had been hiding. . . . They took a lot of moving pictures of me, and some of them asked for dates, etc. (Naturally I refused!).
>
> They were all nice Army officers and men. After they finished with some of the pictures, an army corporal by the name of David Conover told me he would be interested in getting some color still shots of me. . . . He said he would make arrangements with the plant superintendent if I would agree, so I said okay. He told me what to wear and what shade of lipstick, etc., so the next couple of weeks I posed for him at different times. When ever he could get over to the plant.

Conover called her a few days later at her job to tell her that the photos had come out amazingly well, and he urged her to take up modeling. He told her he wanted to take more pictures of her and even told her he would get her in touch with some of his contacts to get her more work.

> I told him I would rather not work when Jimmie was here so he said he would wait, so I'm expecting to hear from him most any time again.[41]

Indeed, Norma Jeane did hear from Conover within days. And about three weeks after that letter, one of his photos of her appeared on the June 26, 1945, cover of the Army magazine *Yank*. By June 1946, the still brown-haired Norma Jeane had appeared on the covers of thirty-three popular magazines, including *Laff, Stars and Stripes,* and *Family Circle*. In August 1946, she signed a contract with 20th Century Fox and by September 1946 was divorced from Jim Dougherty. Then she dyed her hair blonde and changed her name to Marilyn Monroe.[42]

BUILDING SHIPS

Shipbuilding was more difficult for women to break into than the aircraft industry, in part because it had such a long history as an all-male workforce. Again, necessity started to change that. In 1942, the Brooklyn Navy Yard lifted a 141-year ban on hiring women.[43] Commenting on the need for an additional 30,000 workers in shipyards along the Gulf of Mexico in 1943, Thomas M. Woodward, a member of the U.S. Maritime Commission, said, "women seem to be the answer, the only one, to the problem."[44]

Susan B. Anthony II (the niece of the famous women's rights leader) spoke about women infiltrating the industry in her 1943 book, *Out of the Kitchen— Into the War.*

> Shipbuilding is no picnic. That more and more women are going into it is obvious. Henry Kaiser alone is hiring thousands out on the West Coast. Government Navy Yards, pioneers in hiring women, are taking on more all the time. Commercial shipyards are bound to follow suit as the man supply dwindles.[45]

Henry Kaiser owned the Kaiser Shipyard in Richmond, California, near San Francisco, one of the largest shipyards in the country. With no experience he entered the shipbuilding business at the start of war production, trying to make cargo ships more quickly than usual to supply the military. Anthony described how Kaiser's company modified shipbuilding and so was able to accommodate newly minted women workers in ways many other shipbuilders could not. "Formerly a custom-building industry chiefly requiring skilled workers, Kaiser's innovation of mass production methods, the use of welding and prefabrication, has telescoped the element of skill, so that more than half of the shipyard workers can be trained now in less than three months." [46] And Kaiser's Liberty Ships went from taking a month to assemble, to a week, to four days. [47]

Katie Grant moved to California in 1943, after leaving Oklahoma with her husband, Melvin, and their young daughter. When they arrived, Melvin joined the Marine Corps and went to fight in the Pacific. Katie trained as a welder at Kaiser. Many of the women who took war production jobs migrated, alone or with their husbands, to the centers of defense production on the East and West coasts and then along the Gulf of Mexico.

> I took classes on how to weld. I had leather gloves, leather pants, a big hood, goggles and a leather jacket. They said you weld like you crochet. Well, I did not know how to crochet, but I could sew and make a neat stitch. So I thought of that when they taught us to hold a welding rod with one hand and the torch fire in the right hand. We placed the rod in a seam and melted it down in a small bead seam and brushed it off with a steel brush. They put me forty feet down in the bottom of the ship to be a tacker. I filled the long seams of the cracks in the ship corners full of hot lead and then brushed them good and you could see how pretty it was. The welders would come along and weld it so it would take the strong waves and deep water and heavy weight. I liked it pretty good. [48]

The analogy with traditional women's work such as sewing was a common one noted by both employers and the women themselves, as shown in a poetic account of shipbuilding called "Welder." Written by a welder named Irene Carlisle, it was published in *The Saturday Evening Post* on February 3, 1945.

> *Under our gloved hands and hooded eyes*
> *The blue arc stitches up the patterned steel.*
>
> *Over the hulls, between the clanging cranes,*
> *We climb and kneel and seam the ships together,*
> *Women are always sewing for their men,*
> *It tides the heart through many a bitter weather.*

The chattering rivets button up the shell,
The waiting bay is laced with windy foam,
The molten stitches glow beneath my hand,
This is the ship on which he may come home.[49]

Working on a ship meant enduring cold weather, burning steel, heavy lift-ing, and constant noise. Despite that, Nova Lee McGhee Holbrook, who moved from Arkansas with her husband to California, wanted to do the job. Both she and her husband worked in the Kaiser shipyard.

> They offered me office work, but I said, "I want to be a welder." They said, "It's going to be dirty."
> "I can wash it off," I said. I went down and took a welder's test, flat, vertical and overhead, and passed, so there I was a journeyman welder. . . . I welded down in the hatches, boiler room, and every-where else the men did. . . . I worked right with the men doing the same jobs, and I enjoyed every bit of it.

A main hazard of welding was burns.

> I got one very bad flash burn during this time, but got over it and went back as soon as I could see again. No one can explain how much those burns hurt, but they are very painful.[50]

Mary Todd Droullard remembered the tough conditions in a Seattle shipyard where she worked as a welder.

> Sometimes when you're welding, over your head, sparks would fly and burn through your brassiere. I have a lot of scars there. I would be working on the decks in the awful cold and damp, and would often get electrical shocks because of the electric welding. I'd climb up and down the ladders and go down in deep tanks and work down there all by myself in the dark.[51]

Perhaps it is not surprising that such work seemed to counter so much of what people believed women could handle. But in their successes, at least a few women must have felt some giddy moments of conquest, like the liberat-ing incident that Augusta H. Clawson, a ship welder, described:

There is nothing in the training to prepare you for the excruciating noise you get down in the ship. Any who were not heart and soul determined to stick it out would fade right away. Any whose nerves were too sensitive couldn't take it, and I really mean couldn't. When those chippers get going and two shipfitters on opposite sides of a metal wall swing tremendous metal sledgehammers simultaneously, you wonder if your ears can stand it. Sometimes the din will seem to swell and engulf you like a treacherous wave in surf-bathing and you feel as if you were going under. . . . It makes you want to scream wildly. And then it struck me funny to realize that a scream couldn't even be heard! So I screamed, loud and lustily, and couldn't even hear myself. It was weird. So then I proceeded to sing at the top of my lungs . . . and I couldn't hear the smallest peep. . . . I decided to make the most of it, so I hauled out my entire seafaring repertoire and sang "Rocked in the Cradle of the Deep," "Anchors Aweigh, My Boys," and "The Landlubbers Lie Down Below." You could almost doubt your sanity sitting in there making an unholy din and not even hearing it.[52]

Katie Lee Clark Knight worked at the Kaiser shipyard in Richmond as a shipfitter, another shipbuilding job that many women took up. She started out marking where the portholes on the ships were to be cut out, using a tape measure. But, she remembered, "It got so cold there at Richmond, and the wind would come across the bay and nearly freeze me to death." She asked to be transferred inside and was then given the job of marking off where the bulkheads would go. "You'd get a template—it was like a lady's pattern for a dress. And you'd lay this on a huge sheet of steel and then take the little center punch and your hammer and punch little imprints of that center punch."[53]

Even in the midst of tackling the physical demands of industrial labor, women were always under a kind of pressure their male counterparts never had to negotiate. They were constantly admonished not to become too masculine. One article in a Navy shipyard newsletter counseled women to "be feminine and ladylike even though you are filling a man's shoes." At Boeing, charm courses were scheduled for women workers.[54]

Another complaint against women workers as the war went on was that they missed too much work. But many were merely having a difficult time juggling dual roles as homemakers and workers, with little or no acknowledgment or assistance. In answer to a questionnaire given to women war workers in 1943, the number one unmet need they cited was help in caring for children. Other top needs included better shopping hours, shorter working hours, and better transportation.[55]

Child care was resolutely considered the mother's responsibility and concern. So if mothers worked, it was indeed a major need during the war. But the government, industry, and working mothers and fathers never came together to solve the problem adequately. Most employers and the all-male War Manpower Commission advocated federal child care, but did little to consult or take to heart the advice of child care professionals or mothers themselves. Therefore, the whole effort to address the problem hit many pitfalls and ultimately did not live up to its potential.

In 1942 Congress passed a bill called the Lanham Act, which provided government funds for the establishment of child care centers in communities most affected by increased war production. It provided for day care and after-school-care funding for children two to fourteen. It was a start toward addressing the problem of child care for mothers who worked. But the whole concept of public child care was new and frightening to most Americans. The process of getting Lanham Act funds was steeped in bureaucracy. Local governments that did receive funding were expected to foot part of the bill as well. In addition, society and mothers themselves generally did not trust the idea of public child care. Local school boards often had charge of the daily operation of Lanham child care centers.[56]

Even when centers were established, some either did not take off or there were not enough of them to keep up with the exponentially increasing number of working mothers in need at the height of war production. Some of the centers failed because they were located inconveniently for women or had hours incompatible with war work.[57]

By 1945, when funding for the Lanham Act was discontinued, the government had spent $51.9 million on 3,102 child care centers. They had served 600,000 children in the largest commitment to public child care in America's history.[58] But the system never adequately addressed the need. Only 10 percent of working mothers used the centers. Many of those were mothers who had moved from their hometowns for war work and did not have a community to draw upon for help with their children. The rest of the working mothers generally turned to haphazard but time-honored networks of family, friends, and neighbors to care for their children while they were on the job. *Fortune* pointed out glitches in the federal program in 1943.

The government assumes that local communities can and should bear most of the responsibility for child care. Whether they can or not, it is quite apparent that few, if any, are. If the present makeshift conditions are not cleared up, the effects can easily be imagined: a rise in absenteeism, worry, lowered morale—all of which means less production—not to mention permanent scars on the bodies and minds of American children. . . . But the problems do not stop with child care. A working mother still has marketing, cooking, laundering, and cleaning to attend to. These stretch her working day another four to six hours. Unless she receives concessions, not normally given, it is questionable how long she can stand up under a twelve- or fourteen-hour day.[59]

Those kinds of concessions are just what were provided for working mothers at two Kaiser shipyards in Oregon and California. Twenty-four-hour day care centers were established, some of the only such company-run centers in the country. The centers were located at the shipyard site and accommodated all three shifts women worked. They also provided women with a hot meal when they picked up their children after work. This kind of company support for working mothers was thought to contribute to the productivity of the Kaiser shipyards, which were noted for producing large numbers of ships quickly.[60]

Frances Keller Blanchet worked as a shipfitter in the Kaiser shipyard in Portland, Oregon. Her mother and father also worked in the shipyard. And she was able to take her children, a two- and three-year-old, to the day care there.

I had to walk about six blocks to catch the bus, took my kids to the day nursery and let them off right there at the gate, and walked down the hill to the shipyard. . . . They had a beautiful day nursery. . . . On my way home, I'd pick up my children and come home.[61]

Other companies also operated or subsidized day care for their employees' children, including Grumman, Curtiss-Wright, Hudson, and Douglas. And some companies set up shopping, laundry, and other facilities to help working women until the war was over. But the majority of working women were left to their own devices to cope with child care and other family and personal duties outside the workplace.[62]

MUNITIONS

Producing bombs and ammunition was some of the most hazardous war work. Plants were usually located in rural areas away from major population centers, where an accidental explosion would cause the least harm. The labor pool was often rural women and men. Black women, in particular, had many jobs in making ammunition. Women in munitions plants even started an organization of their own called Women Ordnance Workers, or WOW. All it took to join was perfect attendance on the job and at chapter meetings for three months. The reward was a WOW insignia and a special WOW uniform.[63]

Despite that effort to give the work some measure of allure, it was a tough job, in part because of its tedium. As one ordnance worker wrote:

> There isn't any glamour and excitement in making bombers and shells. . . . [It is] a job to be done day after day . . . doing it exactly the same way, maybe a hundred times a day, or a thousand times or five thousand times. . . . There is no glamour in pressing a lever five thousand times a day.[64]

Susan B. Anthony II said:

> One of the biggest woman-employing industries today is small arms ammunition. Women form almost half of all the workers trimming bullet jackets, annealing case parts and assembling bullets and cartridges. In big ammunition—artillery—women form more than a third of the workers. Many of these ammunition plants are set up in rural areas where no trained workers are available; so women have had to be recruited from surrounding cities and states. . . . Employers testify that, once on the job, the women learn quickly. Today they are making and loading powder bags, assembling and loading shells and cartridge cases, and assembling small parts such as fuses, boosters, primers and detonators. . . . Weighing smokeless powder for fixed ammunition and pouring powder into the cartridge cases is dangerous work. But it's got to be done.[65]

Lillie Cordes Landolt worked at a plant that made bullets in Des Moines, Iowa. She had five kids, and her husband also worked in the plant.

Making bullets was interesting. I had a huge machine. The ammunition is made in many parts, and the part we worked on was the bullet, which started out as brass, maybe a half inch across, quite thick, and not very deep, just kind of a cup. It went through a series of punches. . . . We made armor-piercing and incendiary bullets.[66]

In Huntsville, Alabama, the local paper reported on an "all-girl" crew at one arsenal:

> These girls are all handling a man's job. Every-one of them believes she has a personal stake in this war. Their morale is about the highest at the Arsenal. They are expert press operators, ball table operators, and they handle these 124 pound to 150 pound pallets with the ease and efficiency of old timers. . . . Each one of them is capable of substituting for the other in case of need. . . . This spirit of knowing their assigned job well, and the job of the girl working next to them has made every one of them valuable operators.[67]

Some women worked for the military in what was essentially quality control—inspecting ammunition and bombs made by contracting companies. Bessie Stokes worked for the Army inspecting bombs at a former steel mill in McKeesport, Pennsylvania. Bessie remembered that on her first day at the new job she met her friend Alfreda at the bridge outside the plant, and the two started to go in together.

> I said to her, "Have you seen any girls going in?"
> And she said, "No, but there's an awful lot of men going down in there."
> When we got down in that mill it was huge area with a straight line that seemed almost two miles long to where we had to report at the Army general's office. And we walked that line and the fellows were whistling and hollering. And Alfreda was kind of bashful. She didn't get married till late in life.
> And she said, "Bessie, what are we going to do?"
> I said, "Just ignore them."
> We found out later we were the first two girls in that mill. The next day, other girls started arriving and then more, and we started making bombs. They were about the size of a grapefruit around. I was in the department where the big bomb shells were made.

Bessie said the adjustments the men had to make in seeing women doing their jobs sometimes meant the women came in for fairly harsh treatment. After Bessie had met with Army officials who were inspecting the plant the day before, a supervisor for the plant had teased her for her thoroughness. The Army official had instructed her to throw out almost half of the bomb-shells she inspected because he said they were dirty. So she did what she was ordered to do. But the supervisor did not like that and took it out on her. The next day he gave her a present in front of his entire, mostly male crew.

> [He] said, "Hey Bessie, I have a gift for you." And he had this little box all done up in nice paper with a ribbon on. And when I opened it, it was a magnifying glass. He said because I pushed off so many shells that had even the smallest speck on them, I would need the magnifying glass.
>
> And he said, "Yeah, and right now I'm going to rename you. You're the flyshit inspector." That place went crazy. Even though all I was doing was what the officer asked. But that's all [he] ever called me from then on. "Flyshit."
>
> Soon the other fellows started calling me that too, and I finally got mad. And I went home and I cried. And my husband, Spike, said, "Bessie, you're doing a man's job. You're getting a man's salary." He said, "You have to act like a man."
>
> I said, "But they cuss me. And I don't like that."
>
> He said, "The only way you're going to stop it is to cuss right back to them."
>
> Well, I was a good church member at that time and I didn't want to do any cussing. But about four days later, one of them started cussing me up and down and I called him everything I could think of. That stopped it. They knew that I wasn't going to take it anymore.[68]

Not always being valued for their work could also be reflected in the wages many women workers received. In many jobs that women infiltrated during the war years they were paid less than men doing the exact same work. Some-times the same jobs were given different names depending upon whether a man or woman was doing them to justify a different pay scale. For instance, in the Brooklyn Navy Yard, women were called "helper trainees" and men were called "mechanic learners" for the same job. But helper trainees made less money.[69]

In 1942, the National War Labor Board, which had heavy union representation, issued a declaration that women should receive pay equal to men's for the same work. It was not a law, but it did influence some workplaces. For instance, the Army and Navy implemented equal pay in their own munitions plants. But many companies ignored the equal pay idea. Others hired women at the same starting salary for entry-level jobs, such as riveters or welders, but then gave them no chance of advancement to higher-paying jobs, when men could expect to move up within months.[70] By 1944, the average weekly wage for female manufacturing workers was $31 a week while it was $55 a week for men. Part of the reason for that gap was the lack of upward mobility for women once they got entry-level manufacturing jobs.[71]

Some union organizations, such as the CIO, promoted a policy of equal pay for equal work, but not all local unions did much to back it up for women members. In fact, women and labor unions had a rocky relationship during the war. In 1940 overall union membership was at 7.3 million. During the war the membership rose to 12.6 million. In 1944, 3.5 million of those union members were women. Female union membership threatened many male members because it meant women might angle for male jobs after the war. So while most unions opened their ranks to women in manufacturing, a few, including the railroad, mining, and construction unions, did not. And after the war, many that had opened to women managed to get rid of female members.[72]

During World War II, women taking war jobs raised many issues that persisted through to the next century: equal pay, child care, equal job advancement opportunities, juggling home and work obligations. As William Chafe said in his 1972 book, *The American Woman*:

> Female participation in the labor force was essential to victory in the war, but it also raised serious questions about the nation's social values and the future direction of male-female relationships. It was one thing to encourage women to work as a temporary device to meet a manpower shortage and quite another to view females as permanent jobholders with the same rights as men. The achievement of economic equality required more than simply the decision to hire women as replacements for men gone to war. It also entailed the establishment of a uniform standard of pay, equal access for females to the higher ranks of business and government, and, most difficult of all, the development of community services to ease the woman's dual role as worker and homemaker.[73]

OTHER WAR JOBS

The unprecedented inroads women made in industrial manufacturing jobs during the war sometimes overshadow the complete picture of women's wartime employment. Of the more than six million women who joined or rejoined the workforce from 1940 to 1945, a little more than 2.5 million worked in defense production. That was a significant leap. But more than two million new female workers went into clerical jobs.[74] In fact, a telling recruitment poster depicting three smiling female clerical workers had the caption "Secretaries of War." Still, women workers' greatest gain in terms of percentage of total workers in an occupation was in agricultural work, where women made up 8 percent of total workers in 1940, and 22.4 percent of total workers in 1945, a 14.4 percent increase.[75]

There was also a big push to fill what were called "essential civilian jobs" that had lost workers, both male and female, to higher-paying, higher-status defense industry jobs or to the military. As the writer Dorothy Parker said in an article urging younger women to take civilian jobs in *Mademoiselle* magazine in May 1943:

> The first thing to do to win your war is to lose your amateur standing. Girls and young women are needed badly and immediately for the daily jobs that must go on if our world is to go on. . . . Somewhere, right near you, there is an empty job that must be filled; a job a man has left to go where he was told to go. He may have driven a bus, a taxi or a trolley; he may have worked in a bank, a drugstore or a telegraph office. If he can do what he is doing now, certainly you can do what he used to do. For God's sake—are we women or are we mice?[76]

Women responded to this call as they had to the call to industrial jobs. *Fortune* said in 1943:

> Women are working as barbers, butchers, taxi drivers, slaughterhouse workers, railroad track tenders, fire fighters. . . . Commercial airlines have women ticket sellers, mechanics, cargo loaders, and checkers.[77]

Mary Jo Davis Owens took a job as a movie usher at the Missouri Theatre in St. Louis. It was formerly an all-male occupation and so there were no uniforms for women.

They must have thought it was only temporary, because they didn't order uniforms for us and we had to make do with the same ones the men wore. My friend and I were the only ones tall enough to wear the "greatcoat" with all the gold braid.[78]

Winifred E. Tanges delivered milk with her mother in New York State. Her father owned the company and had a hard time keeping male delivery drivers, because they always knew they could find higher-status work elsewhere. So she and her mother pitched in.

The customers loved us. They all thought it was great, the two women, mother and daughter, delivering milk. We wore slacks. . . . We worked from a route list that told us where to put the milk. Sometimes we would go into the house and put it in the refrigerator. We would also deliver eggs and butter, but we had to make sure we got the ration coupons for the butter.

. . . We had to pick up the empty bottles and take them back to the milk plant, unload them at the pasteurizing plant, then take them back to our garage. . . . We had to roll forty-gallon milk cans full of milk onto the truck and take it to the pasteurizing plant, unload the truck. Nobody helped us. It was our job. . . . The job reinforced the feeling that I was the equal of any man.[79]

GOING BACK HOME AGAIN

As the war wound down after D-Day in 1944, men returned home and industry started gearing up for the postwar world. Their visions did not include female workers.

By the time the war ended in August 1945, the American war industry, with the help of women workers, had produced 296,429 airplanes, 102,351 tanks and guns, 87,620 warships, 47 tons of artillery ammunition, and 44 billion rounds of small arms ammunition.[80] From 1940 to 1945, the proportion of women in the American workforce rose from 25 percent to 36 percent. By 1945, nearly 20 million women were in the labor force, up from 11.5 million in 1940.[81]

Many women would not have the option of continuing to work when the war ended. The promise from the beginning of the war, that these jobs for women were only temporary until the men came home, was being fulfilled.

Women were asked to move aside and go back to their rightful place in the home, with their families. As quickly as Rosie the Riveter had been created, an equally effective campaign was launched to cast her aside.

A newsletter for war employees published by Boeing in October 1944 in Tacoma, Washington, gave an example of a model female worker's new attitude.

> Lorraine Blum, riveter, 684, likes to build Boeing bombers to help knock out the Nips and Nazis. "But as soon as it's curtains for the Axis, it's going to be lace curtains for me," says Lorraine. "I want to establish my own home and stay put." [82]

Charlcia Neuman was laid off in September of 1945 from her job as a riveter at Vultee Aircraft in the Los Angeles area. She had been at the work since 1942.

> I just got a slip of paper saying that I wouldn't be needed again. . . . The idea was for the women to go back home. The women understood that. And the men had been promised their jobs when they came back. I was ready to go home. I was tired. . . . I knew that it would be coming and I didn't feel any letdown. The experience was interesting, but I couldn't have kept it up forever. It was too hard.
> . . . The women got out and worked because they wanted to work. And they worked knowing full well that this was for a short time. We hoped the war would be over in a very short time and that we could go back home and do what we wanted to do. So that was what I felt. [83]

But not all women workers were as easily dissuaded from their jobs. Ottilie Juliet Gattuso, who worked for Grumman in New York, wrote a letter to President Harry Truman in 1945 after she had been laid off.

> I happen to be a widow with a mother and son to support. . . . I would like to know why after serving a company in good faith for almost three and a half years, it is now impossible to obtain employment with them. I am a lathe hand and was classified as skilled labor, but simply because I happen to be a woman I am not wanted. [84]

President Truman might have expected such a reaction, since in 1943, while still vice president, he said: "Let no one imagine that the women will permit themselves to be shunted out of these jobs which they have demonstrated so well their capacity to do." [85] Secretary of the Interior Harold Ickes also had said in 1943, "I think that this is as good a time as any . . . to warn men that when the war is over, the going will be a lot tougher, because they will have to compete with women whose eyes have been opened to their greatest economic potentialities." [86]

Naomi Craig worked at Federal Products in Providence, Rhode Island, making gauges and precision instruments for war equipment. She described the problems for herself and other female war workers in converting back to prewar attitudes about women and work.

> The women who worked did change. They had gotten the feeling of their own money. Making it themselves. Not asking anybody how to spend it. And then when their husbands came home, it was kind of like, "Oh." You had to ask for money. You had to begin to curtail the things that you would have been buying, had it been your own money. The war taught them how to stand on their own two feet. So, when their husbands came home, a lot of them didn't know how to be wives anymore because they had gotten kind of bossy. It was hard to get adjusted to somebody telling you "do this" when you've been doing what you want. [87]

William Mulcahy supervised women war workers in a factory in Camden, New Jersey, with a contract from the Navy to assemble sensitive electronic parts for ships. He remembered the scene as the war wound down:

> Despite the skill and patriotism the women had displayed, we were forced to lay them off. I will never forget the day after the war ended. We met the girls at the door, and they were lined up all the way down Market Street to the old movie theater about eight blocks away, and we handed them a slip to go over to personnel and get their severance pay. We didn't even allow them in the building, all these women with whom I had become so close, who had worked seven days a week for years and had been commended so many times by the Navy for the work they were doing. [88]

Katherine O'Grady worked in a woolen mill during the war making blankets and other clothing for soldiers. She saw a direct connection between the war years and the social transformations that followed for women in the workplace.

> After the war things changed, because women found out they could go out and they could survive. They could really do it on their own. That's where I think women's lib really started. I think it made us more aware. We were very sheltered up until 1941.[89]

But riveter Barbara Walls, who had worked in New York at the same plant as her mother, believes that though many women exited the factories, something from their war work stayed with them.

> Some of the Rosies did very heroic things. And they didn't want to give up what they had experienced or achieved during their war work. But even as they left their jobs, I'm sure that a seed was planted, that women can be heroic.[90]

A lot of such seeds were planted during the war that would germinate and flower in the years to come. Edith Sokol, anticipating her husband's return from fighting overseas, sweetly foreshadowed a sea change in a letter to him near the end of the war in 1945:

> Sweetie,
>
> I want to make sure I make myself clear about how I've changed. I want you to know now that you are not married to a girl that's interested solely in a home—I shall definitely have to work all my life—I get emotional satisfaction out of working; and I don't doubt that many a night you will cook the supper while I'm at a meeting. Also, dearest—I shall never wash and iron—there are laundries for that! Do you think you will be able to bear living with me?
>
> > I love you.
> > Edith[91]

The men who had gone to fight in World War II to preserve the American way of life would come home to a place where, for many women, that way of life had been transformed. Masses of lower- and middle-class American women had tasted a kind of freedom they had never known before. For some it was sweet, for others more bitter. But the genie was out of the bottle.

Women had had a taste of making their own money and having their own life outside the home, and many had liked it. Although society in general could not discern it right away, in hindsight it is clear that no matter how hard anyone tried to coax her, that genie was not going back in. A revolution had begun in working life and home life in America.

Saipan
Tuesday, July 10, 1945

DEAREST FAMILY:

I've been intending to write you about . . . the shows that come to this island—the USO shows . . . Since I've been here Gertrude Lawrence and her show, Joe E. Brown and his show, "This Is the Army," and several other shows with lesser-known stars have been here . . . I'd read Joe E. Brown's book when I was at the Digest in which he kept repeating over and over again that the men he'd given shows for had thanked him for always presenting clean material. And as far as I can make out that seems to be the prevalent opinion out here. The men (and especially the ones who've been out here for a long time for some reason or other) seem to resent it terrifically if a show depends on risque material for humor. The Marines (and that too came as a surprise to me since you think of Marines as the roughest, toughest fighting men) particularly resent it, and they've been known to boo performers off the stage and get up and walk out.

. . . And while we're on the subject of celebrities I must also add that I've met Tyrone Power out here. He's in the Marine Air Corps and I met him one night at a Marine party. . . . He'll kid with the fellows and promise to fix them up on dates with Lana Turner and Betty Grable. And they all think he's all right.

CHAPTER THREE

Putting Up a Good Front

FEMALE ENTERTAINERS, FICTIONAL CHARACTERS, AND ICONS

A lot of guys don't have any girl friends to fight for. I guess you could call us pinup girls kind of an inspiration.

BETTY GRABLE[1]

National Archives

THERE ARE MOMENTS when a voice, a song, an image or some sort of news has the power to touch a person so deeply that it spurs his or her life in an uncharted direction. For Jean Ruth, such a moment came on January 16, 1942, just after America entered the war. She had boarded her flight home to Denver from New York City, heady with a newfound sense of herself. Not only had she just been featured on a national radio show but she was going back home with inklings that Hollywood might soon be calling, asking to buy the rights to a movie about her life. Only months before, Jean had become one of America's first female disc jockeys, filling in for the male voices who had gone off to war. A woman in the job was such a novelty that on January 5, 1942, *Time* magazine ran a story about the twenty-four-year-old's early morning radio show in Denver.

> Of the many pretty girls to whom the Army looks for the joys of life, few have merited as much mass devotion as a cheerful, blue-eyed little number. . . . Known as "Beverly" on Denver's station KFEL, she is directly responsible for the fact that 28,000 Army men at Fort Logan and three other Army posts get up willingly before sunrise. Her hour-long program, "It's a Date at Reveille—with Beverly" goes on the air at 5:30 every weekday morning.

The article went on to describe the fan mail she was receiving, including a letter from a soldier that said, "You couldn't seem any closer than you do coming into this big barracks room. Your voice is all sort of warm and sparkling." Army morale officers even began sending her announcements to read each morning as the best way to guarantee their troops heard them. Jean—going by the on-air name of "Beverly" because it rhymed with "reveille"—was not quite sure what to do with this sudden whirlwind of attention. But when her plane stopped off in Chicago to refuel that day she heard the sad news that crystallized her commitment to her wartime radio life.[2]

Early that morning, Carole Lombard, one of the most popular actresses in America and Clark Gable's wife, had been killed in a plane crash just outside Las Vegas, Nevada. Lombard was on her way back from the first official

Hollywood campaign promoting the sale of government bonds to raise money for the war cause. Just after Pearl Harbor, the Treasury Department had enlisted the Metro-Goldwyn-Mayer studio to recruit stars to sell war bonds state by state. M-G-M approached Gable, who was head of the actors' division of the Hollywood Victory Committee, and asked him to kick off the first drive somewhere in the heartland of America. But Gable was about to begin shooting a film with Lana Turner, so his wife agreed to go instead, making Lombard the first star to embark on a bond drive. As a bonus, she decided to start it all in her home state of Indiana, where she was especially revered. It was just the kind of classic middle-American place the studio had requested. Lombard's mother went with her, and on the last day of the tour, in Indianapolis, Lombard raised $2 million. Triumphant, she hurried home to her husband on the ill-fated plane, instead of aboard the train on which they had been scheduled.[3]

Lombard's death shocked most everyone in America that morning. "She was my favorite actress," Jean Ruth remembered. "She was *the* star, in my mind." Most of the other passengers on Jean's plane decided not to reboard in Chicago after hearing of Lombard's crash, and instead took a train to Denver. But Jean pushed on. Aboard the flight, she tried to read but could not concentrate. Her mind kept turning back to Carole Lombard, who many were calling the first female casualty of the war. "Here was a woman with everything to live for," thought Jean, and yet she went out and died doing her part for the war effort. The sacrifice had a profound effect on Jean, who was beginning to decide just how she was going to contribute to the war effort.

> I was already quite committed. I knew I was going to stay in something for the armed forces. . . . But that sort of cemented it. It was coming home to Denver that I decided I had to stick to the microphone for the guys. I kind of wanted to get married and have kids, except for the war. . . . Suddenly multitudes wanted me. And I thought, well this is what I have to do and want to do. So I was prepared. By the time I got to Denver . . . I had pretty much decided that I had to stay by my microphone.[4]

Hollywood concurred with her decision. Almost immediately after returning to Denver, Jean Ruth signed a contract with CBS radio and moved her show to Los Angeles, where it was broadcast throughout the country. Soon it was sent all over the world by Armed Forces Radio, which the government started in 1943 to broadcast news, music, and information to American troops abroad.

Before the war, no one imagined a woman's voice could be influential. Radio announcing had been left to men. But soldiers loved Jean, and the other women disc jockeys. That love was not something trite or whimsical. For many of the troops the voice of a woman, the image of a woman, were all they had to cling to for comfort amidst the bleak terrain of war. A sailor once wrote to Jean saying simply: "I'm with the Seabees out here in the Pacific. . . . There are no women out here and it does us good to hear your voice."[5]

At the beginning of her show on Armed Forces Radio, called *GI Jive*, a man's voice introduced Jean in the snappy lingo of the time: "Leading the line of march today is one of the best-looking swing sergeants you ever laid an optic on. She's the lovely radio personality, the reveille gal, Beverly." Jean's patter between songs also reflected the zippy tone she was charged with maintaining on the air: "Hi there, men from the U.S.A. This is Beverly. We're ready with the stuff that makes you swing and sway. I've just finished loading the turntables with platters that are busting with bounce. Ready, and I mean ready, so let's let a few of them loose."[6]

By 1943, the film based on Jean's life was produced. Called *Reveille with Beverly*, it starred Ann Miller as Beverly, and featured Duke Ellington and an up-and-coming singer named Frank Sinatra in one of his first film appearances.

Like many women in wartime entertainment work, Jean saw her job as boosting the men's spirits. Often she played requests sent in by soldiers who she named on the show. The songs and performers were the era's most popular, such as Artie Shaw's "Begin the Beguine," Tommy Dorsey's "I'll Be Seeing You," Ella Fitzgerald's "Three Little Words," Doris Day's "Sentimental Journey," as well as Benny Goodman, Glenn Miller, and Harry James. "I didn't talk too much about the war," said Beverly. "I managed to put a lot of sympathy in my voice when dedicating to men in the hospitals. . . . But I generally kept it up, up, up. . . . The music was the important thing."[7]

Indeed, the women singers of the time felt a special obligation to bring sentiment and the love of the women back home to the men in combat. Jo Stafford was one of the most popular female singers of the war years and her versions of wartime ballads like "Long Ago (And Far Away)" and "It Could Happen to You" were often featured on radio shows for troops. She recalled: "For many guys, I was a conduit—from them to me to Joanne or whoever their girl was at home. Something about my sound made them glad to be sad. . . . That nostalgic sadness was the last thing they wanted to hear before they went to sleep at night."[8]

On the home front, radio was also the public's main source for music, as well as for news and information. By 1944, estimates based on the U.S. Census reported 88.9 percent of all families in the country had radios. An earlier *Fortune* magazine poll ranked radio as the recreation enjoyed the most by Americans (18.8 percent), with going to the movies (17.3 percent) second, and reading magazines and books (13.8 percent) third. But when asked, "If you had to give up either going to the movies or listening to the radio, which one would you give up?" the results heavily favored keeping radio—with 79.3 percent saying they would give up movies and only 13.9 percent willing to give up radio.[9]

Just as the Office of War Information had worked with the magazine industry to try to influence information about the war and promote government causes, so the OWI created the Radio Bureau as a liaison with the radio industry. One of the Radio Bureau's responsibilities included writing and producing short radio spots promoting the war effort that were broadcast between shows. War-related announcements on almost all radio programs effectively helped keep the civilian sense of obligation to the national good foremost in the minds of most Americans. On February 1, 1944, for instance, CBS radio had *Kate Smith Day,* featuring one of the most popular and patriotic singers of the day. She made fifty-seven appeals in support of the war throughout the day's programming and raised a total of $112 million for the war effort.[10]

Some of the announcements that ran regularly had an almost campy tone, as with this DRB script for a nonspecific spot about women's role in the war:

ANNOUNCER: (Forceful) Woman Power!

WOMAN: (Poetically) Woman power! . . . The power to create, and sustain life. The power to inspire men to bravery, to give security to little children. A limitless, ever-flowing source of moral and physical energy—working for victory! *That* is woman power![11]

BOND DRIVES

Perhaps that notion of woman power would not seem quite so overblown if it were applied to the way female movie stars succeeded in selling war bonds, an investment that gave a sort of loan to the government to finance the war. Actress Hedy Lamarr once sold $17 million worth of bonds in one day, with one kiss going for $25,000. Lana Turner charged $50,000 a kiss.[12] A pair of stockings once worn by Betty Grable netted $110,000 at a bond drive in Virginia.[13] And Dorothy Lamour was reported to have sold $30 million worth of bonds in four days, and raised a total of $350 million through kisses, autographs, and appearances during the war.[14] Her success prompted *Modern Screen* magazine to say in 1943, "Dottie Lamour has swept the country like a forest fire. If you haven't bought a bond from Dottie, you ain't lived."[15] Lamour remembered one of her most lucrative bond tours in New England:

> In most places there were as many as twelve- to fifteen-thousand people lined up on the streets. I had set up where I would sell the bonds and had someone with me to count the money. I made a deal with the Treasury Department that I would not take pledges, only cash. That way I got the money before they got the autograph. I was extremely proud that in the first four days, I brought in $30 million.[16]

Marlene Dietrich, a German-born actress, was a zealous war bond salesperson. She had immigrated to the United States to make films and became an American citizen before the war in 1939.[17] Perhaps more than any other American entertainer, Dietrich's dedication to the war effort was deeply personal and especially risky. Her outspoken presence as a visible supporter of the Allied cause provoked Hitler himself to put her on his personal hit list. Some of her family were still living in Germany during the war. She had been asked by the German government to come back to Germany to support the Nazis as war broke out in Europe, but had refused. So it is especially noteworthy to see what a Nazi newspaper in Berlin said in a caption to a photo of her taking her oath of American citizenship in 1939. In what was perceived as a further slap in the face to the Nazis, the judge who administered Dietrich's oath was the kind of person the Nazis hated most. He was Jewish.

> The German-born film actress Marlene Dietrich spent so many years among Hollywood's film Jews that she has now become an Ameri-

can citizen. Here we have a picture in which she is receiving her papers in Los Angeles. What the Jewish judge thinks of the formula can
be seen from his attitude as he stands in his shirtsleeves. He is taking
from Dietrich the oath in which she betrayed her Fatherland.[18]

By the time of Pearl Harbor Dietrich was ready to do whatever it took to defeat the menace she saw in her homeland. She was tireless in her work to sell
bonds. She remembered some of her early bond tours in the U.S. accompanied by Treasury Department officials:

> Our tours were exhausting—six to eight hours a day, and sometimes
> also an evening performance. I had to go into factories and call upon
> workers to give a certain percentage of their salaries as a loan to the
> government. I gave speeches according to instructions, and even
> went so far as to pit one factory against another as rivals. This
> strategy proved very productive. All by myself, I raised a million dol-
> lars, which flowed into the Treasury coffers. All that effort was sup-
> posed to contribute—at least in my eyes—to the ending of the war as
> quickly as possible.[19]

Dietrich was also known for embellishing some of her stories for dramatic
effect, which could have been the case with an account she gave of one bond
sales tactic. She said that the Treasury Department had a deal with the bank-
ing system giving it access to current records of all accounts, any time of the
night or day. Dietrich said she would take a Treasury official with her when
she performed at a nightclub. And when a patron wrote Dietrich a check for a
bond, in order to give the official enough time to check out his account, she
said she would "sit in the donor's lap and wait until I got a nod from the Treasury Department agent signaling that everything was in order—or that we
had been hoaxed."[20] Whether it is true or not, it shows that Dietrich took her
role in the war seriously, and so, presumably, did the government.

Along with the individual star efforts, bands of stars would also tour the
country raising bond money for the war cause. In spring 1942, the Army-
Navy Relief Fund put together the Hollywood Victory Caravan to raise
money for the families of men killed overseas. The troupe included Olivia de
Havilland, Claudette Colbert, and Merle Oberon, as well as Bob Hope, Cary
Grant, Bing Crosby, Groucho Marx, and others. Occasionally guest stars, such
as Marlene Dietrich, would travel for a few days with the group.[21]

Bob Hope started his lifelong tradition during World War II of visiting troops both at home and overseas and bringing along attractive female performers. World War II was also when Hope became famous for his gentle but ribald sense of humor. And the women around him played along, such as when Dorothy Lamour joked with him onstage in front of an audience of soldiers. The joke played off a line in Johnny Mercer's popular 1944 wartime song "Accentuate the Positive," which spoke of eliminating the negative and latching on to the affirmative, but not messing with "Mr. In-Between." So Lamour made her own light quip about something mundane and then in front of all the soldiers she said innocently, "Don't take me seriously, Bob, I was just pulling your leg." Hope reportedly replied with a glint in his eye, "Listen, Dottie, you can pull my right leg and you can pull my left leg, but don't mess with Mr. In-Between." [22]

Another female star who caused a sensation and became an adept bonds saleswoman was Lana Turner. She was known as "the sweater girl" during World War II because of how her shapely figure filled out the tight sweaters she wore. Turner remembered riding from town to town selling bonds from the train at small stations along the way. Many of the places had munitions plants where workers would come out to see the celebrities. "At every stop," she said, "we were greeted by wildly cheering crowds, often mostly women. That sea of female faces—you knew that the men had gone to war." [23]

Also in 1942 the Hollywood War Activities Committee and the Treasury Department organized Stars Over America, a massive tour of celebrities to raise money through war bond sales. [24] There were 337 actresses and actors who took part, including Bette Davis, Myrna Loy, Ginger Rogers, Gene Tierney, Dorothy Lamour, Greer Garson, Veronica Lake, Jane Wyman, Hedy Lamarr, Irene Dunne, and Paulette Goddard. The tour started on the steps of the Treasury Department in August and celebrities fanned out in seven different groups across the country to visit more than 300 cities and towns during the next month. When Bette Davis was boarding the train at the beginning of the tour she said, "I think it is outrageous that movie stars have to wheedle and beg people into buying bonds to help their country. But if that's the way it is, I'm going to squeeze all I can out of everyone." [25] The tour ended in New York with a show at Madison Square Garden that included most of the stars who had participated. The whole tour had raised $775 million, and that final night in New York brought in $86 million for the Treasury. [26]

Carole Lombard's death had woken up Hollywood early to both its power and obligation to work for war victory. *Modern Screen* magazine in February 1943 remarked on the movie industry's efforts.

> Believe us, nobody has to ask what Hollywood is doing in this war! To date, its War Bond sales amount to $838,250,000! Among the things that this sum can buy are 8 battleships for your sons! Or 24 cruisers for your brothers. 670 sub chasers, 120 subs, or tanks, bombers or fighters! Our boys aren't going to die for lack of equipment, ever again, and we can thank our "stars" for much of the good work![27]

THE STAGE DOOR CANTEENS

Another way entertainers contributed to the war effort was through opening and performing at a string of canteens in large cities across the country, where they would entertain the troops, serve them food, and dance with them. The first of these Stage Door Canteens, as they were called, was in New York. The idea sprung from a group of Broadway theater women who had banded together to assist the British War Relief Society before America entered World War II. The tradition of actors helping the war effort had started in earnest during World War I when playwright Rachel Crothers and six other women formed the Stage Women's War Relief to collect food and clothing, sell Liberty Bonds, and entertain soldiers. Rachel Crothers was one of the most prolific and successful playwrights of the early twentieth century. She not only wrote but also produced and directed plays on Broadway. Most of her plays looked at women's position in American society, often using humor to point out the double standards under which women lived. They included *A Man's World, The Three of Us, As Husbands Go,* and *When Ladies Meet.*

As World War II approached, Crothers again called on the women of Broadway to help. Actor and director Antoinette Perry (the woman for whom the Tony Awards are named), Helen Hayes, Lynn Fontaine, Tallulah Bankhead, and others joined with Crothers in 1939, when the war started in Europe, to raise money and to knit clothing for French and British refugees. When America entered the war in late 1941 the group named itself the American Theatre Wing for War Service. Along with Crothers, Antoinette Perry is credited with being a main motivator behind the Stage Door Canteen, which opened in March 1942, set up in the basement of the 44th Street Theatre on 44th Street between Broadway and Eighth Avenue in the heart of New York City's theater district.[28]

The Canteen was just down the street from the St. James Theatre, where a young, unknown hopeful was working as an usher. Her name was Lauren Bacall.

> The Stage Door Canteen was about to open in New York and it needed hostesses. Only theatre folk qualified. I signed up for Monday nights. I was to dance with any soldier, sailor, or marine who asked me—get drinks or coffee for them, listen to their stories.
>
> Many of them had girls at home—were homesick—would transfer their affections to one of us out of loneliness and need. Some would come every Monday night to see the same girl. It was really very sweet and sad and fun, a natural set-up for a dreamer. There was always music, and stars would appear each night to entertain or talk to the boys from the small stage. My first night there I couldn't believe it—Alfred Lunt and Lynn Fontaine were washing dishes and serving coffee. Helen Hayes too. Betty Kalb and I had signed up together. Each of us was so busy watching the famous stars coming in that there wasn't time for us to compare notes until the end of the evening.
>
> On Monday nights there was fierce jitterbugging. Many a time I found myself in the middle of a circle—everyone clapping to the music—while I was being whirled and twirled by one guy, then passed on to another, non-stop, until I thought I would drop. Judy Garland and Johnny Mercer came in one night and sang some of Mercer's songs—John Carradine came in—and many, many others. It wasn't much to do for the war effort, but it was something. At least the boys had a place to go that was clean and fun and a relaxing change for them.[29]

Branches of the canteen, run by the American Theatre Wing, were soon set up in Los Angeles, Boston, Washington, D.C., Philadelphia, Cleveland, Newark, San Francisco, London, and Paris. Celebrities mingled with average soldiers, waited on them, danced with them, and cleaned up after them. A weekly radio show sprang from the canteens in 1942 and a movie called *Stage Door Canteen* came out in 1943. It featured many cameo appearances by actors and musicians including Ethel Merman, Katharine Hepburn, Gypsy Rose

Lee, Merle Oberon, Mary Pickford, Helen Hayes, Tallulah Bankhead, and Ethel Waters.[30] Perhaps it was just an oversight that in America military women were not allowed in the canteens, or were kept segregated from the main areas reserved for men. The reason given was because no romance was permitted in the canteens. Overseas canteens, however, did allow servicewomen.[31]

Maxene Andrews, one of the famous singing trio the Andrews Sisters, remembered the circumstances of the many canteen appearances she and her sisters made.

> No one simply performed at the Canteens. You sang or danced or told jokes or played a musical instrument, whatever your specialty was, but you also waited on tables, danced with the guys or gals, and provided a friendly or sympathetic ear whenever the occasion arose in conversation, which was often.[32]

Andrews also remembered that singers were discouraged from playing any songs that were too evocative of less positive wartime feelings. There was a no-play list for the canteens that attempted to focus the performers on singing only upbeat material. Some of the songs shunned in the canteen included "Remember Pearl Harbor," "When the Lights Go on Again," "Dear Mom," "White Cliffs of Dover," and even "God Bless America."[33]

After visiting New York's Stage Door Canteen on a bond drive, actor John Garfield got the idea to open a similar canteen in Los Angeles. He enlisted Bette Davis to make it happen. She is credited with instigating the highly successful and active Hollywood Canteen and keeping it going.[34] The February 1943 *Modern Screen* magazine called Davis "the lady Bob Hope." The magazine said she was "the gal who completed a Bond tour, ill . . . worked like crazy to make the Canteen grow! Said Canteen has fed 300,000 boys, used 3,000 lbs. of java, 60,000 gals of orange juice, 150,000 packs of cigs!"[35]

Hedy Lamarr remembered Bette Davis calling her at the last minute to work at the canteen one fateful night after a long day working at the studio. Lamarr was reluctant—having already climbed into bed exhausted. But Davis's ardent pleas drew her in.

> Several actresses who had promised to work that night, for one reason or another couldn't make it. I protested but Bette was insistent. . . . I dragged myself out of bed and went back to the Canteen.

Lamarr said she headed for the kitchen and began to make some sandwiches, when she spotted about 200 unwashed cups piled in the sink. Bette smiled and said, "I washed the last few hundred. Now it's someone else's turn." Davis directed the actress to work with an actor Lamarr had never met before who was standing nearby, John Loder. The two took to the dishwashing, and to each other it turned out. Hedy Lamarr and John Loder married a little while later in May 1943.[36]

Davis made sure the focus stayed on their true mission. It was a measure of the general feeling of support for the war effort that permeated the entertainment community that celebrities who were used to such pampering in the rest of their lives could be found putting the soldiers' needs first during the war years. And just to make sure they stayed on task, Bette Davis would sometimes send out directives, like the memo she dispatched to hostesses at the canteen about dealing with wounded soldiers.

> Forget the wounds, remember the man. Don't be over-solicitous, nor too controlled to the point of indifference. Learn to use the word, "prosthetics" instead of "artificial limbs." Never say, "It could have been worse." And when he talks about his war experiences, *listen,* but don't ask for more details than he wants to give.[37]

The image of the women of Hollywood in particular, just like women in real life, had to undergo a transformation to stay in step with the mood of the war. The October 1944 *Daily Variety* pointed out this shift.

> No longer are actresses pictured as leisurely, luxury loving dolls. Today's femme star or player is as virile as the men—shown washing dishes in canteens, sweeping, hefting five-gallon coffee cans, doing hundreds of other things to prove she can take it, that she's doing her share in the war effort. Jewels, clothes, luxury are out—screenlady today is war conscious . . . minimize theatrical qualities, magnify human attributes.[38]

The participation of female stars in promoting government war aims was just about universal. It became a job requirement for most all female players. Evelyn Keyes, who had portrayed one of Scarlett O'Hara's sisters in *Gone With the Wind* in 1939, remembered that the studios asked for war support from their contract actresses:

I worked almost steadily during the war . . . the war effort and selling bonds was a continuation of what we were doing. For publicity they'd send you out with other pictures, even if they weren't yours, just so your name got in the paper or on the radio. . . . We did what we were supposed to do. But we were so welcome everywhere and so eagerly sought. People were besieging us to come here or there.

When I was in California, I had a regular night when I went to the USO, and so did everyone else. Every city had a canteen, and so every time I went to a city, I would go to that too. The boys always behaved themselves. They treated us with huge respect. Since television, it has changed, because now they know you're real people. But at that time, you weren't quite a real person. You weren't really a girl.[39]

USO TOURS

The United Service Organizations was formed in February 1941, with President Roosevelt as its honorary chairman. It brought together six well-established civilian service organizations under one umbrella to provide a connection to civilian life for soldiers—the Young Men's Christian Association, the Young Women's Christian Association, the National Catholic Community Service, the National Jewish Welfare Board, the Travelers Aid Association, and the Salvation Army. President Roosevelt said he wanted "these private organizations to handle the on-leave recreation of the men in the armed forces." The government was to build the buildings and the USO was to raise private funds to carry out its main mission—boosting the morale of the military. The first national campaign chairman was Thomas Dewey, who raised $16 million in the first year, before becoming governor of New York (and later running a close second to Harry Truman in the 1948 presidential race). The second USO campaign chairman was Prescott Bush, future U.S. senator, father to one future president, and grandfather to another.[40]

Many of the principal foot soldiers in the USO's morale mission were women, charged with providing friendly diversion for U.S. troops, who were mostly men in their teens and twenties. The USO operated centers all over the United States and in all the theaters of war, recruiting female volunteers to serve doughnuts, dance, and just talk with the troops. In October of 1941, the USO created an affiliate organization called Camp Shows to furnish live

entertainment for the soldiers. It was funded by the USO but run by a separate board of directors consisting mainly of executives from the entertainment industry. Camp Shows negotiated with all the major unions, including
the Screen Actors Guild, Actors' Equity, and musician's unions to waive pay
and working condition requirements so entertainers could more readily perform for troops in the uncertain conditions of wartime, under the auspices of
the USO.[41]

Three traveling circuits of performers were set up domestically to provide
shows for troops at 640 large military bases, smaller outposts, and military
hospitals.[42] *Modern Screen* magazine in February 1943 reported:

> Stars on nationwide tours have traveled one million miles. Two such
> are Betty Grable and Rita Hayworth. Rita visited 6 camps, auto-
> graphed by the thousand, came back from Texas with a full-fledged
> nervous breakdown from over-enthusiasm! Betty's camp total was 5;
> she Canteen-queens it every spare second.[43]

The popular World War II singer Margaret Whiting remembered performing
a sentimental song called "Dream" for an audience of 100,000 troops at an
Army base in Arizona about to be sent off to combat in the Sahara. She characterized the reception the men gave her as "thunderous" and "full of emotion."

> I knew they were being sent overseas the next day. I sang in the pour-
> ing rain. It was very dramatic. That taught me a great deal about per-
> forming. I really learned my craft during the war.[44]

Many performers spoke of the disheartening emotions they felt when
they were supposed to be lifting the spirits of the troops. Maxene Andrews remembered seeing troops off as they boarded a ship in Seattle heading into
combat in the Pacific. She and her sisters had been requested to sing their hit
song "Don't Sit Under the Apple Tree" as the men pulled away from shore.

> We stood down on the pier, looking up at all those young men lean-
> ing over the ship's rails, waving and yelling and screaming . . . It was
> happening countless times every day in groups large and small all
> over the country in 1942[,] one thought nagged at you: How many of

the young men shipping out wouldn't come back? I can still see the mothers and sweethearts standing on that dock and singing along with us as the ship sailed away to war.[45]

Andrews also remembered when she and her sisters performed at a military hospital in San Francisco, after being told by a nurse that it would be very different from anything else they had ever seen. "The most important thing," the nurse told them, was not to break down. "The last thing the boys needed," she said, "were tears."

> We walked into the first ward and it was very quiet. When we were announced, there wasn't any applause at all. It was a very long ward. We were ushered into the middle. There were beds in front of us, beds behind us. We finally looked. The sight was terrible. We saw boys with no arms or legs, with half-faces. The three of us held on to each other, because we were afraid we were going to faint. The terrible thing is to hold back the tears.[46]

Singer and dancer Ann Miller described performing for badly wounded soldiers in Florida at the Coral Gables Hotel, which had been converted into a military hospital. She did forty-eight shows for broken soldiers, who were mostly lying on stretchers in the lobbies of hotels, watching as she entertained them. During her last show she collapsed and had to be taken home on an Army airplane.

> We went from ward to ward to ward, singing and dancing and trying to boost the morale of these men. It was just hell. . . . I just fell apart and I think the shock of seeing those men with their arms and legs blown off—it was just frightening. But when you do it, you do it. You try to help them, try to sing and dance. You try to keep their spirits up. It's heartbreaking.[47]

Eventually, Camp Shows expanded its operations overseas with what it called the Foxhole Circuit. One of the first women to go overseas was actress Merle Oberon, who was accompanied by Edward G. Robinson, Al Jolson, and a singer named Patricia Morrison in 1942 on a tour of Britain, entertaining Allied troops.[48] But many of the female entertainers who performed for the troops were relative unknowns who spent years overseas on the Foxhole Circuit.

One such unnamed female USO entertainer in New Guinea described in a letter the conditions she endured, which were similar to those many combat soldiers saw. The food she described was the standard fare of "C Rations . . . dehydrated potatoes and eggs and the ever-present Spam and bullybeef." She also mentioned having "broadcast from a jungle radio station," and being "wakened in the middle of the night by a rat scampering across my face." She went on:

> We've played to audiences, many of them ankle deep in mud, huddled under their ponchos in the pouring rain (it breaks your heart the first two or three times to see men so hungry for entertainment). We've played on uncovered stages, when we, as well as the audience, got rain-soaked. We've played with huge tropical bugs flying in our hair and faces; we've played to audiences of thousands of men, audiences spreading from our very feet to far up a hillside and many sitting in the trees. . . . We've played to audiences in small units of 500 or so, and much oftener to audiences of 8 to 10,000. Every night we play a different place.

She echoed another point made by many USO performers when she said, "Don't try to fool a GI with a Hollywood face and very little talent; above all, don't underestimate him by thinking all he wants is a leg show and dirty cracks." The men got the reputation for only wanting the lowest common denominator of entertainment. But one special services performer who worked for the Army remembered a scene in Burma when opera singer Lily Pons began to perform a serious song for the men. At first they jeered and asked for more accessible female entertainment. But as she kept going a respectful quiet fell on the audience. By the time she finished, the men were silent. Then suddenly, after a few seconds during which no one moved, an applause erupted that stunned even the most seasoned performers.[49] In her letter, the USO performer in New Guinea explained her interpretation of that kind of reaction. "Every woman back home wears a halo now," she said, "and those who represent her had better keep theirs on too."[50]

In October 1944, a soldier named Harold, also stationed in northern Burma, sent his mother what he called "an editorial which I wrote several nights ago, after seeing a USO-Camp Show." He expressed some of the emotional effect the women performers could have on downtrodden male soldiers.

Last night for the first time in a long time, the men here in Northern Burma were satisfied; satisfied to the extent that they hit the hay, practically normal humans once more. . . . Five girls put laughter and memories into the hearts of nearly 500 lonely GIs—GIs who haven't seen a beautiful American girl in two years, some cases longer.

. . . A mighty spontaneous roar went up when the girls pranced on the stage. The men clapped and stamped; yelled and screamed; howled and whistled. The din was terrific—months of pent-up emotion blew out in one instant. . . . The girls sang, danced, teased the boys—and made them like it. Every song, every word called for more screams and howls. . . . To these men who have suffered intolerable tortures from Mother Nature and the Japs—it was a miracle—a temporary Shangri-La—where their cares and worries could be dispersed. No greater play or musical received such an ovation. A half hour after the performance the men were still sitting in the rain, still applauding.[51]

To be sure, USO performers saw some harrowing circumstances. But the performers seemed to sense that they had better not complain out loud, since they always remembered that the troops in combat had it worse. In October 1944, a radio reporter described the conditions under which many camp show performers worked overseas:

For five weeks now these performers have been playing here in Germany, right in the front-line area. Sometimes they live out of trucks and tents and put their make-up on in a muddy field under an apple tree. Other times they live in houses—broken houses with no windows and sometimes the house next to them gets hit by enemy shell fire. . . . They may not be the biggest names in show business back home, but they're headliners here, and if you could see the faces of GIs watching their performance, you would see why.[52]

Big names did tour the Foxhole Circuit. And like all female performers they were instructed by the USO's *Guide to the Foxhole Circuit* to dress for their stage shows like "girls back home on an important Saturday night date."[53] In late 1942, Carole Landis set out on a heralded tour of Europe and Africa with performers Martha Raye, Mitzi Mayfair, and Kay Francis. Landis chronicled what was supposed to be a six-week tour, but turned into a five-month journey, in her book, *Four Jills in a Jeep,* which also was made into a film. In one scene, Landis described a night at a military camp in Africa when she and her fellow performers were having a cup of coffee in the canteen hut just before a show.

> We were all dressed to the hilt for the boys, with our last remaining pair of silk stockings, high-heeled shoes and the best dresses we could muster. Suddenly, all hell seemed to break loose. The kids who were serving us didn't wait for any officers to materialize. They just grabbed us and flung us out of that building so fast we didn't know what had happened to us. Across the pitch-black field, with the ack-acks blazing away like sixty, they dragged us headlong, in our silly high-heeled shoes, with our gas masks banging against us. . . .
> We stumbled, fell and were flung into a hole, and crawled the rest of the way through the mud on our hands and knees. . . .
> We were in a trench that had been boarded up overhead for protection against shrapnel. At either end of the trench was an entrance, and the boys kept piling in from both sides, with the four of us in the middle. Kay and Mitzi were lucky; they were wearing their trench coats. But I had on my silver fox and Martha was wearing her mink. And we were sitting in about three inches of mud.

Then one of the boys asked Martha Raye to sing a song. Next they asked Carole Landis to sing. And soon, everyone in the trench sang together as the bombs dropped overhead. That intrepid singing went on for about an hour until the all-clear siren sounded and everyone emerged caked in mud. The women had mud all over their faces, in their hair, their mouths, and their ears. But they soon dried out and cleaned up, and they hit the stage to get on with the show.

> When we got out on the platform we received a terrific yak from the boys, the kind of reception everybody in the theatre dreams of. The fact that we had gone through an air raid with them and were still there with a song and a dance and a laugh, the relief they felt within themselves that they were still there to enjoy it—well, they just tore the place down with applause.[54]

Marlene Dietrich dedicated herself to entertaining Allied troops for the USO throughout the war. Her first performance was for an audience of 1,200 soldiers in Fort Meade, Maryland.[55] In her autobiography, she reported what General Patton told her when she began her mission to entertain overseas.

"It'll do the soldiers good to know that you're at the front. They'll tell themselves the situation can't be so bad if Marlene Dietrich's there. If we were all going to be mowed down here, the old man certainly wouldn't expose her to such danger."

Dietrich knew that it was risky for her to go anywhere near German-held territory. But she pushed on with her work through Europe regardless. She was always conscious that Hitler saw her as a particularly despicable traitor to her country and to his Nazi cause. She reported how Patton reacted when she told him of her fears.

"I'm not afraid of dying, General, but I am afraid of being taken prisoner. . . . Perhaps the Germans know that I am in the European theater of operations? . . . if they catch me . . . they'll shave off my hair, stone me, and have horses drag me through the streets. If they force me to talk on the radio General, under no circumstances believe anything I say."

The general smiled, turned around and took a revolver out of his windbreaker. "Here, shoot rather than surrender! It's small but it's effective."

Dietrich said she carried Patton's revolver with her for the rest of the war, but luckily she never had to use it.[56]

By the end of the war, the USO reported that it had put on 428,521 live shows for the men and women of the armed services, at home and abroad. More than 7,000 performers had appeared in USO shows. And thirty-seven died in the line of duty, including singer Tamara Dreisen, who was killed in a plane crash in Lisbon in 1943, along with twenty-three other entertainers. Jane Froman, a popular singer, survived that crash with major injuries but recovered and went back to performing with the USO.[57]

ALL-GIRL BANDS

Most orchestras in the prewar years were exclusively male, with females on hand to perform vocals only. But as male musicians joined the military, openings came for women. Sherrie Tucker wrote a book called Swing Shift, about the all-girl bands that arose during the war:

It was a time when serious professional musicians were seen as temporary war workers simply because they were women. . . . Women musicians were consumed as visual entertainment, primarily as representations of the idealized sweethearts that wartime propaganda and entertainment relentlessly encourages servicemen to miss or imagine. Bandleader Ada Leonard recalled telling her musicians, "Because you're a girl, people look at you first, then listen to you second." The emphasis on glamour was sometimes a hard pill to swallow, especially for women who thought of themselves as professional musicians and who traveled with all-girl bands solely because other bands would not hire them.[58]

The term "all-girl" was used without any sense of inappropriateness. Calling adult women "girls" was standard during the war years. Perhaps using "girl" as a qualifier can be interpreted as a subliminal reflection of the diminished status a female presence gave to previously all-male professions. Viola Smith, a respected drummer with seventeen years of professional experience, tried to counter that prejudice in an editorial in *Down Beat* magazine in 1942:

In these times of national emergency, many of the star instrumentalists of the big name bands are being drafted. Instead of replacing them with what may be mediocre talent, why not let some of the great girl musicians of the country take their place.[59]

That seemingly innocent and logical suggestion sounded outrageous to many jazz fans like William Peri, who wrote a reply letter to *Down Beat* in 1942 entitled "Who Said Girl Musicians Could Play?" He raged, "Girls should leave this kind of business to persons who know what it's all about. And I mean men."[60] Another reader said in reply to Viola Smith: "Who's going to supply the music when the men go? Well, it won't be women! The older generation, Joe Sullivan, George Wettling and their buddies still jive better than fanatical housewives."[61]

Sherrie Tucker reported on a female musician who, years later, compared attitudes toward women musicians before and during the war.

Trumpet player Jane Sager characterized the difference between playing in the 1930s and the playing in the 1940s as a shift from being perceived as professionals to being seen as companions for soldiers. In the 1930s, "everything was how good we sounded and how the arrangements were and what kind of performance we put on. We had a lot of pride in our work. We didn't want to sound crummy, because there was so much prejudice against women musicians to begin with." In the 1940s, however, musical expertise took a back seat to celebrations of the patriotic "girl next door." . . . While a reputation for supporting "our boys" may have carried positive connotations for a patriotic public, it also carried a promise of impermanence—"good girls" would happily put down their horns when the troops came home.[62]

Despite the musicians' ambiguous feelings surrounding this new opportunity, a number of all-girl bands played the USO circuits throughout the war. Each member received a salary of $84 a week. Some of the most popular who played stateside were Ada Leonard's All-American Girl Orchestra, Eddie Durham's All-Star Girl Orchestra, and Virgil Whyte's Musical Sweethearts. On tour for the Foxhole Circuit overseas were Sharon Rogers' All-Girl Band, D'Artega's All-Girl Orchestra, and the International Sweethearts of Rhythm.

An added pressure for these women was they had to wear glamorous clothes, such as strapless gowns and high heels, as part of the job, making wielding large instruments difficult. Doris Jarrett, who played bass with a female band called the Queens of Swing, said her clothes were particularly impractical for bass players. She mentioned a problem male bass players never had to face. "You would try to pin the dress to your bra," she said. Still, sometimes the dress would slip down, exposing her bra or more. "I was behind the bass trying to get my chest covered," she said, while also trying to keep up with the band. Similarly, female saxophone players complained of neck straps cutting into their low necklines. And for many female musicians, standing through a whole set in high heels was particularly difficult—another problem male musicians never encountered. As soon as drummer Bobbie Morrison got to her drums after walking onstage in a pair of heels, she would change into a pair of flat shoes she kept hidden behind her drums. Otherwise, it was almost impossible for her to work the drum pedals in heels. "I've seen girls do it," Morrison said. "I don't understand it because it totally changes the leverage.[63]

Not only were bands often segregated by gender, but most all-female bands were racially segregated as well. One notable exception was the International Sweethearts of Rhythm, a predominantly African-American band from Mississippi that hired a few white female musicians. They played throughout the U.S. and were tapped to play for African-American units in Europe during a USO tour at the end of the war.[64]

Some female musicians, such as Maurine Longstreth, a baritone saxophone player, managed to play in predominantly male bands. She had played in an all-girl orchestra in Dayton, Ohio, before the war and then took her boyfriend's place in a Dayton dance orchestra in 1943 when he joined the military. After training, he was stationed at Bergstrom Air Force Base near Austin and in early 1945 they married and she moved to Texas. As the war was winding down and many of the male musicians were leaving the military, she was the only woman playing in his Air Force band. She said the other musicians were welcoming. But she remembered one uncomfortable incident of that time when she and the band had to play backup music for Gypsy Rose Lee, the famous stripper and entertainer who had performed for troops throughout the war. Longstreth got no sympathy for her discomfort from the commanding officer:

> They had this big auditorium with thousands of men. I never saw so many men in my life. Here I am the only woman. I kept telling the major that I didn't belong in this. I just did not feel that I should be there with a bunch of men in a striptease. I was the only other woman besides Gypsy. But the major just said no, you're playing. So I played. But when Gypsy came out, man, if you've ever seen anyone slide down in the chair underneath the music stand and still play a horn—I was embarrassed. She had on one of those netsy body suits that your imagination could play a lot. The men were going crazy. They weren't even looking at me I'm sure. As soon as that was over I got the heck out of there. I was gone.[65]

By virtue of her talents being recognized and used for the first time in a world of men during the war, women like Longstreth found themselves face-to-face with some of the other women who had inhabited a man's world before the war, mainly in roles like Gypsy Rose Lee's. There had always been a place for women who used their bodies to titillate men, but generally that had been a clandestine role. During World War II, women's sexuality was more out in the open than almost any other time before in America. That presented new problems as well as new freedoms for women and men. Gypsy Rose Lee was one of the more racy entertainers allowed to perform for American troops. But overtones and undertones of sexuality were almost always close by whenever male soldiers considered women. Sometimes those currents found very public ways of expressing themselves among the men in the military.

PINUPS AND NOSE ART

Some of the most influential females during the war years were not real women at all. They were the female images fostered in the media to pin down the often contradictory expectations of women during World War II—or to pin them up. Drawings and photos of supremely available women that men pinned up on their barracks walls reportedly helped divert them from the horrors of war. Some of the most notorious of these pinups during wartime were the Varga Girls—drawings by a Peruvian-born artist named Alberto Vargas and featured in *Esquire* magazine (the "s" at the end of his name was taken out to appear less South American). Because of the Varga Girls' supposed positive motivational effect on the morale of the fighting men, Bob Hope was heard to say, "Our American troops are ready to fight at the drop of an *Esquire*." [66]

But not everyone felt that these *Esquire* renderings of slightly dressed women in suggestive poses were a good thing. That is why *Esquire* went to court in 1943 when the Post Office tried to censor its racy content. A look at the substance of that controversy shows key points about changing attitudes in the nation during the war regarding women and sexuality. The postmaster general at the time, Frank Walker, took formal action against *Esquire* in 1943, threatening to revoke its second-class mailing status because of its "obscene, lewd, and lascivious character." The Varga Girls were singled out as particularly offensive. If *Esquire* could not win and had to mail its magazine at first-class rates, it would have cost the magazine an additional $500,000 a year. So the magazine mounted a fierce battle, calling thirty-eight nationally known educators, writers, scientists, and other experts including two women—child welfare activist Edith B. Cook of the Connecticut State Welfare Association, and social worker Rae L. Weissman of the New York City Committee on Mental Hygiene—both of whom said the magazine was not indecent. [67] And, it was pointed out, at the Army's behest, *Esquire* had supplied extra copies for isolated military outposts and military hospitals, thereby supporting the magazine's claim that its content boosted the spirits of America's soldiers. [68]

GIs responded to the *Esquire* case with passion. A Navy lieutenant wrote a letter to his congressman saying, "*Esquire* magazine is an aid to the morale of the fighting men." He told of a soldier in his unit who died in a foxhole grasping a picture of a Varga Girl. The lieutenant said, "He had not wanted to risk leaving his picture in his tent for fear the enemy would get it. These boys have so little; they have and hold foremost their memories."[69]

The Post Office panel ruled in *Esquire*'s favor, but the postmaster appealed, eventually to the U.S. Supreme Court, which, in 1946 after the war had ended, ruled unanimously for *Esquire*.[70] Obviously, the Varga Girls' popularity was unaffected by the Post Office case. The drawings even became the templates for the sexy images of women that proliferated on the noses of military planes throughout World War II. Most B-17, B-24, and B-29 bombers were adorned with such "nose art" paintings of voluptuous, Vargas-inspired fantasy women in various stages of undress. The tradition grew that these drawings were accompanied by names that military pilots would pick for their planes, usually a play on women's names or body parts—names like "Dinah Might," "Iza Vailable," "Any Time Annie," "Eager Beaver," "Booby Trap," or "Miss Conduct."

The pinup evolved on its own during the war. Other magazines got into the act, and Hollywood picked up on the trend. Even the military began soliciting pinup art for distribution to the troops. Some women artists also hit it big in the illustrating business during the war, especially Zoë Mozert, Pearl Frush, and Joyce Ballantyne. Mozert was her own model, posing in front of a mirror to draw alluring likenesses of herself. She was known for her more realistic, but still sexy, depictions of women. She also specialized in drawing Hollywood starlets for covers of magazines like *Screen Book, Romantic Movie Screen,* and *True Confessions.* But most of her drawings were done for calendars, as was much of the pinup art of other artists.[71]

Yank, a magazine published by the military for the troops, went beyond the pinup drawings and began running photographs of real female celebrities in sexy poses. The Hollywood studios also began to require such pinup shots of its women contract players. Actress Evelyn Keyes remembered:

> We females spent hours posing in bathing suits, negligees and shorts, jumping out of candy boxes for Valentine's Day. . . . We donned our sexiest threads and visited army camps, always with a photographer present. . . . I spent a great deal of time in bathing suits for pinups.

Even that was part of the war effort. It's funny when you think of it, because our careers were built on the war-camp walls.[72]

In the mix of all this, the most famous and popular pinup photo of the war emerged: Betty Grable's famous bathing suit shot, taken from behind as she looked over her shoulder. Shot by a publicity photographer at 20th Century Fox, the studio estimated it had sent out five million copies of the celebrated pose to soldiers by the end of the war.[73]

One soldier wrote to Grable:

> There we were. Out in those damn dirty trenches. Machine guns firing. Bombs dropping all around us. We would be exhausted, frightened, confused and sometimes hopeless about our situation, when suddenly someone would pull your picture out of his wallet. Or we'd see a decal of you on a plane and then we'd know what we were fighting for.[74]

Other actresses became popular pinups as well, including Rita Hayworth, Jane Russell, Ann Sheridan, Lana Turner, and Veronica Lake. And in those days, even pinups were segregated by race, so Lena Horne became the most popular pinup for black soldiers.

Ladies' Home Journal and other women's magazines had set forth the ideal image of women as homemakers, like Betty Crocker, who became every soldier's perfect mother. *The Saturday Evening Post*'s Rosie the Riveter, drawn by Norman Rockwell, became the icon of competent females in the workplace, and every soldier's consummate sister figure. *Esquire* magazine put forth another fanciful image of women as compliant sex kittens—the pinups, every soldier's ultimate girlfriend or wife. For many women during the war years, there was some pressure to emulate all three of these widely publicized icons, often all at once. And it was Betty Grable who came the closest to doing so publicly. She could be the sexy siren, yet she was always portrayed as the wholesome girl next door, especially after she married bandleader Harry James in 1943 and had children. By the end of the war she was the highest-paid woman in America, showing her professional mastery as well. Other women listened to Betty Grable and trusted her, and men loved her.

FICTIONAL WOMEN

The creative minds who came up with fictional characters did not stop at the actresses and illustrations that populated magazines. They went on to find plenty of other ways to portray female figures who fit into the molds created by the various requirements society was demanding of wartime women.

With so many new feelings, roles, obligations, and reactions swirling around an upended society during wartime, one place people turned to try and make sense of it all, or to escape the confusion and sadness, was to the movies. Messages about national spirit and morale were seen and heard throughout the films made during World War II, and they were not there by accident.

The Office of War Information's Bureau of Motion Pictures had set up camp in Washington and Hollywood soon after the war began, and worked with studio executives to influence their output. In 1942 it published a guide for moviemakers on U.S. policy called *The Government Information Manual for the Motion Picture*, which had suggestions about how to influence audiences. Early in 1943, the OWI's director, Elmer Davis, said:

> The easiest way to inject a propaganda idea into most people's minds is to let it go in through the medium of an entertainment picture when they do not realize that they are being propagandized.[75]

Evidence of that charge can be seen in most films made during the war. One of the most ardent and early films to carry a strong war-related message was *Mrs. Miniver*, which came out in June 1942. It set forth a portrait of the obligations of women, as well as men, to the war effort. Directed by William Wyler, it starred Greer Garson as the English housewife in the title, enduring hardships during Germany's repeated but ultimately unsuccessful assaults on Britain. In one scene, an English minister gave a sermon after the deaths of a choirboy, the stationmaster, and Mrs. Miniver's daughter-in-law. He said:

> This is not only a war of soldiers in uniform. It is a war of the people—of all the people—and it must be fought not only on the battlefield but in the cities and in the villages, in the factories, on the farms and in the homes, and in the heart of every man, woman, and child who loves freedom.

President Roosevelt and British Prime Minister Winston Churchill both loved the film. Roosevelt directed that the movie be rushed to theaters. The Voice of America radio network broadcast the minister's speech from the film, magazines reprinted it, and it was copied onto leaflets and dropped over German-occupied countries. Churchill sent a telegram to studio head Louis B. Mayer that read: "Mrs. Miniver is propaganda worth 100 battleships." The film won six Academy Awards.[76]

Many other films that followed featured women, and concentrated on war themes, always reinforcing the mission of the war and of citizens and soldiers alike. In 1943 Hollywood released films like *First Comes Courage* starring Merle Oberon, and directed by one of the only female directors of the time, Dorothy Arzner. Ginger Rogers starred in *Tender Comrade*. A film about women nurses called *So Proudly We Hail!* starred Claudette Colbert, Paulette Goddard, and Veronica Lake.

In 1944, Rita Hayworth starred in *Cover Girl,* and Tallulah Bankhead played war photographer Margaret Bourke-White in *Lifeboat.* Also in 1944, *The Doughgirls* came out starring Ann Sheridan, Alexis Smith, Jane Wyman, and Eve Arden. And another classic film from 1944 echoed *Mrs. Miniver: Since You Went Away,* starring Claudette Colbert, Jennifer Jones, and Shirley Temple, showed a family weathering wartime sadness and hardship, this time on the American home front.

In the 1943 film *Stage Door Canteen* war themes and the female entertainer's role were the focus of the plot. Eileen was a young actress who began working at the Stage Door Canteen, where she met a soldier about to be shipped overseas. Despite the ban on romance at the canteen, Eileen, played by Cheryl Walker, ended up proposing to him and they were to get married at the end of the film before he left for war. As she waited for him, another soldier showed up at the canteen where her fiancé was supposed to meet her to tell her that he had to ship out suddenly and could not meet her. Katharine Hepburn, playing herself in a significant cameo, heard all this and went to comfort Eileen. In the process, she gave an impassioned speech that celebrated the female actresses who volunteered at the Canteen as well as sent the audience the same message of sacrifice and support for the war that had been put forth in *Mrs. Miniver.*

EILEEN: It isn't fair.
KATHARINE HEPBURN: You bet it isn't fair, but it's happening.

EILEEN: Oh Miss Hepburn, I just heard . . .

KATHARINE HEPBURN: Yes, I know. He sent you his dearest love and said he hoped you'd be his Mrs. when he got back.

EILEEN: I can't stand it. I've got to get out of here.

KATHARINE HEPBURN: Wait a minute. Why'd you volunteer for this work?

EILEEN: Because I wanted to help.

KATHARINE HEPBURN: Help what?

EILEEN: I wanted to help my country.

KATHARINE HEPBURN: Why do you think your country needs your help?

EILEEN: We're in a war and we've got to win.

KATHARINE HEPBURN: Yes, that's right. We're in a war and we've got to win. And we're going to win. And that's why the boy you love is going overseas. And isn't that maybe why you're going to go back in there and get on your job?

Look, You're a good kid. I don't wonder why he loves you. He knows what he's fighting for. He's fighting for the kind of world in which you and he can live together in happiness, in peace, in love.

Don't ever think about quitting. Don't ever stop for a minute working, fighting, praying until we've got that kind of a world. For you, for him, for your children, for the whole human race.

Eileen then kissed Hepburn's cheek and bravely marched back onto the dance floor to take up her work again.

Apparently, that dedication to the war effort was not just acting. Hepburn talked about the importance of the war in her offscreen life as well. In letters to a friend from her college days, Robert McKnight, who was serving in the Army in North Africa, Katharine Hepburn spoke of her personal feelings about being a woman unable to join the fight on the front lines. She told him that she felt amazed at his being so far away and doing such courageous things. She contrasted his military service with her life, and said her daily routine on the home front felt "like some mad dream" compared to the life she imagined him living. She said that when she played tennis or did any of the other things she did each day, she felt "as though I've been left behind on a another planet." She told McKnight she realized that he might consider her lucky for being so far away from the bloody battlefront of the war. But as time went on, she said, she felt more and more that it is only good to be "a vital part of the most active world—however horrible—to feel that you are really functioning to your best capacities." She added, "So in a way I envy you."

This idea that men were doing active duty and women were not might have been more acute for Hollywood women because so many of the men they worked with in the industry were going off to join the military, while none of the women were encouraged to do so. In another 1943 letter to McKnight, Hepburn mentioned some of the male stars in Hollywood who had done stints in the military. She said George Cukor was promoting the film *Gaslight* with Ingrid Bergman and Charles Boyer. Hepburn said Cukor had been a private in the Army for eight months. And she wrote, "He enjoyed the experience, and enjoyed even more getting out." Hepburn also reported that George Stevens was a major, and had worked as a photographer in Africa, Egypt, Palestine, and Moscow. Then she reported that Spencer Tracy (whom she referred to as "Spence T.") was about to leave for an entertainment tour in Alaska, and had just finished a film called *A Guy Named Joe*.[77]

Tyrone Power was another star who joined the military as a private in the Marines. When he enlisted in 1943, *Motion Picture* magazine wrote a story about his wife, Annabella, and the effect his leaving had on her and their marriage. Even through the tone of the magazine, some of the same mixed feelings about being left behind that Hepburn had mentioned can be detected. The article described the moment when Tyrone decided he had to join the battle. "As any true woman would," the magazine said, "terror or no, she loved him for it. . . . The decision was his own, Annabella stayed on the sidelines." Then the magazine went on to discuss Annabella's feelings about being a woman at a time of war.

> Now, for the first time in her life she wants to be a man. Because, during wartime, girls are doing the best they can, but still they are just second. Second to men. Well then, since you can't be a man, at least you must not make it difficult for him, already it is tough enough. The girl has to help, but not to suggest and advise—which is, perhaps, to confuse and irritate. It is he who takes the danger, it is he who must make the decision. So when Tyrone talked, she listened. When he asked, she answered.[78]

That article was supposed to echo the lives of real women all across the country sending their men off to war. But there was one realm of popular culture in which the issues that average women faced were always on the front burner: daytime radio dramas, the soap operas. Twenty million women listened to the daytime dramas.[79] Between 10:00 A.M. and 6:00 P.M. a variety of fifteen-minute soap operas were heard by about 40 percent of American women.[80]

A radio soap opera was relatively cheap to make, costing about $18,000 a week to produce and generating about $35 million a year in advertising revenue during wartime.[81] Historian Sherna Gluck said soap operas "showed women how to survive, 'how to take it.'" She explained:

> These forms of popular culture did not portray women as weak and dependent. Buried in the melodramatic stories of hardship and romance, rather, was a depiction of women as strong and largely competent. This was the time of day when a woman could define—or redefine—her world. Women were in the forefront and men, at best, were de-emphasized. . . . Women could be in charge—as long as they didn't stray too far from their prescribed roles.[82]

Although the war was not always mentioned directly in the soap operas, some plot lines included wartime circumstances such as rationing. But very few of the harshest wartime hardships penetrated the daytime world. Ma Perkins, the heroine of a favorite soap, did lose her son in the war. Stella Dallas, another popular lead soap opera character, took a job in a war plant. And writers of the soap opera *Life Can Be Beautiful* worked with the Office of War Information to include wartime themes.[83]

Women were also depicted in comic strips. Aside from the daily strips that appeared in newspapers on the home front, at least two female characters were created solely for military publications. One was a character named Lace in the comic strip *Male Call,* the other was the title character of the comic strip *Winnie the WAC.*

Lace, who first appeared in 1943, was a sultry dark-haired woman who lived near a military base. She was a pal to the soldiers—sexy but still wholesome, risqué in dress or undress, while still somewhat innocent in spirit. Her creator, Milton Caniff, never got paid for his creations. It was his donation to the war effort. *Male Call* was seen in more than 2,000 military newspapers and no civilian papers. In 1946 Caniff won the Cartoonist of the Year award from the National Cartoonists Society. Here is how Caniff described the creation of the main character:

Miss Lace became the single central figure, both because she had one and because a pretty girl is a nice thing to look at even if she is a paper doll. The name "Lace" sounded feminine, it was short and easy to remember. The strip's title was suggested by the Camp Newspaper Service for its obvious twist on the familiar phrase.

In one *Male Call* comic strip Lace receives a letter from a GI that read: "Dear Miss Lace—Since you are the only glamour girl most of us guys ever see, we'd appreciate it if you'd show up in real pinup outfits—you know—like the movie stills. —Dogface Dan" In the next frame, Lace, standing reading the letter in a black bra and underwear and garter belt and stockings, reacted by trying to figure out how to accommodate the soldier while still observing the proper decorum. Then she appeared in the next two frames in revealing skimpy outfits, joking that she was showing how she couldn't possibly dress. She said that if she were to dress as she was in the middle two frames, the soldiers would "chase me (purely in the line of duty of course)." In the last frame, back in her original skimpy outfit she wrote a reply to the soldier: "Dear Dan, I guess you're stuck with me the way I am—Not pinned-up. Approximately yours, Lace."[84]

Winnie the WAC was created by Vic Herman, a corporal in the Army who was asked to create a weekly cartoon for his own camp paper after the editor heard he was an illustrator. The cartoon was eventually picked up widely among camp papers. In one representative cartoon Winnie is standing in an apron in a mess hall kitchen, holding a dish towel amidst a pile of broken dishes, with other dishes piled beside her waiting to be dried. She looks up at an angry senior officer and asks, "Do you mean to tell me I'm not fired?"

Actress Carole Landis wrote an introduction to a collection of Winnie cartoons in 1945, in which she described Winnie as:

> Cute, blonde, pert, pulchritudinous, pinupy—that was Winnie. . . . She wasn't any one WAC in particular; just all WACs rolled into one, and one WAC representing all. . . . The WAC who for so long now had been doing quiet, conscientious, thorough jobs, and receiving only a pittance of the praise they deserved . . . a cartoon character glorifying them, laughing with them rather than at them.[85]

One of the most enduring female creations of World War II was the comic book character Wonder Woman, created in 1941 by a male DC Comics consultant, psychologist, *Ladies' Home Journal* columnist, and feminist, Dr. William Moulton Marston. He believed there were not enough strong female role models for little girls. Wonder Woman began life as an Amazon princess named Diana, from an all-female land called Paradise Island. The plane of an American pilot, Captain Steve Trevor, was shot down near Diana's island. She rescued him, nursed him to health, fell in love with him, and followed him back to America, where she would also fight against threats to American ideals by the Axis nations. She took on an alter ego of U.S. Army nurse Diana Prince, who eventually quit nursing and joined the WAC, becoming a secretary for a colonel, who was an associate of Captain Steve Trevor.

All the while, as Wonder Woman, she fought heroically against Nazism and Fascism and became the first female inducted into the DC Comics superhero's League of Justice. But even though her superpowers exceeded those of most of the men in the League, she was only allowed to be the League's secretary, taking notes for the men.

Wonder Woman was first introduced as a feature in an issue of *All Star Comics,* along with stories from other superheroes. Within six months she had become so popular that she was one of only a few superheroes, and the only female, considered a strong enough character to be featured in her own comic book. (In the early 1970s Wonder Woman would appear on the first cover of *Ms.* magazine, because editor Gloria Steinem said she was the best female role model available for girls who grew up in the 1940s and 1950s.)

Wonder Woman's appearance in 1941 seemed to foreshadow some of the changes that came with the war in the limitations traditionally placed on women. Wonder Woman embodied many of the ironies in the expectations placed on women during the war. And the introduction written by Marston for Wonder Woman's first appearance in a comic book reflected the alterations occurring in at least some of the minds and hearts of the many women who were discovering their previously unrecognized powers and undeveloped skills during World War II, even if no one else could see them:

> At last in a world torn by hatreds and wars of men, appears a <u>woman</u> to whom the problems and feats of men are mere child's play. A woman whose identity is known to none, but whose sensational feats are outstanding in a fast-moving world! With a hundred times the agility and strength of our best male athletes and strongest wrestlers, she appears as though from nowhere to avenge an injustice or right a wrong! As lovely as Aphrodite—as wise as Athena—with the speed of Mercury and the strength of Hercules—she is known only as Wonder Woman.[86]

PART II

Honolulu
Tuesday, May 8, 1945

Another important event today was receiving another letter from Tom—and he enclosed a story which he'd written—I read it tonight and Dotty Brown read it too. It quite catches the spirit of this life out here—all about some nurses on a Pacific Island. We enjoyed it hugely.

> Sam's discovery was basically simple, natural, reasonable. He had discovered that nurses lived in the long, yellow house. He had discovered two large windows in the middle of the second-story front. . . . He had discovered (the telescope is a powerful glass and the room was well illumined by sunlight) that the windows belonged to the bathroom. It is, of course, redundant to say that he had also discovered a nurse in the shower stall in the far left-hand corner of the room. All of this would seem to be a model of logic, of sweet reasonableness: what could possibly be more logical than that there be a hospital at this base, that there be nurses attached to this hospital, that these nurses lived in a house, that this house have a bathroom, that this bathroom have windows, that these nurses bathe? Nothing you would think. And yet to these signalmen and quartermasters (who had last seen a white woman, probably fat, certainly fully clothed, perhaps fourteen months ago) this vision was literally that, a vision, and a miracle, and not a very small miracle, either. Like Sam, they were stricken with reverence in its presence, and like Sam their remarks were reverent; those who could speak at all. "Holy Christ!" a few of them managed to breathe, and "Son-of-a-bitch!" That was all. Those are the only legitimate things a man can say when suddenly confronted with the imponderable.*

---

* Tom Heggen, *Mr. Roberts* (New York: Houghton Mifflin, 1946), pp. 97–98.

CHAPTER FOUR

This Man's Army

WACs

You are the pioneers. There were many bets against you when you first came . . . that you couldn't take it with the boys; that American women couldn't endure Army discipline; that you'd use your femininity when the going got rough; that you'd break within a year. Everyone who bet against you, lost.

CAPTAIN MARY A. HALLAREN,
Commander, First Women's Army Corps Separate Battalion,
England, 1945 [1]

Women Veterans Historical Collection / Dorothy Gribble

Up until World War II, nursing was the only job women were allowed to do in the United States Army and Navy. But as America joined the fight in the early 1940s, it became clear that winning such a massive war on several fronts would require more military manpower than ever before. Just as it had in industry, the idea of employing women in less traditional jobs gained momentum in the Army and Navy. Women, the reasoning went, could take the place of the able-bodied men performing noncombat military work, so that those men could be sent to battle.

Yet at just about every turn, the idea was met with resistance in public opinion and, by extension, in Congress. Opposition was generally based on some mix of both disdain and protectiveness toward women. And one unwavering proviso always remained: women were not to go into combat. That meant taking a step back from some of the skills women had already proven in past wars, when their soldiering was covert, or at least less conspicuous than it was during World War II.

Perhaps the earliest and most famous American war heroine was Molly Pitcher, who got her name because she was said to have carried water in a pitcher to her husband and his fellow soldiers on the front lines during the Revolutionary War. When her husband collapsed from the heat, Molly Pitcher took his place at the cannon and heroically finished the battle for him. She was either based on a real woman, or perhaps was a symbolic representation of the deeds of many of the women who participated in the Revolutionary War.[2] Also during that war, and in the Civil War as well, stories were told of women disguising themselves as men in order to be allowed into combat.

During World War I, a bill was introduced in Congress to enlist women in the Army. It was rejected by then secretary of war Newton D. Baker, who said in a memo that the idea of women in the Army had "never been seriously contemplated" and was "considered unwise and highly undesirable."[3] Still, about 1,000 American women worked with the Army in France during World War I, with civilian status, as translators and telephone operators. In addition, briefly during that war the Navy and Marines managed to enlist nearly 13,000 women for clerical jobs in the U.S. and U.S. territories overseas. These women were given full military status. But as soon as the war ended, female Navy and Marine units were disbanded, and the women who had served were given no lasting benefits, such as hospitalization, pensions, or veteran status.[4]

Since women did not have the right to vote in America until just after World War I, it stands to reason that they also would have been denied other rights and responsibilities of full citizenship, such as joining fully and permanently in the armed forces. But after women finally secured voting rights in 1920, it was still a slow march to May 1942, when Congress passed the bill allowing women to serve as auxiliaries to the U.S. Army.

The staunch opponents to women's infiltration of the military gave in during World War II, but not without ensuring strict limits on women's options and status within the ranks of the military. Thus, women were given some of the trappings of military service for the first time ever. But not only were female soldiers in the Army not allowed to carry or use weapons, the essential equipment of war, but female naval personnel were not permitted to serve on the open sea, only on shore duty. And while women Air Force pilots could soar anywhere above the United States in military planes, they were not allowed to fly those planes outside American airspace. The sort of acrobatics of compromise those paradoxical opportunities demanded required a special strength of character and state of grace, which seemed to be at the essence of every early military woman.

GETTING WOMEN INTO THE WAR

While male soldiers were left to engage in the physical combat of the war, those early military women often found themselves at the leading edge of another type of fierce war—a war against their very existence within the Army and Navy. The first big battle of that war was the political skirmish that secured women their right to be in the Army at all. Politicians drew the battle lines and set the tone for women's tenure in the military during World War II.

Along with their new voting rights, World War II became the first war during which women had a political presence in government. Joe Martin of Massachusetts, minority leader in the House of Representatives, appointed Maine representative Margaret Chase Smith to the Naval Affairs Committee and Connecticut representative Clare Boothe Luce to the Military Affairs Committee. Martin said female members were picked for the assignments because the men on the committees had a "realization that women of the country take an important part in the war effort."[5] And it was some of the few new female politicians at the time who drew up and pushed through legislation that brought approximately 350,000 women into the military as soldiers during the war, and began to grant military women additional rights throughout the 1940s.

In spring of 1941, U.S. representative Edith Nourse Rogers of Massachusetts made it known she was about to introduce a bill to establish a women's branch of the U.S. Army. Army Chief of Staff General George C. Marshall asked her to delay. The Army's motives were set forth in an internal memo to Marshall from Brigadier General Wade H. Haislip, his assistant chief of staff, in April 1941:

> Congresswoman Edith Nourse Rogers has been determined for some time to introduce a bill to provide a women's organization in the Army. We have succeeded in stopping her on the promise that we are studying the same thing, and will permit her to introduce a bill which will meet with War Department approval.
>
> Mrs. Roosevelt also seems to have a plan.
>
> The sole purpose of this study is to permit the organization of a women's force along lines which meet with War Department approval, so that when it is forced upon us, as it undoubtedly will be, we shall be able to run it our way.[6]

The result of their study was a call for establishment of a Women's Army Auxiliary Force (WAAF), a civilian group, not part of the Army. Later, the proposed name was changed to the Women's Army Auxiliary Corps (WAAC), since it echoed the already established British WAAC, thereby making it more palatable for some. Rogers and other women advisers objected because the name was too close to the word "wacky." But they put aside such concerns and took a more tactically expedient route.

Rogers first introduced a bill at the end of May 1941. She said she had wanted the bill to give women full military status, with the same pension, disability protection, and rights as the men, but realized she could not secure that. "The War Department," she said, "was very unwilling to have these women as part of the Army." In early summer 1941, Congress referred the bill to a committee that did not act on it.[7]

By fall of 1941, General Marshall was starting to do an about-face. At that time, the armed forces consisted of only a few thousand military nurses and just more than one million enlisted men.[8] As Marshall became convinced that a manpower shortage would develop in the Army if America went to war, he began to consider women more favorably as part of the answer. Although he did not see an immediate need for women, he wanted to get the approval of Congress out of the way, so when and if he did want to call upon women, he could.[9] Colonel John H. Hildering, a top member of Marshall's staff, said that by the end of November 1941 General Marshall became adamant, once shaking a finger at him and saying, "I want a women's corps right away and I don't want any excuses." Hildering went to work in earnest.[10] After Pearl Harbor, the effort was speeded up.

Rogers reintroduced a similar bill on Christmas Eve 1941. Hildering remembered that the bill drew a volatile fight as it made its way to the attention of Congress. "It was a battle," he said. "In my time I have got some one-hundred bills through Congress, but this was more difficult than the rest of the hundred combined."[11]

The gauntlet of ridicule was indeed intense during debates on the floor of Congress in the first half of 1942. Legislators spoke on the record against women in no uncertain terms. One congressman said: "Take the women into the armed service . . . who then will maintain the home fires; who will do the cooking, the washing, the mending, the humble homey tasks to which every woman has devoted herself; who will rear and nurture the children; who will teach them patriotism and loyalty; who will make men of them, so that, when their day comes, they, too, may march away to war?"[12]

In February 1942, with military preparedness foremost on his mind, General Marshall named Oveta Culp Hobby as the first director of the WAAC, even before the bill establishing the WAAC had been approved. Hobby was thirty-seven years old, a lawyer, and married to former governor of Texas William P. Hobby, publisher of the Houston Post. Oveta Culp Hobby was an executive at the paper herself, president of the Texas League of Women Voters, and a mother of two. For the year leading up to her appointment she also had been serving in the office of General Marshall as chief of the War Department's Bureau of Public Relations—Women's Interest Section. Hobby was named the director of the WAAC, a nonmilitary title.[13]

On May 14, 1942, the bill establishing the WAAC was approved by the Senate and President Roosevelt signed it the next day.[14] At that point, Hobby's title was still director, but that title was made equivalent in rank to a colonel in the Army, while her pay was only equivalent to that of a major.[15] The public-relations-minded Hobby did not have time or much inclination to quibble about titles and pay. She knew she had a fine line to walk in establishing a women's corps and getting public support for it. As with so many endeavors women undertook during the war, the WAAC had to be perceived as tough, but not unfeminine. It had to be taken seriously, but not seen as threatening. At the beginning of her term of office Director Hobby said: "WAACs will neither be Amazons rushing to battle, nor butterflies fluttering about."[16]

Recruiting began swiftly. Not everyone was pleased. Religious leaders criticized the new WAACs. *Time* magazine reported in June 1942: "The rush of enlistments in the Women's Army Auxiliary Corps (WAACs) has perturbed the Roman Catholic pulpit and press." One bishop had reportedly told his congregation "that he hoped no Catholic women would join the WAACs, as it was opposed by teachings and principles of the Roman Catholic Church." A Catholic periodical in Brooklyn said the WAACs were "no more than an opening wedge, intended to break down the traditional American and Christian opposition to removing women from the home and to degrade her by bringing back the pagan female goddess of desexed, lustful sterility."[17]

Yet the fact remained: women had entered the U.S. Army as soldiers for the first time in American history. And once that beachhead was secured, it was only a matter of months before four other women's military branches were established. In July 1942, the Navy established the WAVES (Women Accepted for Volunteer Emergency Service). Then in November 1942, the Coast Guard formed the SPAR (Semper Paratus, Always Ready). In February 1943, the female Marines came into being, with no catchy acronym. And in August 1943, the WASP (Women Airforce Service Pilots) was formed when the WAFS (Women's Auxiliary Ferry Squadron) and the WFTD (Women's Flying Training Detachment) merged.

A main difference between the women's Army bill and the bills establishing the other women's services was that from the outset, the WAVES, SPAR, and Marines were set up as members of the military, not auxiliaries to it. Those women were accepted *in* the naval forces. Members of the WAAC and the WASP were still civilians serving *with* the Army.

That precedent was set by the Army and Navy nurses, the only other women's branches of the military in existence before the WAAC. The Army Nurse Corps was established in 1901 and the Navy Nurse Corps was established in 1908. At the start of World War II, nurses were still civilians serving with the military. And neither nurse corps had any kind of equal pay policy until 1944.[18] Perhaps as a hazard of being the first during the war to establish a new women's military branch, the authors of the WAAC bill had, in the name of political expediency, asked for less than did those who drew up the bills establishing the subsequent women's services.

But the fact that the others secured military status eventually served the WAAC. Because within a year of establishing the WAAC, Congress relented, granting their members military status. In September 1943, the word "auxiliary" came out of their name, and the WAAC became the Women's Army Corps (WAC). Still, all these military women never quite received pay, rank, or benefits equal to that of their male counterparts during the war.

Additional differences between the WAC and the other women's services remained for most of the war. From the start, the WAC bill allowed for separate units composed of black women, just as the Army Nurse Corps had done. The Army was racially segregated at that time, and the WAC and the nurses were no different. But the WAVES and the SPAR did not admit black women until late in the war. And the short-lived WASP never allowed black women, while the Marines did not admit black women until after World War II. In addition, as with the nursing corps, the Army's bill allowed WACs to go overseas, whereas the new bills establishing the other branches prohibited overseas service for women.

OFFICERS AND ENLISTED WACS

Through the course of the war, WACs were deployed to the three main parts of the Army. Forty percent were assigned to the Army Air Forces in such jobs as weather observers and forecasters, radio operators and repairwomen, control tower operators, and aerial photograph analysts. Another 40 percent of WACs went into the Army Service Forces, working as cryptologists, photographers, telephone operators, mechanics, medical lab technicians, and other more clerical jobs. And 20 percent became part of the Army Ground Forces, which was the area of the Army most reluctant to deploy women. The WACs assigned to the ground forces mostly worked in secretarial jobs and motor pools.[19]

On July 20, 1942, the initial group of WAAC officer candidates arrived at a hastily put together WAAC training camp called Fort Des Moines, in Iowa.

The first 440 women had been carefully selected from a pool of 30,000 applicants who responded to the call for women officer trainees. Although no higher education requirement existed, most of the 440 officers had at least some college. Ninety-nine percent had been employed in civilian life, with many holding professional jobs such as college deans, lawyers, editors, and teachers. A few days after they arrived at Fort Des Moines, Director Hobby addressed the women officers.

> You are the first women to serve. . . . Never forget it. . . . You have given up comfortable homes, highly paid positions, leisure. You have taken off silk and put on khaki. And all for essentially the same reason—you have a debt and a date. A debt to democracy, a date with destiny.

Hobby also wanted the women to be mindful that they would be under a microscope, with any individual's misstep reflecting on all women soldiers.

> You do not come into a Corps that has an established tradition. You must make your own. But in making your own, you do have one tradition—the integrity of all the brave American women of all time who have loved their country. You, as you gather here, are living history. . . . From now on you are soldiers, defending a free way of life. Your performance will set the standards of the Corps. You will live in the spotlight. Even though the lamps of experience are dim, few if any mistakes will be permitted you.[20]

The first WAACs set out to prove their worth, not only to the military or the nation, but to themselves. Enlistment went quickly. Other classes of officers and enlisted women went through training in Iowa.

Margaret Porter Polsky remembered arriving at Fort Des Moines in September 1942 from Missouri, where she had been a schoolteacher. She was part of the third class of officers to go through training. When she found her barracks on her first day in the Army she reacted with a bit of shock to the bed that was assigned to her.

> I thought gee, this is the bleakest, coldest bed I ever saw, in this room that is equally bleak and cold. But it was not frightening to me. I had made this decision. So I thought, "I am here to handle this, and I must. And I will see it through." It was a whole new world.

Polsky said the first weeks of training were a blur of all the things she needed to know to be a part of "the Army life." She learned military protocol, how to salute, and all sorts of military terms. She learned that "when you run into a man walking across the camp who has three stars on his shoulder, you salute." She attended classes and took lots of exams. And she learned to march.

> I enjoyed the drill field. I really enjoyed marching and being trained. I liked the band. Maybe it was the sense of music and rhythm. In the Army you were really living a disciplined existence in contrast to the freedom you had known before. It was a new thing for most women. But the discipline was good. I enjoyed having companies that I could train to march. It was fulfillment to have them well-trained.

After her officer training, Polsky was assigned to the newest training camp for enlisted women in Daytona Beach. She commanded a company of recruits, in charge of everything to do with "feeding them to clothing them, and drilling them. All personal issues came to you," said Polsky, "homesickness, weariness, blisters and anything else." But she enjoyed the work. "It's a sense of accomplishment. Train these people. Train them well and right and prove to them that they can do it too."

Within six months Polsky was sent to an Army Air Force pilot training base in Columbus, Mississippi, to command a company of WAACs, and later to Maxwell Field in Alabama and then briefly to Fresno, California. Polsky also met her husband during her time in the WAC. When they met, he was a lieutenant at the base in Columbus, and so was she. She was promoted to captain and then they married. It was one of the first times a bride outranked her groom in the U.S. Army. "The first question everyone asked us was whether I made him salute."

Even as Polsky continued to be in charge of so many other women, she was also aware of changes taking place within herself from being an officer in the Army.

> It was a liberation for me. I enjoyed what I was doing. I liked the hard times as well as the easier times. It was my liberation from a limited existence. Before, I had never really traveled. My world was restricted. It expanded greatly in the WAC. I met people from all over

and had to get along and work with them. At the same time I was learning, I felt I was accomplishing something, and contributing something.

But she said one of her greatest satisfactions through it all was watching the effect that being in the military had on the enlisted women under her command.

> I saw women who maybe had been dissatisfied with their own lives—feeling that they hadn't lived up to their potential or done what was most interesting to them. I saw women blossom. And it certainly made me feel good. What they were doing was valuable and I was helping them do it. At the same time they were being productive for the nation, they were also realizing a personal sense of contribution and fulfillment. I'd watch them grow.[21]

Typical of such early recruits in Daytona Beach was Dorothy Wain. Before her decision to join the WAAC, Wain said: "I was a good solid citizen in a small town, and it was taken for granted that I would be there the rest of my life." She described her longtime office clerical job as stable, a little too stable perhaps. "I had become a permanent fixture there—just like the desks, chairs, filing cabinets." She described herself as always having been the good daughter, sister, and aunt. "In fact," she said, "I was becoming the Old Maid Aunt of the family. . . . I was a good person to borrow five dollars from." Yet, she felt little sense of purpose, especially as the war heated up.

Once she enlisted and received her orders, Wain realized she really was going off to war. From training camp in Daytona Beach, which she described as "the Land of Women—10,000 of them," Wain wrote in a letter to her family: "I have never been away from home for more than two weeks at a time, and I suppose I shall be a little homesick at first." In basic training in Daytona Beach, Wain took classes in such subjects as military customs and courtesies, map reading, and "how the Army is run, in three easy lessons." Wain told of having learned "to get up at the blast of the bugle and get dressed in five minutes and be on line in time for Reveille. We have learned that when the Army tells us to be at a certain place at a certain time, they mean fifteen minutes earlier." After basic training, Wain went on to serve in England until the end of the war.[22]

MARSHALL'S EXPERIMENT

One of the earliest tests of women's usefulness in the Army was a secret experiment initiated by Army Chief of Staff General George Marshall in 1942. The service was still the WAAC and the experiment fell under the auspices of the Army Ground Forces. Two WAAC companies, including ten officers and more than 200 troops, were assigned to a mixed-gender antiaircraft tactical unit in Washington, D.C. Lieutenant General Dwight D. Eisenhower had reported to Marshall that he had seen women used successfully in British antiaircraft units. Marshall's experiment tested how well women could function in many non-arms-firing positions, such as tracking enemy planes by using radar, height finder, and searchlight machinery attached to the antiaircraft guns. Since Congress had specifically stipulated that women were not to be in combat, these experimental WAACs were never to fire guns and were given no arms training.[23]

Lieutenant Elna Hilliard was one of the WAAC officers assigned to the experiment that was conducted in late 1942 and early 1943. She remembered the visit in February 1943 of an Army general who came to observe the women tracking and targeting a test plane to see how well they could calculate and convey the moment at which the gun needed to fire to hit the plane. It was not an exact science. The time was measured between when a spotter called out that a plane was in range and when the gunner would fire. The amount of time that tracking took, and whether the gun would hit its target, were the marks of how efficient and successful the crew had been. Hilliard remembered that the assistant to the visiting general "punched the stopwatch when the crew chief, Lt. Dorothy Mitchell, called out that the plane was in range, then stopped it when she called out, 'On target.' "

The general then "looked at the stopwatch and said, 'Impossible.' " Hilliard was standing next to him and asked, "What's impossible, Sir?" He told her the mixed-gender WAAC test crew had just equaled the top time of the best male antiaircraft crew on the entire East Coast. He asked the crew to repeat the test twice more, and both times they performed faster and more accurately than his best male crew.[24]

Those kinds of results were common during the experiment, but they were never publicized. In fact, Army officials were protective of the secret experiment and its results for many years beyond World War II. They felt if word got out that Army women were anywhere near guns or that Army women were working with men, it would seriously hamper WAAC recruit-ing. Also, they thought such news might impede passage of the bill to make the WAAC a part of the Army—an action the War Department was advocat-ing by early 1943. In an internal War Department memo from May 11, 1943, asking to continue Marshall's experiment and add more WAACs, it was noted, "any publicity as to action recommended herein might endanger pas-sage of contemplated congressional bills to make WAAC a component of the Army of the United States."[25]

The antiaircraft experiment was discontinued in mid-1943. The report on the experiment concluded that WAAC personnel in mixed-gender units were "superior to men in all functions involving delicacy of manual dexterity. . . . They perform routine repetitive tasks in a manner superior to men." The re-port also mentioned the morale of the women being higher than most male units and attributed that enthusiasm to "the fact that they felt that they were making a direct contribution to the successful prosecution of the war."[26]

But General Marshall had to weigh the success of the women with public opinion and the Army's most urgent wartime needs. The official reason given to stop the experiment and not deploy women to antiaircraft units was that the women would be taking the place of men in the unit who were mostly "limited service personnel"—meaning they had some sort of mild disability that precluded them from combat. Therefore, WAACs in antiaircraft units would not be freeing men for battle. It was felt that WAACs could be used more efficiently in other positions where they would be taking the place of men who could go into battle.[27]

WACS TO NORTH AFRICA AND EUROPE

By summer of 1943, at the end of the first year of the WAAC, about 60,000 women had enlisted. Most were hoping for overseas service, to see and be a part of the war and the world beyond their homes. The first WAAC battalion was sent overseas in early 1943.[28]

In fall 1942, Marshall had appointed then Lieutenant General Eisenhower as commander of Operation Torch—the invasion of North Africa in Novem-ber 1942. By November 11, American and British forces had secured control of Morocco and Algeria.[29] Within the month, Eisenhower began asking for WAACs to staff his office as stenographers and for French-speaking WAACs to operate switchboards in the North African theater. Marshall was ready to send Army women overseas for the first time ever, even though he was concerned that because the WAACs were still civilians they would not have the same protections if hurt, captured, or killed overseas accorded male members of the Army.

General Marshall and General Eisenhower were bullish on the use of women soldiers throughout the war. They were spurred at first by their positive observations of British WAACs, who counted Prime Minister Winston Churchill's daughter, Mary, among their ranks.[30] General Marshall went ahead with fulfilling Eisenhower's request for North Africa. But he made his frustrations about the women's status known to Congress in a December 1942 memo to the Military Committee of the House of Representatives:

> The law provides that these women shall not be employed in combat service. They will not be. However, in their present status they do not enjoy the same privileges that members of the Army do who become a prey to the hazards of ocean transport or bombing. I arranged that no individual should go who did not volunteer for this purpose.
>
> At a later date it is the purpose of the War Department to submit to Congress a request for a modification of the law to make this Corps a part of the Army, but in the interim I wish members of the Committee to be aware of the action I have taken.[31]

By the end of 1942, the first WAAC officers were sent to Africa, and in January 1943 the first company of enlisted women arrived in Algiers. That initial group was composed of handpicked and highly qualified volunteers. Many of the women were bilingual and most were eligible for officer candidate school.[32]

Miriam E. Stehlik wrote to friends in the WAAC back home in 1943 after arriving in Africa to work on Eisenhower's staff. In this new setting, even routine tasks seemed special to these first American women soldiers serving overseas.

> At the end of my working day, I slowly walk home in the gorgeous sunset, knowing in my heart that "paper work" is just as important in this business of war, as is ammunition and supplies—and no day is too long for me to work. I am on the General's staff.

. . . All of us feel very privileged in being part of this great North African Campaign, and we know that that is something that no one will ever be able to take away from us. For in her small way, each of us over here has helped to write the history of this war, that will be written in books that our children will read.[33]

After WAACs were sent to North Africa in January 1943, the European theater began to get an influx of women soldiers too. They started out in Great Britain, with the first WAAC battalion arriving there in summer of 1943.

By December 1943, WAC Captain Gretchen Kroch found herself facing a Christmas Eve far different from any she had seen before. Stationed in the United Kingdom, she wrote home to her parents in Chicago about that first holiday season American female soldiers spent abroad.

Darlings—

This is war—and War is Hell. It's Christmas Eve—and instead of being at home with you, amidst gaiety and happy clamor, I'm in the bleak waiting room of the railroad station in Maxton, waiting to put a coffin on the train. A nice young flyer was killed last night when his glider plummeted to the ground. He was to have been married tonight.

Of course, women had encountered the dead and dying in past wars. American nurses with the military had witnessed and cared for the results of many a front-line battle since the Revolutionary War. By the end of the war, Captain Kroch had served in France and occupied Germany. Still, in the early stages, Kroch was learning to cope with how war looked and felt up close, in the same way all soldiers have had to learn:

I whom you brought up carefully and tenderly, sheltering me from life's vicissitudes, look now upon broken bodies and bloody corpses without flinching.
. . . I long for your comforting presence tonight. I am bitterly lonely. . . . Yes, this is War.

Grace Porter came to England to work as a WAC cryptographer at the Eighth Air Force headquarters in Hertsfordshire. She worked with one other WAC and four GIs in the basement of the castle that was their ultra-secure headquarters.

Specially reinforced concrete walls at least three feet thick surrounded us on top, bottom, and all four sides, with no outside windows or vents. To enter, we had to pass through three guarded doors,
then knock on the code room door and be identified by voice before
we were allowed to come in. The door was always locked immediately after we entered. We worked around the clock in shifts with
two people always there to receive and send secret messages. . . . We
decoded or encoded them and sent them on to the proper persons.
. . . Many of the codes were in long series of five-letter groups:
MCMOD RFVLO CDRMA, and so on. Accuracy was essential. One
letter wrong, and the meaning of the whole message could be lost.
. . . It was work that took a great deal of patience and concentration.[34]

Porter remained in England through 1943 and into 1944. In the months leading up to the Allied invasion of France her work in the code room intensified.

In those hectic days just before D-Day, we could barely keep up with
the huge volume of classified messages coming in and going out at
all hours of the day and night.[35]

One of the hazards of service in England were the German air raids. By
1943 and 1944 the Germans were sending "buzz bombs" to attack the British.
They were unmanned planes that flew in, turned off suddenly, and then
crashed and exploded on their targets. Corporal Libba Cobb from Georgia
was a radio operator at the Eighth Air Force headquarters. On August 4, 1944,
she wrote to her husband about narrowly surviving a buzz bomb attack.

All heaven and earth joined together in one gigantic, deafening explosion. . . . All the blood in my body rushed to my head, and since I
could neither see (lights went off with the explosion) nor hear, I decided I was dead. No, I'm not kidding! I thought the explosion had
killed me and this was the transition. Just as I had begun to worry
about some of the more serious charges in The Book against me,
someone lighted a cigarette lighter.

The buzz bomb had made a direct hit on the house next door, destroying it
completely and also destroying her roommate's car and their garage. No one
in her house was hurt, except for some minor bruises.

In the house hit directly, a little three-year-old girl was killed instantly—a child I had talked with a few hours before . . . I've never really believed that I was in danger. . . . This was a bit different![36]

Within weeks of D-Day in June 1944, WACs were sent into France for the first time. On August 6, 1944, Patricia Rand McGalliard wrote to her family in Ohio about her life on the brink of the battle.

> We are now somewhere in France. We are bivouaced in tents in an apple orchard, and are rapidly learning what the term "field conditions" really means. It is definitely on the rough side, but none of us mind very much. We are getting pretty used to accepting whatever comes our way. . . . We are living three women to a tent. We wash in our helmets and sleep in our clothes. The nights are freezing cold; it's getting toward fall. . . . We have just begun to receive our mail again, thank goodness. It is so important to us. Time for bed now, so I'll close. I think of you all constantly. You are so very dear to me. I am not afraid, really I'm not. I know God is taking care of "me, and mine and all."[37]

Gertrude Pearson Cassetta was in a mobile communications unit of the WAC as part of the First Tactical Command Air Force serving in Vittel, France, during the Germans' last big offensive against the Allies, the Battle of the Bulge.

> The winter of 1944 and 1945 in Vittel was an important time in our military careers. We had been accepted into the First TACAF against the wishes of some who felt women belonged in the rear areas and were unsuitable for the type of work assigned to us. They felt that women were incapable of enduring the hardships and rough conditions of a combat area. However, our success and outstanding work changed many attitudes. We had remained reliable and stable while on duty under stressful conditions. It was the roughest winter any of us had experienced, and we were eager to go on.[38]

By the time the Battle of the Bulge was winding down, Grace Porter, who had worked as a cryptographer in England, was sent to Belgium. She worked with the Ninth Air Force in their headquarters in Charleroi, Belgium, decoding messages sent to and from U.S. and British units. Occasionally Germans would get access to Allied code lists, in which case the codes would be changed immediately and Grace or one of her colleagues would have to venture out to remote units in Belgium or Holland to give them new code lists. They were transported there in jeeps by armed drivers.

> GIs in these isolated units had not seen an American woman for months. As soon as our jeep drove into their area, word would spread quickly that a real, live American girl was in camp. Lines of soldiers would form on both sides of the road as we drove in. "Are you really American?" "Where ya from, Corporal?" "Say something in American!"
>
> I learned to grin at all of them and keep a fast line of banter going with the crowd as my driver and I dashed to find the unit code officer. As soon as the information was delivered, we were always invited to the mess hall for coffee or lunch. There is nothing that can do more for a girl's ego than having lunch with several hundred men, all vying for her attention. On the ride back to Charleroi it was hard to keep from crying as I remembered all those homesick guys craving some small reminder of home before many of them would be wounded, or captured or killed.[39]

WACS IN THE PACIFIC

The first WACs arrived in Australia in May 1944. WACs were not sent to the Pacific earlier, partly because already close-by Australian women were filling many of the jobs the American WACs would have done. The WACs who did come to the Pacific soon fanned out to camps in New Guinea, and finally to the Philippines. The conditions in the Pacific were rough, since disease was more common than in Europe. Also, the clothing the WACs were issued for the Pacific was inadequate. Because of malaria-carrying mosquitoes, everyone was required to wear long sleeves and pants. But the only long-sleeved clothing the WACs had were the herringbone twill coveralls they had worn on board the ships that transported them overseas. The heavy material was known to cause skin irritation in the United States but was especially inappropriate in the hot, damp jungle climate of New Guinea.

As a result, many WACs in the Pacific developed skin diseases, especially dermatitis, or "jungle rot," which was so prevalent that it became the leading cause of medical leave from the Army for women in the Pacific theater. When the women wore short-sleeve shirts to deal with the heat they exposed themselves to mosquitoes, and the lack of the kind of footwear that would protect the women from the damp rainy ground also was thought to have contributed to a high rate of respiratory problems among WACs in some areas. Attempts to supply the approximately 5,500 women in the Pacific with light khaki pants and appropriate shirts and shoes for the rainy, hot climate took much maneuvering by the Army. Without the right clothing WACs often had an especially hard time getting their work done.[40]

Irene Brion was a WAC cryptographer in Hollandia, New Guinea, from late 1944 through 1945, where conditions were some of the most treacherous.

> At times the heat was oppressive. It increased slowly but intensely until by late morning it was extremely uncomfortable. Normally, I perspire very little, but by noon the back of my shirt would be drenched. . . . One of the officers . . . warned us about mosquitoes. After telling us how to identify the malaria-carrying anopheles (it bites with its proboscis at a right angle to the skin) she stressed the importance of keeping our sleeves down and buttoned at all times.

Brion took a pill which most service personnel in the Pacific took called Atabrine to protect against malaria. Its chief side effect was that it turned skin yellow. Atabrine and quinine were the main protections against malaria, along with clothing to cover the body. But Brion did not escape skin disease.

> Our chief medical problem was "jungle rot," a term that covered a wide spectrum of fungal infections. Sooner or later most of us got it, usually the mild variety that was treated with gentian violet. I got some between my fingers, which cleared up quickly, but Marge Wilhelm and Edith McMann had cases that required hospitalization. Marge broke out in sores all over her legs. Mac's was the most serious—the type that attacks the optic nerve and causes blindness— and she had to be shipped home. We learned later that she lost 90 percent of her vision.[41]

Sergeant Edna Gene Cox worked in a finance office in New Guinea from which she wrote her family in October 1944.

At most times, the jungle seems far away from this GI oasis hewn
from malaria-infested swamps.... But sometimes, and tonight is
one of them, the jungle seems to draw nearer. A warm breeze rustles
the palms with a sound like rain on the roof. I am working late, and
when the clatter of my Australian comptometer ceases, the silence
hangs heavy in the air. The cries of strange birds are heard occasionally; I have never heard a bird sing in this place—they crow or bark,
chatter or scream like animals. New Guinea stars are wonderfully
bright and beautiful—but they are unfamiliar stars, and one is often
oppressed with a vague loneliness and nostalgia when twilight falls.
However, we work too hard to have much time for brooding. The
hours are long and the pace terrific.

... There is a strange reaction I notice to this environment—most
of the women take great pains with make-up, cologne, hair, etc.—
even more than in the States. A natural attempt to preserve femininity, I suppose—and the men we work with are greatly appreciative of
our efforts to remain feminine and at the same time do our jobs as
well as any man.[42]

The Army tried to make sure the women in the Pacific were not accessible
to many men, so WACs were locked in barbed wire compounds and only able
to leave with armed guard escorts. No leaves were allowed. Off-duty, women
were forbidden spontaneous or private dates. Curfew was at 11:00 P.M. and
some WAC units also were subject to bed checks. All this was attributed to
the massive numbers of men in the area compared to the low number of
women. Also, some military historians have said the policy had something
to do with an irrational fear on the part of some in the military that black
American soldiers serving in segregated units in New Guinea would have
raped white women WACs if they were not guarded. Some women protested
that they were being treated like children and were living under protective
custody only afforded male soldiers who were court-martialed. But the lock-
down policy for WACs and other American women serving in the Pacific did
not change much throughout the war.[43]

Still, somehow, love, or something like it, did bloom. There were
company-approved dances and group activities for the women, who could attend when accompanied by armed guards. Josephine Downey was a French
and Spanish teacher at St. Paul High School in Minnesota before joining the
WAC in 1943. She was sent to the Pacific in 1944 and wrote with some humor

in a September 7, 1944, letter to her family about the social circumstances of her new world, where men far outnumbered women.

> New Guinea is a girl's paradise for gold diggers. The fellows are so eager to meet them that they come with offerings, like Columbus bribed the natives with bright jewelry. . . . Our principal amusement is entertaining the GIs. They can go to the movies with us, or toss in the waves, if we invite them and they can get cleared through the M.P. gate into our area. It's diverting and in the barracks we're awfully silly about the whole thing. The question isn't: "Did you have a good time?" It is: "What did he bring you?" It's a racket but the boys evidently feel that their chances are better for seeing us again if they bring things. My specialty is the mess sergeant; neat, isn't it? I won the jack pot last night—ten candy bars, chewing gum, two cans of grape fruit and a fish sandwich. In the afternoon I only got three bananas, but not a bad haul.[44]

Some WACs apparently had their own pinup pictures of male celebrities like Cary Grant, Clark Gable, Tyrone Power, and even General MacArthur.[45] The WAC had few restrictions against marriage, yet it was hardly common. Only 121 of the 5,500 WACs in the Pacific theater married during wartime.[46] And like the famous "Dear John" letters male soldiers had always received, some WACs got "Dear Jane" letters of rejection from their prewar boyfriends who had met and married other women while they were apart.

WAC private Betty "Billie" Oliver of Chicago was not one of them. She served in New Guinea as a mail clerk starting in August 1944. Three days after she arrived, she met Mike Donahue, whom she married a few months later in late December 1944 in New Guinea. She wrote to her parents, "your gal is engaged to the sweetest guy in the world." But a wedding and a honeymoon during wartime had special challenges. So as most other women in the WAC did at some point during their service, Oliver wrote home in December 1944, asking for some clothing she could not get in New Guinea.

> Will you please get me a real sexy nightgown. You know, the kind a bride would wear? . . . After all, I will have to get married in uniform. I'd like to let my boy know he's got a woman, not a soldier.[47]

BACKLASH

While just about every woman who joined the Army did so with a sense of patriotism and commitment, a concerted slander campaign against Army women arose in 1943. Rumors had been circulating about the moral character of women who joined the WAAC during the first year of its existence. The talk came to wider public notice when one of the rumors was reported in a nationally syndicated column called *Capitol Stuff* by John O'Donnell of the *New York Daily News*. O'Donnell had opposed most of President Roosevelt's policies, and on June 8, 1943, said that WAACs were being issued condoms as a matter of course. The columnist mocked the WAACs, Director Hobby, and even the president and first lady when he wrote:

> Contraceptive and prophylactic equipment will be furnished to members of the WAAC, according to a supersecret agreement reached by high-ranking officers of the War Department and the WAAC Chieftain, Mrs. William Pettus Hobby. . . . It was a victory for the New Deal ladies. . . . Mrs. Roosevelt wants all the young ladies to have the same overseas rights as their brothers and fathers.[48]

Other destructive rumors had been spreading up and down the East Coast through the spring. In early June 1943, the War Department asked the FBI to investigate their sources. Some thought perhaps German operatives had spread the rumors to damage WAAC recruiting, since it was widely publicized that WAACs were intended to free more U.S. soldiers to fight on the front lines. One rumor said large numbers of WAACs had to be returned from North Africa because they were pregnant, a condition that meant immediate dismissal from military service. Another rumor said that 90 percent of WAACs were prostitutes and 40 percent had gotten pregnant while "servicing" male troops. Word had also spread that all applicants for the WAAC who were found to be virgins during Army physicals were immediately rejected. And numerous obscene jokes about WAACs' anatomical specifications went around among Army men at home and overseas. Many stories circulated about WAACs openly soliciting and engaging in sex acts in public and WAACs spreading venereal disease.[49]

Leisa D. Meyer in her book *Creating GI Jane: Sexuality and Power in the Women's Army Corps During World War II* said terms used to classify past female participation in the military, before World War II, such as "camp followers" or "cross-dressers," were usually derogatory. They had the same implications of female immorality as the direct rumors of World War II did. Meyer said they reflected a long-held notion "that only immoral women would associate with the military, and that the only valuable service a woman could provide the military was sexual in nature." [50]

Among WAACs and their families the rumors, and especially the article about condoms, caused tumult. An officer reported that right after the article appeared, long-distance calls from parents came in telling their daughters to come home. Morale was hurt. Younger women were in tears while older WAACs were bitter that lies could circulate so widely. One WAAC said she acted immediately to counteract the rumors and try to appear proud in the face of the slander.

> I went home on leave to tell my family it wasn't true. When I went through the streets, I held up my head because I imagined everybody was talking about me, but when I was at last safe inside our front door, I couldn't say a word to them, I was so humiliated—I just burst out crying, and my people ran and put their arms around me and cried with me. I couldn't understand how my eagerness to serve our country could have brought such shame on us all. [51]

In fact, the rumors were just that. The WAAC had a venereal disease rate so low as to be virtually nonexistent, much different from the relatively high VD rate among male Army personnel. WAACs were never issued any contraceptives or given any information about using contraceptives, unlike the extensive program to issue military men condoms at all military installations. The pregnancy rate among unmarried WAACs was also extremely low— about one-fifth that of the rate among unmarried women in civilian life. [52] And it was estimated that more than half of the low rate of WAAC pregnancies in the North African theater, for instance, was among WAACs who were married and had seen their husbands on leaves. [53]

The War Department and Director Hobby reacted as swiftly and effectively to the slander as they could. Secretary of War Henry L. Stimson said in June 1943:

> Sinister rumors aimed at destroying the reputation of the Waacs are absolutely and completely false. Anything which would interfere with their recruiting or destroy the reputation of the Corps, and by

so doing interfere with increase in the combat strength of our Army, would be of value to the enemy. The repetition of any unfounded rumor . . . is actually an aid to the enemy.[54]

Pressure on columnist John O'Donnell from the president, the War Department, and others forced him to retract his report on condoms being issued to WAACs. The Army issued a report on investigations into the rumors. Instead of finding enemy operatives as the source, it was concluded that the rumors stemmed mainly from Army personnel who opposed the existence of the WAACs. Yet the damage had been done. Recruiting of WAACs was hindered. Most of the resistance to joining stemmed not from women themselves, it was found, but from negative reactions by the men in their lives to the idea of women joining the military. Army censors reported that letters written home by soldiers who had heard the rumors spread them back to their families. Most soldiers had little if any contact with WAACs, but they had strong opinions nonetheless. While many expressed some support of the idea of women in uniform, most were less than enthusiastic about their own female family members joining.

One soldier wrote, "Join the WAVES or WAC and you are automatically a prostitute in my opinion." Another wrote: "Any service woman—Wac, Wave, Spar, Nurse, Red Cross—isn't respected." A soldier wrote his sister saying: "It's no damn good, Sis, and I for one would be very unhappy if you joined them. . . . Why can't these Gals just stay home and be their own sweet little self, instead of being patriotic?" A husband told his wife: "Darling, for my sake don't join them. I can't write my reasons because the censors won't let it through." And another husband threatened his wife with divorce when he heard her idea of joining the WAC.[55]

Ultimately WAC leaders took the badmouthing in stride. One WAC officer commented, "Men have for centuries used slander to keep women out of public life." Years after the worst effects, Director Hobby said she believed the slander was inevitable. "No new agency requiring social change," she said, "has escaped a similar baptism. I feel now that nothing we might have done could have avoided it."[56]

POSTWAR WAC

By the end of the war, WACs had served in every theater of operation. Sixteen WACs were awarded Purple Hearts.[57] Many of the WAC missions had been called experimental—so that, like a bad boyfriend, the Army would not have made any permanent commitment to continuing a women's corps after wartime. The women had signed up just like the men, for the duration of the war plus six months. And many people assumed that after the war the WAC would be disbanded. But Army generals such as Douglas MacArthur, who commanded the Pacific forces, and Eisenhower, who ran the European and African theaters, as well as General Marshall, were all in favor of keeping the WAC as part of the Army.[58]

Colonel Mary A. Hallaren became the third director of the WAC in 1947, after Director Hobby resigned in 1945 and her replacement, Colonel Westray B. Boyce, resigned in 1947. Hallaren testified in the Senate in 1947 in favor of permanent military status for the WAC. She stressed it was merited because women had duly proven their worth during the war. "In the future," she said, "we won't have to worry about recruiting women or convincing the men. When the house is on fire, we don't talk about a woman's place in the home. And we don't send her a gilt-edged invitation to help put the fire out."[59]

Despite some public reaction against it, three years later in 1948, Congress finally passed a law making women a permanent part of the U.S. Army. Slowly, attitudes had been chiseled and the idea of a woman soldier became a less jarring prospect. Major General Orlando Ward, the Army's chief of military history, said in a foreword to the Army's official history of the WACs in 1953:

> The WAC did not always understand the Army—its customs and traditions, its organization and necessary chain of command. The Army did not always understand the WAC—its needs and temperament, and the many other things that man, being the son of woman, should have known but did not, much to his continued embarrassment.[60]

CHAPTER FIVE

On Duty at Home

WAVES, SPARS, MARINES, AND WASPS

The girl in a job equally open to men, had to be better than the ordinary man to prove her capacity. When she had done so, she was often commended as though she had performed a miracle. . . . The surprise of men at the accomplishment of women was not flattering, but it was fun.

LIEUTENANT COMMANDER
MILDRED MCAFEE HORTON, U.S. NAVY,
Director, WAVES, 1946[1]

WOMEN IN THE MILITARY during World War II entered new territory. Even if it was well trodden by men, any entry had a sense of conquest to it. When they decided to volunteer, these women were given indefinite assurances that they would be doing something worthwhile. And indeed they ended up successfully filling a wider range of jobs than it was assumed they could handle before the war began. The early women in the Navy, Coast Guard, and Marines and the first women pilots with the Army all broke new ground, an achievement in itself. But the foot soldiers of constructive change do not always do the dramatic or sensational. They often perform quieter, less obviously heroic feats, and endure boredom or sometimes humiliation. They learn to master the art of finding private enthusiasm for their unacknowledged deeds of daring, and personal meaning in their unrecognized acts of triumph. To overlook those small, individual acts is to miss an appreciation for the true components of change—the particular human thoughts, heartbeats, and feelings that propel the larger collective transformations war brings.

NAVY WOMEN—THE WAVES

In creating the name for the new women's Navy, Lieutenant Elizabeth Reynard, a former Barnard College professor, said she knew the name had to include a W for Women and a V for Volunteer, since the Navy wanted to emphasize that these women were not drafted but volunteered for service. She came up with WAVES—Women Accepted for Volunteer Emergency Service. Reynard said she used the word "emergency," thinking it would "comfort the older admirals, because it implies we're only a temporary crisis and won't be around for keeps." [2]

Approximately 86,000 women joined the Navy as WAVES during World War II, starting in July 1942. The Navy was just as reluctant as the Army to admit women at first, but was motivated to do so for the same reasons the Army was. A manpower shortage developed in the Navy and women became the best alternative. But the Navy had learned what not to do when drawing up legislation for a women's branch from the Army's example. So the Navy's women's branch, from the beginning, was not an auxiliary to the Navy but was incorporated into the Navy.

About 150 women were commissioned by the Navy to become its first officers. Most all of them had come from professional jobs in civilian life. Mildred H. McAfee, the president of Wellesley College in Massachusetts, was named the director of the WAVES. As with the WAC director, McAfee was given a civilian instead of a military title. "My first assignment," she said, "was just getting enough women there to start doing something, and what they were to do was as vague to me as it was to all the rest of the Navy at the time."[3]

Perhaps because of McAfee's academic background, WAVES training camps were usually set up at college campuses. Officers were sent to Smith College in Northampton, Massachusetts, and later to nearby Mount Holyoke College as well. Enlisted women went to training camps at University of Wisconsin—Madison, University of Indiana—Bloomington, and Oklahoma A&M College in Stillwater. By February 1943, one large and permanent boot camp for all enlistees was set up at Hunter College in the Bronx in New York City. The training took six weeks. New classes arrived every two weeks and usually consisted of about 1,600 women.[4]

In March 1945 *Time* magazine described the training WAVES underwent at Hunter College.

> In those six weeks they became trim and sharp—factory-made old salts who referred to walls as "bulkheads," windows as "ports," and floors as "decks." . . . They had absorbed Navy tradition, had had a quick but thorough briefing on naval operations, naval weapons, history and current affairs. They were also imbued with the idea that if a WAVE quit, it was the same as a battlefront casualty.[5]

The article went on to explain the way the Navy deployed the women to free the men for battle during the peak years of the war.

> WAVES had released more than 70,000 men for combat, which was the same as adding 70,000 men to the Navy's muster. . . . In such routine jobs as Navy storekeeping, clerical work, stenography, the Navy's women were at least as competent as the Navy's men. In ad-

dition they have taken over jobs which no one had thought anyone could do but men. They weather-briefed Navy pilots, made weather observations and forecasts, directed air traffic from flying field control towers. They instructed Navy pilots in instrument flying ... taught Navy airmen to shoot. They had become metalsmiths, radiomen, aviation machinist's mates, truck drivers, laboratory technicians, decoders and cooks. There are some 1,000 naval installations in the U.S. and at roughly half of them WAVES are at work.[6]

Ruby Messer Barber was one of six sisters, and had grown up in La Grange, Georgia, just south of Atlanta. Almost as soon as she heard about the WAVES she knew it was something she wanted to do, even though some of her sisters did not want to join and others were too young to consider it.

> It was a choice of adventure. I didn't have any brothers, and I thought that's something I can do, one way I can make a contribution. My sisters thought it was great, but they were not interested. There was too much discipline and routine involved. I felt like it would be a challenge, to step forth and do it, to see what it was all about. It gave a sense of confidence. At the time girls just didn't join the WAVES or go into the military. But my dad, he said, "You'll be O.K."

Barber went to training in the Bronx and then was assigned to the Atlanta Naval Air Station, where she lived in barracks and worked in Personnel for two years. "I was doing a job that needed to be done," she said, "for my country." In the camaraderie she felt with her fellow WAVES, Barber found some similarities to her time growing up with five sisters. "We became so attached to each other," she said. "We were all there together, doing the same thing, dressed the same way. We had the same responsibilities, the same pressures. I met people from all over. We were compatible. There was a respect for each other."[7]

Dorothy Cole Libby was in the WAVES from January 1943 to February 1946. She served as secretary to Commander William J. Sebald, head of the Pacific Section, Combat Intelligence Division. He had practiced international law in Japan for ten years and was the Navy's top authority on the Japanese.

> Everything our office handled was top secret—ultra. And security was tightly controlled. Each day my boss dictated an enemy intelligence report that was delivered by officer courier to the President

and returned to our office the following day. . . . Occasionally both President Roosevelt and later President Truman penciled comments in the margins. It was a source of special pride to me knowing that the President read my typewritten words![8]

Margaret Lindeen Routon joined the WAVES in late 1942 and was among the first to be trained at Hunter College. From there, she did her yeoman's training in Georgia. Then she was assigned to Great Lakes Naval Training Station, north of Chicago, where she worked in the base's public relations office.

> There was one other WAVE in my office. But the thing I noticed at the very first was how much the men resented us . . . because we were taking their jobs, which meant they were going to sea. They were comfortable in their jobs. They were all advertising men, radio personalities, newspapermen.
>   But it didn't take them long to like us. It seems that once they got to know you and saw your work, they thought, "This is really silly. It's not her fault I have to go to war." . . . I felt I could probably do the job better than they could because it was office work and women have done that forever. In fact, I thought, "What are men doing in an office? That's sort of silly work for a man to be doing. All right for women, but not for men."

One of Routon's main duties in public relations was to interview returning servicemen and write reports on them to send to their hometown newspapers. Sometimes she would go out and speak about the Navy or the WAVES to groups in the community. Or she would speak to potential recruits. She said the reception she got from civilians was generally favorable. "I remember every once in a while some guy would say, 'I wouldn't let my girlfriend go in the military.' But most people seemed to be pretty accepting." Later Routon was transferred to another public relations office in Detroit. She stayed in the service until 1944, when she married and had a child. But Routon felt her time in the WAVES expanded her horizons. "It gave me a freedom that I had never experienced before, and a purpose."[9]

With so many uphill battles to acceptance, public relations was an important element of growth and survival for the women's services. A 1943 book called *The WAVES: The Story of the Girls in Blue,* said:

A few months ago the very word WAVES was a kind of joke, and the thought of women in uniform was barely acceptable to the so-called protective male animal. But the organization is functioning now, developing surely and fast, and wiping out laughter about itself as it goes.[10]

Indeed, the Navy began to recognize the value of women members and expanded not only the duties they were asked to perform, but also the places they were able to serve. In 1944, Congress ruled that Navy women could serve outside the continental United States in American territories. The greatest need was in Hawaii, where WAVES began arriving in early 1945.

Marie Cody, a member of the WAVES in Washington, D.C., was considering trying to go to Hawaii. Since she was unmarried, she said she saw no reason not to travel farther afield than the continental U.S. She wrote to a friend in March of 1945:

I have nothing here that makes it necessary for me to stay. Mother will miss me, and so will the children. God knows how much I'll miss them but yet, they will understand. You see, they are used to the idea by now of my streak of restlessness or wanderlust or whatever you call it and, happily for me, tolerate it.[11]

WAVES Lieutenant Lillian Pimlott was sent to the Navy Yard at Pearl Harbor to work in Personnel in April 1945. She wrote her mother in July 1945 about all she had seen and learned in her first months on the island.

I am fascinated by the ships which are making history in every battle. I've talked to seamen and I've met flyers—from Iwo, from Okinawa, heroes from every encounter. I know now what war means and my heart goes out to every one of them. Among them I am making, I hope, lifetime friends, for their experiences mean everything to my self-satisfaction. . . . As long as they fight on, I have no desire to return home, for I feel I belong here. . . . I have learned much in these 3 brief months about life and living. And I know I have already changed in many ways and many viewpoints. . . . It is truly a most broadening experience and I shall never outlive it![12]

Military life did open the worlds of many women during World War II. But for those who had already had some measure of accomplishment, it also pointed up most clearly the hurdles women still faced in overcoming rigid views of their proper role in American society. WAVES director McAfee, with some sadness, noted the differences between her work in a women's university and in the military. "Life in the Navy," she said in 1945, "has taken me out of the cloister in which a woman was unaware of limitations on her freedom or individuality and has thrust me into the big world where women are women and men are men." [13]

NAVY WOMEN—THE SPAR

Just before World War II, the whole Coast Guard was transferred from the auspices of the Treasury Department to the U.S. Navy. With that move, the smallest of the military branches expanded rapidly. One way the Coast Guard coped with its need for extra personnel was to establish a women's reserve in November 1942 called the SPAR. The acronym was based on the first letters of the Coast Guard's Latin motto, "Semper Paratus," and the first letters of its English translation, "Always Ready." About 11,000 women joined the SPAR for shore duty in the U.S. during World War II. [14]

The general public had a bit of trouble distinguishing between the many new women's military branches and their acronyms. It was a problem many women in uniform encountered throughout the war, and was especially challenging for women in the smaller, less-well-known service branches. In their 1946 book, *Three Years Behind the Mast: The Story of the United States Coast Guard SPARs,* Mary C. Lyne and Kay Arthur recounted facing that public confusion.

> We tried to be understanding, tried to tell ourselves that we were once civilians too. But it didn't help. Civilians . . . couldn't tell the difference between a WAVE and a SPAR. In fact, it seemed to us that civilians took a keen, secret pleasure in remaining ignorant of the differences between uniforms, dismissing the whole subject with a simple, "I just can't tell them apart!"
>
> . . . To civilians we were figures of fun wherever we went. We grew accustomed gradually on streetcars, buses, and trains to the frank stares, the furtive scrutiny, even the smiles and giggles. Just walking down the street in our conservative navy blue, we were about as inconspicuous as a brass band.

. . . Doubtless misled by recruiting posters describing "the fresh-faced girl in the trim navy blue with her jaunty hat," civilians expected us at all times to maintain an attitude of cheerful briskness. This role was often exceedingly difficult. We could not permit ourselves the luxury of sagging in public—even if we had been up since 0600, had put in a hard day at the salt mines, and had drawn the duty for that night. Normal expressions of fatigue were usually interpreted by civilians as signs of frustration, boredom or dislike of regimentation.

. . . Men . . . protested longly and loudly that they didn't care for "women in uniform." We knew that, and didn't expect them to care for us collectively. What man cares for women as a group anyway? . . . Men's prejudice often took the form of what in civilian life would be called slander. Attacks upon the morals of the SPARs were common. . . . Either we had to grin and bear it or fall into the trap of becoming embittered ourselves.

. . . Perhaps, after all, we and not the civilians were the ones to be regarded as curiosities. But after our thorough indoctrination into a new way of life, we lost our perspective for a while, forgot for the time being that actually we were a comparatively small, unique group. We learned how slowly new ideas trickle down into the public consciousness, for we were a new idea to America. Yet, when all is said and done, America finally responded with vigor to the phenomenon of women in uniform—even to the point of imagining tenderly that we had all been stationed either in jungle bivouacs or the tails of B-29s.

When the great histories of the war are written, historians will not overlook the part we played—but they'd better not call us WAVES or we'll sic our grandchildren on them![15]

In fact, some of the confusion may have come from the fact that the first 153 enlisted SPARs were formerly WAVES. And the first fifteen SPAR officers were former WAVES as well. The director of the SPAR was former WAVES Lieutenant Dorothy Stratton, who had previously been dean of women at Purdue University.[16]

The first SPAR recruits trained in Oklahoma, Iowa, and with the WAVES at Hunter College in New York City. The early officers trained at Smith College with the WAVES officers. But in June 1943, the SPAR set up its own training station at the Biltmore Hotel in Palm Beach, Florida. "The thought of boot camp in Palm Beach was particularly intriguing in January!" said Boston native Alice Jefferson, who had at first contemplated joining the WAVES, but instead was swayed by location to enlist in the SPAR in January 1944. "I also felt," she said, "that there might be greater opportunity for advancement in the smaller service." [17]

Most of the SPAR recruits served in Coast Guard district offices or bases in the U.S., near the ocean coasts, and along the inland Mississippi River coast as well. Many were sent to the Coast Guard's main headquarters in Washington, D.C., and some remained in training stations helping to train new recruits.

Doris McMilan, a SPAR stationed in New Orleans in 1943, had an encounter on a city streetcar one day that echoed reactions other women in uniform sometimes faced from angry family members of servicemen. It was an example of how the original justification for women in the military, taking the place of men so they could be sent into combat, did not always stand the women in good favor with all of the public. A woman on the streetcar suddenly began to hit Doris with her umbrella and scream at her saying, "It's your fault that my son is now at sea. If he's killed, it's your fault!" Doris was shocked. "Tears were streaming down her face and mine," Doris said. "I did not know how to handle the situation. I finally took her umbrella and left the bus at the next stop." [18]

One top secret mission the SPAR undertook during the war was called LORAN, or long-range aid to navigation. It is an electronic system that was developed when many lighthouses were disabled during the war by coastal wartime blackouts and dim-outs required to avoid enemy attack. The LORAN system, developed at MIT, would transmit simultaneous radio signals from two opposite points, with a ship traveling between them. The signals were picked up on the ship's LORAN receiver, which then calculated the ship's exact location by measuring the amount of time each signal took to reach the ship. LORAN monitoring stations along the Atlantic Coast of the U.S., Canada, Greenland, and Great Britain were set up to make sure the system worked.

One of those stations was staffed entirely by SPARs. Lieutenant Vera Hamerschlag was the commanding officer of the all-woman unit. The whole LORAN system was kept top secret for the entire war. About twelve women made up the staff of the only all-female monitoring station in the U.S., located in Chatham, Massachusetts. "The selection of the SPARs was unique," said Hamerschlag. "LORAN was so hush-hush that not even the training officer had any conception of what the duties of these SPARs would be." [19] Most of the women had some experience in radio or telephone work and learned the LORAN system in an intensive training course at MIT.

"All our class work, paperwork and notebooks had to be confiscated every day, and secured," said Marion Withe, a SPAR who worked on the LORAN project in 1944 and 1945. Another member of the unit, Anita Freeman Eldridge, said the SPARs were told not even to mention the word "LORAN" outside the Coast Guard station. "Everybody hated us," she said. "They thought we were snobs because we couldn't talk to anybody." [20]

But, Hamerschlag said, the SPARs on duty were excited by the work, even though it sometimes could be tedious. They had to sit in a darkened room for four hours at a time and watch and record the LORAN signals every two minutes. "The thought that we were participating in a system," said Hamerschlag, "that was playing such an important part in winning the war, gave us a feeling of being as close to the front lines as was possible for SPARs." [21]

Eventually, like the WAVES, SPARs were allowed to be deployed outside the continental United States in 1944. But only a few SPARs made it to Hawaii and Alaska before the war ended in 1945. By mid-1946 most of the SPARs had been discharged. And when the other services gained more permanent admittance into the military a few years after the war, the SPAR was not included in the legislation. That was because after the war, the Coast Guard was no longer under the auspices of the Navy, but had gone back to being a part of the Department of the Treasury. [22]

NAVY WOMEN—THE MARINES

When the Marines finally admitted women in early 1943, the acronym craze had all but played out, and its female members were simply called Marines. Although plenty of suggestions were made for cute monikers, such as WAMS, Femarines, Glamarines, and Submarines, Marine Commandant Thomas Holcomb told *Life* magazine in 1944, "They are Marines. They don't have a nickname and they don't need one. They get their basic training in a Marine atmosphere at a Marine post. They inherit the traditions of the Marines. They are Marines." [23]

The first classes of Marine officers went into training at Smith and Mount Holyoke colleges, where the WAVES officer training facilities were. Ruth

Cheney Streeter became the first director of the female Marines, a civilian title. She was a forty-seven-year-old mother of four from Morristown, New Jersey, who had never held a paying job before, but had been a prominent volunteer leader in health and welfare organizations in her home state. Three of her sons were in the military, and her husband was an accomplished businessman. In addition, she had earned her private and commercial pilot's license just one year before becoming head of the Marines.[24]

Enlisted Marines first trained at Hunter College in New York, alongside WAVES and SPARs. But in June of 1943, all training was moved to the largest Marine training base on the East Coast, Camp Lejeune, North Carolina. The Marines were the only branch to train male and female enlistees and officers in the same location.[25]

The uniforms of the Marines were also a little different from those of the other services. The women wore the forest green of their male counterparts, with their jackets tailored to be more feminine. And as with the WAVES, female Marines were encouraged to wear lipstick and fingernail polish, but it had to complement the red trim on their uniforms. Elizabeth Arden designed a shade of lipstick in honor of the female Marines called Montezuma Red, with that goal of color coordination in mind.[26]

Women in the Marines eventually were allowed to fill more than 200 job categories. And some Marine women were trained in a few combat skills, although they were never allowed to use those skills outside of training. On June 30, 1943, *The New York Times Magazine* ran a feature article, "Toughening Up the Women Marines."

> A tougher training course for the feminine counterpart to the hard-hitting marines . . . is indicated by the announcement that henceforth all the new recruits will be trained at Camp Lejeune. . . . One entire regimental area of the large Marine Corps base has been set aside for women marines. Beginning July 12, new classes consisting of 525 girls will start training every two weeks. During their six-week indoctrination period they will be shown all phases of marine combat training to give them a better understanding of their tasks.

The article's accompanying photos showed women learning such combat skills as antiaircraft gunnery and parachute jumping. The caption below a photo of a female parachutist said, "Marine daredevil—A trainee tried the 'shock harness drop' from the high parachute tower." Another somewhat awkward and even silly-looking photo showed two women in full uniform (skirts, button-down long-sleeved shirts, hats, oxford shoes, and beige cotton stockings) engaged in what appeared to be a wrestling match. The caption read, "Self-protection—Women are taught the art of Judo, a combination of ju-jitsu and rough-and-tumble. Two girls demonstrate for their sisters in service." [27]

Perhaps because of the acclaimed macho image of the Marines, women who joined that branch of the military came in for some particularly blatant ridicule. The male Marines themselves apparently were the biggest offenders. Since the women had no acronym equivalent to the WACs or the WAVES, the male Marines came up with a less-than-affectionate acronym of their own for the women in their ranks. Many male Marines called their female counterparts BAMs, which stood for "Big-Ass Marines."

Mary Amanda Sabourin served in the Marines starting in 1945. By then, she said, the women had learned to stand up to some of the harassment. "You're always going to find some people that . . . resent you. And some of the men resented [us] because we took their place and they had to go fight. . . . They would have their wise remarks," she said. But Sabourin and other women Marines had found a fairly tart retort. When called a BAM to her face, she remembered, "I would say, 'And you're a HAM.' " The H, she said, stood for Half. [28]

But the top official of the Marines had a more direct response early on. In 1943, when word of such open hostility from male Marines toward women reached Marine Commandant Thomas Holcomb, he wrote a pointed directive to male officers:

> Information reaching this Headquarters indicates that some . . . officers and men of the Marine Corps treat members of the Women's Reserve with disrespect . . . coarse or even obscene remarks are being made without restraint by male Marines in post exchanges, moving picture houses and other places in the hearing of members of the Women's Reserve. . . . This conduct . . . indicates a laxity in discipline which will not be tolerated. Commanding officers will be held responsible. [29]

Overcoming the similarly resistant attitudes of friends and family was a challenge for Marine women, as it was for members of the other women's services. Mary McLeod Rogers had grown up on a farm in Taylorsville,

North Carolina, and was the youngest of nine sisters. Her mother had died when Mary was five and she had no brothers. Mary's decision to join the Marines when she was twenty-three years old perplexed and troubled some of those around her. "Being the youngest, everybody just assumes they can give me orders. The youngest gets that. And going in the Marine Corps was the first thing that I had ever done on my own. . . . My father didn't want me to go . . . but I didn't ask anybody."

She said she chose the Marines partly because of a man she had dated for a while who "came up from Camp Lejeune just for the weekend. It was not any big love affair or anything. I just admired him so much, the way they looked in their uniforms and how proud he was of the esprit de corps. I thought, 'Well, I'd like to have that.' "

Another man also influenced Mary's decision. "A boy I was supposed to be engaged with," she said, "had gone off in service, and he came home and brought me a ring. He never asked me if I wanted a ring or anything. And because he was a soldier, I hated to hurt his feelings. So it wasn't really an engagement that was going to work anyway. But he said, 'If you go in the service, I am through.' " He was put off by the bad reputation military women had among soldiers. But for Mary, that attitude provided a convenient out. Mary said that when he told her, "I'm just not going to have anything to do with you if you go in the service," she replied, "Fine." She told him she intended to join up anyway, and the engagement was off. "It was a nice way to end that relationship," Mary said, "without being personal about it."

In February 1944, Mary did not tell anyone in her family, she simply took the bus to a recruiting office in Charlotte. "I remember thinking that ordinarily I would be very nervous." Instead, she found herself calm, confident, and resolved. "I felt, 'I've made a big step in my life, and I'm looking forward to it.' For the first time in my life I was independent, and I liked it."[30]

By the end of World War II, nearly 20,000 women had served in the Marines. And the male Marines had begun to accept their female counterparts.

AIR FORCE WOMEN—THE WASP

Only one branch of the military never officially accepted women into its ranks during World War II—the Army Air Force. A pilot shortage early in the war had spurred the Air Force to use women civilian pilots for help ferrying planes from manufacturers to military bases in the U.S. The women also helped train male combat pilots and antiaircraft gunners. But Congress never granted the Air Force women military status, as it had done with all the other female military branches that began during World War II. Yet the fact remains: women who flew for the military in World War II defied more than just gravity when they took to the skies in military training planes, fighters, and bombers. They defied the prevailing social mind-set that said women were not capable of making their own decisions and taking full responsibility for their own fate. A pilot must do both.

That was one of the reasons World War II pilot Lillian Epsberg Goodman loved flying solo most of all. There was something so magical and freeing for her about the feeling of being up among the clouds all alone, totally in control of her own destiny. "It was so much fun," she said. "No one knows the pleasure of it, the beauty and the quiet, until you do it." Goodman had grown up in New York City, and in the years just before the war her boyfriend sparked her interest in flying. He was taking flying lessons and she would go with him to flight school in Staten Island. "I would sit out there and watch," she said, "and wish I were doing it." Goodman finally got her chance through a government initiative started in 1939 called the Civilian Pilot Training Program, which awarded full scholarships to flight training courses at colleges and flying schools around the country. The program was started to boost the number of civilian pilots, with an eye toward training more pilots who might serve in the military if America were forced to join the war brewing in Europe.

Goodman enrolled in a six-week ground school course in Staten Island with other men and a few women. At the end of the course they all took an exam to determine who would be awarded the ten CPTP flight school scholarships. Nine were to go to men, and one to a woman. Lillian Epsberg Goodman was the woman chosen, and she went on to get her private pilot's license. That put her on a list of about 2,000 women in the U.S. who had private licenses at the time. By late 1942, most of those women, including Goodman, received a letter from a well-known female pilot named Jacqueline Cochran. She was contacting as many women pilots as she could find and inviting them to a training school at an all-female military base in Sweetwater, Texas, where they would prepare to become pilots with the Army. "I just couldn't believe it," said Goodman, "because there was no such thing as women pilots in the U.S. Army." So by March 1943, Goodman quit her job, left New York for the first time, and took a train to Texas. "To me it was like candy, this opportunity," she said. "It sounded so exciting." [31]

By the beginning of the war, Jacqueline Cochran had become one of the country's premier female pilots. Most notably, she was one of the first women to win the prestigious Bendix Race in 1938, beating all the men and setting a speed record for flying nonstop between Los Angeles and Cincinnati. When war broke out, Cochran began to believe that women pilots had a place in the military. "With the start of the war," she said later, "I became convinced that there was a sound, beneficial place for women in the air—not to compete with or displace the men pilots, but to supplement them—and I never let up trying to establish in practice the birth of my belief." [32] She contacted Hap Arnold, commander of the Air Force, and began to talk to him about starting a women's air corps, with a training program similar to the one the military provided for men. Arnold was open to the idea but did not see the need at first. He promised Cochran, however, that if the Army ever did start a women's air corps, she would be its leader.

As that was happening, another accomplished woman pilot, Nancy Harkness Love, was brewing an idea of her own. Before Pearl Harbor, and without any knowledge of Cochran's idea, Love had contacted the Ferrying Division of the Army Air Force's Air Transport Command with her own idea that women could be useful in ferrying planes within the United States, freeing male pilots for combat. Love's idea was less ambitious than Cochran's, since it involved using only the most experienced female pilots and would not have been very concerned with training. Love's idea was not adopted then. But in the spring of 1942, Love moved with her pilot husband, Robert Love, to Washington, D.C., where he was to become the deputy chief of staff of the Air Force's Ferrying Division.

Nancy Love got a civilian administrative job with a Ferrying Division operations office in Baltimore. She commuted to her job from D.C. in her own plane. By summer of 1942, as airplane production for the war was increasing rapidly, the Ferrying Division was having great difficulty finding enough qualified male pilots to handle its workload. Around that time, the head of the division's domestic wing heard about Nancy Love's flying to work each day, and began to realize that female pilots were an untapped resource. [33]

Early that fall, another pivotal female advocate of the use of women pilots in the military spoke out. Eleanor Roosevelt had been a friend of famed pilot Amelia Earhart and had enthusiastically received Jackie Cochran's ideas on women pilots in the military during the years before Pearl Harbor. She finally made her feelings known publicly when she wrote in her *My Day* column, syndicated to newspapers across the country, on September 1, 1942:

> I believe in this case, if the war goes on long enough and women are patient, opportunity will come knocking at their doors. However, there is just a chance that this is not a time when women should be patient. We are in a war and we need to fight it with all our ability and every weapon possible. Women pilots, in this particular case, are a weapon waiting to be used.[34]

By September 10, 1942, the Air Transport Command announced it had formed the WAFS (Women's Auxiliary Ferrying Squadron), with Nancy Harkness Love as its leader. Love recruited an elite group of twenty-eight of the most highly qualified female pilots. They had to be high school graduates, with a 200-horsepower rating, and have 500 hours flying time. Male candidates for the ferrying posts had to have only three years of high school and 200 hours flying time. The women would be paid $250 per month, $50 below the pay of the less experienced male pilots. The first WAFS began reporting to New Castle Army Air Base in Delaware in September.

Jackie Cochran read about the WAFS in *The New York Times*. Thinking she had been double-crossed, she went straight to Hap Arnold. It turned out that miscommunication had caused the formation of the WAFS. A new head of the ferrying command had approved the WAFS and recruited Love, unaware of Arnold's promise to Cochran. Still, the damage was done. Within days, the Air Force announced that a separate training program for women who had less flying time than the WAFS would be started with Jacqueline Cochran as its head. It would be unofficially called the WFTD (Women's Flying Training Detachment).

The first classes began training in late 1942. Cochran wrote in a newsletter to her women pilot trainees in March 1943:

> Now, we are on the verge of seeing this whole dream blossom into reality in a truly big way. . . .
> What will be the ultimate result—good or bad—will be up to the girls themselves. You of the first classes will have the real responsibility. By your actions and results the future course will be set. You have my reputation in your hands. Also, you have my faith. I have no

fear—I know you can do the job. After graduation, I will be following you with anxious and proud eyes, and your success will be my satisfaction.[35]

In August 1943, all female active duty and trainee pilots merged together into the WASP (Women Airforce Service Pilots). Jackie Cochran maneuvered into the position of director, and Nancy Love headed up the Ferrying Division of the WASP.[36]

The WASP trained at Avenger Field in Sweetwater, Texas, 200 miles west of Dallas. It was the only all-female pilot training base in the country. Often these daring women seemed somewhat alien in the world of the 1940s and in Texas small-town life. A little girl who lived in Sweetwater during the war remembered seeing the glamorous-seeming female pilot trainees at a local swimming pool in the summer.

> These "high class" women held a powerful fascination for me. . . . I observed them keenly. . . . They were tan; lithe; bold in appearance, speech, and behavior. They were aloof, self-contained, self-assured, and self-sufficient; at least so it seemed to me then. Their hair and their make-up had an elegance, a just-rightness, which no local beauty shop could produce. Their clothes were unlike anything found in J. C. Penney, Sears Roebuck, or even the elite Levy's Department Store. They wore jewelry, even while swimming, the likes of which had never been seen in Sweetwater. They spoke boldly and in hard, Northern-sounding accents. They used words we didn't use in Sweetwater—some long and fancy words, some short and pungent words.[37]

Adaline Blank began her training in Sweetwater on July 15, 1943. She was part of the class 43-W-8, meaning she was a member of the eighth WASP class in 1943. During her training she wrote a number of letters to her older sister Edwina exhibiting the heady excitement most of the female pilots felt. As Adaline told her sister early on, "I still get a thrill out of hearing the planes take off. Even Reveille and Taps give me a little shiver. I'm already sun burned and rugged looking."

Adaline described how the women lived in "bays," rooms with six cots and lockers. There was one bath for two bays, and eight bays in a barrack. Adaline's July 18, 1943, letter described her roommates and their quarters.

My bay mates are swell: we have lots of fun and are very congenial. It's a good thing because any semblance of privacy is strictly "taboo." Actually we are so busy that we aren't in the bay very much, but it seems that when one is here, *everyone* is here. We might as well not have a door on the bathroom at all. Often there is someone in the shower, someone on the "john," and still another one of us washing socks in the sink—all simultaneously. Just one big happy family.

One girl is from California; she is married and her husband is in the Air Corps somewhere in the Pacific. Another girl used to be on a newspaper in Oklahoma City. . . . Adele, my favorite, is from Iowa. . . . There is one girl from our class who was evacuated from the Philippines before Pearl Harbor; her father has been reported missing since Bataan. There are salesgirls, college girls, teachers, stenographers. Every type and size but we all have this in common—our hearts are in flying, so come what may, nothing else matters.

By September Adaline was learning more and more about flying the training planes called BTs, or Basic Trainers. On September 10, 1943, she wrote her sister about her first solo cross-country flight.

It was a real thrill to set out in a BT entirely on my own for a long flight. It is a mighty sweet ship; after you get her trimmed right you can relax and cruise along beautifully. There really isn't anything in this world that compares with the contentment that comes with flying. Sis, it even beats horseback riding.

The best fun out of a cross country is landing . . . at some strange air field and seeing the surprised expressions on the officers' faces when a mere girl climbs out of that plane. They just can't casually accept our being able to fly these army planes. Most of them are proud and very interested in what we are accomplishing. But occasionally you run into an officer who assumes an attitude of superiority and can't resist making a sarcastic remark. I really think they are jealous and innately resent our infringement upon masculine territory. There is your old double standard for the sexes again.

By the end of September Adaline had passed most of her tests, or flight checks, while some of the other women had washed out—failed and so could not qualify to become part of the WASP and had to move out of Sweetwater immediately. The training was rigorous and only about 50 percent of the trainees made it to graduation, where they would have their wings pinned on.[38]

Adaline Blank passed all her flight checks, completed her training, and graduated in December 1943. Of the 25,000 women who applied to become WASPs, only 1,830 women were accepted into training, and 1,074 made it through training. WASP trainees logged 210 hours of flying time during thirty weeks of rigorous preparation in Sweetwater. Upon graduation the women knew how to fly any size trainer plane—primary, basic, or advanced—and had the basis to learn to fly combat planes. Many of the women went on to ferrying jobs. But some worked as test pilots, or flew planes that towed targets behind them for use in training men to become antiaircraft or combat gunners.

Some WASPs also learned to fly bombers like the B-17 Flying Fortress and the B-26 Marauder, usually to assist in the training of male pilots. The women who tested repaired airplanes were doing what male pilots were reluctant to do—risk their lives in making sure maintenance crews had completed their repair work successfully. The men felt if they were to risk their lives, it should be in a more masculine way, in combat. Women were also trained on pursuit planes.[39]

Florene Miller was one of the first women to join the WAFS and later, as a WASP, was trained to fly pursuit planes. At flight school one day, she saw the double standard under which women pilots operated.

> There were about fifty men and four girls in our class. We always knew that we had to do a better job of flying with a minimum of mistakes or we would come under scorn from the men. One time I was standing in a group of men students and instructors at the school when a girl bounced her plane—a little, not badly—when she landed. The men, not remembering that I was there, ridiculed the landing and said that girls should not be flying. Right behind her a male student landed his fighter and bounced so badly several times that it appeared that he might really crash. The same men said, "Well, it looks as if old Joe is having a bad morning!" Nothing was said about his not being fit to fly.[40]

Iris Cummings Critchell also was in the early WAFS, and was sent to pursuit school in Palm Springs, California, to learn to fly fighter planes, including P-38s, P-51s, and P-61s. She went on to deliver them from the manufacturer in California to a base in Newark, New Jersey, where they were loaded onto ships and taken across the Atlantic for use in the European theater. "The

P-38," said Critchell, "is a pretty exciting airplane. It has a style all its own. I loved flying it."

Critchell was particularly representative of the kind of self-reliant spirit innate in most all of the women who served in the WASP. She had become a pilot in the first class of the Civilian Pilot Training Program in 1939 when she incorporated flight lessons into the curriculum for her physics and math degrees at the University of Southern California. After graduating she earned her living as a flight instructor with the CPTP and then was among the first women to join the WAFS.

> Flying attracts women who are going to be a little bit more independent or are interested in trying something different. It was a spirit of adventure and a spirit of challenge. Of course that is one of the things that attracted me. But I was already on the road back in 1935, doing things that put me on this track.

In 1936 Critchell was a U.S. national women's swimming champion. And in 1936, at fifteen years old, she joined the U.S. team and traveled to Berlin to compete in the Olympics. Adolf Hitler was the host, and Critchell caught glimpses of him when he attended to watch his country's athletes compete.

> We could see him and we could see the crowds and the way they were being whipped up by the general Nazi spirit. Hitler had to call off some of his foolishness because he wanted to put a good face to the world. But in spite of that, of course there were swastika banners and Nazi pride displays. We didn't know we were going to fight a war over it. But we knew the world was in trouble with this one. He had already made some moves that were unacceptable, about the superiority of the Aryan race.

That Olympic experience just added to the patriotism and sense of purpose Critchell felt seven years later as she began to ferry planes toward the battlefront, which would help the Allies win the war. "I knew that it was a huge privilege," she said of her time in the WAFS and WASP. "I think the most thrilling part of it was to realize that it was making a difference."[41]

By 1944, a particularly large type of bomber had rolled out of the factories, ready for action in the Pacific. The B-29 Superfortress was twenty-five feet longer than the B-17 Flying Fortress, which had been used to establish air superiority in Europe. The wingspan of the B-29 was forty feet wider than the

B-17, and the plane was twice as heavy. Pilots who flew B-17s and B-24s were hearing alarming stories about frequent engine fires in the bigger plane. Unlike the B-17, the B-29 had not gone through the years of rigorous testing and modification. Some bomber pilots were extremely reluctant to train on the B-29 Superfortress, which was intended to win the war in the Pacific with its ability to fly long distances with heavy payloads.

More than a year before anyone knew that the most famous B-29 of them all, the *Enola Gay*, would carry the most potent weapon ever, the Air Force was struggling to convince pilots of the handling qualities and reliability of the mammoth bomber. A twenty-five-year-old lieutenant colonel in the Army Air Force, Paul W. Tibbets, was a major champion of the B-29, and would ultimately pilot the *Enola Gay*, named after his mother, which dropped the atomic bomb on Hiroshima in 1945. But in mid-1944 he was charged with convincing male pilots to learn to fly the plane, and he thought the WASPs could help him with that. He figured men would be less reluctant to pilot the planes and would think them less dangerous if they saw women flying them. Tibbets recruited two WASPs, Dora Dougherty and Dorothea Johnson, from Elgin Field in northern Florida, where they were towing targets for gunnery practice. Both women had flown twin-engine planes, but not the four-engine bombers.[42] Dora Dougherty remembered how Tibbets taught them to fly it in just three days and also served as their check pilot.

> This new bomber, built especially for the long-range bombing desperately needed in the Pacific theater, was considered a "killer" or a "beast" by the men pilots assigned to train in it.[43]
> . . . We were surprised when we sat at the controls. It was so well-engineered. . . . Although it was a large plane, it was easier to fly than some of the twin-engine planes.[44]
> We completed our checkout by the end of the third day (despite an engine fire during the first flight) and thereafter demonstrated our ship, Ladybird, at the very heavy bomber training base at Alamogordo, New Mexico. After a short time, the purpose of the flights had been achieved. The male flight crews, their egos challenged, approached the B-29 with new enthusiasm and found it to be not a beast, but a smooth, delicately rigged, and responsive ship.[45]

Cornelia Fort was one of the original WAFS to join with Nancy Love in 1942 and begin ferrying planes for the Army. But Fort, a seasoned pilot, had seen the war from the air right at its very beginning. In her role as a flight instructor in Hawaii, she had been conducting a flying lesson over the Pacific on the morning Pearl Harbor was bombed. She had seen the Japanese planes fly past and watched as they dropped their bombs. It made her more determined than ever to use her flying to help the war effort. She went home to Nashville to find a way to get into the war. The WAFS was her answer. She became one of its most zealous fliers, and one of the most eloquent in expressing the emotions she and her colleagues had about their work.

> I have yet to have a feeling which approaches in satisfaction that of having signed, sealed, and delivered an airplane for the United States Army. The attitude most nonflyers have about pilots is distressing and often acutely embarrassing. They chatter about the glamour of flying. Well, any pilot can tell you how glamorous it is. We get up in the cold dark in order to get to the airport by dawn. If the weather is good we fly all day, usually without lunch. We wear heavy cumbersome flying suits and 30-pound parachutes. We are either cold or hot and you can't change clothes very well in the air. We get sunburns and windburns and if female your lipstick wears off and your hair gets straighter and straighter. You look forward all afternoon to the bath you will have and the steak. Well, we get the bath but sometimes we are too tired to eat the steak and we fall wearily into bed.
>
> None of us can put into words why we fly. It is something different for each of us. I can't say exactly why I fly, but I "know" why as I've never known anything in my life.
>
> I knew it when I saw my plane silhouetted against the clouds framed by a circular rainbow. . . . I know it in the dignity and self-sufficiency and in the pride of skill. I know it in the satisfaction of usefulness. . . . For the first time we felt a part of something larger. . . . I, for one, am profoundly grateful that my one talent, my only knowledge, flying, happens to be of use to my country when it is needed. That's all the luck I ever hope to have.[46]

On March 21, 1943, Fort was flying in formation with other pilots, when she and a male pilot began flying more closely to each other than was considered safe. His landing gear sliced off part of her left wing. She lost control of the plane and it crashed, killing her. The male pilot survived. Rumors had circulated that he was trying to impress Cornelia by doing such a risky maneuver, but no concrete evidence of that existed. The conclusion of one of Cornelia's

officers in the WAFS was that the collision that killed her was purely accidental. The twenty-four-year-old Fort was the first American woman military pilot to die on duty. Knowing the hazard of what she was doing, she
had written a letter to her mother in case she died, declaring her love of her
work.

> If I die violently, who can say it was "before my time"? I should have
> dearly loved to have had a husband and children. My talents in that
> line would have been pretty good, but if that is not to be, I want no
> one to grieve for me.
>   I was happiest in the sky—at dawn when the quietness of the air
> was like a caress, when the noon sun beat down and at dusk when
> the sky was drenched with fading light.[47]

In 1943, a group of the best-performing women from an early graduating
class at Avenger Field was chosen to go to Camp Davis in North Carolina to
fly planes that towed targets behind them for men learning to be antiaircraft
gunners. There were 50,000 men at that base and about twenty-five women at
first. Hostility toward those early WASPs was out in the open, from the major
in charge of the base to the enlisted men.

In August and September of 1943 two WASPs were killed in crashes, and
a third was injured, narrowly escaping death, all in somewhat mysterious
equipment failures. A concerned Jacqueline Cochran went to Camp Davis
after the first death and found the women fearing for their lives. The climate
of hostility toward the women might have contributed to the deadly consequences, although no direct link was ever found to specific males. Still, the
WASPs were highly disturbed at the shoddily maintained planes and lax
attitude of the male officers toward their safety. And they were insulted by
constant affronts to their competence. Cochran noted their complaints, but
fearing negative publicity, did little to change things. Then, after the second
death, she launched an investigation. In the engine of the second downed
plane investigators reported they had found enough sugar to make the plane
malfunction. Although disturbed by the findings, Cochran decided not to
make the stark evidence of apparent sabotage public, or to investigate further, believing that such information would endanger the continuation of the
entire WASP program.[48]

Cochran's decision was one of a few that the majority of women in the
WASP did not know about at the time. Most had assumed that the concern

for their safety, and appreciation for their dedication, that was foremost in the minds of those who oversaw them would override any political considerations. Ann Darr finished her training in 1943, and ended up flying B-26 bombers at a gunnery school for male combat trainees in Las Vegas. She would tow a target, or sleeve, behind her plane and men in B-17 bombers would fly beside her and shoot at the target, "firing live ammunition at the sleeve we towed. After a target run, we dropped the sleeve on the desert. The ammo had been dipped in colored wax, and the rim of the holes showed which gunner had hit the target." With men literally gunning at her, Darr developed a particularly close kinship with her fellow female pilots. "I will never forget the camaraderie," she said. "Friends . . . to share the anxieties, aching bones. . . . Living close-in, with all the ups and downs."

But during Darr's time in Las Vegas, a fellow WASP was killed while copiloting a plane that was towing a target for gunnery practice. The way the Army handled her death sent chills through all the WASPs, as it had done in the case of each of the thirty-nine WASPS who died in the line of duty during the war. Not only did the Army not pay for the transport of her body, or her burial, or give her family a flag to drape on her coffin, but her parents were given no gold star to signify the loss of their child in military service.

"The male pilot's body was sent home to be buried with honors," said Darr. "The female co-pilot . . . the Army said it was not responsible. The Civil Service said it was not responsible. We took up a collection to send her body home." [49] Darr was distressed. "I was so humiliated that our government could treat us that way." [50]

Such dismay existed. Yet most of the women who encountered it found a way to live with it and get on with their work nonetheless. And many women never ran into it. Lillian Epsberg Goodman, who had joined the WASP in 1943 after getting her private license in Staten Island with the CPTP, said she was glad she did not realize that some people were so adamantly opposed to her doing what she loved so much.

> I never felt like they were challenging us. I just didn't see it. I guess I was going around with blinders on thinking everybody was proud of us. There were a lot of people who complimented us. I guess the ones that didn't, didn't come right out and tell you themselves. . . . But I was so happy. It seemed to me that every place we went we were popular. . . . I was amazed when I learned later that there was this animosity. [51]

By early 1944 Jacqueline Cochran and Hap Arnold were ready to push for militarization of the still civilian WASP, just as the WAC had done successfully the year before. On March 22, 1944, congressional hearings began on a bill that would make the WASP an official part of the Army Air Force and finally give the women pilots military status and benefits. Hap Arnold was the only witness to testify. Previous experience had taught that a commanding general deeming an action necessary for winning the war was all Congress needed to pass a bill.

Arnold made a strong case. But militarization proponents had miscalculated, both in their timing and in their political maneuvering. They did not allow for the stage that the war had reached. By spring of 1944, Allied air superiority had been established in Europe, especially after brutal bombing campaigns using B-17s over Germany by the Eighth Air Force and other Allied bombing groups. Many of the combat veterans were returning from battle and the shortage of pilots on the home front was decreasing. As a result, the Air Force had closed down training programs for male civilian pilots, leaving 900 flight instructors and 5,000 trainees out of work as pilots. Many of those men had enlisted to teach in the cadet training programs to avoid the draft until they got enough flight time to be assigned as pilots. But they were suddenly being assigned to ground positions.

The perception that women pilots were not as valuable as they once had been was growing. Before the WASP militarization bill was introduced, a virulent letter-writing campaign by a small but vocal group of civilian pilots got the attention of many in Congress. Arnold tried to counter the idea that WASPs were depriving these men of flying commissions. He did not see the logic in giving work to men who were less experienced than the women. He pointed out that the Air Force had always had a policy that any man who could meet the Air Force requirements would be trained and deployed. He also pointed out that the WASPs had been held to and met the highest, most stringent military standards, while the male civilian pilots were allowed to fly with much less experience and training. Still, the bill to militarize the WASPs was defeated in the House of Representatives by only nineteen votes on June 21, 1944, despite the fact that such prominent proponents as Representatives Lyndon Baines Johnson, Clare Boothe Luce, and Margaret Chase Smith all voted in support of WASP militarization.[52]

The bill's defeat meant the WASP would have to be disbanded. It was left to Cochran and Arnold to tell the women. In late fall of 1944 each active

WASP and WASP trainee got letters from both Arnold and Cochran telling them their mission had been completed. Arnold said, "You have freed male pilots for other work, but now the situation has changed and the time has come when your volunteered services are no longer needed. The situation is that, if you continue in service, you will be replacing instead of releasing our young men. I know that the WASP wouldn't want that." [53]

Lillian Epsberg Goodman remembered how hard she and her colleagues took the news. "We were just all done in to have it end so abruptly," she said. "Nobody was prepared for it. We thought it would go until the end of the war." After her time in the WASP, Goodman never piloted a plane again. [54]

Pilot Ann Darr remembered that during the congressional debate on militarization the WASP were told not to speak out, that General Arnold would do the talking for them. "We were advised," Darr said, "to act like 'ladies'— and keep silent." But she also remembered how differently she and others handled lingering resistance decades later, in 1977, when Congress finally granted the women who had served in the WASP military status.

> More than 30 years later when another bill came up in Congress to give us the title of "veteran" retroactively, we ended our silence. WASPs came from all over the country to make our case. Even though the committee chairman said publicly to . . . a former WASP pilot, "I promise you this, young lady, the bill will never leave my committee." When the final vote was taken, we had our place in history. We now had recognition and a burial plot. No GI bill, no insurance, but we had the name we'd fought for: veteran. [55]

In the three years of the WASP's existence, its pilots flew more than 60 million miles and ferried more than 12,000 aircraft between factories and military bases. [56] In a report on the WASP in August 1944, Jackie Cochran said, "their job is to do the routine, the dishwashing flying jobs of the AAF, that will release men for higher grades of duty." [57] Iris Cummings Critchell, the Olympian, continued to fly throughout her life. "We stepped up and pushed the envelope," she said. "And then had to back up a little bit and wait for total acceptance. Society wasn't ready." [58]

Saipan
Friday, June 1, 1945

Vega and I spent the day over at the B-29 base. . . . But the real excitement for the day—in fact for the stay on Saipan so far came tonight as we were driving home. We'd both heard many rumors about the "Japs in them thar hills." We'd seen the innumerable signs "Restricted Area, Keep Out, Danger Japs." And we've heard lots of stories. But tonight, about 9:30 driving back to our quarters on a busy, but still somewhat isolated road that cuts across the middle of the island right through the "Jap-infested" hills, we got as much proof as I want to get that there are still Japs here. We were shot at by a Japanese sniper, who fortunately was a very poor marksman. The fellows we were with have been here on the island for some time now, and being shot at by Jap snipers is not a new experience for them. And they both said, as soon as we heard the shot, "Jap 25." Vega and I decided that henceforth it's wiser not to wear white shirts at night.

CHAPTER SIX

Save His Life and Find Your Own

VOLUNTEERS, LAND ARMY, RED CROSS GIRLS, AND NURSES

You gain strength, courage and confidence by every experience in which you really stop to look fear in the face. You are able to say to yourself, "I lived through this horror. I can take the next thing that comes along."

ELEANOR ROOSEVELT[1]

Save his life... and find your own

FOR THE MANY WOMEN who stayed on the home front, volunteering through such organizations as the Red Cross, the USO, and the Office of Civilian Defense was their avenue to war involvement. These women were also less threatening to the status quo than their military counterparts, though they discovered a similar kind of satisfaction in using their skills and talents in public life.

Females in the women's branches established during World War II ran into some opposition—at least in part because they went against traditional notions of womanhood. But military nurses endured much less stigma or backlash. In fact, nursing was considered such a feminine job that men were not allowed to be military nurses during World War II. Similarly, women who went overseas with the Red Cross, a quasi-military civilian service group, were able to rise above some of the negative feelings against women in uniform, since they seemed to conform more closely to the traditional ideas of feminine nurturing and support than did regimented military women.

But nurses and Red Cross women often came closer to the rigors of battle than any other groups of women. "Red Cross girls," as they were called, started going overseas to help in Great Britain's war effort before the U.S. entered the war. And they sometimes were allowed up to the front lines, even up to foxholes, if only to deliver coffee, doughnuts, and good cheer to the men. Military nurses were sent abroad with male troops once the U.S. joined the Allies in battle, and traveled closely with the military units to which they were assigned.[2] By the end of the war, 35,000 Army and Navy nurses and 7,000 Red Cross girls were serving overseas.[3] In the course of the war, 255 nurses died at home and abroad, sixteen as a result of direct enemy fire, and twenty-nine Red Cross women died on duty overseas.

HOME FRONT VOLUNTEERS

With so many admonitions to do their part in the war effort, women on the home front often searched hard to find outlets for their energy and their will to help. One of the most popular was working with the Red Cross in the U.S. More than 3.5 million women volunteered in the various divisions of the Red Cross on the home front during World War II. Two of the most well-known divisions included Nurse's Aides and Gray Ladies, who volunteered in military hospitals, providing assistance to medical personnel and morale boosts to patients. The production division oversaw another famous job women had done with the Red Cross since its unofficial beginnings during the Civil War: rolling bandages for use in military hospitals at home and abroad. During World War II, Red Cross volunteers were said to have produced 2.5 billion of these surgical dressings. Volunteers also put together food packages and shipped them to POWs in Europe and the Far East, at one point assembling 1.4 million packages per month. In addition, they produced comfort kits, or care packages, for soldiers at home and abroad, containing hand-knitted items and food.

Women volunteering for the newly formed blood banks of the Red Cross worked in one of the organization's most vital services during World War II. Red Cross volunteers collected blood and plasma donations all over the country and shipped them to hospitals caring for soldiers wounded in battle. By the end of the war the Red Cross had collected 13 million pints of blood. The blood and plasma were essential to saving lives in the field. After D-Day, plasma was dropped by parachute to evacuation hospitals treating the wounded. General Eisenhower said, "If I could reach all of America—there is one thing I would like to do—thank them for blood plasma and for whole blood. It has been a tremendous thing."[4]

Another well-known Red Cross endeavor fell under the Home Service division, which notified servicemen and servicewomen of births, weddings, and other important news from home. The Red Cross notified families of the status of their wounded loved ones in hospitals around the world. During the war the Red Cross sent approximately 42 million such messages.[5] In addition, Red Cross volunteers ran canteens, provided first aid training all over the country, and maintained a motor corps.

At twenty-two, Billie Banks Doan was not old enough to go overseas with the Red Cross when she joined at the beginning of the war, so she was sent to Miami Beach to help coordinate recreational activities for returning servicemen who were taking some mandatory time off. "I really felt I had to be in the war. It was part of my personality. Where the action was, that's where I wanted to be. . . . It was an opportunity to move out in the world and learn something about it."

Many of the men who ended up in Miami Beach were bomber pilots who had flown and survived their mandatory twenty-five missions. "It was called redistribution," Doan said. "Some of the people went overseas again. Some of them went home." She was assigned to one hotel for enlisted men, and along with another Red Cross girl organized dances and beach parties and played pool and Ping-Pong with the men. Her boss was a male Red Cross worker who oversaw all the Red Cross workers in Miami Beach. The hotels there had been taken over by the military for soldiers who needed time to rest.

> We organized baseball games. We had parties. We called the weenie roasts we would have on the beach "singe binges." If you were going to have a dance you ordered so many girls, so many cases of beer. All up and down the beach they did this. You ordered forty girls. You may not get them. These were girls who lived in Miami, who came to all the parties. We always got our quota of girls, because of the kinds of parties we ran. They were lively. But I would not date any-one. Because I was there for everybody. I had GIs get drunk and come up to me hating the Red Cross because the only things you women want to do is to find somebody and get hooked. So I said I wouldn't date anyone. I wasn't that interested in men because I hadn't grown up yet. I wasn't that young, I just hadn't grown up yet.

Doan was serious about her work, since she felt it was contributing to the well-being of the men who were fighting for the country. Later in the war, she went overseas to India and worked as a Red Cross girl there too. "I didn't feel I was saving the country," she said, "but I am incredibly proud of what I did." She said she made life a little more bearable for the men. "That was what I had to give. And that was necessary." [6]

The United Service Organizations operated approximately 3,000 clubs in the U.S., where women volunteered as hostesses, dancing partners, played cards and Ping-Pong, or just socialized with soldiers. "When I volunteered to be a dance partner at the USO," said one woman, "I found out that the boy who's going there really wants companionship, a feeling that he's being accepted as a human being." [7] Other volunteers helped wounded soldiers write letters, sewed on buttons, and distributed books and magazines at military bases. In the 1942 book *Calling All Women*, about volunteer opportunities for women in wartime, a chapter on the USO said, "The U.S.O. needs women workers. It can use you if you are young and pretty, if you are young and not pretty, if you are middle-aged, if you are old and gray. All it asks is co-operation—willingness to do what you are asked to do." [8]

Nancy Potter was a student at Tufts University during the war, but found time to do volunteer work in the midst of her studies. She had entered college at sixteen, so she was younger than most college students.

> I did work as a volunteer in a hospital in Boston to relieve civilian nurses. We were very convinced that everyone ought to be tremendously involved in the war effort. I enjoyed the hospital volunteering, but I found the experience absolutely terrifying. I had been sheltered, and I had not realized that there was as much pain and misery in the world. The hospitals were very short staffed and seemed to me that there was always too much to do. I think the responsibility was really too much for me at that age.
>
> There were entertainment centers called "Buddies Clubs" or USO Clubs, which came a little later, and this meant that typically on a Saturday if you were a good patriotic young woman, you would go to a Buddies Club and you would serve doughnuts and coffee, and you would sit and talk with servicemen and sometimes servicewomen. There would be a tremendous opportunity to meet people from very different parts of the country. Servicemen were very lonely, very homesick, and they simply liked to sit and talk with someone. They would like to show photographs of their homes and their parents and their girlfriends and talk about all that. [9]

Louise Aukerman worked in Charleston, South Carolina, at the USO club with her husband, who was an employee of the USO. One of her most memorable tasks was operating an audio recorder for servicemen, leaving for war or coming back, who wanted to send messages, recorded onto special record-like disks, home to their families.

> Since I was about 28 at the time, the fellows felt comfortable talking to the record in front of me. . . . When a hospital ship came in, we would have injured servicemen coming into the club, men who were on crutches or bandaged. They would go in . . . and they would have to tell wives or their mothers that they had lost a limb or an arm. . . . They were trying to explain to their families what had happened, so

that when they got home it wouldn't be a shock. It was awfully hard to listen to these men. . . . They would break down and weep and cry. But it was a wonderful service, because they could get this out and communicate. Sometimes it was very sad because sometimes they had just gotten a "Dear John" letter or something, and they were answering it.

. . . We did a lot of counseling or just listening, besides providing the dances and church services. One night, for instance, it was almost midnight and this young fellow came rushing in. He said to me, "Oh, I don't know what I'm going to do. My wife is coming from Washington, the state of Washington, all the way across the country on the bus, and I'm to meet her. We just got orders that we are shipping out in an hour!" You can imagine how hard it was for me to meet that bus, meet that young woman who had traveled all the way across the country, only to tell her that her husband had just shipped out.[10]

Another umbrella organization under which women volunteered was the Office of Civilian Defense, founded in May 1941, with former New York City mayor Fiorello La Guardia as its director. The OCD directed thousands of programs to protect and serve citizens on the home front. Though the OCD did not specifically organize programs for women, many of their volunteers were female. The local planning and organizing arms of the OCD were the Defense Councils, which, in turn, formed Civilian Defense Volunteer offices in communities throughout the country. Those offices became clearinghouses for citizens who wanted to volunteer. They were best known for training and deploying air raid wardens in neighborhoods all over the country. Also they trained and assigned block leaders in neighborhoods who organized scrap metal salvage drives, war bond campaigns, nutrition programs, child care services, and other activities that supported the war effort. The OCD also helped to reinstate the idea of Victory Gardens, which had been a successful concept in World War I. By 1944, there were an estimated 18 million Victory Gardens throughout the U.S.[11]

A January 1942 article about female volunteers in *Time* magazine, "Civilian Defense," mentioned war-related activities of other volunteer women's groups such as the American Legion Auxiliary, the Junior League, and the Woman's Christian Temperance Union. The article talked about how the groups administering volunteer jobs, such as the Red Cross, the USO, and the OCD, had designed military-style uniforms for their female volunteers.

Uniforms blossomed on all sides. *Vogue* ecstatically proclaimed: "This is our new life. This is what we have to do. . . . And whatever our duties are, one of the symbols of our new double-duty lives is the uniform. The uniform stands for our new spine of purpose, our initiative in getting women working, splayed out into hundreds of different jobs, to find talents which have been mossed over. It means that we know that it is time to stop all the useless little gestures, to stop being the Little Woman and be women."

The *Time* article mentioned one volunteer group that had already mobilized by the time America joined the war. The American Women's Voluntary Services (AWVS), founded in 1940, was modeled after the British Women's Voluntary Services. The intent of the AWVS was to prepare for the bombing of American cities. The women who founded it were upper-class, and so were often derided in the press as frivolous. Indeed, in the *Time* article the AWVS was called the volunteer group "that made the most noise." [12]

Many of the naysayers outside the press were isolationists, who objected to readying the country for a war that they felt America was better off not joining. Until Pearl Harbor the women of the AWVS were ridiculed as alarmist. Nonetheless, the AWVS set up 350 branches all over the country in its first two years. It made concerted efforts to involve women from all walks of life and all ethnic backgrounds, another reason they were often met with resistance and ridicule, including from the Ku Klux Klan. One of the first duties the AWVS took on was patrolling the East Coast watching for enemy planes, a job later taken over on both the East and West coasts by the WAC. Since the full-scale bombing of American cities never came, as it had in Britain, the AWVS settled into being another clearinghouse for potential volunteers, funneling them to the Red Cross and the Office of Civilian Defense, as well as into its own protection and service programs. Through the war, more than 325,000 women volunteers were trained by and worked through the AWVS in such jobs as driving ambulances, operating mobile kitchens, driving in motor pools for the military and other public and government agencies, selling war bonds, working in canteens, photography, radio work, typing, and emergency switchboard service. [13]

WOMEN'S LAND ARMY

By the summer of 1942 American farmers were facing a labor shortage. Not only had many farmer's sons and male farmhands gone off to war, but farmhands not heading to war were finding higher-paying jobs in defense plants. Black sharecroppers in the South, in particular, started a migration north toward better working conditions and pay. And thousands of Japanese-American farmworkers on the West Coast had been rounded up and sent away to U.S. government internment camps. In agriculture, as in so many parts of the war economy, the labor pool shrank. Once again, women suddenly became one of the best available untapped labor sources.[14] At first, farmers' daughters and wives took up the slack. While less than one percent of the officially reported farm workforce was female before the war, by 1942, 13 percent was female.[15]

But the need grew, and the U.S. Department of Agriculture responded by creating another quasi-military civilian group called the Women's Land Army, which trained and sent thousands of urban and suburban women to work on farms.[16] The program was modeled after the Women's Land Army begun in Great Britain a few years before. The U.S. program was set up by the federal government, but recruiting and coordination were left to each state. Involvement took many forms. Some women spent their two weeks' vacation from regular jobs working on a farm in the summer. Others worked for the entire summer. Some housewives rode buses to the country to spend a few hours working on farms each day, between about 8:30 in the morning and 3:00 in the afternoon. That gave them time to send their families off to work and school in the morning, and to be home in the afternoon to do food shopping or meet children returning from school.[17] A 1945 Department of Agriculture pamphlet described the program.

> The women who did not commute often lived with specific farm families or in housing set up in centrally located areas from which they would go out to work on different surrounding farms, according to need. These workers were paid the going rate for farm labor, which generally meant they made no profit after paying for food and boarding. But, of course, the women had the option of buying and wearing the official Women's Land Army uniforms.[18]

A *New York Times* reporter followed one group of Women's Land Army recruits from New York City in 1943, "bound for the fruit country of the fertile Hudson River Valley." The writer observed that "most of them had no farm experience beyond reading 'Grapes of Wrath.' . . . 'Birds' were the sounds with which they greeted teams that opposed the Dodgers. 'Corn' was cliche music of the sweet variety." As the women settled into their work they found that "life had much in common with that in the Army. They lived and ate as a unit. The sun knocked them out and they slept untroubled. They rose early. In one of the cabins a girl played a fife to wake her companions. She didn't know reveille, so at 4:45 A.M. the tune wafted out on the gentle morning breeze was Taps." [19]

Some farmers had a hard time accepting the idea of putting expensive farm equipment and livestock in the hands of city women with no rural experience. But necessity and the work ethic the women displayed seemed to win out. Of the New Yorkers who came to work his land, one strawberry farmer told The New York Times, "I like them better than the men for the simple reason that they're not gripers. Men are always complaining." A lettuce farmer said, "We expected at first they would give up . . . [go] home after the first week. They . . . insisted on staying here until the last leaf went to market on Labor Day." [20]

In 1944, the Women's Land Army reported it had placed about 400,000 women workers on farms across the country, and it estimated about the same number of additional women workers were recruited by farmers directly. A 1945 Department of Agriculture pamphlet implored women to stick with it. "Women are urgently needed again this year . . . to offset the greatest farm labor shortage since this war began. . . . So the Women's Land Army urges women everywhere to join . . . help farmers reach crop goals to produce our country's food, a basic weapon of war." [21]

The daughter of a farmer in New Hampshire said, "I decided not to join the WACs or the WAVES, but to do farm work and help in farm production." She added, "I believe this is just as important to the men in the armed forces." [22]

That spirit of finding satisfaction in self-sacrifice and putting the men first, which was encouraged and lauded in so many women during the war, was evident among the Land Army volunteers as well. As one woman worker explained, "No matter how heavy the hay we pitched, how our backs ached from weeding, or how stubborn the team we were driving, we always had the secret joy that we were helping the war effort." [23]

RED CROSS GIRLS OVERSEAS

The American Red Cross sent some 7,000 women overseas to staff 1,800 clubs near wherever troops were stationed. Soldiers showed up for rest, food, dancing and other recreation. Some Red Cross women ran clubmobiles, which were traveling kitchens from which they served coffee, freshly made doughnuts, and any other refreshments available. Red Cross girls made more than 1.6 million doughnuts during the war and reportedly served 400 a minute during 1944 and 1945. The women operated their clubmobiles in the North African, Mediterranean, and European theaters. Many times these women were close to the front as they followed the troops on all the major campaigns. For that reason, the percentage of Red Cross women who died overseas was the highest of the three groups of women who went abroad— even though the number of Red Cross women who served overseas was much lower than the numbers of WACs and nurses.[24]

Red Cross women were all college-educated. None of the military services required a college degree, but the Red Cross did. In addition, Red Cross girls had to be at least twenty-five years old. The idea that college-educated women, twenty-five and older, were called "girls" and were sent overseas to serve coffee and doughnuts and organize dances may strike many people today as a misuse of their skills and mischaracterization of their value. But at the time, joining the Red Cross was an opportunity for adventure and challenge never before available to women. It was the only organization besides the USO entertainment troupes that sent large groups of women overseas without the stern regulation of military service or the grim responsibilities of nursing. Red Cross girls often reported that every moment of their work and life at war seemed infused with meaning and depth that belied the auxiliary, or sometimes even trivial, surface appearance of the duties they performed.

Jean Archer had been a schoolteacher in the U.S. before she joined the Red Cross in 1945. She was sent to Guam in May of that year to work at a Navy on-post club. She described her duties in one of her first letters home from Guam to her parents in New Jersey on May 23, 1945.

> My "work" consists of taking turns at doing everything in the club.
> Right now I'm working on a soldier talent show for Thursday night.
> . . . The sailors are grand and they certainly appreciate the club. It is

always full, never enough chairs for all. We are busy every single moment, playing cards, Ping-Pong or just talking, but we never stop talking and listening. I've seen hundreds of pictures of best girls, wives, children. I've had any number of boys say to me, "Do you know you are the first girl (or white girl) I have talked to in 22 months?" . . . I wouldn't be any place else. It is the hardest and most tiring job I've ever had, not even a rest hour, but it is also the most interesting and satisfying.[25]

In another letter a few days later she briefed her parents on the kind of security surrounding the Red Cross women.

Did I ever tell you about the restrictions under which we live? After six in the evening, we have to be accompanied by two officers, one of whom is armed. We have to be in by ten and no exceptions. That suits me fine. In the first place I work every evening but one and then we have to get up by 6:30 to get breakfast. Mother, the sailors certainly get a kick out of my little red and white apron you made.

"Just like home," they say.[26]

In some ways, that was the main mission of the Red Cross women. They were to bring the men a little bit of home.

Margaret Kelk joined the Red Cross in 1943. Like all Red Cross women going overseas, she went through a few weeks of training in Washington, D.C., where she said she was told to "take care of the enlisted man. He is the one who is facing the guns and fighting the war." Female Red Cross workers overseas were civilians, but were given honorary officer status so they would be treated more charitably if they were taken prisoner. The Army Special Services unit was the liaison with the Red Cross women in the field. Kelk said she was told to "always obey the army. You cannot ever double-cross them. But, on the side, if the army cannot provide you with what you want, then you are a civilian; you may go out and talk to the navy or someplace else. You need a can of paint and the army hasn't got it, find the navy; they've always got paint." Kelk said she realized that "we could moonlight, we had rights, things that we could do that army personnel could not do."[27]

Kelk was wary also of a kind of class division she and others saw between the officers and the enlisted men. One day, while stationed in Noumea, New Caledonia, a few hours off the east coast of Australia, Kelk was asked by the man in charge of her Red Cross unit to accompany Chester Nimitz, the admiral of the entire Pacific Navy, to a party. "I said, 'No way. Forget it fast. I will not even consider it.' Because every time a Red Cross girl fell into that little mess, the GIs turned against her because there was this very different division—officers, GIs. . . . I never went to an officers' club. I never dated officers."[28]

Alice Pennington was a Red Cross camp director in the Pacific from 1944 until after the war. She first landed in Milne Bay in New Guinea on October 2, 1944, after a three-week ocean voyage on a troopship with only two other Red Cross girls.

> We were wearing our tropical uniforms, light gray seersucker, and the first words we heard as we disembarked were, "You can't wear dresses here, General MacArthur's orders. You have to get GI shirts and pants." We had to go to the post tailor to get fitted, and of course nothing fitted me. Then again, nothing fitted anyone else very well either. We were housed in small huts with roofs made of palm fronds. Within the huts there were four army cots and that was the extent of the furniture. We had no indoor plumbing, so when we wanted to take a shower we . . . would take our helmets to a place in the compound where there was water and fill the helmet. Then we went out to the bathing area, a spot that was somewhat enclosed and that had a little hook for the helmets. The procedure was quite simple: first you hooked the helmet over the hook; then you sat under it and tipped it over on yourself. That was a bath.

Eventually Pennington was sent to Sydney, Australia, to oversee recreation activities at a club where Army officers came for two-week leaves. She was taking another Red Cross club director's place and met her predecessor when she arrived. The woman was anxious to leave and gave Pennington only a quick good-bye and a piece of paper with vague notes listing the main activities and outings she had organized for the men. Then, as she was walking out the door, she gave Pennington one last bit of instruction. "Army buses will be provided for your trips," she said, "and condoms are in the left-hand drawer of the old desk. When a man asks, 'May I have a box?' give the condom box to him and show him the door to the next room. He will take what he needs and return it to you. You need to keep it filled."[29]

Red Cross clubmobiles followed men at the front, to provide a bit of respite from battle. Clubmobiles were a new concept in World War II. They traveled in units and had enough supplies to last for fifteen days away from a base of supply. Each individual clubmobile was staffed by three Red Cross girls. The vehicles were General Motors trucks, and each one was named for an American state or city, or had a name with patriotic or symbolic meaning for Americans, such as *Pathfinder, Magnolia,* or *Daniel Boone.* The women staffing them were allowed to move through combat areas with more free-dom than many soldiers or journalists, as they brought coffee and doughnuts right up to the GIs in camps and sometimes in foxholes. Many Red Cross girls were anxious to staff clubmobiles, for a firsthand look at combat as troops made their way from the English countryside through France, Belgium, North Africa, Italy, and into Germany.[30] But most of the twenty-nine Red Cross women who died overseas in World War II were killed in the course of this dangerous kind of work. The first died during the fighting in Anzio, Italy.[31]

Soon after D-Day, Mary Metcalfe served on a clubmobile officially named *President Lincoln,* but usually just called *Abe,* that followed the First Army's 49th Anti-Aircraft Brigade through France, with its approximately 52,000 soldiers. She said she and the other two women worked in shifts starting at 5:00 A.M.

> We made doughnuts until about 11. Since it took some 15 pounds of flour to make 275 doughnuts, we used almost 100 pounds of flour each day. We brewed about 120 gallons of coffee in the 15-gallon urns that we carried on board. The five 35-gallon water tanks had to be filled with fresh water that we got from a designated "water point." The Red Cross was responsible for keeping us supplied with doughnut flour and coffee and the army took care of refueling Abe. At times that was a problem, since there were so many combat vehi-cles used in operation. But as acute as the fuel crisis would become, the army always saved enough to fill Abe's thirsty tank—he only got about seven miles to the gallon.
>
> . . . As we traveled along we passed Nazi tanks and vehicles that had been knocked out and abandoned. In some places the stench of death was nauseating. . . . We tried to visit four or five different bat-teries each day, serving the men doughnuts and coffee. We fre-quently did not have time or were not allowed, because of the position of the unit, to turn on the record player and loud speaker. But the men really loved that jive music when we could play it!

We were required to be back at camp by 10 P.M. because the Nazi Luftwaffe, nicknamed "Bed Check Charlie," began his nightly bomb runs at eleven.

But before going to bed the women had to clean out the greasy ranges they had used to make doughnuts all day. Dirty and exhausted, and with no bath or shower facilities, they sometimes found ways to degrease themselves. "In desperation," said Metcalfe, "we often boiled water in the large tank on the field range and sponged ourselves off. It was remarkable how good that little bit of water felt." And if they had any more water left over they would do their best to clean their dusty, greasy blouses.

Within a few weeks Metcalfe and her two partners on the clubmobile *President Lincoln* received a surprise commendation from the First Army, written by a colonel commanding one of the units of the 49th Brigade. It said the "efficient and charming manner in which" the three women "served the members of this command, including those located at isolated gun sites, has been an inspiration to each of us and a further reminder of the principles for which we are fighting." The women had visited more than 130 remote firing units in their first week on duty and covered more than 600 miles in the process.

One night, upon returning from their work, Metcalfe and the others found "singer Dinah Shore sitting in our tent writing to her husband, something she told us she did every day. She had come to give a USO show for all the units of the 49th Brigade. We were the only American women in the area with a place for her to rest before her show. She was very nice and we were delighted to have the opportunity to visit with her. One of the GIs found a full-size mirror that he brought for her to use. After she left, we continued to use it. Having a mirror made such a difference." [32]

Mary Haynsworth Mathews served with the Red Cross in England, France, and Germany. She was twenty-seven when she joined the Red Cross in 1944.

In the spring of 1945, I was afraid the war was going to end and I would never get anywhere near the front. I wanted to be in the clubmobiles and get where the action was (being young and foolish). So I applied for a change to the clubmobile. . . . And where did they send me? To Le Havre, which was further from the front. But that was interesting because . . . of all those GIs coming in that had been prisoners of war and men still arriving from the States going to fight. We met every plane, train, and ship that came or went. The guys were herded into a huge warehouse (to await the next assignment) with two orchestras, one playing at one end and one at the other. We were told when to be where, to meet what ship or what plane, and then we would be two gals at a time, usually . . . in the warehouse jitter-bugging with the GIs. That was the main thing we did. Of course, they liked the coffee and doughnuts, but they liked the jitterbugging more.

The Red Cross captain in charge of Mathews's unit in France was named Elizabeth Richardson. She was from Wisconsin and had graduated from college in 1940 and worked in advertising at a department store in Milwaukee. In 1944, she joined the Red Cross and headed for England. Then she was sent to head up the unit in Le Havre, France. Richardson was everyone's favorite captain, Mathews said, "the one we really adored. . . . She was tall and not good looking, but such charm. When she would get dressed in the morning she would go to the mirror and she would say, 'Mirror, mirror, on the wall, who is the fairest of them all? Elizabeth Richardson.' That's the kind of gal she was." [33]

Captain Richardson's good cheer was on display in a letter she wrote her parents on August 9, 1944.

> This is our day off. I have never appreciated a whole empty day as much as I am right now. We have been working 12- and 14-hour days, and I almost weep when I hear the word doughnut. . . .
>
> All joking aside, we mix a mean doughnut, and the coffee is certainly better than the GI variety. Our Clubmobile is a converted Greenline bus, fixed up with a lounge, sink, doughnut machine, and serving facilities. Also a British driver and us.
>
> We start out about six in the morning, either make our doughnuts parked outside the local Red Cross Service Club or else we make them at camp with ten million GIs and an occasional colonel watching the operation. Then we turn on our recording machine and serve, all the time smiling like mad and dividing our time between doughnuts, the mess sergeant, the coffee, and a sea of faces.

In May 1945, Richardson, still in Le Havre, witnessed the end of the war in Europe. Within days, she wrote to her parents that as part of her work she was learning to enjoy flying as a passenger in the small planes like the Piper

Cub, in which she could see France from above. She told her parents that she had "taken to the air in a big way and, after flying, other means of transportation seem dull indeed. . . . The Piper Cub is to my liking, soaring low on the Seine, climbing over the nearly wooded hills and looking down on the toy villages and the scars of two wars." [34]

About two months later, on July 25, 1945, Richardson boarded a Piper Cub for an official visit to Red Cross headquarters in Paris. The plane encountered bad weather and crashed near Rouen. "She and the pilot were killed," said Mathews, "that was terrible. The loss of Elizabeth was dreadful. Of course, we lost plenty of pilot friends, but it wasn't like knowing them that well." [35] Elizabeth Richardson was one of the last women to die overseas during World War II.

Gysella Simon, a Red Cross club director in England and Europe, wrote to a friend back home about the changes she saw in herself in the time since she had joined the Red Cross. The letter, from Wales, is dated May 21, 1944, just a few weeks before D-Day, and seems to speak for most of the women who served overseas in World War II.

> At last, here in this forgotten place, I have found myself. For 5 months I have lived with men preparing for combat. I have eaten with them, laughed with them, cried with them, have shared their fears and anxieties, hardships, etc.—and wonder why I didn't get in this sort of work sooner. Of course, I have my moments too, but most of the time I feel I am doing a real worthwhile thing and it makes me glow with satisfaction. I should like to share this feeling with every American girl back home. [36]

NURSES

The Army Nurse Corps and Navy Nurse Corps were the oldest female branches of the military, having been formed in 1901 and 1908 respectively. Early military nurses were given limited military status. They had the responsibilities and obligations of military service, but were still civilians working under contract and had few benefits and no military ranking. [37] They were the first group of women officially recognized as a part of the military, even if they were not recognized as being *in* the military, only as civilians serving *with* it.

It was not until 1920 that Army nurses were given ranking relative to Army men. Navy nurses did not get relative ranking with men until 1942. And neither corps had any kind of equal pay policy until 1944.[38] The greatest reward nurses seemed to garner in the whole equation was praise. They were often lauded as "angels of mercy" for taking up such a self-sacrificing, nurturing job. Yet of all the American women in uniform, nurses had the least-sheltered experience of war. Often, it was instead the most brutal.

Nurses on the Home Front

A great number of nurses in the Army and Navy nurse corps never went overseas. Instead, more than half of the Army and most of the Navy nurses served in military hospitals in the U.S. The Navy nurses worked at forty hospitals and 176 dispensaries around the country. These domestic naval nurses cared for Navy, Coast Guard, and Marine personnel and their dependents.[39]

One of their responsibilities was to train the male medical corpsmen who would perform as assistants to nurses in the field and would tend to troops in areas where women were not allowed, such as aboard battleships. On the home front, Army and Navy nurses served at military hospitals around the country, often caring for men sent back from war who needed long-term or specialized treatment. As threats of nursing shortages occurred in both civilian and military hospitals through the war, Congress passed a bill to give free tuition to women who wanted to train to be nurses. Representative Frances Payne Bolton, a Democrat from Ohio, introduced the bill that established the Cadet Nurse Corps in June 1943. Posters sprang up around the country urging young women to take up nursing, with slogans like "Save His Life . . . And Find Your Own. Be a Nurse."

Female high school graduates between the ages of seventeen and thirty-five were eligible for the Cadet Nurse Corps. Due to the lower age minimum than that of the other military nursing corps, the cadet corps attracted many younger women. Cadet nurses were given free tuition to nursing school. Their living costs were covered and they received a stipend of $15 a month. When they graduated, cadet nurses were obligated to serve in a military or civilian hospital until the end of the war. More than 124,000 nurses were trained through the program, which was run by the Public Health Service and continued until 1948.[40]

Doris Wofford Armenaki joined the Cadet Nurse Corps in 1943 and did her training in Georgia. After graduation, she was sent to work, from January to June 1945, at Kennedy General Hospital, a military hospital in Memphis, Tennessee. Although she never served overseas, she was not spared the dark face of war.

> We had very few private rooms. They were large, open wards, with fourteen to as many as thirty something on a ward. . . . We were caring for amputees. Some head wounds. . . . The amputees could really get to you. We just had so many of them, and they segregated them. They had all right-arm amputees on one ward, left-arm amputees, right-leg, both legs.
> . . . The hardest time was when we had to unload convoys. . . . They would fly planeloads of patients back from Europe. . . . Seeing them come off the plane in the middle of the night, very malnourished, in pretty bad shape. . . . when we started getting the guys from the Pacific, I think that bothered me a great deal because they not only were malnourished, they had malaria, they had what they called "jungle rot." Their feet were constantly wet over there, and their feet, the skin on their feet was sometimes gone completely. That was pretty tough.
>   Got a lot of prisoners from Europe. We got one group of prisoners from Dachau. And one of the prisoners . . . when they freed the prison, they took his picture and it was on the front of *Life* magazine. So it was a big to-do. I never took care of him, never nursed him, but we all knew who he was, and followed his career then, as a patient. I think he was there about two years. He had no injury, but he was a skeleton.

For Armenaki, a particularly affecting group of patients at Kennedy Hospital was some of the nurses who had been held in Japanese prisoner of war camps for more than three years in the Philippines. Not only did she consider them colleagues, but their plight had been well publicized throughout the war, and their rescue by American soldiers in 1945 was big news.

> We got the nurses that were freed in the Philippines . . . twenty-five of them. I was in the detail that helped unload them. I never really took care of the women after they were there as patients. Saw them later in the officers' club as they began to improve. Their problem was just pure malnourishment. . . . They were in prison right after

Bataan and Corregidor. They were there a long time. . . . Some of them were able to be mobile, but I think the release of knowing they were free, a lot of them just sort of collapsed physically.

. . . We had a cadet nurse. She had graduated from high school, gone to nursing school, and was at Memphis. She had a sister in that convoy that was freed that [she] had not heard from all those years. Her sister had no idea that her younger sister had done all this, and they met at Kennedy for the first time in five years.[41]

Pearl Harbor Nurses

Within minutes of the first bombs dropping on Sunday morning December 7, 1941, all twenty-nine nurses stationed in the Navy hospital at Pearl Harbor reported for duty. The mangled men arrived at a receiving station set up in the old nurses' quarters, which were empty because they were about to be torn down to make way for a pier. On that day, the vacant building served as an emergency center. Early casualties were unloaded from ambulances, trucks, carts, limousines, anything on wheels. The broken soldiers were laid on mattresses lined up in rows on the floor. Page Cooper, in her 1946 book, *Navy Nurse*, described the scene.

> Most of them were from the ships in the harbor; boys with flesh torn by gunshot wounds, arms and legs blown off by bomb fragments, and above all, bodies covered with burns foul with thick black oil. . . .
> A group of doctors and nurses gave them morphine to ease the pain and quiet their nerves. . . . One nurse replenished the solution of morphine . . . another took care of the tray of hypodermic needles kept sterile in alcohol. Others gave first aid and tagged the patients. . . . All morning the work went on. Occasionally a nurse rested her tired back by stretching and looking out at the ships blazing in the harbor, took a deep breath to clear away the stench of charred flesh, then returned to the job.
> . . . To these doctors and nurses straining to keep up with the flood of injured men, time ceased to exist. . . . Nurses at the receiving station kept on without relief. In the ward the work went at the same relentless pace, and in the operating room the anesthetist and the nurse who was supervisor of dressings tried to keep pace with four teams that worked at the same time in four relays, a system they were to maintain for three days and three nights. No one went to bed that night. Fortunately the supplies did not give out.
> . . . In the restroom a dozen mattresses had been laid on the floor,

and on these the nurses snatched a two-hour rest period in their uniforms, but it was impossible to sleep with machine guns popping outside somewhere in the dark. . . . The scores of deaths added to a rough total which showed that the Navy had lost more men in three hours than during the whole of the first World War.[42]

Two thousand four hundred and three Americans died in the attack on Pearl Harbor. The 1,178 wounded were treated in Army, Navy, and civilian hospitals all over the island.[43] There were 119 military nurses serving in those military hospitals in December 1941. At the Hickham Field air base hospital, Army nurse Sara Entrikin had gotten a firsthand look at the Japanese bombers.

> Hearing the explosions I ran outside and saw the red sun on a plane that was coming in so close that I could see the faces of the pilots. One of them looked at us and smiled. I rushed to the hospital. Casualties were coming in fast and furious because the barracks were right along the runway and that's where the bombs hit first. Our hospital was close to the runway also, and we had a lot of noise and smoke from shells. . . . There were only seven of us nurses, and we couldn't possibly begin to take care of all the wounded and dying men. . . .
>   Not too far from the hospital there was an American flag flying, and after the Japs dropped their bombs, one plane came back and circled, shooting until the flag was torn to shreds. That night we put up black window covers; we were told that if captured, to only give our name, rank and serial number.[44]

At the beginning of World War II there were only a few thousand military nurses. But within six months of the attack on Pearl Harbor, almost 10,000 nurses joined the Army Nurse Corps alone. By the end of the war, 59,000 nurses had served in the Army Nurse Corps, and 11,000 nurses had served in the Navy Nurse Corps. Among the Army Nurse Corps members, more than 30,000 women went overseas. Only 1,200 of the 14,178 nurses in the Navy Nurse Corps went overseas. Originally, the Red Cross oversaw the recruiting of military nurses, but the government took over recruiting as the war progressed. When planning for D-Day went forward in 1944, the high number of anticipated casualties prompted the War Department to try increasing the number of nurses serving in the military. Even with the Cadet Nurse Corps, finding more women to serve was a challenge, and as the war went on, nurse shortages were projected to continue. In his January 1945 State of the Union address, President Roosevelt proposed that nurses be drafted. And it did not take Congress long to draw up a bill, which passed the House and was only one vote shy of approval in the Senate when Germany surrendered in May 1945. By then, the additional 10,000 nurses needed had already enrolled in the military.[45]

Prisoners of War

On December 8, the day after Pearl Harbor was attacked, U.S. military bases on Guam, Wake Island, and Midway were also attacked. Five Navy nurses on Guam were taken prisoner by the Japanese. Also on December 8, U.S. bases in the Philippines were attacked and casualties overwhelmed the hospitals. Of the one hundred or so Army nurses in the Philippines at the time, most were stationed at two hospitals in the Manila area. The bombings were to the north, close to another U.S. military hospital. By the end of December 1941, all the nurses stationed outside Manila had been evacuated to the city except two Army nurses far to the north. Japanese soldiers landed on the mainland and were moving south. Along the way, the two Army nurses were taken prisoner. General Douglas MacArthur, commander of the U.S. Army in the Far East, ordered all nurses to move across Manila Bay to the Bataan Peninsula, or onto an island to the south of the Bataan Peninsula called Corregidor. They were to set up hospitals there to cope with the casualties from heavy fighting. The Allies hoped to hold Bataan and Corregidor until supplies and reinforcements could arrive from the United States. Eleven Navy nurses stayed behind in Manila. On January 2, 1942, the Japanese entered Manila and took those Navy nurses prisoner.

First Lieutenant Dorothea Daley Engel was one of the Army nurses sent from Manila, just before it was invaded, to work in the jungles of Bataan. She remembered what she encountered landing there in late December 1941 in an article she wrote for *The American Magazine* in October 1942.

> Bataan! It meant very little to me then. Little did I dream that I would soon be trying to care for patients on beds set in the middle of a sandy river bed, that snakes would hang down from the bamboo and mango trees which sheltered us from Japanese bombing, that monkeys would chatter through the trees and try to steal what little food

we had, that we would bathe in a creek. That we would always be hungry, always frightened. That we would grab shovels and help dig fox holes so we would have some shelter to crawl into when the dive bombers came. That we would all suffer from malaria and dysentery and diarrhea. It was a good thing for all of us that we had no idea what we were getting into.

. . . From the moment of the first bombing I lost my appetite. At Bataan I lost 30 pounds. . . . We nurses did try to make ourselves as presentable as possible. We had been able to bring along some rouge, powder, lipstick, and our toothbrushes. . . . We all kept clean and neat, and the men whom we cared for used to tell us we were the most beautiful things in the world![46]

After months of bombings and casualties, and running low on supplies, on April 9, 1942, all seventy-two Army nurses, one Navy nurse, twenty-six Filipino nurses, and a few other civilian women had evacuated Bataan for Corregidor to the south. Bataan was surrendered to the Japanese at 6:00 A.M. that day. By 1:00 P.M. all American and Filipino women had arrived safely in Corregidor. They continued their work in the Malinta Tunnel Hospital. Some of the nurses, including Dorothea Daley Engel, were evacuated to Australia. But when America surrendered Corregidor to the Japanese on May 6, 1942, the fifty-four remaining Army nurses were taken prisoner along with the rest of the American forces still on the island. In all, seventy-seven Army and Navy nurses were held as prisoners of war in the Philippines from 1942 through February 1945, when Allied forces began to retake the Philippines and freed them.[47]

The 1943 film *So Proudly We Hail!* dramatized the nurses' plight on Bataan and Corregidor. It told the story of a few who got away just in time, as Dorothea Daley Engel had done. The movie, starring Claudette Colbert, Paulette Goddard, and Veronica Lake as nurses, celebrated all the women who served in the Philippines. The movie received four Academy Award nominations, including the best supporting actress nomination for Paulette Goddard. When the movie was released, though, the real-life nurses left behind were still prisoners of war.

Among them was Madeline Ullom, an Army nurse who had been stationed at Sternberg Hospital in Manila before being evacuated to Corregidor and then becoming a prisoner in May 1942. In July, the nurses were taken back to Manila and sent to a prison camp at University of Santo Tomás. Ullom said in the first year of captivity there were classes offered by other internees from all over the world. But as time wore on, conditions worsened.

> Our rations were cut back whenever the U.S. took over another island. We had to bow to the Japanese every time we passed one of them. We had classes on how to bow, and it had to be done correctly, or it would have to be done a second time. . . . We received mail three or four times during those years. . . . We were only allowed to send letters twice, and didn't know if they were actually sent.
> . . . Many people were dying of malnutrition and starvation. I remember one twenty-four hour period when we had seven deaths. A civilian doctor was head of the camp medical department, and he wrote on death certificates, "Cause of death: Starvation." The Japanese tried to get him to change it, and he wouldn't, so they put him in the camp jail until we were released. Dead bodies piled up for days, and footlong rats ate their toes off. The cemetery in camp grew bigger and bigger. Food was so scarce, the last ration we received in the camp was two bags of moldy rice for over four thousand people.[48]

In February 1945, after the weak, emaciated internees had spent three years in captivity, the Americans finally rescued them. Navy nurse Mary Harrington Nelson had been imprisoned in Los Baños, in the countryside outside Manila.

> In early 1945 we heard rumors that the Americans were coming. . . . The day we were rescued (February 23, 1945), there was a heavy rumbling before daylight. You could feel it and hear it. We got up and dressed as usual. . . . Once we looked out from the balcony, we saw a parachute coming out of a plane that was flying just a little distance from the camp. . . . Soon we could hear paratroopers coming up the road. Tanks were breaking the bamboo wall that surrounded the area. . . . There was a lot of shooting for a while. . . . Those GIs looked so big and nice and healthy when they came out of those tanks. One old lady went over and hugged and kissed every one she could get her hands on.[49]

Navy nurse Margaret Nash was very ill when the rescuers finally came. But she had no idea until later how close she and the other prisoners had come to death, when the Japanese captors had realized the prisoners were about to be freed. "After we were rescued," she said, "we found out that the Japanese had planned to execute everyone in our camp the morning we were rescued."

The nurses were transported to American military bases on other Pacific islands before arriving in America. Many had serious diseases, but all had survived the camps. Nash said during her captivity she had suffered jungle rot, typhoid, the plague, and beriberi, a disease caused by malnutrition. After arriving on the mainland from Honolulu she had her first checkup in America, during which she was diagnosed with health problems from her Philippines captivity that would continue to affect her throughout her life.

> When we flew into San Francisco, there were ceremonies for us with all the food in the world, but we couldn't eat it. Everything I ate, I would throw up. We were given physical examinations, and I had it all. I was still swollen from beriberi, and they discovered I had tuberculosis.[50]

The Pacific and China-Burma-India Theaters of War

In part because of the crises in Bataan and Corregidor, through the first half of the war most nurses in the Pacific were kept farther back from the front lines than were nurses in Europe and the Mediterranean. They were fenced in and guarded in the same way the WACs in the Pacific had been. In the latter part of the war as Allied troops began to take more Pacific islands, nurses in the region followed close behind. When the Allies took the Marianas Islands in June 1944, nurses came in right away. By February 1945, nurses in newly established Marianas Islands hospitals in Guam, Saipan, and Tinian began receiving wounded and dying soldiers from the battle of Iwo Jima. More than 18,000 wounded arrived in a single month. Okinawa was next. The heavily disputed island, which marked one of the Allies' last steps toward the mainland of Japan, saw heavy fighting. In a three-month period from June to April 1945 more than 50,000 troops were wounded and 15,000 died. Most of those casualties were evacuated to the Marianas, where nurses worked twelve-hour days, seven days a week. When the Okinawa battle was coming to an end, a general hospital was established on Iwo Jima.

The first stop for wounded men from the front line was either the mobile field hospitals or the evacuation hospitals. Field hospitals were usually set up in tents, and moved with the combat troops as they advanced or retreated.

Doctors and nurses performed triage at the receiving tent of field hospitals. Those who needed immediate care were sent directly into surgery. The patients who were strong enough were moved on to evacuation hospitals, a little farther from the front. Those who needed immediate care but were too weak for surgery and not strong enough to travel from the field hospitals were sent to what was called the shock ward. A field hospital could perform up to eighty operations a day and those operations had an 85 percent survival rate.

Evacuation hospitals were usually set up a few miles from the front once the troops had cleared an area. They were somewhat more permanent than field hospitals but still transitory, depending on need.[51]

It was after the Allies invaded the Philippines, in October 1944, that Army nurses in the Pacific began caring for patients nearer to the front lines again. Between January and February 1945 more than 19,000 patients were admitted to hospitals on Leyte Island in the Philippines.

Station hospitals were next in the line of evacuation, after field and evacuation hospitals. Station hospitals were usually in semipermanent locations with running water and electricity. Often, at the start of a new offensive in Europe or the Mediterranean, nurses were sent ahead to nearby areas to set up station hospitals in abandoned buildings or schools or even bombed-out, abandoned hospitals. Station hospitals received incoming casualties needing surgery and specialized treatment. The general hospitals were the last stop in the line of evacuation. They received the soldiers who needed more detailed or specialized care. They also treated servicemen and women who had non-battle-related needs, including those suffering from contagious diseases, and insect-borne diseases such as malaria.

To get the wounded troops from battle to medical care, Army nurses served on hospital trains, and Navy nurses served on hospital ships with comforting names like *Benevolence, Tranquility, Solace, Relief,* and *Rescue.*[52] Hospital ships were clearly marked. An international agreement had established that medical ships were immune from enemy attack because they were not allowed to carry cargo, only wounded patients. Still, some hospital ships were bombed or torpedoed with nurses on board. On April 28, 1945, a Japanese suicide plane bombed the hospital ship USS *Comfort* off Leyte Island. Six nurses were killed in that attack, along with medical personnel and patients.

World War II was the first war in which airplanes were used to evacuate the wounded. The planes used for transporting wounded soldiers also carried cargo, and so could not display hospital markings. Therefore they were vulnerable to enemy fire. Both Navy and Army nurses served on air evacuation planes, which usually had one nurse and one medical corpsman for up to twenty-five patients. Nurses on these planes were usually former airline hostesses, since early airline stewardesses were all registered nurses. These flight nurses took on the greatest risks of any nurses assigned to transport wounded soldiers.

Navy flight nurses arrived at Iwo Jima on March 6, 1945, in the midst of combat there. They helped load wounded men onto planes and evacuated them while coming under mortar attack. Then they went on to Okinawa. Between the two places, Navy flight nurses saved thousands of lives by their swift treatment.[53] The success rate among the 500 Army and Navy nurses who worked in the thirty-one air transport squadrons worldwide was impressive. Of the 1,176,000 patients evacuated by air to a medical facility during the war, only forty-six died en route.[54]

Far higher than the number of battle casualties in the Pacific war and the war in the China-Burma-India theater were the number of people admitted to hospitals with diseases such as malaria, dengue fever, and typhus. In the Pacific, it was once calculated that one casualty from battle was admitted to a hospital for every five patients admitted with diseases. In the China-Burma-India theater that rate was one battle casualty for every 120 admitted for disease.[55]

LaVonne Telshaw Camp was an Army nurse in the China-Burma-India theater. Her memoir, *Lingering Fever,* described a day when she heard that one of her fellow nurses named Ingrid had come down with what appeared to be typhus.

> It was alarming to hear that one of our own had fallen to this most feared malady of the jungle. We had all had bouts of dysentery, a few women had malaria, and I know of one nurse who had been discharged with active tuberculosis, but among the nurses who now staffed the hospital, no one had contracted anything as life-threatening as typhus.
>
> Ingrid was loved by all of us. . . . She was Scandinavian, platinum blonde with skin so white that you could see the tiny blue veins at her temples. Atabrine had turned her skin such a bright yellow that her hair looked more gray than blonde. Ingrid was really dedicated to the profession. . . . We used to refer to her as Florence Nightingale.

There was a possibility that Ingrid did not have typhus. The official diagnosis had been FUO (fever of undetermined origin), a diagnosis used when doctors were not yet sure what the trouble was. If a patient had symptoms such as chills, high temperature, severe headaches, muscle and joint pain, vomiting, and sometimes delirium, Camp said, "we had to put some name on his misery, and FUO was as good as anything, until the laboratory could identify the organism responsible for his illness." Ingrid was transported to another hospital and then flown back to the U.S.[56]

Camp also faced another frightening danger while overseas that sometimes plagued troops in the jungles. She was asleep in her bed one night after a long, hard day of work. She shared the *basha*, or hut, with another nurse named Mitzi. Camp woke up suddenly because she felt "something with warm breath" pushing at the mosquito netting that surrounded her bed.

> The deep, low, throaty rumble of an animal was coming from the same place as the breath, coming directly into my face. I smelled the wildness, the unfamiliar odor of an animal's mouth. . . . He continued to push the netting all up and down my body, as though smelling. I lay paralyzed with fear, for I quickly decided the beast was a tiger. I remembered the stories that were told of men working on the Ledo Road being attacked by tigers, viciously mauled, then brought to the hospital. . . . I thought my heart would rupture my chest with its violent pounding. . . . I wanted to call out to Mitzi on the other side of the bamboo partition, but my mouth was bone dry, and the terror in my heart had turned my tongue to concrete. I feared that any sound, any movement, would precipitate an attack. I knew that I was going to die; there was no escape from this beast who was so close that I could feel his fur. . . . I visualized this beast sinking his long, sharp teeth into me, pulling me off the cot and into the jungle. My parents would be horrified to learn that I'd been eaten by a tiger. Maybe no one would ever know what happened.

Camp stayed still for hours as the creature prowled the small area around her cot and then perched on the shelf where her clothing was stored. She felt she was his prisoner. As the light of the morning came she saw it was not a tiger but a smaller, jet black beast with "wide set narrowed yellow eyes."

Then, "as the morning light increased, he jumped silently from his perch and walked out between the two limp curtains that we called a door. I started to cry." The guard who patrolled the area did not believe Camp at first. But later the animal prints coming out of her hut were identified as those of a black leopard, and the nurse's basha was then equipped with a door which could be shut at night.[57]

Nurses in North Africa and Europe

Army nurse Lieutenant Ruth Haskell was among the first women to come ashore just hours after the first Allied troops invaded North Africa on November 8, 1942. Within a few more hours she was at a makeshift hospital, inside an abandoned home, tending to the many casualties, and all the while dodging sniper fire. When she entered the first, blacked-out room with all the wounded men on litters—or stretchers—she was struck right away by the smells.

> The unmistakable odor of filth and dirt, mixed with the odor of old blood and stale ether. There was a suppressed groan here and another there. . . . One of the boys flashed on his light, and I shall never forget the sight that spread out before my eyes in that room. Rows upon rows of American boys lay on litters all over the floor. Just barely enough room to step over them to get around. There were pools of blood beside some of them, where dressings had not been changed since the first shock dressing was applied in the field. I don't know how the other girls felt, but I experienced at once a violent anger—bitter, surging anger—against a people that, out of greed and power and lust, would cause such things to happen to young manhood. . . .
>
>   . . . We climbed the moldy stairs to the second floor. It was very cold up there, as most of the windows had been blown out, and unlike the first floor all the openings were not covered with blankets. Rats were nosing about at will, but we hardly noticed them.

A soldier then looked up at Haskell and asked for water. Even though the quart of water in her canteen was meant to last her for a long time, she could not refuse the wounded man at her feet. After he drank a bit with her help, he collapsed back onto the floor. There were a few moments of silence, when suddenly he said: " 'My God! A woman, an American woman! Where in heaven's name did you come from?' He was almost sobbing as he finished."

When she flashed her light down to see him more clearly she realized he was a boy of about twenty. She saw "his face contorted with pain, his lips bleeding where he had bitten them to keep from crying out, but his eyes bright and unafraid. He had a bullet wound, grazing his groin—a horrible thing to look at." She saw that his dressings had not been touched since they were applied in the field hours before. "There were bits of dirt, shreds from his trousers, all buried deep into the tissue of the soft part of his groin. It had evidently bled quite a lot at the time, and great clots of blood oozed out from around the dressing." She kept going down the rows of men singling out the men who were the most seriously wounded and getting them treatment. Then she ran into another nurse. "Kelly, a girl in her middle thirties from Wilmington, Delaware, was saying, 'I have worked in the accident room of a city hospital, and I've never seen anything to compare to the horrors I've seen in the last twenty minutes.' "[58]

Nurses also waded ashore with, or just behind, Allied soldiers when they moved from North Africa into Sicily in July 1943, and onto the Italian mainland and up the west coast of Italy to Anzio in January 1944. In February and March of 1944, six nurses were killed in three separate enemy attacks at Anzio. Despite the danger of the brutal Italian battles, the nurses were kept with the forces because they were needed so badly. In the six months from January to June of 1944, field and evacuation hospitals at Anzio admitted more than 25,000 wounded in battle, 4,200 injured accidentally, and 18,000 patients with diseases.[59]

In May 1944, the surgeon general, Norman T. Kirk, wrote an article for *The American Magazine* titled "Girls in the Foxholes," about nurses who worked near the front.

> This is the first war in which it has been necessary to take our army nurses, in Evacuation Hospital Units, to within 3 to 6 miles of the front. On occasion the nurses have been caught in the actual fighting, where, under shelling and bombing, they have conducted themselves as coolly as the most hardened veterans. . . . It has been necessary to take women so far forward, even to land them on contested beachheads, because of the swiftness with which the front advances in mechanized warfare.

Kirk went on to tell how wounded men reacted to the nurses working in the field and evacuation hospitals.

> It is here, too, for the first time since they entered battle, that they see army nurses—and I consider the deep glow of pleasure, the sense of

security and the feeling of home that comes with the sight of these American women more important to recovery than any psychological factor in the course of their treatment.

It is not only blood plasma, the morphine . . . and the miraculous sulfa drugs that are responsible for saving 97 percent of our wounded—twice more than in the last World War—it is also the tender and sympathetic and indefatigable attention given these wounded men by the women at the front.[60]

As they had done in North Africa and Italy, nurses followed invading soldiers into Normandy, just four days after D-Day. Captain Jean Truckey of the 67th Evacuation Hospital was near the front lines in France when she wrote to her sister back home in Detroit on June 18, 1944, about the aftermath of D-Day.

We were lucky to reach here safe and sound—dirty and tired. We've been working with another evacuation unit but move out in the morning, farther up, to set up our own hospital and be ready for patients by noon.

. . . The artillery fire is getting louder with night coming. At 11 p.m., the Jerry bombers come over and then the fun starts. I never could imagine such noise in my life. Like the Fourth of July multiplied a million times. The ground trembles.

. . . As for our soldier boys—words fail me. None of you back home could ever understand. . . . These boys never complain. They are quiet and patient. I was by one as he died this afternoon—just after an operation. His trachea had been completely severed. No need to go into details, for you just can't grasp it. At least we are happy to be doing all in our power to help. There are eight brain operations scheduled for this evening so I'm going to call it quits.

On June 20, 1944, Truckey wrote again about witnessing the effects of war.

Yesterday was an eye-opener. Drove right through places where the battles had raged a couple of days previously. Here are a few hasty impressions, gleaned in transit. . . . Villages completely destroyed. Newly-made graves. German and American helmets and equipment strewn everywhere. Colored parachutes dangling from trees. Gliders smashed to kindling wood. . . . Dead cattle and horses. . . . Overturned tanks and trucks. Tired, dirty, unshaven soldiers whose faces broke into smiles at the sight of American nurses.

And on June 26, Truckey wrote her sister:

> The other night during a huge influx of soldiers . . . I went to as many cots as I could to remove the men's big, heavy, dirty shoes. It sounds so trivial, but many had not had their shoes off in 18 days and they were so grateful just to wiggle their toes.
> . . . My nurses are wonderful girls. We work from 16 to 18 hours a day. . . . One young boy told me the other night I was the first one to tuck him in since he left the States. Just like little boys. My first thought when one has passed away is his folks back home. We surely do all we can for them.[61]

As the Allied forces pushed into Germany in 1945, nurses followed. One of the Army nurses, Lieutenant Mary H. Smith, cared for German POWs and began to witness the horrors of the Nazi regime. She wrote to her mother in New Hampshire from Germany in March 1945.

> I thought we followed the front fast in France but this takes the cake. At least the war should end shortly after we finally get across the Rhine. . . . We continued to work on the Germans for two days and what a dirty mess. Their dressings were three or four days old and gas gangrene had started in the wounds. Their bodies were covered with lice, hadn't been bathed for years by the odor, and several of them who had lost hands, etc., feel it was all right as it was for Hitler. They told us the American soldier does not feel for his country as do the Germans. . . .
> We are living for a day or two in a concentration camp where the Germans kept their forced labor, Russian, Polish, French, Belgian, and Dutch men and women. The stone, windowless barracks are filthy and bugs of all sizes and descriptions are crawling around the long rooms. Double wooden bunks with straw mattresses and small closets are the only furnishings with a very small stove at one end for heat. Some of the laborers have been in camps from two to five years, marching for an hour and a half to work, digging ditches, fox-holes, etc., for eight hours, then marching home to be shut in the barracks until the next day, always guarded by soldiers. Their food was rotten pea soup, a piece of bread, and a little sausage. No pay nor

clothing. And they never knew any war news. At present there are ten babies that have been fed on sugar and water. A six-months'-old child is about the size of a two-weeks'-old baby.[62]

Some nurses went into the concentration camps where Jews, Gypsies, homosexuals, and others had been imprisoned and killed in gas chambers. Army nurse Esther Edwards remembered her time at Dachau concentration camp outside Munich, just after Germany surrendered.

> We saw the horrible barracks and the crematorium, where there was a room filled almost to the ceiling with bodies, waiting to be burned. Bodies were everywhere, hundreds of them. It was unbelievable.
>
> There were some freed prisoners still there, waiting to be processed and hundreds were dying every day from starvation, cholera, and typhus. . . . Three American hospital units were there trying to bring order. . . . We lived in rooms in barracks where the prison guards had lived, and were quite comfortable. The whole camp was extremely depressing. We were there a month.
>
> Most of the patients had been prisoners in the camp and were not able to move, and many had no place to go. . . . Mostly German and Polish, the patients were difficult to communicate with. They hid what they could not eat for fear they would get no more. They were just skin over bones.[63]

Lieutenant Frances Y. Slanger was an Army nurse serving in the ETO (European Theatre of Operations) in Belgium. She wrote this letter to the military newspaper *Stars and Stripes* at 2:00 A.M., from "Somewhere in Belgium," on October 20, 1944:

> It is 0200, and I have been lying awake for one hour, listening to the steady, even breathing of the other three nurses in the tent. . . .
>
> I am writing this by flashlight. . . . The GIs say we rough it. We in our little tent can't see it. True, we are set up in tents, sleep on cots and are subject to the temperament of the weather. We wade ankle deep in mud. You have to lie in it. We are restricted to our immediate area, a cow pasture or a hayfield, but then, who is not restricted? We have a stove and coal. We even have a laundry line in the tent. . . . What with the wind howling, the tent waving precariously, the rain beating down, the guns firing, and me with a flashlight, writing. It all adds up to a feeling of unrealness.

Sure, we rough it, but in comparison to the way you men are taking it, we can't complain. . . . you, the men behind the guns, the men driving our tanks, flying our planes, sailing our ships, building bridges and to the men who pave the way and to the men who are left behind—it is to you we doff our helmets. . . . After taking care of some of your buddies, comforting them when they are brought in bloody, dirty with the earth, mud and grime, and most of them so tired. Somebody's brothers, somebody's fathers, and somebody's sons, seeing them gradually brought back to life, to consciousness and to see their lips separate into a grin when they first welcome you. Usually they kid, hurt as they are. It doesn't amaze us to hear one of them say, "how 'ya babe," or "holy mackerel, an American woman," or more indiscreetly, "how about a kiss?"

. . . We have learned a great deal about our American soldier, and the stuff he is made of. . . . The patience and determination they show, the courage and fortitude they have is sometimes awesome to behold. It is we who are proud to be here. Rough it? No, it is a privilege to be able to receive you, and a great distinction to see you open your eyes and with that swell American grin, say "Hi 'ya babe." [64]

Just one day after writing and sending that letter Lieutenant Slanger was killed by German shell fire on October 21, 1944. She was one of sixteen nurses killed overseas during World War II as a result of enemy attacks. Hundreds of soldiers replied to Slanger's letter in the *Stars and Stripes* newspaper. One soldier pointed out, in what remains a poignant eulogy to her spirit, that nurses volunteered, while enlisted men were drafted. His reply to Slanger might also stand as a tribute to every woman who volunteered in World War II, in both military and civilian service.

To all Army nurses overseas: We men were not given the choice of working in the battlefield or the home front. We cannot take any credit for being here. We are here because we have to be. You are here because you felt you were needed. So, when an injured man opens his eyes to see one of you . . . concerned with his welfare, he can't but be overcome by the very thought that you are doing it because you want to . . . you endure whatever hardships you must to be where you can do us the most good. [65]

CHAPTER SEVEN

Jane Crow

AFRICAN-AMERICAN WOMEN

I have read much about the tasks and duties of mothers in wartime.
Mine is a big job—much bigger than that of some mothers, for I am
a Negro mother; and first, in order to keep that pride and love of his
country alive in the heart of my little boy, I've got to fight against the
resentment and discouragement that wells up sometimes in my own
heart.

LETTER TO THE EDITOR ENTITLED
"A Mother's Faith," from a woman identified as "Georgia,"
Redbook magazine, 1943[1]

National Archives

I N LATE SUMMER OF 1943, twenty-two white women walked off their jobs at a Western Electric plant in Baltimore after one black woman was transferred into their formerly all-white department. The white women vowed they would not return to work until the company provided separate bathroom facilities for black and white workers, as it once had done. The white women said they did not want to use the same toilets as black women because it would subject them to a high risk of catching venereal disease, since black women were so unclean. The company, citing new laws requiring integrated bathroom facilities, said it could not go back to the segregated toilets.

The women returned to work but, along with white male leaders of their independent labor union, circulated petitions through the plant gathering enough votes to call for a strike, even though some black workers were dues-paying union members. The independent union had been formed to keep out national unions, which had somewhat more progressive policies on race. Desegregated bathrooms were the flashpoint around which white union leaders were able to whip up white workers' deeper resentments of the increasing number and mobility of black workers, both male and female, during the war years. Before the war, only 2 percent of the workers at Western Electric's Baltimore plant were black. By 1943, 29 percent were black.

The federal War Labor Board held hearings in November 1943 and ruled in favor of keeping the company's bathrooms integrated. But on December 13, 1943, about 70 percent of the company's workers went out on strike over the women's toilet issue. That percentage just about corresponded with the percentage of white male and female workers at the plant. And most all of the company's black workers crossed the picket lines. Within a week, the situation was considered serious enough that President Roosevelt ordered the Army to take over the plant, which produced communications cables essential to the war effort.

Even though the Army was stretched to its limits fighting a war abroad, troops manned the Baltimore plant for three months. Sharing restrooms with black women was one wartime sacrifice the white women at that plant were not willing to make. And their white male cohorts did not want them to have to suffer such an indignity either. Unable to force the steadfast white workers back to their jobs in a plant with integrated bathrooms, the Army turned the plant over to company control again in March of 1944. The company gave in as well, fearing a race riot like the one in Detroit the summer before, in which gangs of white people had invaded a black neighborhood and attacked residents, leaving twenty-five black people and nine white people dead. So in the Baltimore plant, Western Electric set up segregated bathroom facilities once again and instituted stricter seniority policies to limit promotions of the newer black workers.[2]

Also on a Saturday afternoon in March of 1944, a group of mostly female students from Howard University in Washington, D.C., started trickling in to a popular cafeteria on Pennsylvania Avenue, a few blocks from the White House. In groups of two and three they took trays and waited in line to be served. The white employees behind the counter refused to give any food to these students from one of America's most elite black universities, even though a few of them were members of the military. The cafeteria, Thompson's, was part of a national chain, and like all the other restaurants in the area had always been for whites only. Unfazed, the determined students proceeded to tables in the dining area with empty trays, sat down together, and began calmly reading textbooks, poetry, and newspapers. When the management asked them to leave, they politely made it known that were staying—quietly, peacefully—until they were served. Soon there were more than fifty black students there. And outside on the sidewalk an orderly picket line of a few more students formed, carrying placards that read, "We Die Together. Why Can't We Eat Together?" and "Are You for Hitler's Way (Race Supremacy) or the American Way (Equality)? Make Up Your Mind!"

A crowd gathered. A woman spat at the businesslike protesters. Some soldiers jeered. Some WACs and WAVES cheered. By dinnertime, only about half the regular number of customers came in to eat at the restaurant. Finally, the perplexed management called their main office in Chicago asking what to do. The word came down: serve the black students. A few waitresses balked. So the restaurant manager and the chain's district supervisor stepped in and brought food to the students.

Pauli Murray, one of the three female leaders of the protest and a law student at Howard, later wrote that she and other law students had scrupulously studied Washington's laws of disorderly conduct and picketing before the protest. The students had also pored over and practiced the nonviolent tenets of Indian leader Mahatma Gandhi. Each student had signed a pledge not to fight back against any taunts or threats. Murray wrote in November 1944, "Howard may be proud of those students who have led the way toward a new, and perhaps successful technique to achieve first class citizenship in one area of life in these United States."

It was a new technique. But it would be another decade or two before the same kinds of tactics would be used widely to combat racial segregation in America, especially as codified in the Jim Crow segregation laws that had sprung up after the Civil War and created a caste system in America based on race. Jim Crow was a famous minstrel show character who embodied long-held stereotypes about black people's inferiority. In 1954, the Supreme Court declared school segregation, the idea of separate but equal schools for blacks and whites, unconstitutional in its *Brown v. Board of Education* decision (partly influenced by a brief written by lawyer Pauli Murray). The 1944 Howard demonstration was also eleven years before Rosa Parks peacefully refused to give up her seat in the whites-only front section of a Montgomery, Alabama, public bus in 1955. Her arrest is considered the beginning of the civil rights movement led by Martin Luther King, Jr., whose guiding principle was based on Gandhi's idea of nonviolent resistance. And the Howard protest was sixteen years before students at a black university in Greensboro, North Carolina, started sit-ins at lunch counters that would not serve them in 1960, sparking a decade of such challenges to racial segregation in public gathering places all over the South.

Throughout her time at Howard, Pauli Murray had kept up a lively friendship with Eleanor Roosevelt that continued for the rest of Mrs. Roosevelt's life. It started when Murray began writing letters to the first lady and eventually began to have tea with her at the White House. Murray went on to influence, and push, and sometimes even anger the Roosevelts on issues of race. In 1940, when Murray was arrested and thrown in jail for refusing to give up her seat on a segregated Greyhound bus in Petersburg, Virginia, Mrs. Roosevelt intervened for Murray by contacting the governor of Virginia. And in 1944, when Murray graduated cum laude from Howard, one of the largest bouquets in the auditorium was from Eleanor Roosevelt for Pauli Murray. Also in 1944, Murray went on to apply to Harvard Law School, but was refused not because of her race, but because Harvard did not admit women.

Almost twenty years later, in 1963, she became the first black woman to receive a Ph.D. in law from Yale University. She went on to become one of the founders of the National Organization for Women.

While America was fighting against Fascism and Nazism abroad during World War II, it was still engaged in its own antidemocratic policies and practices regarding race at home. Black men had questioned whether they could fight, and perhaps die, for a military that practiced racial segregation throughout its ranks. In such stirrings of black people against America's internal hypocrisy and injustice during World War II can be seen the seeds of the massive upheavals in the civil rights movement of the 1950s and 1960s. Those seeds were often planted by women. Black women, perhaps more than any other group, saw and felt American hypocrisy most distinctly, since they often found themselves at the bottom of the social and political barrel, dealing with both racism and gender discrimination. Pauli Murray once described that double bind as "Jane Crow."[3]

BLACK WOMEN WAR WORKERS

In January 1941, A. Philip Randolph, president of the Brotherhood of Sleeping Car Porters, the only large labor union for black workers in the country, called for a march on Washington, D.C., to protest job discrimination against black people in America. Along with Walter White, head of the National Association for the Advancement of Colored People, Randolph planned to rally 50,000 black people to the nation's capital to demonstrate the urgency of their message to the government. The idea of such a march made politicians nervous. President Roosevelt called a meeting with Randolph, White, and other black leaders to ask them to call off the march and negotiate instead. Randolph refused. Roosevelt then issued an executive order that said, "It is the policy of the United States to encourage full participation in the national defense program by all citizens of the United States, regardless of race, creed, color, or national origin." Roosevelt also set up the Fair Employment Practices Commission (FEPC) to enforce his order. In a show of good faith, Randolph called off the march.[4]

But since it was enforcing an executive order, and not a full-fledged law, the FEPC did not have as much power as it needed to fight the virulent racial discrimination that existed in industry. Some significant changes did occur in fairness practices toward black workers. But for black women, the effects trickled down. When manpower shortages occurred in war, black men and white women gained opportunities first. Only then did industry turn to black women, who left the low-paying domestic service jobs they had always done to move into the better-paying factory work. As one black woman said, "Hitler was the one that got us out of the white folks' kitchen."[5]

From 1940 to 1944 the proportion of black women in domestic service declined from 59.9 percent of all black women in the workforce to 44.6 percent. Almost all of the white women who had done domestic work before the war left for the factories too. The result was a shortage of maids and cleaning women during wartime. But those women who were left behind to do such work were almost all black. Black women also vacated farmwork to go to work in factories. In fact, the number of black women who worked on farms was cut in half during the war. That was part of a larger migration of black people, both male and female, from the rural South to better jobs in the industrial urban North in the 1940s.[6]

In all, the proportion of black women employed in industrial work rose from 6.5 percent before the war to 18 percent during the war.[7] But black women still often got the dirtiest or most dangerous jobs within industry, such as handling explosives in munitions factories; work others refused to do in meat packing plants; or sweeping and shoveling spilled coal and dust from conveyor belts or leftover ore from the bottoms of unloaded supply boats.[8] In writer Shirley Graham's 1945 story "Tar," a black woman named Mary quits her work doing sewing for white women in New York City to sign up for a course in defense work. She hopes to get a job like the one she had heard advertised on the radio, in a factory making airplanes.

> She thought . . . How wonderful it would be to make even the tiniest part of a great plane! . . . Because Mary was skilled at cutting cloth on a bias and fitting uneven edges, she did exceptionally well in the sheet metal class. She took the advanced course. Then showed her certificate proudly. . . . But Mary didn't get into that factory. Nothing daunted, she tried another and another and another. She stood in long lines day after day—clutching her certificate.

Eventually Mary put her certificate away and went back out to apply for work, armed instead with a letter of recommendation from the husband of a former employer that called her "honest" and "a personable negress."

Mary got a job—filling vats with tar. She stood and poured tar all night—going on twelve and returning in the morning spattered with tar. . . . "I'll move on up soon. Everybody has to start with tar."[9]

But she never did move up. That kind of experience was not unique. In a 1943 article for *Opportunity,* "Negro Women Are American Workers, Too," George E. Demar wrote:

In spite of proper training and wise counseling, and clinging to faith in America, the aspirations of the Negro woman worker are frequently "dimmed out" at the factory employment offices when company representatives say: "There must be some mistake"; . . . You are smart for taking the courses, but we do not employ colored"; "We have not yet installed separate toilet facilities"; "A sufficient number of colored women have not been trained to start a separate shift"; . . . "My wife needs a maid"; "We have our percentage of Negroes."[10]

But some black women did break through. Fanny Christina Hill was able to get a job building airplanes at North American Aviation in Los Angeles during the war.

There were some departments, they wouldn't even allow a black person to walk through there let alone work in there. Some of the white people did not want to work with the Negro. They had arguments right there. Sometimes they would get fired and walk on out the door, but it was one more white person gone. . . . They did everything they could to keep you separated. They just did not like for a Negro and a white person to get together and talk. . . . And they'd keep you from advancing. They always manage to give the Negroes the worst end of the deal.[11]

Black women who wanted to take on civilian jobs left open by manpower shortages also were turned away. When Maya Angelou, a well-known poet and writer, graduated from high school during wartime, she decided she wanted to become a streetcar conductor in San Francisco, where she was living with her mother. Some white women had gotten the job, since the men who had done it were off fighting the war.

I wanted to become a streetcar conductor . . . because I had seen women in their suits with the sharp little cap. So I went down to the streetcar offices, and the people just laughed at me. They wouldn't even give me an application. I came back home crying.

My mother asked me, "Why do you think they wouldn't give you an application?" I said, "Because I'm a Negro." She asked, "Do you want the job?" I said. "Yes." She said, "Go get it! I will give you money. Every morning you get down there before the secretaries are there. Take yourself a good book. Now, when lunchtime comes, don't leave until they leave. But when they leave, you go and give yourself a good lunch. But be back before the secretaries, if you really want the job."

Angelou did as her mother said. For many days she merely showed up at the office, waiting for an application.

Those people did everything but spit on me. I took Tolstoy, I took Gorky—the heavy Russian writers—and I sat there. The secretaries would bump up against my legs as they were leaving. They stood over me. They called me every name you could imagine. But finally I got an application. Within a month I had a job. I was the first black conductor on the streetcars of San Francisco. It cost me the earth, but I got the job.[12]

Black women also made limited gains in white-collar work, mostly in government clerical jobs in Washington, D.C. The Post Office, Treasury, and Justice departments remained 98 percent white during the war, but the War Department and other new agencies were more open to blacks. In the South, black teachers' pay increased in hopes that black schools' deceptive "separate but equal" status could be passed off as real if the Supreme Court ever took up the cases that the NAACP was threatening to bring against inequities in those schools. The average salaries of black teachers, many of whom were women, went up from 51 percent to 85 percent of what white teachers earned in the rural South during the 1940s, and pay rose from 60 percent to 93 percent of white pay in the urban South. But in the private sector, black women were still virtually shut out. Through the 1940s gains by black women in sales jobs and clerical work were almost nil. The Bell companies hired their first black female telephone operators only in 1944.[13]

Black women war workers like Hortense Johnson, who inspected boxes that carried ammunition at an arsenal in New Jersey, strove to maintain dignity and faith when faced with the maddeningly slow progress they were making at overcoming their country's deeply ingrained wrongs.

> We resent the racial injustices that we meet every day of our lives. But it's one thing to resent and fight against racial injustices; it's another thing to let them break your spirit, so you quit this struggle and turn the country over to Hitler. . . . America can't win this war without all of us, and we know it. . . . I'm not fooling myself about this war. Victory won't mean victory for Democracy—yet. But that will come later . . . maybe a long time after the war is over, maybe a hundred years after.[14]

BLACK WOMEN ON THE HOME FRONT

As America was preparing to join the war, President Roosevelt made a famous speech setting forth four essential human values that he said were so worth fighting for that they formed the basis for America's entry into the war effort. They were: freedom of speech and expression, freedom of every person to worship God in his own way, freedom from want, and freedom from fear. These became known as the four freedoms. But for many black people in America, those four freedoms sometimes seemed hollow in the face of all the rejection, abuse, and insults swirling around the United States in the early 1940s. So despite a deep patriotism, sending a son to put his life on the line for this country must surely have taken a toll on many black mothers even greater than the toll white mothers bore in sending their sons to war.

In an article called "One Blue Star," in the National Urban League magazine *Opportunity,* a black mother, May Miller, spoke of the day her eighteen-year-old son got his draft letter. She described how she had to push away her own misgivings, and soothe his, in order to give him the courage to do what the country was calling on him, and her, to do.

> "Come on, Ma, don't carry on like that. You're not sick, are you? You want me to fight, don't you—fight for those four freedoms we live for, don't you?"
> "Yes, son, yes I do."

... "And this time there'll be no quibbling. We mean those four freedoms for everybody, everywhere—for Negro boys like me right here in America."

His voice faltered; the grand pronouncement dribbled to a pitiful personal plea; and I felt a gnawing pain for the doubt that clouded his great vision. He must go to battle freed from nagging doubt. He must keep throbbing within him the promise of a better world. His untried youth must nurse a dream, if he is to fight for fulfillment. And eager to quell his inward questioning, I answered quickly, "And that's something well worth fighting for. I shall be proud of you, my son." I had given him up. . . .

His eyes cleared; the dear swagger returned as he reached in his pocket to draw out a bit of cloth. "Look," he said boyishly, "after I got the letter, I went out and bought this for you to hang in our window."

He tossed in my lap a tiny white silken banner bearing in its center a single blue star.[15]

And the wives who sent their husbands away had many of the same feelings. But as nurse Mabel K. Staupers, who advocated for black women in nursing, said, "Negro women continue to meet the challenge of helping America develop full democracy for all citizens. It is impossible for Negro women to permit their men to return from battlefields and find lack of privilege and opportunity."[16]

One of the ways many black women on the home front worked toward that goal was through volunteer organizations. Black women were not accepted in all the volunteer agencies that welcomed white women, but they still had a will to serve. The Women's Army for National Defense (WAND), founded in Chicago in 1942, stated its mission as providing "an instrument through which our women could serve in this great crisis, with dignity and pride." Mary McLeod Bethune, director of the National Youth Administration's Division of Negro Affairs, was enlisted as an officer. The organization worked in much the same way as many other volunteer organizations during the war, selling war bonds and getting involved in civilian defense projects, but WAND also ran day care centers for black women workers and set up a housing facility for black WACs in Chicago.

Black women were also active in the USO, which usually had separate clubs for black and white people. And black women became a part of the American Women's Volunteer Services (AWVS), which always stated its intention to reach out to women from all backgrounds and walks of life. In Harlem, in New York City, three AWVS units were established. Integrated units also sprung up in Texas, Atlanta, New Orleans, Tucson, Chicago, and Pittsburgh. A black member of a Gary, Indiana, AWVS unit said:

> We want our Negro soldiers to realize that American Negro woman-hood is willing to give its all-out in building up and sustaining the morale of young Negro America. We had and still have many odds against us. . . . But Negro soldiers are our boys, and if they are will-ing to die for a country which denies them full participation in the freedom accorded other groups, they must know that Negro Ameri-can womanhood glories in their loyalty.[17]

BLACK WOMEN IN THE ARMY

Of all the women's branches of the military that existed during World War II, exactly one accepted black women from the very beginning: the Women's Army Corps. But even in the Army, black women were not allowed to serve with white women. Black women served only in segregated units, just as black men in the Army did during World War II. While white WACs were concerned with adjusting to a newly feminized Army, black WACs had the added adjustment of living with their second-class status in the new group.

Marjorie Randolph joined the WAAC in February 1943. She had grown up in Passaic, New Jersey, and unlike WAACs who came from Southern states she had never experienced Jim Crow segregation. So it was a shock when Randolph arrived in Fort Des Moines, Iowa, for her training and realized she would be living and eating and working in a world that shadowed her white counterparts.

> I knew about segregation but it went right over the top of my head because I didn't grow up with it. . . . It didn't occur to me that I was going to be in a black unit. Then I realized, we're separate. There is this invisible line drawn. So then I began to take notice. . . . They had two of everything, two service clubs and two theaters. And the the-aters were different. They were not as nice. Everything was sepa-rated, different but not equal.

Randolph began to see that as a black woman in the U.S. Army she would be doing battle against more than Hitler and the Japanese emperor, Hirohito.

> Of course, you fought the war between the men and the women. . . .
> Then you had the racial thing that you were facing. Then you had
> the war the you were fighting between the overseas and the United
> States. So you were fighting these three wars at the same time, and
> that was very difficult.

Later Randolph served in San Antonio. She remembered a concert at an auditorium downtown with a popular big band that both blacks and whites enjoyed. With time she had forgotten whether it was Count Basie or Duke Ellington playing that night. But the one thing she never forgot was the folly of the evening, as segregation policies invaded even the lighter moments of her life in the military.

> In this big ballroom, they had put two rows of chairs back to back.
> One bandstand, but the chairs were through the center of the dance
> hall back to back. That was the funniest thing to me. . . . Whites
> were dancing on this side of the chairs, and blacks were dancing on
> this side. . . . They'd sit down in the chairs back to back . . . and they
> were touching each other. They could talk to each other, but they'd
> better not turn around and face each other. . . . Other people felt of-
> fended by it . . . but I couldn't even feel offended because I thought it
> was so stupid. . . . I think segregation is stupid. I don't see any reason
> or sensibility to it. So, to me, that was so funny.[18]

The first black women trained were officers. Of the 440 women in the earliest WAAC officer training class in 1942, thirty-nine were black. That ratio was no accident. The bill establishing the WAAC set up a quota for black enlistment, just like the quota that existed on the male side of the Army. The percentage of blacks in the WAAC was not to exceed 10.6 percent of the total number of WAACs, because that mirrored the percentage of the U.S. population that was black. So those first thirty-nine black officers became known as "the ten percenters." The quota situation provided a special challenge for WAAC recruiters, both black and white. The fact that black women were allowed in the WAAC at all meant some white women would not volunteer, and would instead choose one of the other women's military branches that excluded blacks. But the fact that the WAAC was segregated meant that many black women would choose not to join either. They did not want to subject themselves to the humiliation they had heard about from their brothers, husbands, and male friends who had to endure segregation policies after being drafted into the men's military.

A War Department policy on Negro WAACs stated in 1942: "There is a definite reluctance on the part of the best qualified colored women to volunteer in the WAAC. This is brought about by an impression on their part that they will not be well received." Such resistance, the Army stated, could be overcome by an intensive recruiting campaign aimed at getting "the desired class of colored women" interested in the WAAC. Thus, recruiters were sent to black colleges around the country "in order to secure the proper class of applicants." [19]

The black press was diligent in monitoring and speaking out against discrimination in the military during World War II. They got behind what was dubbed the "Double V" campaign, victory against Nazism and Fascism abroad and victory against racism at home. Newspapers such as the *Chicago Defender,* the *Pittsburgh Courier,* the *Philadelphia Afro-American,* the *New York Amsterdam News,* and the *Atlanta Daily World* formed a black press pool in 1943 to report on the war from the perspective of black Americans. For the black press, another sticking point about the WAAC was the choice of Oveta Culp Hobby as director. She was not well known in her own right and was viewed with skepticism by the black press because she was a Southern white woman. [20]

As the black WAACs began getting their job assignments, reports came out in the black press that black WAACs with college degrees were being assigned to clean floors and latrines and perform laundry duty at Army posts around the U.S. By the end of 1942, the black press demanded that a black woman be assigned to the director's office to monitor and address any complaints of discrimination in recruiting or practice within the WAAC.

Director Hobby responded by appointing one of the first black WAAC officers, Harriet M. West, to advise her on racial issues. In April 1943, West had presented her stance on the WAAC in a radio address urging other black women to enlist. She said that while the segregated WAAC "does not represent an ideal of democracy," joining it was not "a retreat from our fight," but instead was "our contribution to its realization." [21] But her influence on issues of race lasted only a few months. West soon was transferred to a job overseeing a black WAC typing pool that sent out letters to families of soldiers who had been killed or were missing in battle.

During the Depression, West had worked as an aide to Mary McLeod Bethune. Along with Eleanor Roosevelt and Representative Edith Nourse Rogers, Bethune was one of the primary crafters of the bill that created the WAAC. An influential leader among black women, Bethune is credited with making sure black women were included in the WAAC from the beginning. She had founded the National Council of Negro Women (NCNW) in 1935, which was a coalition of several black women's organizations and was dedicated to addressing race and gender issues, especially in the workplace. Although sometimes criticized as too accommodating because of its preference to influence from within instead of agitating from outside, discrimination against black women was a concern from the beginning for the NCNW.

And discrimination in the WAAC was of particular concern to Bethune. The WAAC was monitored from the beginning by other black organizations such as Alpha Kappa Alpha sorority, Delta Sigma Theta sorority, the National Urban League, and the NAACP.[22] Bethune became the primary civilian adviser to the women's army on race, always working toward eliminating segregationist policies in the military altogether. As she said in a statement to the WAAC in August 1943, "Full integration is the goal we seek." Harriet West was meant to carry on that mission from within the Army.[23] In the process West was one of only two black WACs promoted to the rank of major during World War II.

The other was Charity Adams, the commander of the only black WAC unit to serve overseas during the war. The 6888th Central Postal Directory Battalion, a unit of more than 800 black WACs, was sent to Birmingham, England, and later to Rouen, France, and Paris to work through huge backlogs of mail to troops. Keeping up with the rapid troop movements of D-Day and the Battle of the Bulge meant mail delivery became more complex at just the time when the experienced mail personnel were shifted away from postal work to other more pressing needs. So the mail, some of which was more than a year old, went undelivered. When the women arrived in Birmingham in February 1945 for their first assignment, they found a building packed with mailbags stacked to the ceiling. They were to get the long-delayed mail to the European theater's more than seven million American troops, including people in groups affiliated with the military, such as the Red Cross. Some of the mail was dirty and damaged, with barely legible addresses. Some had been water-soaked on ships and mildewed. Some packages contained food that had gone bad and was infested with worms.[24]

Myrtle Rhoden, a clerk in the 6888th Battalion, said one room held all the packages that had been sent for birthdays and Christmas containing cookies, cakes, and other perishable gifts. In some of the packages families of rats had moved in. Some had even died and were rotting inside the packages. The smell was horrible. "Some of the rats were as big as cats in there," said Rhoden. "This was not the cleanest job. Girls wore certain types of water-repellent clothes that would protect them from the wetness and stuff. They also wore a certain type of boot. They repacked anything that was salvageable, such as jewelry, socks or anything wearable . . . and sent them to the soldiers."[25]

The job was supposed to take the battalion six months to complete. But working around the clock in three rotating shifts of eight hours, the women sorted the mail in three months. Then they were sent on to France to do the same with another mass of backlogged mail. They knew they were being judged and any misstep would reflect on all black women. And even though they were given one of the dirtiest and most monotonous tasks in the European theater, they were determined to do it with gusto. They took to heart the idea that the mail they were working on was going to boost the morale of the soldiers on the front. The unit broke all previous records for redirecting mail. Each eight-hour shift averaged more than 65,000 pieces of mail.[26]

But Major Adams was dismayed to find that racism had followed them overseas. Within weeks of arriving in Birmingham, England, the unit began receiving requests for black WACs to come visit the homes of local hostesses. Adams was happy to comply, thinking it would be enriching for the women to experience British culture and that it was good public relations for the WAC to reach out to the people of an allied country. Soon, more and more of the invitations included an additional request. The hostesses wanted the women to stay beyond their 11:00 P.M. curfews to 12:30 A.M. They always emphasized 12:30 A.M.

Adams became curious and decided to see why keeping them out past midnight was so important to the British hostesses. It turned out that white American male servicemen had told the women of Birmingham, many of whom had never met a black person before, that all Negroes had tails that came out at midnight. "Some of the good citizens of Birmingham," said Major Adams, "wanted to see for themselves."

But eventually, the WACs began to break through such falsehoods. The *Birmingham Sunday Mercury* reported in a surprised tone, "These WACs are very different from the coloured women portrayed on the films where they are usually either domestics of the old-retainer type or sloe-eyed sirens given to gaudiness of costume and eccentricity in dress. The WACs have dignity and a proper reserve."

As Major Adams said years later of her overseas battalion, and of the approximately 6,500 black WACs who served in World War II: "The women of the 6888th had ventured into a service area where they were not really wanted . . . they had survived racial prejudice and discrimination with dignity. They were proud and had every right to be."[27] She concluded: "Women had never served in the military before. . . . The whites didn't want the blacks. The men didn't want the women. We fought all of those battles, and we still won the war."[28]

BLACK WOMEN IN OTHER MILITARY BRANCHES

The Army Nurse Corps was reluctant to admit black women as the war was starting in Europe. Very few black male soldiers were to be allowed into combat. And true to the segregationist policies of the military at the time, no black nurses would be allowed to care for white soldiers. So, the rationale went, since there would be so few black men to treat, there would be no need for black nurses. But the NAACP protested. So did the National Association of Colored Graduate Nurses (NACGN), which was founded in 1908 to break down discrimination against black nurses and segregation in nursing schools, nursing jobs, the military, and nursing organizations. Black nurses were not welcome in the American Nurses Association at the time. The head of the NACGN during World War II was Mabel K. Staupers, who lobbied throughout the war for acceptance and greater latitude for black nurses in the military.

The Army gave in to some of the pressure when it admitted fifty-six black nurses into the Army Nurse Corps in 1941. That number was a result of a strict quota system implemented to limit the number of black women in the nurse corps. The Navy, however, would not admit any women into its nurse corps. Staupers worked throughout the war to have the quota system lifted, finally succeeding in 1944 after almost all other avenues had been exhausted in the face of what appeared to be a severe nursing shortage. The first black nursing unit to go overseas went to Liberia in March 1943 to care for segregated units of black soldiers.

The Cadet Nurse Corps, the training program for student nurses set up by the government in 1943, began with a more open policy about black nurses than the regular nurse corps. It accepted black women from the start. Representative Frances Bolton included a policy banning racial discrimination in the bill that established the cadet nurses. As a result, more than 2,000 black women enrolled in nursing school under the program.

But for black women who already had their training and were practicing nurses at the beginning of the war, merely trying to enlist was sometimes quite a maneuver. In many states a nurse had to be a member of the state nursing association before she could join the military, but many state associations barred black women. When Ruth Jones Earl, who had finished her nursing degree, went to enlist, she said the Army stalled in admitting her.

> They did not have the right to say directly, "I'm not going to take you," but they would do things like flunk you on your physical. . . . I'd had a complete physical before I even went to see them, so I knew there was nothing wrong. But they kept calling me back for X-rays and all types of things. I went right up to headquarters and told them that I was not going to accept that type of treatment.

After pointing out that they were wasting valuable X-ray materials that could be used better on soldiers overseas, Earl asked them to stop delaying. She was sworn in to the nurse corps two days later.[29]

By the end of the war, about 500 black nurses had served in the Army, a small fraction of the almost 60,000 who were Army nurses. Only five black nurses served in the Navy Nurse Corps during World War II, out of a total of about 14,000. The five had been accepted into the ranks in early 1945, when the Navy finally opened up to black women.

The Navy also was more reluctant than the Army to open its other branches to black women. While the WACs accepted blacks from the onset, the WAVES opened to black women only in October of 1944 and the Coast Guard's SPAR admitted their first black woman only in March of 1945. Fewer than one hundred black women served in the WAVES out of the total 86,000 who enlisted during World War II. And only five black women served in the SPAR out of 11,000 total. The Marines never opened their ranks to black women during the war. The reasoning each of these groups used for delaying or denying the entry of black women was similar. They said the black women were not needed, because there were not enough black men going overseas for them to replace. The Navy did not allow black men to serve at sea until late in the war and the Army sent black units overseas only late in the war. An article on black men and women in the Navy in *The Journal of Negro Education* in the summer of 1943 concluded, "The segregated patterns of training and usages to which Negroes are subjected in the Navy hurt the morale of Negro fighting men. This issue involves the moral standing of America in the concert of world nations."[30]

The WASP never admitted black women into its ranks, even though some black female pilots applied. Janet Harmon had gotten her private pilot's license in 1934 and had written about aviation for the *Chicago Defender*. In 1943 she applied to join the WASP but was rejected because she was black. Since she had gotten her nursing degree in 1929 and worked as a nurse in Chicago, she then applied to join the Army Nurse Corps in 1943, hoping to become a flight nurse, but was told they had reached their quota for black women. Harmon ended up in the Civilian Pilot Training Program at Tuskegee Airfield in Alabama, where the famous unit of black male pilots called the Tuskegee Airmen trained. She earned her commercial flying license there but was never allowed to fly in the military.[31]

Jackie Cochran, the director of the WASP, said that she had a personal meeting with another black woman who was qualified to go to Sweetwater and train to become an Army pilot. But Cochran said she told the woman that while she had no particular prejudice herself, she could not admit her because admitting a black woman would risk a downfall of the whole WASP program. Since so many were having a hard enough time accepting women pilots, Cochran said, they would have an even harder time accepting black women pilots. "This fine young Negro girl," said Cochran, "recognized the force and honesty of my arguments, stated that first of all the women pilot's program should be stabilized and strengthened, and she withdrew the application. . . . She also saw to it, I believe, that I was left alone thereafter so far as this particular issue was concerned."[32]

ENTERTAINERS

Black people in the segregated Army needed entertainment just as much as the white people. The USO responded to that need by establishing a circuit of black performers who would entertain the black troops. The biggest star in that realm was Lena Horne. She became the Army-approved answer to Betty Grable for its black troops. But Lena Horne did not feel it was an honor to be America's number one pinup girl among Negro soldiers during World War II.

> If the officers were white it was hardly safe for a Negro soldier to put up any of the fifty white lovelies, ranging from Grable to Lamarr. They did not have fifty or so Negro lovelies to choose from. They had little ol' me. I therefore chose not to accept my status as a pinup queen as a compliment. It was, rather, an afterthought, as if someone had suddenly turned to the Negro GIs and said: "Oh, yes, here fellows, here's a pinup girl for you, too." [33]

Horne had been known for her singing career and had only recently broken through to film roles. In 1942, she had signed one of the first long-term contracts between a black actress and a major studio, M-G-M. In her contract she had stipulated that she would not play maids or the jungle native roles that were typically the only opportunities for black actresses at the time. As a result Horne often was relegated to being a singer only, without any speaking part, so that her segments could be cut out of the versions shown in Southern movie theaters. Audiences in Jim Crow states apparently could not tolerate seeing black people on the screen with white people except as servants or in other second-class guises. So Horne began to take more comfort in her increasingly prominent role in the touring USO shows. And while she was glad to go, she became fed up with the blatant discrimination she saw and felt in her travels.

> I was always expected to entertain the white soldiers first, then the Negroes—often under the most degrading conditions for both the soldiers and me. I was getting full—up to here—with the whole situation, but I wasn't about to quit USO work, for I was genuinely lovingly received by the men of both races and I wanted to be with them. At least when we appeared we gave the guys a little recreation,

a little respite from the Army and, for the Negro soldiers, a respite from the special hell to which they were assigned.

I guess I should have known that I could not go on forever in this way. The stuff hit the fan at Fort Riley, Kansas.

That was an army base where Horne believed she was going to perform for all the troops together, black and white. Horne and her band were backstage waiting to go out into the big auditorium on the base when she took a peek at the audience. As usual, the white officers were in the place of honor in the front rows of the audience. Behind them were the enlisted white soldiers. But she did not see any black soldiers in their usual designated place at the back of the auditorium. She asked where they were and was told that she and her band were to spend the night and perform for them the next morning in their mess hall, because the Negro soldiers were not allowed in the base auditorium. Horne was indignant. She could not see why they should be excluded, or why she and her road-weary band should have to stay overnight and do an anticlimactic morning show when they could do one big nighttime show for everyone. "The inconvenience of Jim Crow always seemed to hit me first," said Horne. "I suppose it's the way I made personal, inner logic out of something that's so sick and stupid."

She started to shout that she wouldn't do it. Her band members calmed her down enough so she could go onstage that night. And the next morning they headed over to the much smaller Negro mess hall.

They had improvised a little platform for us to work on and I looked out and saw the Negroes were all there all right. Except the front rows were occupied by white men.

"Now who the hell are they?" I asked somebody who was standing around there with me.

"They're the German prisoners of war," he said. Now I don't know if this was an insult calculated by some cracker colonel who had heard me blowing off steam the night before or if it was just the usual Army stupidity showing itself. I don't think I have ever been more furious in my life.

I marched down off the platform and turned my back on the POWs and sang a few songs to the Negro guys in the back of the hall. But by the third or fourth song I was too choked with anger and humiliation to go on. I went backstage. Some of the guys came back to

see what was the matter and to ask me to go on. All I could say was:
"I have to go. I just can't."

Horne asked where the local NAACP office was and headed straight for it.

> I got there. It was some very unfancy place upstairs over a store
> somewhere. There was a beautiful woman sitting there at the desk
> when I came charging in.
> "I want to talk to somebody in charge," I said. "My name is Lena
> Horne."
> And she said, "And my name is Daisy Bates. What's on your mind?"

Daisy Bates would later become famous in the civil rights movement for
being leader of the Little Rock, Arkansas, NAACP at the time of the integration of Little Rock Central High School in 1957. Horne said later, "When we
met, she was just at the beginning of her long struggle. But she already knew,
better than I, how to channel her anger, so she could fight effectively."

That day in Kansas, Horne took solace from Bates as they spoke. Horne
felt she had to do something about what had happened at Fort Riley, but was
worried that the black troops might somehow be punished if she spoke out.
Bates allayed her fear. Horne knew she had enough prominence to get herself
heard and was ready to use it. "The whole situation is bad enough, but this
on top—the enemy getting the front-row seats." Finally, Bates encouraged
Horne to do what her conscience urged. "What have you got to lose?" asked
Bates. "Not a damn thing. So yell it out."

At that, Horne sent a telegram to the USO branch in Hollywood saying
she was quitting the tour because of the way she and the black troops were
treated. She then continued to tour military camps through the war, paying
her own way and performing on her own terms.

> I was frequently involved, in my own work, in similar fights—hotels
> that would not let me use the front elevators even though they may
> be bragging that I was the first Negro artist to play their room, or
> who might let me live in the hotel, but not let my musicians stay
> there too. This made me identify, quite naturally, with any cause
> where people or institutions denied rights and conveniences to indi-
> viduals on the basis of color. I suppose I would have gotten into these
> fights even if I had not acquired a certain celebrity. But when you get

a name you are made aware that you can make a bigger noise about a problem than if you are just an ordinary citizen.[34]

Lena Horne gave hope to many who were working to persuade Hollywood to make some changes in the way it portrayed black people onscreen. The clause in her contract barring her from having to play stereotypical black female roles made her the forerunner of what was hoped would be a new era for black performers. In the spring of 1942, an informal alliance began to form between Walter White, head of the NAACP, some Hollywood executives, and the Office of War Information. White spoke of a campaign to persuade Hollywood to portray "the Negro as a normal human being and integral part of human life and activity." He was intent on movies presenting "a new concept of the Negro," and moving away from typical black characters played by actors like Hattie McDaniel and Butterfly McQueen, most famous for their roles as happy, lovable, loyal slaves in Gone With the Wind.[35]

The OWI conducted a study on how black people were portrayed in Hollywood films that were released in late 1942 and early 1943. The results pointed to a stark reality. "In general," the study said, "Negroes are presented as basically different from other people, as taking no relevant part in the life of the nation, as offering nothing, contributing nothing, expecting nothing." By the spring of 1943 the OWI abandoned its commitment to help change the way blacks were portrayed in films. The office was under pressure from Congress, especially Southern congressmen who fully supported Jim Crow segregation laws, to stop being liberal on racial issues.[36]

As pointed out in their analysis of black people and Hollywood propaganda during World War II, historians Clayton R. Koppes and Gregory D. Black said OWI gave up its commitment to portray three-dimensional black characters after its budget was cut by a Congress unsympathetic to such a mission.

OWI's movie reviewers jettisoned their remaining concern for domestic black opinion and instead focused on how the portrayal of blacks would affect the image of America abroad. By May 1943, [reviewers] limited . . . cinematic recommendations to having occasionally a "Negro speak intelligently" and a "sprinkling of average looking Negro people" in crowd scenes or bank-teller lines. OWI thus hoped . . . to imply an essentially false impression to the rest of the world: that blacks were full participants in American life.[37]

A few major films tried to depict black men as more fully human, such as *Casablanca* in 1942, and *Bataan* and *Sahara* in 1943. But the only nonmusical major film in which a black woman had a leading role was *Since You Went Away* in 1944, meant as a tribute to women on the home front. Hattie McDaniel played Fidelia, the happily self-sacrificing black cook, forever loyal to the noble white family for whom she worked, at one point without pay. McDaniel, for her part, had little choice but to portray the stereotypical characters if she wanted to make a living as a black actress in Hollywood. Unlike Horne, McDaniel's M-G-M contract stipulated that she would play maids, and it even forbade her from losing weight since her rotund size was part of what made her so lovable. David O. Selznick, who produced both *Gone With the Wind* and *Since You Went Away*, repeatedly cast her in those roles and no others. The white people loved her that way. McDaniel had been the first black person ever to receive an Academy Award, for her 1939 role as Mammy in *Gone With the Wind*. But the fact that she won it portraying a slave made many black people feel ambivalent about her accomplishment.[38]

Offscreen, McDaniel, the daughter of a slave, was not the genuflecting appeaser she played in films. Of her Mammy character in *Gone With the Wind* she said she worked within the limits of the time. "I tried," she said, "to turn this stock role into a living, breathing character." McDaniel often responded to criticism of her work with a rationale that gave her some power in the unjust and seemingly inescapable trap in which she found herself, caught between the past and the future. "It's better to get $7,000 a week for playing a servant," she would say, "than to get $7.00 a week for being one." McDaniel headed up the Negro division of the Hollywood Victory Committee, organizing shows for black troops. In 1945, she led black neighbors in her well-to-do Los Angeles neighborhood in a fight against a group of white property owners who were trying to force them out of their homes based on laws that said black people were not allowed to buy in certain areas of the city. McDaniel's case eventually went to the U.S. Supreme Court, which struck down the laws, putting an end to racially discriminatory housing codes in Los Angeles and paving the way for other fair housing legislation.[39]

Other black female entertainers of the time who made some strides forward included opera singers Marian Anderson and Dorothy Maynor, jazz singer Ethel Waters, dancer Katherine Dunham, singer and pianist Hazel Scott, and actress-singers Etta Moten, Muriel Rahn, and Hilda Simms. Occasionally white mainstream writers spoke out against the bigotry these black artists had to endure. Elsa Maxwell, the gossip columnist for the *New York Post*, on November 16, 1943, wrote a strong indictment of racism, celebrating the black stars who were facing it down during wartime.

> Let's look this matter of prejudice straight in the eye. I'm sick and tired of all the pussyfooting that's been going on about Jim Crow. Either we are believers in the principles of democracy—as we piously declare, three times a day—or we are a collection of the greatest frauds the world has seen.
>
> For generations the conventional and learned citizens of this republic have stood stolidly silent while the American Negro has been vilified, libeled and denied almost all access to the privileged places of sweetness and light. . . . Democracy has been wayward in the cause of democracy; and its cultural institutions are all of them suspect.[40]

The black press, which had initiated the idea of the double victory campaign, soon found that women could be useful in promoting the cause as well. Each week, the *Pittsburgh Courier* would profile another young, beautiful "Double V Girl," with a picture of her running alongside the article. Usually the young women were in college, like a Tennessee woman portrayed one week.

> Lovely Marguerite V. Roan, co-ed at Tennessee A and I college, Nashville, is the "Double Victory" girl of the week. Miss Roan, native of Cincinnati, Ohio is an ardent booster of the "Double V" program and one of the first to join the movement. She is a talented ballet dancer and has appeared in many concerts in the midwest.[41]

Other photographs showed women wearing Double V dresses and hats and pins. In September 1945, when the war abroad had been won, the Double V campaign was ended. In its place, the Single V remained until 1946, when the idea faded.

During the war, black women found new avenues outside themselves to begin coping with conflicts they often encountered from their place in society, their double burden of race and gender discrimination. And they found the will inside themselves to ask for more from their country, to ask for justice, for appreciation. It often took a lot of faith. But that faith, nurtured during World War II, helped sustain them as they joined with black men after the war in the long fights to end Jim Crow. A black mother expressed a bit of that brand of belief she had developed during the war in a 1943 letter to the editor of *Redbook* magazine.

> When my little boy comes to me with a look of bewilderment in his eyes, and says, "I want to do this, or I want to be that, when I grow up, but Joe says I can't because I am colored. Can't I Mamma?" I point out to him the achievements of the colored artists, musicians, scientists and champions in the world of sports and say: "Where would they be if they had said—'I can't because I am colored'?"
>
> Yes, I have faith in America, and I love it. . . . I believe that America will eventually wipe out this challenge to her democracy, and that the time will come when no person need fear that he cannot become a truly great American because of race, color or creed. I believe that after we win this war, we will emerge as an even greater nation. I will keep this faith alive in my own heart, and in the heart of my little boy.[42]

CHAPTER EIGHT

Behind Enemy Lines

SPIES, PROPAGANDA WORKERS, AND THOSE WHO WORKED FOR THE ENEMY

If I were making arrangements for an ideal war, I would insist that no women were permitted in forward areas. Regardless of the gallantry and dedication of individual women, the injection of sex into a wartime situation establishes an intolerable obstacle to discipline, without which not much of anything can be achieved.

OLIVER CALDWELL,
Office of Strategic Services agent,
from his book, *A Secret War: Americans in China, 1944–1945*[1]

National Archives

W INNING WORLD WAR II took more than soldiers entering combat and workers building the artillery. There was also a war of information, a battle over what messages and ideas went into and came out of enemy territory. Sometimes information proved more potent than bombs or guns in undermining the objectives of the enemy or defending the goals of the Allies. And just as death and destruction were a part of combat, the ways and means by which the information flow was controlled in war sometimes involved less than savory methods. The two official overseers of that part of America's mission were the Office of Strategic Services (OSS) and the Office of War Information (OWI).

These organizations had different missions and different means by which to accomplish their goals, but their tactics sometimes overlapped. Broadly speaking, the OWI was in the business of creating and disseminating propaganda about America for Americans and for foreigners. The OSS, precursor to the Central Intelligence Agency, was in the business of finding out and influencing what was going on in enemy countries and within enemy military operations. But both organizations had one unifying quality for those who worked in them: an air of subterfuge, if not all-out secrecy. That is why less is known about the exact nature of the work done by the OSS and the OWI than is known about some other war work, since the people who undertook it most often were not allowed to talk about what they were doing or why they were doing it.

The OWI operated both a domestic branch and a branch concerned with how America was perceived overseas. The OWI's Overseas Operations Branch relayed information about America and its participation in the war effort to foreign countries. Also, the OWI's overseas branch sent messages into enemy territory designed to inform Axis soldiers and citizens of the Allied side of the war. The OSS mainly focused its work overseas, where it surreptitiously gathered information that helped the Allied war effort. And the OSS aided resistance groups in Axis-controlled countries. The OSS also sent information meant to unsettle enemy troops and civilians and sabotage enemy morale into Axis-controlled countries.

In both the OWI and the OSS women usually were relegated to secondary positions in support of male workers. But some were able to go overseas to work at far-flung outposts, and a few took on substantial assignments, including spying.

OSS WOMEN

More than 4,000 women worked for the OSS during the war, out of a total of 13,000 employees. The women sometimes did more and knew more than their job titles revealed. When asked what they did they were told to say that they were file clerks. Many were. But a few had jobs that gave them some of the most active and direct involvement in the strategic aspects of the war that any American women were allowed. The only catch was, in order to do that kind of work a woman had to become someone else. She had to become a spy.[2]

Probably the most successful female spy of the war was a master at fooling everyone who met her. People in the rural villages of central France to the south of Paris had no idea that the haggard, old peasant woman Marcelle Montagne, who they saw herding cattle and delivering goat's milk in early 1944, was really a vital, thirty-eight-year-old American woman named Virginia Hall who had attended Radcliffe and Barnard colleges. Not even the German troops occupying the area were able to figure out that this frail graying woman, stooped over her walking stick, was the elusive spy whom the Gestapo, the brutal Nazi special police, had called "one of the most valuable Allied agents in France." Yet she was able to move effectively, unnoticed and unscathed, despite the fact that a wanted poster with a drawing of her from the Gestapo vowed, "We must find and destroy her."

By day, Hall used her fake identity as a peasant farm woman to monitor German troop movements and to scope out the French countryside for places where supplies for the French Resistance and other OSS agents could drop by parachute from Allied planes. At night, she went to various haylofts and safe houses, and radioed all she saw to Allied commanders in London. Virginia Hall became one of the most respected OSS spies of World War II, male or female. The Baltimore native supplied crucial information and worked with French guerrilla resistance members to cut off vital German communication lines and escape routes during and after the Allied invasion of France on D-Day. Her code name within the OSS was Diane. But she was known more popularly as "the limping lady," because she had walked on a wooden leg ever since a gun went off accidentally during a hunting expedition in Turkey, hitting her left foot. Eventually that wound caused gangrene, and her leg had to be amputated from the knee down in the mid-1930s.

It would seem that such a handicap might make it impossible for her to go undetected. And to make it worse, after she had successfully set up resistance networks in occupied France between 1941 and 1943, French double agents had been able to describe her appearance in detail to the Germans. But Hall also became a master of disguise. Instead of trying for some extreme alteration of her physical features, as suggested by disguise specialists in the OSS, Hall opted to take on the persona of a much older rural woman. That way, she figured, her limp would be less noticeable and her status would make her more invisible in the world. In addition, she covered her legs with heavy skirts and taught herself to walk with a less irregular gait.[3]

It all worked. Through spring and summer of 1944, Hall managed to keep up radio contact with London; give daily reports on troop movements; engineer numerous supply drops; organize, train, and aid resistance groups that undermined the last efforts of retreating German soldiers, all while maintaining her disguise and moving constantly to evade German detection.[4] During one part of her assignment that she called "difficult," she reported, "I spent my time looking for fields for receptions, bicycling up and down mountains, checking drop zones, visiting various contacts, doing my wireless transmissions and then spending the nights out waiting for the most part in vain, for deliveries."[5] She worked with a group of thirty resistance members in southern France who provided security for her, helped her mark areas for parachute drops, gathered supplies that had fallen outside the places they were supposed to land, and kept her radio going with fresh batteries.[6]

As the Germans' stranglehold on France was weakening, the resistance workers that Hall oversaw in southern France became particularly useful in helping disable the enemy further. They sabotaged German effectiveness by destroying bridges and rail and telephone lines that were sometimes the last remaining arteries connecting the Germans to the crucial supplies and orders flowing from their homeland. In some of her last dispatches, Hall reported that resistance battalions had taken nineteen French people prisoner who had betrayed their own countrymen to the Nazis. In addition, the resistance forces had killed 150 Germans and had taken an additional 500 Germans prisoner. But even during that hectic time, Hall managed to meet the man who would later become her husband, another OSS agent from New York named Paul Goillot, who had entered the country by parachute and become a part of Hall's team in southern France.[7]

Without her own determination and drive for adventure, Hall's talents might never have been able to blossom and she might never have embarked on a career in espionage. Before the war, during the 1930s, Hall worked as a clerk at the State Department, serving in embassies in Poland, Estonia, Austria, Turkey, and Italy. The State Department saw her as having a promising career in the upper levels of its clerical branch, about the only branch in which a woman could aspire to any authority, even a highly educated woman. In fact, Secretary of State Cordell Hull said Hall "could become a fine career girl in the Consular Service." But he rejected her 1939 application to be a foreign service officer, despite the fact that she had passed the test for such work. Women were not generally considered for career positions in the State Department at that time and Hall's physical limitations provided the official reason for her rejection. State Department policy said a missing limb or missing part of a limb was "cause for rejection in the career field."[8]

The documents that Hall would have filed had she stayed on at the State Department would have contained increasingly more important information as the war escalated. But that prospect was not enough direct involvement in the war effort to keep a restless, keen woman like Hall in the clerk jobs the secretary of state thought so appropriate for her. In 1939 she headed for France and joined the French Ambulance Service, but after France was conquered by the Nazis in June 1940 she went to Britain and became part of the British Special Operations Executive (SOE), the counterpart to what would become the American OSS. In the SOE, Hall was trained in weapons, communications, and security measures. She was fluent in French and was sent into France for the first time as a spy in August 1941 by the SOE, with her cover being that she was a reporter for the *New York Post*. The British didn't think of their operatives as spies, since they were not doing as much information gathering as they were setting up networks of resistance. And since America was still neutral at that time, Hall's cover allowed her to report freely and her work was not censored. After America joined the war in December

1941, Hall stayed on in France for an additional fourteen months until she was ordered to leave by the Nazis and narrowly escaped into Spain after an arduous winter trek through the Pyrenees.[9]

In 1943 she returned to England and was awarded the Member of the British Empire medal for bravery. Soon thereafter she joined the American OSS in London at the rank of second lieutenant and was sent back into France as the milkmaid farmhand. At the end of the war, the U.S. government awarded Hall the Distinguished Service Cross, the second highest military award for bravery after the Medal of Honor. Hall was the only civilian American woman to receive that award during World War II.[10]

Another American spy, Amy Thorpe Pack, was best remembered for procuring naval codes from the Vichy embassy in Washington that were useful in the Allied invasion of North Africa in November 1942. The Vichy government had been set up in negotiation with Hitler when Germany invaded and overtook France. In exchange for Germany agreeing not to occupy a large portion of France, the Vichy government was to protect territories in the French empire against Allied invasion. Eventually the Vichy government became a total puppet of Hitler's regime. North Africa was part of the Vichy empire. Procuring Vichy naval codes and thereby knowing about ship movements in the waters surrounding the North African coast was a key asset for the Allies.[11]

Amy Thorpe Pack was the American wife of a British embassy official in Washington, Arthur Joseph Pack. By the time the war started their decade-long marriage was on shaky ground. The trouble seemed to have started when her husband had forced them to give up their first child, a boy, for adoption. Apparently Mr. Pack did not want to be embarrassed in professional circles when people realized that the son had been conceived out of wedlock, since he was born just five months after their wedding. Amy Pack was heartbroken and was said to have never forgiven her husband. They later had a daughter, presumably to compensate for giving up the boy, but the daughter was eventually sent to boarding schools for much of her upbringing. In addition, during the course of their marriage both Amy Pack and her husband had affairs.

Yet, by following her husband on his diplomatic postings around the world during the 1930s, Pack had made contacts among the powerful, gathering information and becoming affiliated with both the British SOE and the

American OSS. In 1941 she was living in Washington, and was asked by the British to go after the Vichy naval codes. She was to form a relationship with a member of the Vichy embassy staff in Washington. She chose a willing partner in Charles Brousse, a Vichy press aide to the ambassador. In order to get access to the codes, Pack and Brousse bribed a night watchman at the embassy, asking him to be complicit in the affair they were having, allowing them to carry on in his office at night, since it was the only place they could meet discreetly without Brousse's wife finding out. That plan, conceived by Pack, would give them access to the codes when few were around. And it worked.

One night, they shared champagne with the friendly Vichy embassy security guard. In his glass they put a sedative, which they also had placed in his dog's water. With the guard and the dog out of commission, they broke into the secure room that contained the codebooks. But they were not able to crack the safe in time to get the books out and photographed and back to the embassy before daylight. On a second night, as the security guard made his rounds, they persuaded him not to patrol their area because they were involved in intimate activities. To convince him to stay away, they arranged that when he walked in on them he would find them naked. That was enough to give them time to let in an OSS safecracker through a window in the code room, steal the codebooks, photograph them, and return them without the guard knowing.

That successful mission was credited with helping the Allies conquer North Africa. But even with that mission completed, the affair between Pack and Brousse continued. At one point they convinced Brousse's wife, who was also an American and whom they informed of Pack's clandestine role on the side of the Allies, to let Pack pose as the couple's daughter so that she could use the Brousses' social position to make important contacts within the Vichy government. Unaware that Pack and her husband were carrying on an affair, Mrs. Brousse played along, on many occasions introducing Pack, who was more than twenty years younger than her and her husband, at parties as her daughter. Mrs. Brousse even agreed to let Pack take on the name of her real daughter, who had died many years before. Mrs. Brousse thought that by supporting Pack's story she was helping the Allies, who, like her husband, she supported wholeheartedly.

The three lived together in hotels, including their detainment in a hotel in Pennsylvania where members of the Vichy government in the U.S. were held at one point. It was there that Mrs. Brousse discovered the true nature of her husband's relationship with their "daughter" when she walked into Pack's room one morning and found them in bed together. She reacted by going after Pack and trying to kill her. Charles Brousse protected his mistress and somehow got his wife out of the room and back to their own room. The resulting argument between the husband and wife was heard throughout the hotel and apparently turned violent, with furniture thrown and with Mrs. Brousse threatening to reveal Pack's spy status.

Mrs. Brousse was effectively kept under house arrest at the compound until Pack could be taken away to safety. Pack stayed in a New York hotel owned by her family and tried to contact and see Brousse, who remained detained in Pennsylvania. Brousse worked to convince his fellow Vichy officials there that he was still a staunch Nazi, so that his and his mistress's cover would not be blown. Finally, Brousse and Pack were reunited in New York City months later and were not heard from again until more than a year later. Their effectiveness as spies had been compromised. Mrs. Brousse was sent to Mexico by the OSS and told she was doing important clandestine work, when actually she was only being held there under watch doing busywork, so that she would not talk to anyone about the work of her husband and his mistress. The Brousses and the Packs both got divorced. Amy Pack and Charles Brousse married after the war and lived together in a French château until Pack died of cancer in 1963.[12]

Pack was once quoted as saying she was never ashamed of what she did as a spy and who it may have hurt.

> I hope and believe I was a patriot. There is no rule of thumb for patriotism. . . . My superiors told me that the results of my work saved thousands of British and American lives. Even one would have made it worthwhile. It involved me in situations from which "respectable" women draw back—but mine was total commitment. Wars are not won by respectable methods. One tries to win any war, any way.[13]

There were plenty of women with far less glamorous or risky work in the OSS than the relatively few who worked as full-fledged spies. The organization was founded on June 13, 1942, and headed by William "Wild Bill" Donovan. It sprang from the former Coordinator of Information Office, which had been a liaison between the disparate intelligence arms of the military and government. The joke around Washington was that OSS stood for "Oh So Social," or "Oh So Snobby," since most of the original employees were educated at Ivy League and Seven Sisters colleges, and came from upper-middle-class and wealthy families. That was partly a function of William Donovan, who had both undergraduate and law degrees from Columbia. Since the OSS had to form quickly and in the utmost secrecy, Donovan took the shortest route to recruiting loyal personnel. He looked among those he knew, who were also Ivy League graduates and from upper-class families. As the OSS was finding its territory within the intelligence community, there was much rivalry with the FBI and other domestic military intelligence departments. Thus, the OSS became primarily involved with overseas operations.

Donovan once called the many women in OSS clerical jobs in Washington the "invisible apron strings of an organization which touched every theater of the war." He said, "they were the ones at home who patiently filed secret reports, encoded and decoded messages, answered telephones, mailed checks and kept the records." He said that "only a small percentage of the women ever went overseas, and a still smaller percentage was assigned to actual operations behind enemy lines."[14] Virginia Hall and Amy Thorpe Pack were two of the few women who worked in the clandestine Secret Intelligence and Special Operations branches of the OSS.

One OSS woman who went overseas with the Secret Intelligence branch was Julia McWilliams, later better known by her married name as one of America's most famous culinary personalities, Julia Child. She had graduated from Smith College in 1934 and worked in public relations in New York City. Child joined the OSS in December of 1942, after being rejected by the WAVES and the WACs because at six foot two she was too tall. "I stood my full height," said Child, "which is a little over six feet. And they didn't take anybody that tall." She never got a satisfactory answer why. She said she had once heard it was because they did not have uniforms that large on hand.[15]

Child then worked briefly in the OWI as a senior typist, but found that work deadly dull. Then she began at the OSS as a junior research assistant in William Donovan's Washington office. "He was a fascinating man," she said. "The whole organization was his brainchild. And the people who came in to see him were very interesting." Child was promoted and transferred a few times by the end of 1943. At one point she worked on a special project that developed a substance to repel ever-curious sharks that had been setting off explosives in the ocean that the Allies had planted to destroy German

U-boats. The substance kept the sharks away, thereby helping safeguard vital Allied shipping routes. It later was used by NASA to repel sharks from spacecraft that landed in the ocean.[16]

By 1944 Child applied for overseas service and was sent to Ceylon (now Sri Lanka), where she worked as head of the registry of records in the OSS office at Kandy. One of her most vivid memories was of the large ship she had traveled over on first approaching the harbor at Bombay, India. "I remember sitting on the boat and being able to smell India coming up," said Child. "I suddenly had a feeling, I wondered why I was there so far away. It was quite primitive . . . steamy. There weren't any tall buildings or anything like that. I had a qualm. I thought, 'What am I doing here? How did I get into this?' That was just a passing qualm though." She realized she was probably feeling the same thing that many people felt when suddenly finding themselves in a foreign country in the middle of a war. "I would think the men would have had it more than the women," she said, "heading off heavens know where."[17]

In talking about her OSS work after she became well known, Child was always careful to make it clear she was not a spy. She did paperwork. "There was nothing heroic about it," said Child, "I was an office worker. They wouldn't have gotten men to do that kind of work, I don't think. They just needed help. It was all that was available for women." But it was not the work that attracted Child. It was the opportunity to go overseas, especially to the East.

> I was very lucky to get in and to be able to go. I was delighted. I don't think we expected much because in those days women didn't get much anyway. We weren't anxious to go out and do a man's job at all. I was not in advance of my time. I accepted my role as a woman. I didn't have any ambition to go out and do secret service things or anything like that. Women supported the men and they supported the effort in doing the kind of work that they could do.[18]

Still, Child's war job required a high security clearance. In Ceylon and later when she was posted to China, she was in charge of tracking, keeping safe, and relaying secret documents and espionage and sabotage reports. In the days before computers this often involved conceiving elaborate filing and indexing systems. While working in Ceylon, Child also met her future husband, Paul Child, a fellow OSS worker. When she was transferred to China

near the end of the war, so was he. They married after the war and moved
to Paris, where Julia Child went to the Cordon Bleu cooking school, thus
launching her cooking career.[19]

Child saw her time in the OSS as a time of growth, but mainly for the
chance to live in the Far East and to work with such smart, interesting people.

> It just expanded my horizons. It didn't essentially change me in any
> way because I had worked before. I think if a woman had never
> worked and had always been held at home in womanly jobs it would
> have been very affecting. People all say that since World War II
> women have felt freer. I think they became a little more indepen-
> dent.[20]

Another OSS woman who served in the China-Burma-India theater was
Elizabeth P. McIntosh, a journalist originally from Hawaii. She had written
for the Scripps-Howard chain of newspapers before joining the OSS and
being sent in July 1944 to work in the Morale Operations division in New
Delhi. McIntosh and another Morale Operations worker, Marjorie Severyns,
embarked on many projects to disseminate morale-dampening propaganda
among Japanese troops in the China-Burma-India theater and even among
their families and leaders in Japan.

That kind of work in the OSS was called "black propaganda," meaning it
was often based on falsehoods or half-truths that would damage enemy spirits. The rumors, lies, or innuendos were usually cleverly disguised to appear
as if they had come from people or media sources inside enemy countries. An
opposite brand of propaganda was called "white propaganda," which involved conveying more of the truth, labeled as coming from the Allies, to
enemy troops and citizens in hopes that they would be converted to the Allied
cause, or at least would be discouraged from their own. The Office of War Information was in charge of white propaganda.[21]

An example of OSS black propaganda carried out by McIntosh and
Severyns was an operation dubbed "Project Black Mail." It involved postcards
written home from Japanese soldiers to their families before going into one of
their last battles in which their unit was defeated by the Allied forces. The
postcards, intercepted by Allied intelligence operatives, had already passed
through Japanese censors and had the proper postage.

Allied intelligence analysts had determined that the postcards contained no information valuable to the Allied military. So they were considered useless until McIntosh and her colleagues thought of erasing some of the messages in the postcards and forging other messages that would convey to people on the Japanese home front the idea that their troops were losing. They knew that since the postcards had already been read and stamped by Japanese censors, they would not be looked at again and had a good chance of getting directly to Japanese families, one of the OSS's propaganda targets. McIntosh felt regret that these Japanese families would not get the authentic last messages that some of the soldiers had written before they were killed or captured in battle, but she had a job to do and set about implementing the task.

She and the rest of the small staff of the Morale Operations office in New Delhi enlisted help from other intelligence workers in the joint American and British South East Asian Translation and Interpreter Command, many of whom were Japanese-Americans with superb Japanese language skills. McIntosh, one of the crafters of the idea, stressed to all that the same messages should be in each card, "like an advertising campaign emphasizing a single slogan." The messages conveyed that the soldiers felt defeated and that people at home were not supporting them enough. "Accuse the people back home of being slackers," McIntosh advised the forgers. "Tell of heartbreak and starvation in the jungles." As they set about their work, McIntosh and Severyns served the men working on the postcards tea and sandwiches.

When they were completed McIntosh took the postcards to an Army colonel in the area and persuaded him to find a way to slip the postcards back into the Japanese mail system. She told him that it would most probably be the first time the OSS managed to get their message into Japan, directly to Japanese citizens. The colonel agreed and a few days later sent a message back saying the mission was completed. The next week when, coincidentally, the entire Japanese cabinet resigned after the resignation of Prime Minister Tojo, a male colleague brought the newspaper bearing that headline into McIntosh and Severyns, showed it to them and said jokingly, "See what you girls have done?" [22]

Another example of OSS black propaganda was its use of radio. Radio was on the cutting edge of information technology during the war. Not only was it used to send coded messages from military commanders to their field forces, but it was also used for propaganda purposes by both sides. [23] Women's voices were a major part of the radio arsenal on both sides. Working with the

British, the OSS set up broadcasts called Soldatensender West, which were able to reach into Germany by broadcast and shortwave radio. The programs ran every night from 8:00 P.M. to 8:00 A.M. and were a mixture of news, talk, and music. The news and information was often accurate, but mixed in would be some half-truths and lies to confuse and subvert the enemy. In late 1944, the OSS recruited Marlene Dietrich to record some songs written in German especially for Soldatensender West to hurt the morale of the German soldiers. She also sang the popular song "Lili Marlene," about a soldier who was thinking about the girl he left behind and how another man had probably replaced him.

The manager of the OSS's Far East Morale Operations was a woman based in the Washington headquarters. Every week she would conduct a "rumor mill" meeting with her staff to concoct misinformation that would be circulated by her staff in Burma, India, Ceylon, China, and Thailand. To sabotage relations between the Japanese and any supporters they may have had in China, the OSS branch in China once circulated a rumor that the Japanese military was planning to lure Chinese pilots into doing kamikaze missions for Japanese suicide squadrons.[24]

The use of propaganda continued through the war, in all the theaters of the war. Often the OSS was responsible. But other branches of the information-propagating artillery also got into the act.

WOMEN IN OWI, ARMY, AND NAVY INTELLIGENCE WORK

The Office of War Information communicated to people on the home front about the war through its Domestic Bureau, which included the magazine, radio, and film boards that exerted influence on purveyors of public opinion in America. But its overseas operations were focused on disseminating propaganda to enemy troops and citizens, and keeping Allied troops and citizens informed of news from America.

In February 1945, 249 women served in the overseas division of the OWI, along with 985 men.[25] But many of those people did not work in overseas outposts, staffing instead large offices in New York and San Francisco that directed the overseas operations aimed at the West and the East. Much of their work involved producing radio propaganda, specially produced newsreels and films, and various publications for dissemination in foreign countries. The audiences of the OWI overseas output were enemy and neutral countries, allies in those countries, and Americans stationed outside the U.S. The OWI supplied news, entertainment, and propaganda. The OWI also produced the *Voice of America* radio broadcasts that were white propaganda broadcasts beamed all over the world to tell America's story.

Another tool the OWI used to accomplish its goals was the employment of journalists, nationals, and social scientists to help monitor and translate the mood and culture of enemy and neutral nations to which the Allied nations were trying to communicate.[26] The OWI used social scientists to help it understand the culture of the U.S. in a time of war. Notably, the OWI turned to two prominent female anthropologists for some of that kind of insight: Margaret Mead and Ruth Benedict. Mead, who was best known for her studies of Samoan culture, was less formally engaged with the OWI than her mentor and friend Benedict. But Mead lectured and engaged in research to find how anthropology could help nations communicate with each other and help the U.S. government communicate with its own citizens.[27]

One window into the kinds of questions Mead considered was revealed in a letter written but never sent to her brother-in-law Leo Rosten, a writer employed by the OWI, about using the study of culture to stem rumors among American citizens that interfered with the war effort. Mead suggested the establishment of "rumor clinics" on university campuses around the country to study the effects of rumors and come up with ways to circumvent and deny rumors that circulated among people, especially in America's heartland. That idea was not taken up, but the fact that Mead considered it shows how seriously false information used as a weapon was taken during wartime. Defense against rumors would have fallen to the OWI, while using rumors offensively was a tactic practiced by both the OWI and the OSS. Mead was involved in the world of information and its uses during the war, as was her husband, Gregory Bateson. Also an anthropologist, he joined the OSS and was stationed in Ceylon during the war, in the same office as Julia Child.[28]

Mead wrote a book in 1942 called *And Keep Your Powder Dry!* about the nature of American culture and national character, and how anthropology could help society in a world at war. The title was taken from a quotation by a World War I commander to his men just before they crossed a river into battle. In the book Mead analyzed the American people's customs and habits in the same way she had done in her famous sojourns to foreign lands. She found that in the American character is a deep-seated need to succeed. She said it helped the country accomplish ambitious things and that it always had to have an outlet. Another national trait she noted was a great belief in the power of science and technology. She also observed a need for a sense of moral purpose in the efforts undertaken by Americans. Those, she concluded, were the terms by which Americans could be motivated to fight a war.

> Although this is not a job for Americans alone we must see it as America's. Americans will not do it—being what we are—unless we feel that for some aspect of it we are better fitted than any people on earth today. We are proud but not sure, anxious to succeed but never certain that we will, willing to go ahead and tackle any job—but it must be our job. If we are to fight, if we are to win, if we are to hold before us as we fight a goal we will count worth fighting for, that goal must be phrased in American terms, in that mixture of faith in the right and faith in the power of science.[29]

That insight seemed to be at play in the way that OWI presented the war to the American people at home and to the soldiers abroad. But OWI also relied on anthropologists such as Benedict to shed light on the culture and character of people in Axis countries. Benedict began such a study of Japan in 1944. She wrote a book based on her findings, *The Chrysanthemum and the Sword,* published in 1946. Calling Japan "the most alien enemy the United States had ever fought in an all-out struggle," Benedict went on to describe the contradictions apparent in the Japanese national character. She said, "the Japanese are to the highest degree, both aggressive and unaggressive, both militaristic and aesthetic, both insolent and polite, rigid and adaptable, submissive and resentful of being pushed around, loyal and treacherous, brave and timid, conservative and hospitable to new ways." In order to conduct her study she said she had to look at how the Japanese acted during war from a cultural standpoint, not a military one.[30]

Because Benedict could not go to Japan during the war she could not base her observations on direct experience of the people in their homeland. Instead, like other social scientists doing similar work during the war, she relied on talking with Japanese-Americans raised in Japan, Japanese POWs, and scholars of Japan, as well as on some reading and on the culture coming out of Japan at the time, especially movies. In one part of the book on the Japanese child, Benedict looked at the cultural climate in which women were raised in Japan, which in some ways might not have seemed too far from what she and other American women of the time had been brought up to believe. "From their earliest memories," she said of young Japanese girls, "they have been trained to accept the fact that boys get the precedence and the attention and the presents which are denied them. The rule of life which they must honor denies them the privilege of overt self-assertion." [31]

Another function performed by both the OWI overseas office and the OSS during the war was the production of publications for distribution in enemy countries. Writers, both male and female, for the OWI and OSS designed the leaflets, containing white and black propaganda respectively, that were dropped over German, Japanese, and Italian towns from bombers and other Allied planes.

Almost six billion leaflets were distributed through Western Europe alone by the British and American air forces based in Britain during the war. The American Eighth Air Force started dropping leaflets in 1943 on its daylight bombing missions and sometimes in special leaflet missions, and by May 1945 had distributed nearly 600 million. The leaflets were designed to persuade individual soldiers to stop fighting a losing battle or to make civilians aid the Allied forces that would soon be their liberators. In addition, leaflets were produced that instructed enemy soldiers how to surrender and promised good treatment when they did. The U.S. Army also set up a Psychological Warfare Division, which helped produce leaflets. After D-Day the OSS, the Psychological Warfare Division, and the British Political Intelligence Department produced "newspapers" that gave current news laced with Allied propaganda and was distributed daily in Germany by Allied planes. [32]

By the time the war was over, a debate had been raging about whether intelligence and propaganda were needed in peacetime America. The OWI was shut down in August 1945 and eventually its functions were performed by what became the U.S. Information Agency. The OSS was disassembled in October 1945 and the CIA was formed two years later to take over its functions.

But when America's propaganda machine was in full force during the war, it was coordinated by the War Department's Psychological Warfare Board, composed of representatives from the State Department, the Army and the Navy, and the OSS and OWI. They met weekly to coordinate overall worldwide propaganda efforts, making sure the black and white propaganda campaigns of the various agencies worked in concert.[33]

The Navy had a division that was especially concerned with code breaking during the war, since enemy ships communicated with commanders on land and at sea by using codes. WAVES worked in the Navy's cryptanalysis department, called OP-20-G, part of the Office of Naval Communications. By early 1944, 2,813 women served on the staff of OP-20-G.[34] A top secret project employed 600 WAVES during the war to help build a machine that could break the German Enigma naval code. Early in the war the British had first made a machine called "bombe" that was able to decipher German naval codes, but the Germans caught on and created more complex Enigma codes. In 1942, German U-boats were sinking too many American and British ships carrying supplies and troops across the Atlantic to and from the United States. So the U.S. Navy engaged the National Cash Register company in Dayton, Ohio, to build a bombe capable of breaking the newer, more complex German code.

The 600 WAVES who came to work on the machine were housed at a National Cash Register company training center for salesmen called Sugar Camp. At first there were not enough accommodations for all 600 women. They were working three eight-hour shifts, keeping the vital production of the 200 code-breaking machines going twenty-four hours a day. So the women took turns sleeping in the bunks. One shift of 200 women slept while another worked. The women soldered together and wired the many parts of each of the 2.5 ton machines, which were ten feet wide and seven feet tall. In the interest of secrecy, each component was assembled in separate areas of the warehouse where it was produced. If a worker assigned to work in one room of the building wandered into another room she would be stopped by a Marine guard.

Secrecy was such a common condition during World War II that it was not only spies and intelligence workers who were involved in subterfuge. The famous slogan "Loose Lips Sink Ships" was well known to everyone in America, so it did not seem odd that none of the WAVES was told what kind of machine they were building. If asked by anyone what they were doing in Dayton, they were to say that they were taking accounting machine courses. "People must have thought we were pretty stupid to be there all that time learning how to run adding machines," said one WAVE who worked on the project, which ran from 1943 to 1945.[35]

"OF COURSE I CAN!

I'm patriotic as can be—
And ration points won't worry me!"

Shortages and rationing altered the lifestyle of all American civilians during World War II, but the impact on women in charge of running a home reached most aspects of their daily routine. *Northwestern University Library*

The first food item to be rationed by the government was sugar. Women and children waited in line at the sugar rationing board in Detroit in 1942. *Library of Congress*

The Office of War Information commissioned patriotic posters and billboards of the home front to promote the sale of war bonds, an investment that gave a sort of loan to the government to finance the war. *Library of Congress*

Homemakers were encouraged to save all fats and greases from cooking to be processed into ammunition for soldiers. *National Archives*

In 1943, a fictional character emerged named Rosie the Riveter. She was everything the government wanted in a female war worker: She was loyal, efficient, patriotic, compliant, even pretty. *National Archives*

We Can Do It!

Norman Rockwell's *Saturday Evening Post* cover illustration of Rosie appeared on May 29, 1943. *Reprinted by permission of the Norman Rockwell Family Agency, copyright © 1943 the Norman Rockwell Family Entities*

Douglas Aircraft, one of the largest aircraft plants in the U.S. in the early 1940s, employed nearly 22,000 women during the war to help build bombers and transport planes used in the air war on both fronts. *National Archives*

Many women who took war production jobs migrated to the centers of defense production on the East and West coasts, and along the Gulf of Mexico like these welders at a Pascagoula, Mississippi, shipyard. *National Archives*

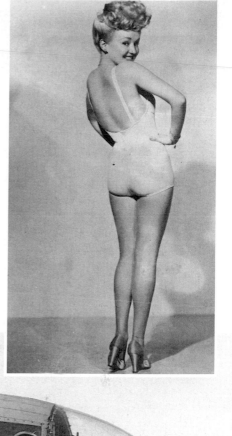

Betty Grable's famous bathing suit shot was taken by a publicity photographer at 20th Century Fox. The studio estimated it had sent out five million copies to soldiers by the end of the war. *National Archives*

Most American bombers were adorned with "nose art" paintings of voluptuous fantasy women in various stages of undress. *National Archives*

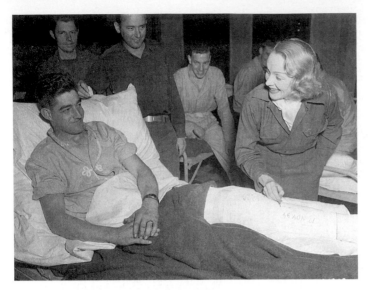

German-born actress Marlene Dietrich had a
deep and especially risky dedication to the
Allied cause that provoked Hitler to put her
on his personal hit list. *National Archives*

Director of the Women's Army Corps Oveta Culp
Hobby and First Lady Eleanor Roosevelt with soldiers
in England in 1942. *National Archives*

For your country's sake today—

For your own sake tomorrow

GO TO THE NEAREST RECRUITING STATION
OF THE ARMED SERVICE OF YOUR CHOICE

In 1942, women entered the U.S. Army as soldiers for the first time in American history. Once that beachhead was secured, it was only a matter of months before four other women's military branches were established. *National Archives*

"I'm proud of my *two* soldiers"

JOIN THE WAC NOW !

THOUSANDS OF ARMY JOBS NEED FILLING !

Women's Army Corps
United States Army

Recruiting women for military service meant going against traditional ideas of women's place in society. *National Archives*

The first women soldiers set out to prove their worth, not only to the military or the nation, but to themselves as well. *Library of Congress*

Starting in July 1942, approximately 86,000 women joined the Navy as WAVES, taking on a variety of jobs including working in air control towers, like these women at Anacostia Naval Air Station. *National Archives*

The Coast Guard established a women's branch called the SPAR in November 1942. About 11,000 women became SPARs for shore duty in the U.S. during World War II. *U.S. Coast Guard*

In the three years of existence of the Women's Airforce Service Pilots (WASP), its pilots flew more than 60 million miles and ferried more than 12,000 aircraft between factories and military bases. *National Archives*

Some Red Cross women ran traveling kitchens called club-mobiles, from which they served coffee and doughnuts very close to the fighting front. *Mary Haynsworth Mathews Collection, University Archives & Manuscripts, The University of North Carolina at Greensboro*

Army and Navy nurses worked in air transport squadrons worldwide. Of the 1.176 million patients evacuated by air to a medical facility during the war, only 46 died en route. *National Archives*

By the end of the war, 70,000 nurses had served in the Army and Navy Nurse Corps. These Army nurses posed in front of their barracks in Australia in 1943. *National Archives*

The U.S. Department of Agriculture created a quasi-military civilian group called the Women's Land Army, which trained and sent thousands of urban and suburban women to work on farms. *Oregon State University Archives, Harriet's Collection, photo #972*

The USO came up with creative ways to make soldiers feel at home, including providing female escorts for church-goers. The sign reads: "If you want to go to heaven, go to church with an angel!" *Virginia Historical Society*

Only after the labor pool of white women and black men was exhausted did industry turn to black women, who left low-paying domestic service jobs to move into better-paying and abundant factory work. *National Archives*

Hattie McDaniel headed up the Negro division of the Hollywood Victory Committee, organizing shows by black entertainers for black troops. *National Archives*

The pinups and photos of girlfriends that African-American male soldiers displayed in their barracks were as racially segregated as the military was during World War II. *National Archives*

WANTED!

FOR MURDER

Her <u>careless talk</u> costs lives

Women were admonished not to share information publicly about their loved ones serving overseas, for fear that enemy spies had infiltrated America and would use any such information against the Allies. *Northwestern University Library*

About two-thirds of the Japanese Americans ordered to move to internment camps were American citizens, and about 60 percent were women and children. They were told that the government was removing them from their homes for their own protection. *Library of Congress*

By June 1944, approximately 120,000 Japanese Americans, many born in the U.S., had been held in 10 internment camps, where they tried to maintain their normal American lives. *National Archives*

Initially, Japanese families evacuated from their homes were assigned to horse stalls at racetracks on the West Coast. *Library of Congress*

Eleanor Roosevelt and Mrs. Winston Churchill appeared together on Canadian radio in 1944. *National Archives*

The terms of a prostitute's employment had always been that the rest of society would look the other way. In return, these women were expected to carry on without complaint in the dirtiest, most degrading war work of all. *University of Minnesota Libraries*

Women were usually implicated publicly as the ones who spread venereal disease, a common condition among enlisted men. *National Archives*

By the end of the war, men were often portrayed as surprised at the newly proven competencies of women. *National Archives*

My mother, Carol Lynn, played a number of the roles that women all over the country played during the war: war bride, military wife, career woman, Red Cross girl. *Yellin family photos*

My mother echoed the sentiments of many women when she said in a 1944 letter that she had joined the Red Cross because she had to "get out and try to do something active and direct when so many other people are doing so much." *Yellin family photos*

In Saipan my mother experienced the uneven ratio of men to women in war zones. She said, "If you don't bear it constantly in mind, you begin to think you're pretty irresistible." *Yellin family photos*

Though none knew exactly what she was building in Dayton, there were some educated guesses among the WAVES. One woman who worked on the heart of the machine, the communicator wheels, said she had a hunch that the work had something to do with codes. "The wheels we soldered," she said, "had 26 points on them, and there are 26 letters in the alphabet. That kind of tipped me off." [36] Eventually some of the WAVES who helped build the computer-like machine were also trained to operate it and were sent along with the machines to run them at the Naval Communications Annex in Washington. They had been schooled in the secrecy of their project in Dayton, but when they got to Washington they were warned from the very beginning that if they told anyone about their work they would be shot. [37]

Such discretion was required of many women who signed up for the military or for civilian jobs with intelligence agencies. But a few women were recruited to clandestine work because of their contacts, and had to choose whether to take the work on, often at great risk to themselves. One was Alice Marble, who accepted her covert mission after a series of personal tragedies.

Alice Marble was a tennis star of the 1930s who had won four U.S. singles titles and the 1939 Wimbledon singles, doubles, and mixed doubles (with Bobby Riggs as her partner) titles. One of Marble's dearest friends was actress Carole Lombard. When Marble heard of Lombard's death in the plane crash as she came home from a bond drive at the beginning of the war, she was devastated. "Losing Carole was like losing a sister," said Marble. "We had such a wonderful kinship, an intuitive understanding of each other . . . she was caring and fun, and had become my closest confidante."

Inspired by Lombard's death to aid in the war effort, Marble felt she had to do something meaningful herself. She began visiting military hospitals and singing and playing Ping-Pong with soldiers at the Stage Door Canteen in New York. One night she began to sing "Take a Chance on Love" with a group forming around a piano at the canteen, when she noticed an Army captain who had joined the singing. That was the start of a whirlwind romance that blossomed into true love and marriage. Joseph Crowley could not tell her what he did in the Army, but he worked in the intelligence branch. So their marriage had to be kept secret until after the war, especially because it would have been big news since Marble was so well known.

While Joe went off on missions, Marble toured more than 500 military bases during the war, playing exhibition tennis matches for troops. The happy couple got together whenever they could and soon Marble became pregnant. One night near the end of 1944, about five months into her pregnancy, she was driving home when her car was struck by a drunk driver. She lost her baby in the accident. Marble decided to wait to tell Joe until a few days later when he was to come home on leave for New Year's 1945. But on Christmas Eve she got a telegram from the War Department telling her that her husband's plane had been shot down over Germany.

> I felt a scream rising in my throat, but when I opened my mouth nothing came out. . . . There would be no more reunions, no more nights of passion, no more plans of a family and our future together. There was no future. . . . At least Joe had died thinking the baby still lived inside me. . . . There was nothing left for me but pain, and I couldn't face that. I had been forced to be strong all my life, and I was tired of it. I didn't want to be strong anymore. I didn't want to *be* anymore.

Marble attempted suicide that night by taking an overdose of sleeping pills, but was discovered by friends who got her to the hospital, and she was released the next morning, Christmas Day. As she began to recover, she slowly began to think about getting back into tennis.

It was soon thereafter, in early 1945, Marble recalled in her autobiography, that Army intelligence contacted her and asked for her help. They set up a secret meeting with her at a warehouse in Brooklyn. She was shocked when they asked her to go to Switzerland and try to reestablish contact with an old boyfriend, Hans Steinmetz, a Swiss banker. Apparently, Steinmetz was harboring treasures in his bank that Nazi officials were smuggling out of Germany near the end of the war. The Army wanted records of the transactions, which included gold, jewelry, money, art, and other valuable assets. They hoped to find the names of the Nazis involved and stop them in their plans to move to South America when Germany lost the war. These Nazis intended to live on the smuggled assets, many of them stolen from Jewish people.

Two Army men said they thought Hans probably kept the assets and the records of them in a vault in his large home. They wanted Marble to "regain his trust" and get the records and take photos of the pages with the names of all the Nazis. Marble told the men she would have to think about it. Hans had been her first love and she had given him up for tennis. Joe had been a truer love and without him the world had lost much of its meaning for her.

> I'd had many sleepless nights since Joe's death, but now Hans intruded on my thoughts. I'd loved him and hurt him before. Could I bring myself to spy on him, to betray his trust? And could I make love with him? . . . I knew "regaining Hans's trust" would mean sleeping with him.
> I hoped that Hans wasn't helping the Nazis, but if he was, then what he was doing was wrong—maybe not illegal in his country, but wrong nonetheless. If I could do what . . . [the Army] wanted, it could hurt the bastards who shot Joe's plane out of the sky. I tossed in my bed as if the Germans had already caught me and were torturing me. I could get killed. Was I prepared to die for my country?

Marble agreed to do it. She felt she had little to lose. She was sent to Switzerland to play some highly publicized exhibition matches with the notion that Hans would contact her if he heard she was nearby. He did. Within a few days he had invited her to move into his home with him for the rest of her stay in Switzerland. Their love affair rekindled.

Marble stayed with Hans for three weeks. He bought her jewels and other expensive gifts. She tried to stop him from spending so much money on her. But one night he said, "When will you accept that I am a very wealthy man, and getting wealthier all the time?" Later that night they returned from a lavish party and Hans was drunk and drinking more. He finally revealed to her that he was indeed harboring money and assets for Nazis in a vault in his home. As if on cue, he told her where the key was.

Marble found a night to be alone and went down to the vault to photograph the records containing names of all the Nazis with whom Hans was doing business. As she was coming up the stairs from the vault she was nearly discovered by a servant. She also realized that Hans had come home earlier than expected. The only way to make her getaway was through the front door. She bolted out and took the Mercedes that Hans had left in the driveway a few minutes before with the keys still in the ignition so the servants could drive it to the garage. Marble narrowly escaped. As she was fleeing out of the country she was shot and almost died but was saved by an Army man who was following her. After the war, when the Nazis were put on trial for war crimes, she recognized some of the names she had seen in Hans's ledger and took some solace in her part in nabbing them. "By helping bring them to justice," she said, "I had, in a small way, avenged Joe's death." [38]

RESISTANCE

Another famous American woman who used her position to help fight the Nazis was the African-American performer Josephine Baker. She had immigrated to France before the war because she was tired of the racism in America and found more acceptance in Europe. In the late 1920s she had become one of the highest-paid women in the European entertainment industry. When the war began, she volunteered to assist the French resistance. As she traveled freely throughout Europe she was able to smuggle information across borders. Messages were written in the margins of her sheet music in invisible ink. Most of her entourage was composed of French resistance workers. The legend of her war work also includes stories about how she attended parties in enemy territory and would write what she heard on notes and pin them in her underwear to smuggle back into France. No one would search or question her, it was said, because everyone in Europe was in awe of her.[39]

Less is known about the German resistance or about American women who may have worked with them, except for Mildred Fish Harnack, an American from Milwaukee who lived in Germany during the war. Her story shows the grave hazards for anyone in Germany who dared to oppose Hitler. Harnack met her husband, Arvid, a German, at the University of Wisconsin—Madison. He was a Rockefeller fellow studying economics and she was an alumna and a young English instructor. They fell in love, married, and moved in 1930 to Berlin, where they watched Hitler's rise to power with trepidation. They became members of a key resistance group that helped German Jews escape the country, distributed leaflets containing President Roosevelt's speeches, and supplied economic and military information to the Americans and the Soviets. As the war began, Arvid Harnack maintained his position as an economist in the Nazi government and Mildred taught American literature at the University of Berlin and translated German literature into English.

Mildred also worked as an English tutor in the home of the American ambassador, where she passed intelligence from her husband to the United

States. In addition, the resistance group began to send coded messages to the Soviet Union via radio transmitters. In June 1941 the Germans intercepted the messages, and discovered the spy ring inside Germany that included the Harnacks. Both Harnack and her husband were arrested in September 1942, along with more than 135 others. The Harnacks were not allowed to communicate with each other in prison, and Mildred was not allowed to see or talk to anyone for most of her time at Plötzensee Prison. According to family, other prisoners, and a biography of Mildred Harnack, Arvid was tortured in prison and Mildred was kept in solitary confinement for most of her time behind bars.

After a secret Nazi trial of thirty-one of the men and eighteen of the women, Arvid Harnack was sentenced to death. Mildred was given a lighter sentence of six years in prison because she was proven to be a wife who simply went along with her husband. The trial in December 1942 was the first time the couple saw each other since their arrest and the last time they would ever see each other again. Three days later, Arvid Harnack was hanged in Plötzensee Prison in December 1942. Because Mildred was an American, Hitler felt her original sentence was too light. He wanted to make an example of her, so he ordered her to undergo a new secret trial in January 1943. He was more satisfied with the verdict and penalty in the second trial, in which Mildred was sentenced to die. In February 1943 Mildred Harnack was taken to a guillotine, on special orders from Hitler. In the same room in Plötzensee Prison where Arvid had been hanged two months before, Mildred's head was chopped off. She was the only American woman executed on orders of Adolf Hitler during World War II.[40]

Inge Havemann, Arvid's sister, had waited outside the courtroom during the trial and heard reports of what had gone on behind the closed doors. She wrote to her mother the day after her brother's death sentence in December was handed down and when they still believed Mildred would serve six years and live on.

> Although we all had secretly anticipated this, it was still a blow. . . . A[rvid] received the verdict with complete composure and exemplary bearing. On one of the previous days he had been able to speak in his own defense, so as to clarify his motives. This was his greatest wish and will have been a great relief to him. For his wife it is dreadful. How nice that they were together again for these five days.[41]

TURNCOATS

Elizabeth Bentley got into the Communist Party while she was a graduate student at Columbia University in the 1930s, in part because her roommate at the time persuaded her to join. Soon Bentley fell in love with a KGB operative, Jacob Golos, and by the time the war started she had become a spy for the Soviet Union in America. The Soviets eventually were allies during World War II, so the Communist Party was not thought of as quite as evil by some as it later came to be seen in America after Senator Joseph McCarthy conducted his famous witch-hunt for Communists in the 1950s. It would be Elizabeth Bentley who supplied some of the first pivotal information about Soviet spy activity in the U.S. that sparked the climate that led to McCarthyism.

At the beginning of the war, she worked as a secretary to her boyfriend. At the same time she worked for the Italian Information Library in New York. She was able to pass on information about the pro-Fascist activity that was being funneled through the library. After that job, she continued with Golos as a courier and spy, getting information for him from his business and social acquaintances.

In 1943, her boyfriend Golos died, but she carried on his work, coordinating a large spy ring in the United States. But since she had lost her main link with the Soviet government, her relations with the KGB frayed. In 1945, Bentley started to talk to the FBI. By the end of 1945 she had given the FBI about eighty names of Soviet operatives in the American government. As the Red Scare and Cold War heated up after the end of World War II, Bentley proved a key source in the prosecution of supposed Communists during the McCarthy era. The newspaper headlines dubbed her the "Red Spy Queen."[42]

Of all the ways in which people's loyalties switched during World War II, one person who was seen as particularly despicable by Americans was a woman named Mildred Gillars. She had renounced her U.S. citizenship and pledged allegiance to Hitler to become a disc jockey at Radio Berlin. Mildred Gillars was born in Maine and studied drama at both Ohio Wesleyan University and Hunter College in New York, hoping for a stage career. It never panned out and she ended up moving to Germany in 1933, apparently following a German-born, married professor from Hunter with whom she had had an affair in New York. He became an official in Nazi radio, in charge of propaganda broadcasts. He enlisted Gillars to his cause.

She went on the air December 11, 1941, broadcasting a show called *Home*

Sweet Home, and referring to herself as Midge. The GIs called her Axis Sally. Similar to what Marlene Dietrich had done for the Allies, Gillars turned on her country's government and aided the other side with her voice. She played American music and interspersed it with talk designed to make the men homesick and discouraged. But Gillars peppered her broadcasts with hateful talk about Jewish people and President Roosevelt. In an interlude between songs she once said, "Damn Roosevelt! Damn Churchill! Damn all Jews who made this war possible. I love America, but I do not love Roosevelt and all his kike boyfriends." Gillars took her work a step further than other female propaganda workers by going into POW camps posing as a Red Cross worker. She then persuaded the American soldiers to record messages that she promised to play for their families back home. Instead she would take the soldiers' words and intersperse her own anti-American, anti-Semitic comments. After a particularly heartfelt greeting from one soldier she said, "It's a disgrace to the American public that they don't wake to the fact of what Franklin D. Roosevelt is doing to the Gentiles of your country and my country."

Gillars continued her broadcasts throughout the war until May 6, 1945. After the war, she was found by the American government and brought back to the U.S. and tried for treason. Her broadcasts had originated in Berlin but reached into Europe, North Africa, and could even be heard in the United States. The Federal Communications Commission had taped most of her broadcasts during the war from a listening station in Maryland. Using her own broadcasts, the government's case against her had plenty of evidence, also including testimony from bitter soldiers who had been interviewed by her in the prison camps. It was noted that she had been the highest-paid broadcaster on all of German radio. She was brought to trial on ten counts of treason, but was found guilty on only one count, based on her participation in one particular broadcast.

On May 11, 1944, just weeks before the June 6 D-Day invasion of Normandy by the Allies, Gillars played an American mother from Ohio in a radio play written by her lover. Called *Vision of Invasion*, the story was set on the Normandy beaches and was broadcast to troops in Britain poised to invade France. The mother had a dream in which her son was killed as his ship crossed the English Channel. He came to her after his death and told her of the horror of it all. In the background, shrieks, moans, and crying men were heard suffering in the bloody battle. The announcer said, in a deep voice, "The D of D-Day stands for doom, disaster, death, defeat."

After the three-month trial, Mildred "Axis Sally" Gillars was convicted of treason and sentenced in 1949 to ten to thirty years in Alderson women's prison in West Virginia, and given a $10,000 fine. No real explanation was ever put forward for what exactly had turned Gillars into a Nazi sympathizer, except that she was under the influence of her Nazi boyfriend. She was granted parole and released in 1961.[43]

On a C-54 cargo plane flying from Honolulu to Saipan
Saturday, May 12, 1945

We slept last night stretched out on the floor of the plane, wrapped in an Army blanket. . . . This afternoon, since Millie and I were the only girls on the plane, we had little trouble in wangling a special invitation from the crew to come up in the pilot's compartment. . . . We listened to Radio Tokyo over the plane's radio. Really an amazing thing. We heard famous Tokyo Rose giving the latest dope on the 500 ships that the Japs had just sunk at Okinawa. . . . It was quite interesting to hear these English-language Japanese propaganda broadcasts. . . . All very confidential, sort of "The Japs don't know I'm saying all this but I want to give you the real inside dope" idea. Really a rather clever device. The prize prediction for the day was that within a few days Russia would declare war on the U.S. and Great Britain, because Russia realizes that Great Britain and the U.S. hate her even more than they hated Germany.

CHAPTER NINE

A Question of Loyalty

JAPANESE-AMERICAN WOMEN

I have gotten used to many things over here and I think in a few more months I will be able to say that I don't mind living in Japan. It has been very hard and discouraging at times but from now on it will be all right, I am sure. But for the rest of you, no matter how bad things get and how much you have to take in the form of racial criticisms and no matter how hard you have to work, by all means remain in the country you learn to appreciate more after you leave it.

IVA TOGURI,
letter to her family, October 13, 1941[1]

MORE THAN ANY OTHER GROUP of Americans, the lives of Americans of Japanese descent were so deliberately disrupted and destroyed by the American government during World War II that it is hard to see how they could remain loyal to a country that treated them with such disdain. But they did stay true, as much as they were allowed to do so.

With all the hate that spewed forth during World War II, the egregious way Americans of Japanese descent were treated by their own country sometimes got lost in the shuffle. After all, the concentration camps American Japanese were forced to inhabit were not as gruesome as the ones Hitler created. No one was being gassed to death in any of the American camps, although a few people were shot and killed by guards for getting too close to the barbed wire fences that kept them imprisoned. And the way that Japanese-Americans were rounded up from their homes, split off from their families, and taken away to concentration camps to live was a bit less vicious than the way the Nazis rounded up the Jews, Gypsies, and other outcast groups to send them off to almost certain death.

America justified its alarmist actions by saying that it was holding an entire race of its citizens captive for the safety of the rest of the country, in case any Americans of Japanese descent still had loyalty to the land of their ancestors, our enemy in the Pacific. In the wake of the Pearl Harbor assault, the national desire for vengeance on the only country that directly attacked America during World War II was high. Add that to the fact that resentment of immigrants from Asia had been brewing for many decades in mainstream, white America. With little time for consideration, fear during war can easily turn to licensed hatred. The internment of Japanese-Americans during World War II, like the segregation of African-Americans, at the very least was an unfortunate oversight at home in the rush to fight injustice, bigotry, and tyranny abroad.

Tragic stories of the fate of Japanese-Americans bearing the effects of persecution during World War II are bountiful. And for the women, who were in charge of caring for their parents', children's, and husbands' physical and emotional needs, the effects on their everyday lives were vast. Even the story of the most notorious and misunderstood woman of them all, the woman branded as Tokyo Rose, was just the beginning in a long line of tales of humiliating injustice experienced by Japanese-American women. Yet through it all they remained steadfastly committed to America.

TOKYO ROSE

In the same way Betty Crocker was created out of the composite rendering of several women, so was Tokyo Rose. But unlike Betty Crocker and Rosie the Riveter, both of whom were fabricated to embody ideals of beloved, virtuous, white American womanhood, the myth of Tokyo Rose was spun from imaginations full of all the hatred that had been allowed to run rampant toward Japanese-Americans during World War II. Tokyo Rose became the quintessential disloyal woman.

It was true that there had been propaganda broadcasts by English-speaking women in the Pacific theater. And most probably some of those broadcasts contained the kinds of personal threats that had been reported to have come from a female announcer called Tokyo Rose. But there was not one woman doing it all. There were a dozen or so women broadcasting propaganda from Radio Tokyo and other outlets during the war. Some were committed to their mission of dampening the morale of Allied troops. But others were covertly defiant of that goal. None of the women on Radio Tokyo was ever referred to as Tokyo Rose on the air. And as it turned out, most of the propaganda broadcasts that came from Radio Tokyo had been undermined by the POWs who were forced to write them. The programs were rigged with innuendo, humor, and double-meaning that the Japanese did not catch, and some programs were delivered by complicit pro-American women among those doing the announcing.

If the concept of truth and justice had entered into it, it would have been clear that Iva Toguri was the wrong woman to blame for treason. Born on the Fourth of July in Los Angeles, she had graduated from the University of California at Los Angeles in 1940 with a bachelor's degree in zoology. She had never been to Japan and did not speak Japanese. But her mother, who was born in Japan, got word that her sister was ill and needed help. Iva's mother was also unwell and could not go to her sister's bedside in Japan herself. So she sent Iva to care for an aunt she had never met. On July 5, 1941, the day after her twenty-fifth birthday, Iva Toguri boarded a boat for Japan on a mission of mercy.

Just before Japan bombed Pearl Harbor, she tried to come home. She was uncomfortable in Japan and sensed that it was not a good time to be an American there. In addition, she wanted to be back home to help her family, since she also was aware that Japanese Americans were coming under more scrutiny in the United States. But complications with passports and booking passage meant she was unable to get out of Japan before Pearl Harbor. And afterward it became increasingly difficult. She had to move out of her aunt's house, since her American heritage meant their neighbors distrusted her and thought she was an enemy spy.

She finally found a part time job at a Japanese news agency and a room in a boarding house. Eventually she was also hired at Radio Tokyo as a typist. Cut off from family and virtually abandoned by her homeland, she was stuck in enemy territory in wartime. She used all her wits to get work and survive. She took Japanese lessons and was visited a few times by Japanese authorities urging her to renounce her American citizenship. She refused, and tried in vain to get back home. In 1943, she was asked by a colleague at Radio Tokyo to become an announcer on *The Zero Hour*. She understood it was propaganda broadcasting but also thought she might be able to find ways to lessen the effects of the propaganda, and instead contribute positively to the morale of American troops.

She took the work, thinking it would be a way for her to help the boys from home. She said later, "I thought I could entertain the American soldiers that way." The American and Australian POWs who worked with her let her know that they were trying to make the program as entertaining as possible and never to think of it as propaganda. That way, they all felt they were not really helping the Japanese accomplish their goals of undermining American morale. In addition, Toguri smuggled in food to the radio station for the POWs, who were often malnourished.

Toguri said:

> I knew that "Zero Hour" was Japanese propaganda for the purpose of lowering the morale of the Allied troops. . . . My purpose was to give the program a double meaning and thus reduce its effectiveness as a propaganda medium. . . . I did not feel that I was working against the interests of the United States.[2]

Many of the troops thought the broadcasts were humorous and Toguri often signaled to her listeners that she was not to be taken seriously.

On February 22, 1944, she started the broadcast with a typical sign-on:

> Hello there enemies. How's tricks? This is Ann of Radio Tokyo, and we're just going to begin our regular program of music, news and the zero hour for our friends . . . I mean, our enemies . . . in Australia and the South Pacific. So be on your guard, and mind the children don't hear. All set? O.K. Here's the first blow to your morale. The Boston Pops playing "Strike Up the Band."

She always started her show with that song because it was the UCLA fight song. And she called herself Ann, since that was the abbreviation for the role of announcer that was written in the script beside what she was supposed to read. On March 27, 1944, she said:

> Greetings everybody. This is your little playmate, I mean your bitter enemy, Ann, with a program of dangerous and wicked propaganda for my victims in Australia and the South Pacific. Stand by. You unlucky creatures here I go. Peter Dawson singing "Old Man River."

And after the song she came back on and said:

> See what I mean? Dangerous stuff that. And it's habit forming. Before you know where you are, you're singing too. And then where are you? Doggone it. There's a war on isn't there? So none of this singing nonsense. Sergeant! Gag those men. We're going to have some music!

Then another song was played and she came back on and lampooned the broken English of the Japanese, something that might have passed over the heads of Japanese monitors, but would have struck a chord with native English speakers such as herself and her audience.

> You are liking please? Well keep honorable ears pinned back and we'll have one more item before your news from the American home front.[3]

Because of the obvious tongue-in-cheek spirit with which she injected each broadcast, Toguri naively believed that her fellow Americans would see that she had worked for the U.S. in Japan during the war instead of against it. In April 1945 Toguri married a Portuguese citizen, Felipe d'Aquino, and when Japan surrendered she was planning finally to go back home to America with her new husband.

When the war ended and Allied forces occupied Japan, the Hearst chain of newspapers and magazines in America, known for sensational reporting and dislike of ethnic minorities, was looking to interview villainous Japanese enemies. Of course they wanted to interview the leaders of the Japanese military and government. But just as urgently, they also wanted to find and interrogate Tokyo Rose, a woman who soldiers had reported was the vicious hostess of Radio Tokyo propaganda broadcasts. She was the woman who had continually taunted the troops, broadcasting threats to their lives sometimes using names of actual soldiers and regiments. It did not matter that in the months before the war ended the Office of War Information had issued a report that said, "There is no Tokyo Rose; the name is strictly a GI invention. . . . Government monitors listening in twenty-four hours a day have never heard the words Tokyo Rose over a Japanese-controlled Far Eastern radio."[4]

Two Hearst reporters, one from *Cosmopolitan* magazine and the other from Heart's International News Service, offered a reward to anyone who could tell them where to find the "Dragon Lady of the Airwaves," Tokyo Rose.

Sure enough, someone came through. His name was Kenkichi Oki. Born in Sacramento, California, and a 1939 graduate of New York University, Oki had moved to Japan before the war and given up his American citizenship to become a citizen of Japan. When America joined the Allies in the war, he was working at Radio Tokyo and soon became production manager of *Zero Hour*. It used mostly Japanese-American women living in Japan to play music and broadcast propaganda aimed at weakening the resolve of Allied troops in the Pacific. Most of the women, for one reason or another, had given up their American citizenship. The one exception was Iva Toguri. Even under pressure from Japanese authorities, she would never denounce her birthright. And it was her steadfast and undying loyalty to the United States that would be her downfall, making her the only one of the women broadcasting from Radio Tokyo eligible to be tried for treason by the U.S., since only citizens could be tried for treason.

Kenkichi Oki told the reporters that Iva Toguri was Tokyo Rose. He took the money and ran. He might have been trying to deflect blame from his own wife, who also had been an English-language announcer on Radio Tokyo and was a Japanese citizen.

Iva was arrested by American occupation authorities on October 17, 1945, at her Tokyo apartment. She was not allowed to notify a lawyer. Three officers of the Eighth Army Counter Intelligence Corps simply took her to a jail in Yokohama. A month later she was transferred to Sugamo Prison in Tokyo, where she was held along with other Japanese war criminals. She was kept there for eleven and a half months in a six-by-nine-foot cell and never charged with a crime.

Six months after her arrest, the Eighth Army's legal section, which had been investigating charges of traitorous acts by her, said: "There is no evidence that [Iva Toguri d'Aquino] ever broadcast greetings to units by names or location, or predicted military movements or attacks indicating access to secret military information and planes, etc. as the Tokyo Rose of rumor and legend is reported to have done." They called her broadcasts innocuous. But that was not enough to free Toguri and clear her name. The military was reluctant to release her even after that report because there had been such publicity about her arrest and they feared a backlash. But once the attorney general restated that she was not Tokyo Rose, Toguri was finally released on October 25, 1946. During her years in Japan her mother had died and her family had left the internment camp and moved to Chicago.[5]

Iva wanted to go home. It had been five years since she left her homeland for Japan before the war. It took another year before the State Department would grant her permission to receive her U.S. passport and be allowed to go home. But as word of her plans to come home surfaced in America, reaction was harsh. The American Legion called for her to stay in Japan and not return to America. The city council in her hometown, Los Angeles, passed a resolution against her return to the U.S. And famous newspaper columnist and radio personality Walter Winchell campaigned for her prosecution. FBI director J. Edgar Hoover publicly began to ask for help in proving she was indeed Tokyo Rose, even though the Justice Department and the Army had found her blameless.

In the interim, Iva Toguri d'Aquino had become pregnant and desperately wanted her child to be born in America, so he too could be an American citizen instead of Japanese. But she was not able to get home and in January 1948 her baby was born in Japan. He died the next morning.[6] The furor around her continued. In August 1948, Mildred Gillars, the former American citizen who had become a German citizen and had been identified as Axis Sally, was arrested in Germany and shipped back to America to stand trial for treason. That added to the drumbeat for d'Aquino's arrest. In late August, a newsreel reporting Axis Sally's return to the U.S. for trial then turned to Iva's imminent arrest, again.

> At almost the same time, another American-born woman who did radio work for the enemy hits the headlines. Ordered arrested in Tokyo is Iva Toguri, a woman known as Tokyo Rose and as Little Orphan Annie. . . . She had a disc jockey program for GIs in the Pacific. Now she too may be ordered back to face the music in the land of her birth.[7]

She was arrested for treasonable conduct again and shipped to San Francisco for trial, arriving on September 25, 1948. Iva Toguri d'Aquino was held for another ten months before her trial began on July 5, 1949, one day after her thirty-third birthday, and exactly eight years after she had boarded the boat for Japan. Her husband was not allowed to follow her into the country, and she was not called to testify until September 7, 1949. A series of witnesses were brought over from Japan at the U.S. government's expense. The bill for the trial skyrocketed to approximately $750,000, making her trial more expensive than any other trial in U.S. history before that time. Iva's father had to pay all the costs for the defense of his daughter, so her side had much less ammunition to fight her case, although her husband was allowed to enter the country to testify on her behalf. He had to post money to ensure that he would leave as soon as his testimony was done. He did so and would never see his wife again.

When Iva Toguri was shipped back to the U.S. and tried for treason, it was Oki's testimony, along with that of another American-born Radio Tokyo worker named George Mitsushio, that would be the basis for her conviction.

Iva Toguri d'Aquino was convicted of one count of treason and sentenced to ten years in prison and a $10,000 fine. She served six years and was released for good behavior on January 28, 1958, more than seventeen years after she had innocently left her home for the first time to go help her sick aunt in Japan. For two years she fought deportation by the government and worked for another fifteen years to pay off the $10,000 fine. And nearly thirty years later, Oki and Mitsushio would admit to an American reporter that their damning testimony was a lie and had been made under threats and pressure from the U.S. government, at the behest of FBI chief J. Edgar Hoover. In

1977, President Gerald Ford, who had fought in the South Pacific during World War II, officially pardoned Iva Toguri d'Aquino of treason, more than thirty-six years after she had first left the country for Japan. She was sixty years old.[8]

TAKEN AWAY

At least four parts of the Bill of Rights of the U.S. Constitution seemed to have been violated when Japanese-American citizens were rounded up and sent away to concentration camps in the wake of the 1941 Japanese attack on Pearl Harbor. There was the Fourth Amendment, guaranteeing against unreasonable search and seizure. There was the Fifth Amendment, guaranteeing citizens would not be deprived of life, liberty, or property without due process of law. Also violated were the Fourteenth and Fifteenth Amendments, which ensured that all U.S. citizens would have equal protection under U.S. law, regardless of race.

Starting on the day of the attack on Pearl Harbor in December 1941, the FBI began rounding up men who had been leading figures in Japanese-American communities on the West Coast. By February 1942, the federal government was holding 1,291 Japanese men without trial or explanation. Actual evidence of criminal or subversive activities was not necessary for arrest or imprisonment, just suspicion.[9]

Chiye Tomihiro was born and raised in Portland, Oregon. On the night of the Pearl Harbor attacks, she and her mother had gone to a social event at their church.

> My father was arrested on December 7 during the FBI roundup. . . . When we came home, they had ransacked the apartment, taken lots of things, and left the door open, unlocked. Then we learned that my father had been taken away . . . by the FBI. . . . It's really silly, the reactions you have. At the time we thought it was because he spoke English well and because he was quite prominent in the community, that they probably needed him for some interpreting or some darn thing like that. Never . . . realizing that he was going to be interned. They stuck him in the . . . county jail, and I went down to see him the next day. Then they brought him back one day to pick up some things, and he said, don't worry, don't worry.[10]

The Japanese-American men like Tomihiro's father who were sent to prisons were mostly of the generation called Issei, which was a combination of the Japanese words for "one" and "generation." The Issei were born in Japan and had moved to the United States, often early in life. Most had married Issei women and were raising families in America. But Issei, even those who had been in the country contributing to the economy for decades, were not allowed to become American citizens.

It was a policy that dated back to just after the founding of the U.S. in the late 1700s, when naturalization laws specified that only white immigrants were eligible to become citizens. Then, after the slaves were freed, the law was amended to include black people. In 1922, a Supreme Court case challenging whether a Japanese-born immigrant could become a citizen ruled that he was not eligible, since "white" referred only to people of the "Caucasian race." In 1924, additional Japanese-born people were banned from immigrating altogether by an "exclusion law" that was passed by Congress. Tomihiro's father had a law degree from the University of Oregon, yet was not allowed to practice law since he wasn't a citizen, but a resident alien. He had used his knowledge of the law to advise other Issei in Portland with legal problems.[11]

The children of the Issei, born in America, were called Nisei and were automatically citizens by virtue of their birth in the U.S. They became the hope of the Issei. Their ability to be American citizens, with all the rights and privileges that go with that, became the reason for any sacrifices made by the Issei. Property was put in the name of the Nisei by their parents, since Western states had passed laws prohibiting land ownership by aliens. Those "alien land laws" were directed at limiting the ability of the Issei to own farms, since white farmers had become threatened by the success of Issei farmers. In 1941, about 77,000 Nisei and 43,000 Issei lived on the West Coast, where about 90 percent of all the people of Japanese heritage in the U.S. lived.[12]

Initially, the Issei were the ones most threatened after Pearl Harbor, fearing their already precarious status in the U.S. would be limited further. But it turned out that no one of Japanese descent was safe. By February 1942, President Roosevelt had signed Executive Order 9066, giving the U.S. Army the power to decide which areas of the country would be declared military zones from which "any or all persons may be excluded." The Army, under the leadership of Lieutenant General John L. DeWitt, head of the Western Defense Command, decided that anyone with even one-sixteenth Japanese blood in their ancestry should be "evacuated" from the Western coastal states of the

U.S. (That meant anyone who had even one great-great-grandparent who had been born in Japan would have to leave the West Coast.)

Even when her father was sent to a prison camp for "enemy alien" men in Santa Fe, New Mexico, as a Nisei, Chiye Tomihiro believed that her government would protect her. "I remember how we tried to be so patriotic, and we were so trusting," she said. But within months she and her mother were also made to leave their homes and go live in an internment camp in Idaho called Minidoka.

> We used to argue with our parents all the time because we'd say. "Oh, we're American citizens. Uncle Sam's going to take care of us, don't worry."
> ... We were so damn naive. I don't think any of us ever believed it would happen to us, I think even as we were being hauled away we didn't believe it was happening to us.... We were just like in a trance.... We were all taught in the history books that our rights were going to be protected and all this other stuff. And I think that that feeling of having been betrayed is the thing that really makes me the saddest of anything.[13]

About two thirds of the people affected by the evacuation orders were American citizens, and about 60 percent were women and children. They were told that the government was removing them for their own protection. They were told that because they would be indistinguishable from invading enemy Japanese in the event of an attack, being in the camps would differentiate and protect them from being mistaken for the enemy. Internment was also said to be a "military necessity" to guard against sabotage, despite the fact that government reports had found there was little to no threatening subversiveness within the Japanese community in America. And while relatively few noncitizens of German or Italian ancestry had been arrested by the FBI initially, no such across-the-board exclusion ever went into effect for those citizens, even though some were recent immigrants from Nazi Germany.[14]

General DeWitt, head of the Western Defense Command of the Army, had declared at a meeting of federal and state officials in January of 1942 that the Western states of the U.S. had "been designated as a theater of operations." He spoke of the nearly 288,000 enemy aliens in the states who were under their watch.

I have little confidence that the enemy aliens are law-abiding or loyal in any sense of the word. Some of them yes; many, no. Particularly the Japanese. I have no confidence in their loyalty whatsoever.

In early February 1942, DeWitt recommended the mass evacuation of Japanese from the Western states.

In the war in which we are now engaged racial affinities are not severed by migration. The Japanese race is an enemy race and while many second and third generation Japanese born on United States soil, possessed of United States citizenship, have become "Americanized," the racial strains are undiluted.[15]

The *Los Angeles Times* got into the act as well, supporting the idea of mass evacuation from California when it said, "A viper is nonetheless a viper wherever the egg is hatched—so a Japanese American, born of Japanese parents— grows up to be a Japanese, not an American."[16] In addition, groups of white people like the California-based Native Sons and Daughters of the Golden West and the American Legion called for full-scale Japanese removal. FBI director J. Edgar Hoover sent a memo to Attorney General Francis Biddle on February 2, 1942, saying, "The necessity for mass evacuation is based primarily upon public and political pressure rather than on factual data. Public hysteria," he continued, has created a "widespread movement demanding complete evacuation of all Japanese, citizen and alien alike."[17] But the hysteria was only on the West Coast. Hawaii, on the other hand, where a large portion of the population was of Japanese descent and where the attack by the Japanese military had occurred, did not feel the need to remove from the island the Issei and Nisei among its residents.

In testimony to a congressional committee a year after Executive Order 9066 was implemented, General DeWitt explained why other people with ancestry from enemy countries did not face mass evacuation. Others of Italian and German descent were detained, but they were dealt with on a case-by-case basis, the way many had hoped the government would deal with suspicions about those of Japanese ancestry.

You needn't worry about the Italians at all except in certain cases. Also, the same for the Germans except in individual cases. But we

must worry about the Japanese all the time until he is wiped off
the map.

After that testimony, DeWitt said at a press conference that the Japanese were
excluded from the West Coast because "a Jap is a Jap." [18]

Akiko Mabuchi was nineteen years old when Japan bombed Pearl Harbor.
She lived in El Cerrito, California, across the bay from San Francisco, her
birthplace, with her Issei parents and two Nisei sisters, Michiko, twenty-three,
and Clara, fourteen. She had graduated from Richmond High School and was
working in El Cerrito, at the Contra Costa Flower Shop, which her family
owned and had named after their home county. Because their home and business was so near to military shipyards in Richmond, her Issei parents were
ordered to move within days from the area. By mid-December they had reset-
tled in Berkeley, in a rented house with four other Issei couples, leaving their
daughters to run the family business. "We were all in shock," said Akiko of
the orders for her parents to leave their home.

> When we heard about Pearl Harbor we couldn't believe it. We knew
> immediately it would affect us. We were just really numb. I'm sure
> the people that had to move were worried. The Isseis don't really
> show much emotion. They hold it in within themselves. They were
> probably worried sick and wondering what to do. They had to leave
> their children. They were helpless. We were just thankful they had a
> place to stay.

All people of Japanese heritage on the West Coast were allowed to travel only
within a five-mile zone of their homes. Akiko and her sister felt lucky that
their parents were able to find a place to live less than five miles away so they
could visit them. The sisters tried to run the flower shop, even though sales
fell because fewer and fewer customers wanted to patronize shops owned by
Japanese-Americans.

> They started slowly not coming. . . . There could have been new cus-
> tomers that would come to the door, see it was a flower shop and
> stop. And we'd go out and wait on them and they'd call us Japs and
> leave. It happened quite often during the period while we were still
> running the shop. It was an awful feeling because we were not to
> blame. Here we were being blamed for something that we didn't
> start. Nobody wanted to buy anything from us.

El Cerrito was mainly an Italian community. People who were once our friends began to shy away from us. I guess they worried that they may be next. It was a difficult and lonely time.

All people of Japanese ancestry were required to turn in any weapons, radios, cameras, or anything that could send signals and information to Japan or Japanese ships offshore. The government conducted random raids without search warrants in many homes of Japanese-Americans, seizing radios, cameras, and other property they considered suspicious. "We got frightened," said Akiko.

We destroyed and burned anything that was Japanese, like records and books. Whatever was Japanese we would just burn. A lot of people destroyed precious things, like swords and antique things they had brought from Japan. They were afraid to keep them. They didn't want to appear like enemy aliens.[19]

But such attempts to bury their heritage did not change the tide. Their faces, their hair, and their skin betrayed their efforts. Signs began appearing on telephone poles around their neighborhood from the Army telling "all persons of Japanese ancestry . . . both alien and non-alien" that they were to be evacuated from the area by a certain date and time. They were also told where to report to be picked up and taken away. By April of 1942, Akiko and her sisters saw the notices that they had to leave within the month. Like many others they had to find a way to close their shop quickly. Many Japanese had to sell their property and belongings at very cut rates. Stores and equipment that were worth $15,000 sold for $1,000. No one knew exactly where they were going or when or if they would ever come back. Businesses and family savings that had been built by the Issei and the Nisei over many decades were lost.

But Akiko and her family considered themselves lucky when the man who owned the furniture store next door to the flower shop agreed to watch their store and their home behind it while they were away in exchange for letting him store furniture in it. A customer agreed to take their two cats. All families had to register at control stations, where each family received the number that would identify them to authorities. The Mabuchis became family number 13451. From then on, each family member had to carry with them or wear the tag at all times with "13451" inscribed on it. The sisters began to pack the one suitcase that each of them was allowed to take to the camp. They were also told to bring their own bedding, towels, dishes, and any other necessities, but only what they could carry themselves. Some sort of mattress was all they were promised would be provided. Family 13451 was to be sent away, just like all the other families, to government-established "assembly centers," temporary quarters to contain the Japanese until relocation centers could be built farther inland.

The sisters met up with their parents in Berkeley one morning in late April and all headed to the pickup spot. There they boarded the bus that took them to Tanforan racetrack, outside San Francisco. On April 7, 1942, the *San Francisco News* reported on people, like the Mabuchi family, who were beginning to leave for the assembly centers in an article entitled "Goodby! Write Soon! Alien Exodus Like an Outing."

> With a few courteous bows and lots of promises to write soon and many sturdy American-type handshakes, the first Japanese involved in the military evacuation orders yesterday said farewell to San Francisco. Elders, steeped in their native traditions, displayed few emotions. . . . College-age boys and girls and their slightly older friends and relatives, most of them American citizens, still laughed, wisecracked in the latest slang, gave the scene the air of an outing. . . . As the buses rolled away friends remaining waved goodby, raised their thumbs in the air, made the victory V signal in final tribute. The younger Japanese responded, broad smiles on their faces; heads bobbed up and down in affirmation.[20]

Upon arrival at the Tanforan racetrack, the Mabuchi family of five was assigned to their stall. It had been occupied by a horse just the week before. That was to be their home, along with 8,000 other people in similar quarters, for the next six months. Akiko was stunned by it all.

> There were bugs and straw all around and we could see our neighbors through the cracks in the stall and hear conversations in the next stall. We slept on straw mattresses. My father made a big mistake when he tried to wash the floor. The dung beneath the boards smelled to high heaven. The latrines were a culture shock. There were two rows of toilets facing each other with no doors. When one flushed, they all flushed. There was no privacy in the showers either. At first we walked across the racetrack to the grandstand for our

meals. It was canned beans and canned wieners, and more beans and more wieners. Later mess halls were built and staffed by our own cooks and food got better. For diversion, we mainly hung out in front of the barracks and talked to pass the time away, or played cards. We had nothing to do.[21]

It was no wonder Akiko and her family were surprised by the assembly center. Like most all of the Issei and Nisei, they had complied with all government orders and trusted assurances that they would be protected and treated well. A March 1942 editorial in the *San Francisco News,* "Their Best Way to Show Loyalty," had told the people of San Francisco the government plans for Japanese residents. It urged strong support of the evacuation order by all citizens and complicity by the Japanese.

> Every indication has been given that the transfer will be made with the least possible hardship. . . . They may be housed in temporary quarters until permanent ones can be provided for them, but during the summer months that does not mean they will be unduly uncomfortable. Their property will be carefully protected by the Federal Government, their food and shelter will be provided . . . and they will be furnished plenty of entertainment and recreation. That is not according to the pattern of European concentration camps by any means.[22]

In the later part of October 1942, Akiko and her family were finally ordered to board the train to Topaz Relocation Center in Utah, the concentration camp where they would end up spending the next two and a half to three years.

> The train was one of those rickety old trains, a real antique. It was awful. It hardly moved and it was hot. And then they made us keep the shades down. I don't know why. Maybe they didn't want us to see anything. We were told we were going to Topaz, Utah. We heard it was in the middle of the desert. But you don't really realize how bad it is until you get there.[23]

Another young woman, Yoshiko Uchida, from Berkeley, also arrived at Topaz from Tanforan with her mother and father and sister, family number 13453. Uchida described in her book, *Desert Exile,* her approach to the camp on a bus that transported her family from the nearest town after their long train journey.

> We were entering the edge of the Sevier Desert . . . and the surroundings were now as bleak as a bleached bone. In the distance there were mountains rising above the valley with some majesty, but they were many miles away. The bus made the turn into the heart of the sun-drenched desert and there in the midst of nowhere were rows and rows of squat, tar-papered barracks sitting sullenly in the white, chalky sand. This was Topaz, the Central Utah Relocation Center, one of ten such camps located throughout the United States in equally barren and inaccessible areas.
>
> The entire camp was divided into forty-two blocks, each containing twelve barracks constructed around a mess hall, a latrine-washroom, and a laundry. The camp was one mile square and eventually housed 8,000 residents. . . . Everyone looked like flour-dusted pastry. In its frantic haste to construct this barrack city, the Army had removed every growing thing, and what had once been a peaceful lake bed, now churned up into one great mass of loose flour-like sand. With each step we sank two to three inches deep, sending up swirls of dust that crept into our eyes and mouths, noses and lungs.
>
> . . . Each barrack was one hundred feet in length, and divided into six rooms for families of varying sizes. We were assigned to a room in the center, about twenty by eighteen feet, designed for occupancy by four people. When we stepped into our room it contained nothing but four army cots and mattresses. . . . cracks were visible everywhere in the siding around the windows, and although our friends had swept out our room before we arrived, the dust was already seeping into it again from all sides.[24]

Both Yoshiko Uchida and Akiko Mabuchi were American citizens, young women in their twenties, and both had to live with their parents and sisters in one small, barren, dusty, makeshift room for more than two years. Like all of their fellow Nisei throughout the ten camps in the interior West, they were prisoners in their own country. They never knew when they might be freed. At most of the camps, dust storms were a common occurrence. The temperatures in the barren desert could range fifty degrees in one day, with hot days sometimes up to 130 degrees and cool nights. Two of the camps were in rural Arkansas, where humid heat and torrential rains were the bane of the evacuees' lives instead of dust storms. Because of the communal bathrooms, showers, laundry, and mess halls, waiting in long lines for basic needs took up hours each day. Women had to wash their family's huge loads of dust-laden clothes and bedding and towels by hand with only a few wooden washboards per laundry room and a sporadic water supply, only occasionally heated. Sometimes, people would be lathered up in the public shower when the water would go out.

Occasionally someone would receive a pass to go into the nearest town, Delta, Utah, and shop in a civilian store or eat in a civilian restaurant. These outings not only rejuvenated spirits but confirmed determination to get back to regular life, where one is allowed to walk freely in public and mingle as citizens in their own country. No shops with clothing were available to the internees. They had not been allowed to bring more than one suitcase. And they were given an allowance of only $3.75 a year for clothing. So the most available and often only source for clothing was a Sears or Montgomery Ward catalogue.

Everyone was required to work in the camps at jobs ranging from cleaning the latrines to cooking in the mess hall to teaching in camp schools. The pay scale was $12 per month for unskilled laborers, $16 per month for skilled laborers, and $19 per month for professionals. It was purposefully kept well below the wage of the lowest level Army private ($21 a month) to avoid criticism that the internees were being coddled. After losing most of their prewar assets and without any way to save at such reduced wages in the camps, most families had little prospect for comfort when and if they were ever released from imprisonment. Middle- and upper-middle-class families like the Mabuchis and the Uchidas were diminished to poverty levels they had never known before. Some of the younger people did manage to get permission to work in canneries or in harvesting sugar beets and other crops in the agricultural areas around some of the camps. Akiko Mabuchi spent one season at a cannery, which was a welcome break from the camp. She also worked in the camp school as a secretary and in the camp canteen as a cashier.

Doctors and nurses of Japanese descent manned the camp hospitals, but the medical facilities at the assembly centers and camps were limited at best. Many of the women in the camps were of childbearing age. Many of the elderly people were more susceptible to illness and disease after being taken from their homes and forced into such inhumane conditions.

Emi Somekawa had graduated from nursing school in 1939 in Portland,

Oregon, where she had been born and where she later met her husband. Her father and her husband were in business together running a fish company in the heart of Portland's Japanese Town. At the time of the evacuation the couple already had one young child and she was pregnant with another. She was appalled at the conditions under which she had to live out the last months of her pregnancy.

> The Portland Assembly Center was terrible. It's just amazing how people can think of putting another group of human beings into a place like that. There was so much horse and cow manure around.

They were put into a horse stall with wooden planks on the floor about an inch apart. Grass would grow up between the planks. They were to fill an empty bag with straw to be their mattress. They lived in the stable from May to September of 1942.

> My son was born in a horse stall. It was terrible, and that stench came up from the ground. . . . So of course we didn't want to stay in it any longer than we had to; we'd just go over there and sleep at night. So most of the time people would spend the time right outside the door . . . there was a barbed wire fence, only about five feet from the outside.

Somekawa and her family were transferred to Tule Lake Relocation Center in northeastern California. She served as a nurse in the camp hospital.

> The hospital facilities . . . were very minimal, to say the least. The camp-based hospitals were not furnished with a sufficient number of bedpans, urinals, or washbasins. We never had enough linens, and we'd run around looking for blankets and pillows. . . . There were a lot of unnecessary deaths in camp. . . . There were not enough people to watch the patients.
>   . . . I remember a pregnant woman came in with just terrible pain, and she was having what we call an abruptio placentae, where there's bleeding in the uterus and it's absolutely necessary to operate right away and do a cesarean section. But there was no doctor to do the surgery. The woman died of a hemorrhage without delivering the baby.[25]

From mid-1942, any men of draft age who were citizens of the U.S. but had Japanese ancestry had been classified as 4-C, "enemy aliens," and were not eligible for the military. Japanese-American women were also excluded from the military, including the WAC and nursing corps. But in January 1943 the War Department rethought that position. The OWI was having trouble combating the perception overseas that the war in the Pacific was a race war. The enlistment of Nisei men, it was decided, would be a good propaganda move. So the Army began to create an all-Nisei unit. At the camps the recruitment efforts were met with contempt and disbelief.

Akiko Mabuchi said she remembered when recruiters came to Topaz.

> Some families thought that was crazy. . . . Some thought it was awful that they should have the nerve to come and draft the people who they put into the concentration camps. Some of the men just wanted to go because they wanted to prove that they were loyal to the U.S. And they lost their lives in doing that.[26]

Yoshiko Uchida said both men and women attended the meeting at Topaz where Army recruiters were answering questions. People were especially suspicious of the idea of making an all-Nisei unit, thinking they were to be segregated so they could be sent into the worst, most deadly conditions. Why, they asked, could the Nisei not be integrated into the Army like white citizens? Why were there not special all-German or all-Italian units? Uchida said the Army answered by saying, "As an all-Nisei combat team . . . their actions would gain special attention, allowing the Nisei to prove their loyalty in a dramatic, forceful way to the whole country."[27]

Many were even more outraged at that answer. And to add insult to injury, the recruiting efforts came just as all internment camp residents above the age of seventeen, citizen and noncitizen alike, were ordered to fill out questionnaires measuring their loyalty to the United States. They were told the information gathered would be used to expedite their eventual release from the camps. Two questions were particularly disturbing. Question number 27 asked, "Are you willing to serve in the armed forces of the United States on combat duty, wherever ordered?" This was vexing to some Nisei men, who had not been allowed to serve in the military previously. Nisei women were asked if they would serve in the WAC or the Army Nurse Corps. Again, because Nisei women had been barred from the military up to that time, the question seemed peculiar. For Issei men and women question 27 made no sense either since they were not allowed to be citizens and so could not serve in the military.[28]

The next question, number 28, was even more troubling to many. It asked both Issei and Nisei if they would swear "unqualified allegiance" to the United States and "forswear any form of allegiance or obedience to the Japanese Emperor, or any other foreign government, power or organization." For the Issei, a yes answer would mean they would be left without a country. For the Nisei, a yes answer implied that they had started out with allegiances to another country besides their own, which they argued they had not.[29] About 22 percent of the 21,000 Nisei men eligible for the draft solved the problem by answering no to both questions. They became known as the "no-no boys."[30] Most Nisei women, like Akiko Mabuchi, answered yes to both questions. "I filled it out the proper way," she said, "because I am loyal to the United States."[31]

The WAC did not allow Nisei women into the ranks until November of 1943. On a much smaller scale and with much less fanfare, the WAC had also sent recruiters to the internment camps during 1943 to determine the interest and loyalty of Japanese-American women. The first Nisei woman inducted into the WAC was Frances Iritani on November 10, 1943. She had not been interned because she and her family were among the few who managed to leave the West Coast before internment was implemented. The first Nisei who had lived in a concentration camp inducted into the WAC was Iris Watanabe, a former resident of Poston in Arizona as well as of Amache in Colorado. Her mother and younger sister were still imprisoned in Amache when Iris was inducted in December 1943.

By mid-February of 1944, only thirteen Nisei women had enlisted in the WAC. In March the WAC increased its recruiting efforts among the Nisei. Soon other Nisei joined, but never in large numbers. The Army Nurse Corps also eventually lifted its ban on Japanese-American women in 1943. But restrictions and loyalty investigations meant not many registered as nurses until after the war was over. The Navy did not admit Nisei women during the war.

But 33,000 Nisei men did join the military, meeting the challenge to prove their loyalty. The all-Nisei 442nd Regimental Combat Team, formed in World War II, became the most decorated regiment in American history. The unit had 9,486 casualties in less than two years of combat participation, a rate higher than that of most units.

But it was not only on the battlefield that Japanese-Americans lost their lives. At least nine people were shot and killed by prison guards at the internment camps for getting too close to the fence. At Topaz, a sixty-three-year-old man was shot and killed by military police in April 1944. The MP said James Hatsuki Wakasa, an Issei, was trying to crawl under the fence and ignored warnings from the guard towers above the camp. The sentry who shot him was a disabled Pacific war veteran. But Wakasa was shot in the chest and would have been facing the guard, so it was hard for residents to understand how he could have been crawling away. Most believed instead that he was confused and did not hear or understand the guard's warnings. Court-martial proceedings were held for the guard, but he was found not guilty.[32]

Akiko Mabuchi remembered the killing. She said the authorities "tried to keep it hush-hush, so there wouldn't be a riot." But everyone at the camp knew about it and there was a big funeral. Since they were under armed guard, Mabuchi said, very few if any internees ever thought seriously of escape. Mostly it was older people and children who inadvertently wandered too close to the fence. It seemed ridiculous to everyone, Mabuchi said, that the guards would think anyone would actually try to escape. "Where would you escape to," she asked, "in the middle of the desert? You'd get bitten by scorpions. And coyotes were there. . . . You'd have to walk a long way to get out of the desert."[33]

By June 1944, after more than two years in which approximately 120,000 Japanese-Americans had been held in ten internment camps in the noncoastal U.S., Harold Ickes, secretary of the interior, wrote to President Roosevelt about his objections to what he saw as their ongoing illegal imprisonment, which he called "clearly unconstitutional." He added, "I will not comment at this time on the justification or lack thereof for the original evacuation order. But I do say that the continued retention of these innocent people in the relocation centers would be a blot upon the history of this country."[34]

When Ickes did finally comment on the situation after the war in 1946, he said:

As a member of President Roosevelt's administration, I saw the United States Army give way to mass hysteria over the Japanese. . . . It began to round up indiscriminately the Japanese who had been born in Japan, as well as those born here. Crowded into cars like cattle, these hapless people were hurried away to hastily constructed and thoroughly inadequate concentration camps, with soldiers with nervous muskets on guard, in the great American desert. We gave the fancy name of "relocation centers" to these dust bowls, but they were concentration camps nonetheless.[35]

Originally Milton S. Eisenhower, the brother of Dwight D. Eisenhower, was appointed as national director of the War Relocation Administration, the civilian organization charged with overseeing the internment camps. But very early into the job Eisenhower had grave doubts about the morality of the evacuation. He resigned in June 1942, telling his successor, Dillon Myer, "I can't sleep and do this job." Ten months later, on the one-year anniversary statement of the WRA, Dillon Myer said:

> Life in a relocation center is an unnatural and un-American sort of life. Keep in mind that the evacuees were charged with nothing except having Japanese ancestors; yet the very fact of their confinement in relocation centers fosters suspicion of their loyalties and adds to their discouragement. It has added to the contention of the enemy that we are fighting a race war; that this nation preaches democracy and practices racial discrimination.[36]

When the evacuees finally were released from their desert imprisonment in 1944 and 1945, many never returned to the West Coast. They had to find ways to make new lives and start over with very little. Akiko Mabuchi was given $25 and a one-way ticket to Chicago in 1945, where she married her fiancé, Mitusuru Toba. They had met and become engaged in the camp. They raised two children and stayed in Chicago. Akiko Mabuchi Toba's sisters and parents returned to El Cerrito, and slowly rebuilt the flower shop into a successful business. Yoshiko Uchida attended graduate school at Smith College after her internment.

It took more than forty years for the government to offer any official apology to the internment camp victims. In 1988, President Ronald Reagan, who had been a captain in the U.S. Army's movie unit during World War II, signed legislation that granted $20,000 to each surviving evacuee.

Akiko Mabuchi Toba said that years later people still wondered why her generation, and the women in particular, appeared so passive in the face of the internment. She said it was important for everyone to understand they were not being complacent at the time. Instead, they believed they were displaying a steely kind of defiance. It was their sole option in those times, given the racial climate of the country and what had been ingrained in them by their Issei parents.

> Our generation was raised never to call attention to ourselves, to work twice as hard as others, and above all never to bring shame to the family. We had a strict upbringing. And women, in particular, were never to cause any waves in society. I think it was because our parents were having enough trouble at the time making their way in America and showing their loyalty, and they didn't want us to make it harder.
> So when the war broke out, the only thing we felt we could do was go behind that barbed wire to prove we were loyal. I lost three years of my life and my parents lost everything they had built up over the years. But I sure hope we proved it.[37]

CHAPTER TEN

Qualified Successes

POLITICIANS, JOURNALISTS, DOCTORS, BASEBALL PLAYERS, AND OTHER PROFESSIONAL WOMEN

The individual woman is required . . . a thousand times a day to choose either to accept her appointed role and thereby rescue her good disposition out of the wreckage of her self-respect, or else follow an independent line of behavior and rescue her self-respect out of the wreckage of her good disposition.

REPRESENTATIVE JEANETTE RANKIN,
REPUBLICAN—MONTANA,
First woman elected to the U.S. Congress[1]

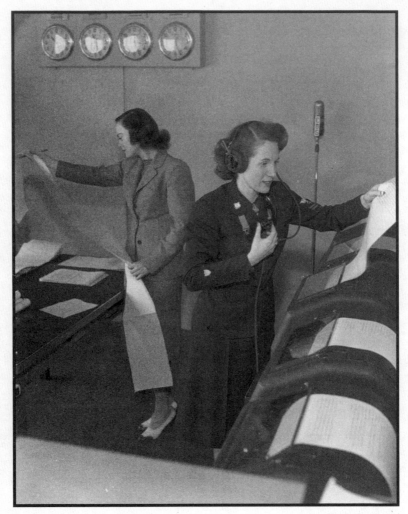

U.S. Coast Guard

T HROUGHOUT THE TWENTIETH CENTURY women made strides into professional and public life like never before. When World War II broke out in the middle of the century, women already pioneering in fields such as politics, journalism, law, medicine, and science found career opportunities that during peacetime they may never have dreamed possible. In the same way that industry and the military opened up for women during the war, women with professional aspirations also made gains while the men were away at war.

TO SIT IN THE HIGH SEATS OF POWER

The effects of women gaining the right to vote in 1920 were starting to be seen in politics during World War II, the first major war in which women had a presence in government. Some of the most tangible early evidence of that played out on the day after Pearl Harbor was attacked.

On December 8, 1941, just as Congress was poised to declare war on Japan, the all-out fervor was dampened briefly by a congresswoman from Montana. In the midst of a hawkish debate on the House floor, Jeanette Rankin, a lifelong pacifist, repeatedly tried to speak out against war. But she was met by shouts of "Sit down, sister" from the gallery, and was ignored by the speaker of the house, Sam Rayburn. During the roll call she finally got a chance to voice her opinion. Everyone knew that she did not believe in war, but she added a twist to her reason for voting against it that could only have come from a female politician at the time. Alluding to the fact that in 1941 women still were not allowed in the military, she stood up and said, "As a woman, I can't go to war and I refuse to send anyone else." Then she cast a lone nay vote, the only politician to register any objection to going to war on either the House or Senate floor that day. Loud boos and hisses erupted.

Minutes later, Rankin was forced to lock herself in a phone booth just outside the chamber for her own protection against the mobs jeering her. From there, she called the Capitol police to escort her back to her office, where she locked herself in for safety. A few days later when the vote to declare war against Germany and Italy came up, Rankin abstained, not voting for war, but not appearing to sympathize with Hitler by voting against it either.

Rankin had gone against the tide before. On April 6, 1917, Rankin had voted against American involvement in World War I. Hers was not the only vote against the war that time, but it was a bold move all the same. Just days before, on April 2, 1917, Rankin was sworn into office as the first woman elected to the U.S. Congress. Even though women did not yet have the right to vote nationally, women had won voting rights in Montana and a few other states. Rankin became the sole female in Congress. So the first vote by the first woman in Congress was against war. Many years later she talked about the meaning of that action.

> I was conscious of my position. This was the first time in the history of civilization that a woman had been elected to a major legislative body in a free country. I was a symbol and a representative, not only of women in Montana or the United States, but of women in all nations and ages.

Expressing her opinion in that antiwar vote in 1917 cost her her seat in Congress in the next election. It would be two decades before she was elected to Congress a second time. And again, her 1941 vote against war cost her her congressional job in the next election. She said later, "Never for one second could I face the idea that I would send young men to be killed for no other reason than to save my seat in Congress."[2]

But not all women were able to make such bold declarations, and not all women agreed with Rankin's stand on World War II. By December 1941, there were seven other female legislators besides Rankin in the House, and one in the Senate, and they all voted for the declarations of war.

The fact that a diversity of political opinion was expressed among women was not a slight to Rankin as much as it was a confirmation of her ideals. Rankin had always fought for the right of women to bring their voices into the political forum. That is why she was active in the long campaign to win voting rights for women in the first place. And Rankin had helped write the Nineteenth Amendment to the Constitution, which granted women's suffrage in the U.S. in 1920.

> We did not labor in suffrage just to bring the vote to women, but to allow women to express their opinions and become effective in gov-

ernment. Men and women are like right and left hands. It doesn't make sense not to use both.[3]

But even with the power of the ballot, the path to power was not always as direct for other women as it had been for Rankin. She was one of the few women in Congress during World War II who got her seat on her own instead of through replacing a husband who died in office.[4] By 1945, fifteen women had served in the House during all or part of the war; six of them had come into office to fill their husband's seat after he died. Only one woman served in the Senate during World War II, Hattie Wyatt Caraway from Arkansas. She also had replaced her husband after he died in 1931 and went on to be elected in her own right in 1932 and was reelected a few more times and served through January 2, 1945.

Edith Nourse Rogers was among the first to enter Congress by replacing her husband when he died in 1925. But Rogers, a Republican from Massachusetts, went on to win seventeen more consecutive elections, racking up thirty-five years in Congress and making her the longest-serving woman in congressional history. One of Rogers's most notable achievements was her championing of women's entry into the military. She introduced the bill in 1941 that established the Women's Army Auxiliary Corps. Originally the bill was frowned upon by most in Congress and the military, but three weeks after Pearl Harbor, on Christmas Eve 1941, it passed. In 1943, Rogers spoke of what drove her to push through the legislation.

> I was convinced that the army and navy would need women to re-
> place men in certain duties after the last world war. But it was
> twenty-five years before I was able to get through Congress a mea-
> sure which created the Women's Army Auxiliary Corps.[5]

Rogers had served in the Red Cross during World War I, and worked on veterans issues in the Harding, Coolidge, and Hoover administrations. She is noted for having helped secure pensions for Army nurses in 1925. Rogers also was among the first in Congress to speak out against Hitler's treatment of Jews, before American involvement in World War II. In addition, she co-authored the landmark GI Bill of Rights, which provided education and other benefits to returning World War II veterans.

Another congresswoman, Margaret Chase Smith, a Republican from Maine, also got her start in politics when she took over her husband's seat after his death in 1940. Like Rogers, Smith was concerned with issues surrounding women in the military. Smith served on the Naval Affairs Committee, and so focused her efforts on the status of the WAVES, SPARs, and Marines. Three times she introduced the bill to allow them, like the WACs, to serve overseas. Three times she was unable to get it passed. It was almost impossible to persuade the men of Congress to authorize Navy women to venture past the shores of the U.S. Apparently, the same mix of protectiveness and underestimation of female abilities that dogged women throughout World War II were the main reasons for Congress's delay. Finally, Smith was able to get a compromise measure passed in 1944, which allowed women to serve only in the "American Area" (North and South America, Hawaii, Alaska, the Canal Zone, and the Caribbean). Smith went on to a Senate seat in 1949, becoming the first woman elected to both houses of Congress.[6]

While the women in Congress were not a huge force, they at least made a showing during the war. In the cabinet of the president only one woman had broken through. Franklin D. Roosevelt appointed Frances Perkins secretary of labor in 1933. She was the first female cabinet member in U.S. history. She is still the longest-serving labor secretary, having held the post for Roosevelt's entire administration through the Depression and World War II, resigning in May 1945 after his death. In that time, Perkins helped usher in FDR's New Deal programs. She was one of the principal architects of the Social Security Act. And she was a leader in enacting the Fair Labor Standards Act, which instituted the minimum wage and the forty-hour workweek.

It was in the early part of the century that Perkins had become committed to social work, after time she spent in Chicago working with social reformer Jane Addams. Perkins was educated at Mount Holyoke, the University of Pennsylvania, and Columbia University. Although married, she kept her maiden name throughout her career, considered a radical move at the time.

Her strong commitment to protecting workers, especially women, was cemented in 1911. She happened to be having tea across the street from the Asch Building in Greenwich Village, when a massive fire broke out in the building, which housed the Triangle Shirtwaist Company. Perkins saw the famous scene firsthand, as 146 people, mostly young girls working in the company's sweatshop conditions, died in less than an hour. Many leapt to their deaths from upper-story windows because rooms in which they worked were locked or narrow stairways allowed them no other escape. The owner had locked the workers in because he was afraid they would try to steal the goods.

That incident gave Perkins a window into the obscenely harsh working conditions that many of the lowest-paid workers endured.

By the time Roosevelt offered her the position of labor secretary she knew she had a rare opportunity to effect change. She said to her friend Carrie Chapman Catt, the well-known suffragist:

> The door might not be opened to a woman again for a long, long time and I had a kind of duty to other women to walk in and sit down on the chair that was offered, and so establish the right of others long hence and far distant in geography to sit in the high seats.

Of her early days in office Perkins said:

> I was apprehensive and on guard at the first official cabinet meeting. As the only woman member, I did not want my colleagues to get the impression that I was too talkative. I resolved not to speak unless asked to do so. . . . My colleagues looked at me with tense curiosity. I think some weren't sure I could speak.[7]

By World War II she had found her voice in government. And occasionally she even used it to speak out against the efforts of some of the women in Congress. Perkins saw clearly that women were not treated equally in the workplace, and she was solidly in favor of equal pay and equal rights for women. She disagreed, however, with the main idea that had sprung up during the two preceding decades to remedy the situation: the Equal Rights Amendment.

After the suffrage amendment gave women the right to vote in 1920, women saw equality under the law as the next constitutional hurdle for women that needed addressing. Suffragist Alice Paul wrote the original version of the Equal Rights Amendment (ERA) in 1923. It read: "Men and women shall have equal rights, throughout the United States and every place subject to its jurisdiction." The ERA went on to be introduced and defeated in every congressional session since 1923. But supporters thought the ERA might have a better chance of passing during World War II, when women were needed in the workplace like never before. The ERA had appeared on both the Democratic and Republican party platforms in the early 1940s. And the war had heightened awareness of the inequities women faced in the workplace and other areas of public life.

In 1943, Alice Paul rewrote the amendment to read more like the Fifteenth Amendment, which gave black people equal protection under the law,
and like the Nineteenth-Amendment granting women the vote. It read:
"Equality of rights under the law shall not be denied or abridged by the
United States or by any state on account of sex." But again in 1943, the ERA
did not pass.

Women's labor groups had aligned with Frances Perkins and worked to
implement protective legislation for women in the workplace, limiting work
hours and extreme conditions. For many years they had been most concerned
with making sure women workers were not exploited in the low-level jobs
they typically held. To Perkins and the labor groups, the ERA seemed antithet-
ical to that mission because they feared its broad wording might be used to
nullify the protections they had gained. Supporters of the ERA were mostly
professional women and women in business who felt any legislation that
set out separate rules based on gender hindered their freedom to advance in
the workplace. It was a tricky bind. Even though liberals in Congress were in
favor of women's equality they tended to support the labor groups and not
the ERA.[8]

By the end of World War II, a new urgency arose for ERA supporters.
Congresswoman Rogers was particularly concerned that the gains women
had made during the national emergency would not all be lost in peacetime.
Rogers said:

> War is like a flood or a hurricane. As soon as it is over people lose in-
> terest in preparing against a recurrence. . . . Because some, weary of
> the strain of war, will want the illusion that all can be as it was before
> the war began. They will try to force all women out of the factories,
> the professions, the armed services, try to relegate them back to
> housework. We must plan to fit a certain number of women into our
> postwar economic life.[9]

In thinking of the fate of women after the war, Rogers teamed with Representative Smith to become the first women to cosponsor the Equal Rights
Amendment in 1945. "Women gained the vote," Smith said, "as free citizens
of the United States in the last war period. It is fitting that the principle of
equal rights should be recognized in this war period."

Up until 1943, the ERA had always been sponsored by men. But once
again, in 1945, the ERA did not pass. (It was introduced in every session of

Congress through 1972, when it finally passed in both houses. The 1972 version of the amendment was essentially the same as Alice Paul had rewritten it in 1945. By the 1970s, however, liberal groups had come to support the ERA, and more conservative elements were against it. Yet once again it did not become law. Only thirty-five of the needed thirty-eight states ratified the amendment in time to meet an arbitrary 1982 deadline set for its acceptance.)[10]

Without legislation to ensure women equal access to the upper levels of power, women began to make more indirect inroads. An influential voice in that realm was Clare Boothe Luce, a Republican from Connecticut. Married to Time-Life owner Henry Luce, Clare Boothe Luce was a playwright and magazine writer as well as a politician. She voiced the need for government to open up to women in an article she wrote for *Woman's Home Companion* in 1943.

> Although in our own country today there are few outstanding women leaders in high governmental and administrative posts, the importance of women's activity in community life and political life is wholly and clearly recognized. Thus in both our major political party organizations we have made room for women. Theoretically in many states they can be elected to any office, though tradition is still against their being elected to the higher offices. . . . The practical politicians in the lower echelons, anyway, have long since recognized the fact that women can play quite as effective a role in party politics as men.
>
> . . . If the government really wants to get women all-out for the war as well as the peace, it is high time it began to put more and more able women into the bureaucratic and administrative end of things in Washington.

Luce was complimentary of a woman many admired, the wife of the Chinese leader Chiang Kai-shek, Mayling Soong, who became known as Madame Chiang Kai-shek. China sided with the Allies against the Japanese during World War II. And the leader's Chinese-born, but Wellesley-educated, wife became a popular ambassador of sorts in America for her husband and their country. In speaking of the value of female leaders, Luce said Madame Chiang had made "an extraordinary and special impact . . . on her own nation and other nations—an impact that could only be made by a woman." Luce said that during Madame Chiang's visit to the U.S. in early 1943 she touched many with her goodwill. "It would be impossible," said Luce, "to conceive of any man speaking in the accents of tenderness and faith and spirituality that Madame Chiang employed during her American visit." Luce added, "And yet these are the very accents in leadership for which the world so sorely grieves at the moment."[11]

In February 1943, Madame Chiang addressed a joint session of Congress. It was one highlight of a U.S. tour that enhanced her popularity among Americans and confirmed the alliance of her country with the Allied forces fighting Japan. She said in part:

> I came to your country as a little girl. I know your people. I have lived with them. I spent the formative years of my life amongst your people. I speak your language, not only the language of your hearts, but also your tongue. So coming here today I feel that I am also coming home.
>
> I believe, however, that it is not only I who am coming home; I feel that if the Chinese people could speak to you in your own tongue, or if you could understand our tongue, they would tell you that basically and fundamentally we are fighting for the same cause . . . that the "four freedoms," which your President proclaimed to the world resound through our vast land as the gong of freedom . . . of the United Nations and the death knell of the aggressors.
>
> I assure you that our people are willing and eager to cooperate with you in the realization of these ideals, because we want to see to it that they do not echo as empty phrases, but become realities for ourselves, for our children, for our children's children, and for all mankind.[12]

Madame Chiang used one of the few influential roles available to women on the world stage at the time, her status as the wife of a male politician. America's first lady, Eleanor Roosevelt, would take that role to new heights during her husband's tenure in office, including during World War II. She used the position to advance the substantive causes she supported and in particular to speak for women.

The first lady was at the forefront of many a change during the war involving the status of women. She advocated for women working in war industries in many ways. Most notably, she pushed the idea of government-supported day care for the children of working mothers, and of after-school care as well. She took stands against discrimination toward black women.

And she advocated on behalf of women in the military. Eleanor said of herself and her relationship to her husband's presidency, "I think I sometimes acted as a spur, even though the spurring was not always wanted or welcome."[13]

In an article in the November 1944 *Ladies' Home Journal* entitled "How to Take Criticism," Eleanor Roosevelt spoke of handling those critical of her outspoken activities as first lady.

> One of the things which my critics most frequently stress is the fact that I am not elected to any office, so it is clear that I must be seeking publicity. . . . The President's wife is not an elected official, but she has certain obligations. . . . In the natural course of events . . . you get to know a good deal about the country and its people, and conditions and situations as they exist. This gives you an opportunity perhaps to be of service and here is where criticism centers.
>
> Should the President's wife, who is not elected to any office, be interested in working conditions, for instance? She can have rare opportunities for knowing about them if she has eyes, ears and understanding. Should she be blind, deaf and dumb?[14]

Eleanor's answer to that hypothetical question was a resounding no. In a letter to a friend she expressed her concern about her son serving in the war. Her words could also have been a motto of sorts for her tenure as first lady. She wrote, "Perhaps we have to learn that life was not meant to be lived in security but with adventurous courage."[15] That was the spirit with which Eleanor took the role of first lady to new realms and influenced her husband in ways first ladies before her had not done. As Anna Rosenberg, a labor adviser to the president and official in the War Manpower Commission, said of the first lady, "He would never have become the kind of President he was without her."[16]

Another Washington wife and future first lady who added to her power base in many ways during World War II was Lady Bird Johnson, wife of Lyndon Johnson, a congressman from Texas at the start of the war. After Pearl Harbor he enlisted in the Navy and went to the South Pacific, leaving his wife to take over and run his congressional office. Lady Bird, who had a degree in journalism from the University of Texas, said that Lyndon Johnson "introduced me to the world of politics. It was his life and his career, and I wanted to serve and help, but it was never really my life." Yet just like other women entering jobs during wartime that they had never had the opportunity to do before, running her husband's congressional office showed Johnson that she had her own talents and skills. "I learned a good deal about self-esteem. It gave me the feeling that I could hold down a job if suddenly I didn't have Lyndon."

During that time Lady Bird also learned politics was not a reliable way to make a living, since it was subject to the whims of the electorate. She and her husband wanted a family, so Lady Bird decided to take matters into her own hands. Her husband came home in July 1942, after the war emergency caused President Roosevelt to order all members of Congress back to Washington. Soon thereafter, Lady Bird took $17,500 of her inheritance from her mother and bought a failing radio station in Austin. KTBS was an unprofitable 250-watt station when Lady Bird came in, losing at least $600 monthly. But Lady Bird turned it around by scrupulously tracking ad revenues, thereby making the business side of the station more accountable and efficient. The station became the cornerstone of the Johnsons' media holdings, which turned profits in the multimillion-dollar range. In the midst of all this, she and Lyndon began trying to start a family. After three miscarriages, Lady Bird finally gave birth to a daughter, Lynda Bird, in 1944.

She had learned a lot from her business success, mothering duties, and taking over her husband's job while he was away during the war. And almost twenty years later, it all served her well, when, as first lady, she became one of the most influential women in Washington.[17]

GOVERNMENT GIRLS

Unlike the relatively few women in politics, most of the women in the halls of power in Washington during the war had no influence on government policy or in shaping the future of the country. They were the clerical workers, called "government girls," who came to town to do the paperwork of war. In November of 1941, Sally Reston wrote an article in *The New York Times Magazine*, "Girls' Town—Washington." The subtitle said, "The capital has been captured and subdued by an army of young women workers, 80,000 strong."[18]

These workers ended a moratorium on hiring women for government jobs that had lasted in Washington throughout the nineteenth century. At the Patent Office women were allowed to do the most menial paperwork and cataloguing, but they had to do their work at home and mail it in, so that they would never show up in the office. They were required to receive their salaries by mail in the name of a male relative, since women's names were not to appear on the government payroll. The government girls were still facing down the legacy of such attitudes when they arrived in Washington in the early 1940s. And their pay was usually far less than any man working in government, despite the fact that the cost of living in Washington was one of the highest in the country during the war years.[19]

Sally Reston's *New York Times* article described what drew the women to the nation's capital.

> These new national defense recruits, like the young men of their own generation being drafted into the new United States Army, came from all over the country. On the whole, they are a pretty unsophisticated lot. They're not as slick as the white-collar brigade in Wall Street, partly because many of them are away from home for the first time and partly because they are younger than the typical New York stenographer. In general they range from 18 to 25 years of age.
>
> . . . Their reasons for coming to Washington are fairly clear. They didn't come down here to beat Adolph Hitler, and they didn't come with any great understanding of the fundamental conflict between the ideals of the youth of Germany and the youth of this country. They came to get a job. They came to get between $100 and $120 a month, because many of them are helping support their families at home. They came for security, because after the six-month probationary period in the government service it's pretty hard to get fired. And they came for adventure just like the stage-struck youngsters who go to Broadway in New York.

The article went on to note some of the problems the young women faced. Because of the monotony of the typing pool, and the housing shortage and single man shortage in D.C. during the war, the spirits of the women needed bolstering. But no one much took it as their task to help the women's morale when they were relegated to monotonous jobs far from home with not many prospects of eligible men, good pay, or comfortable living.

In fact, *The New York Times* predicted a bleak and unencouraging future for the women who chose the route of government jobs. Reston's article ended on a downbeat note:

Most social observers here are of the opinion that just as there were
thousands of unmarried women in the capital after the last war, so,
too, after this one there will be left a new generation of spinsters, living one day on their hard-earned government pensions.[20]

NEWSHENS

In the same way the military had been an all-male bastion before the war, so
journalism had been almost as closed to women. A few pioneering women
broke through the ranks, but they were the exception. When potential young
male reporters were sent to war as soldiers, slowly the field opened up for females. By 1945, the military had accredited 127 American female reporters
and photographers to cover the war overseas for various newspapers and
magazines. Numerous other women took up editorial and reporting jobs
at magazines and newspapers on the home front, vacated by draft-age men
who had gone to war. In 1940, thirty-three female newspaper and magazine
reporters were accredited to cover House and Senate proceedings on Capitol Hill in Washington. By 1944, there were ninety-eight. And of the 400 reporters accredited to cover the White House in 1944, thirty-seven were
women.[21]

But in Washington, women were not allowed into the National Press
Club, a gathering place for journalists where tips and deal making, as well as
important press conferences, took place. In 1919 women had started their
own Women's National Press Club, but it never had the same kind of status
or professional access as the male club. In the 1930s, Eleanor Roosevelt
started weekly female-only press conferences in order to pressure news organizations to hire at least one female reporter. These two organized efforts
to bolster women journalists were no cure-all, but they did foster many of the
serious female reporters who covered the war. One of the leaders among
them was May Craig, a Washington and overseas correspondent for a few
Maine-based newspapers in the Gannett chain and the head of the Women's
National Press Club. "The war has given women a chance to show what they
can do in the news world," said Craig in 1944, "and they have done well."[22]

However, it would be a long time before the gates to male privilege in the
profession opened much farther. The National Press Club, for example, did
not allow women into its fold until 1971. Before that, women who wanted to

cover the many important press conferences and dinners with newsmakers held at the club were relegated to a balcony above the dining area. They would try to catch what was said from the podium. And during dinners they watched as their male colleagues ate and drank, sitting on the main floor.

One stark wartime example of that kind of unfairness occurred in 1944, when May Craig filed an official complaint with the White House Correspondents' Association. The thirty-seven White House correspondents who were female had been excluded from the association's annual dinner. It was the only dinner outside the White House that President Roosevelt attended during wartime. In stating the women's side of the issue, a *Time* magazine article on the exclusion noted that after all other options were exhausted women had made some strides into wartime political press circles in the capital city. "None could dispute," the article said, "that Washington's editors need women reporters and writers. At the bottom of the manpower barrel, they are recruiting more and more women." The article went on to say:

> The newshens cover almost everything. A few have been on the police beat. They help on every major Government bureau beat, and on two—OPA and Agriculture—women alone represent one major press association. The editors' consensus is that they do remarkably well. . . . The girls contend that the traditional greeting of officials at press conferences—"Good morning, gentlemen"—is no longer fit for so many feminine ears.[23]

In 1943 a *Newsweek* article about the increased number of women in the wartime Washington press corps said, "The women have not won their battle for equal rights with men reporters without something of a struggle. It took powerful lobbying for them to get a powder room in the Capitol. Even today they complain that many gatherings at which they might meet good news contacts are usually stag affairs."

The article went on to say that "The ladies of the Washington press differ as widely as their styles of writing." But instead of giving examples of any of their words or accomplishments, it then only described them by their attire and physical appearances. About May Craig it said: "Mrs. Craig, who always wears blue, belies her petite blue-eyed prettiness by being one of the spunkiest newspaperwomen and will argue at the drop of one of the perky hats she perches on her top-knotted long hair." The article described Winifred Mallon as a "veteran correspondent of *The New York Times*," adding only that she "peers with dignity over spectacles which slip down her nose." Then it called Lee Carson of the International News Service, Mallon's "antithesis." The article went on to say that Carson, "in dressy clothes, high-heeled shoes, theatrical hairdo's, and liquid make-up that gives her face a mask-like appearance resembling that of a Balinese dancer, is the siren of the women's group." The *Newsweek* article ended with what seemed to be an attempt at a high compliment. The female journalists, it concluded, were "women who can do a man's job but still look like women in not too severely tailored clothes and becoming hats." [24]

The women who reported from locales outside Washington and New York were less scrutinized for their appearance. In fact, both male and female journalists working overseas had to wear official uniforms. The female version looked much like the WAC uniforms, with an armband that said "War Correspondent." Reporters and photographers were given the honorary rank of captain so that if they were captured and held prisoner they would not be mistaken for spies and would be treated as officers.

One of the most prolific and accomplished of all female World War II photographers was Margaret Bourke-White, who worked for *Life* magazine. In 1941 she showed the world the first pictures of World War II in Russia with Nazis bombing the Kremlin at night. In 1942 she was accredited as the first female photographer in the war and had a uniform designed for her that all female correspondents eventually wore.

> I was allowed to do everything to build up my story: photograph the early dawn briefings, go on practice flights, whatever I needed except the one thing that really counted—go on an actual combat mission. There was not a whisper of a double standard about the decision, but as though written in invisible ink, it was there for all to read. Male correspondents who applied got permission. My requests got me nowhere. [25]

Eventually she made more and more strides. In December 1942, her ship was torpedoed on the way to cover the invasion of North Africa. Bourke-White had taken the ship because she had been denied permission to fly to North Africa as male correspondents had done, since flying was thought to be too dangerous for women. On board the ship with Bourke-White were American and British nurses, five WAACs, and Eisenhower's private secretary, Kay Summersby. Bourke-White had managed to take two cameras with her when she boarded the lifeboat. And true to her reputation as a tireless worker, she snapped photos in the night and as the day dawned. Finally, a destroyer rescued her and the others on their lifeboat. Bourke-White wrote about the experience to accompany her photos of it in the February 22, 1943, *Life*.

> The skipper, an enthusiast about photography . . . helped hold me on the gunwales of the bobbing lifeboat to get as favorable a viewpoint as possible for snapping my fellow passengers. One of the American nurses had unaccountably saved an orange which she passed out generously, section by section, as far as it would go.
>
> . . . After a few more hours we could make out the shape of our destroyer appearing over the horizon and by her interrupted course we guessed that she was picking up other survivors. . . . As soon as we were dragged aboard her we were given cups of steaming Ovaltine. I climbed up to the gun station and photographed the last of the family of lifeboats as their occupants were helped to deck. The man who had died from a cracked skull was handed up strapped to a pair of oars. Another boat yielded a soldier who had died from shock and exposure. Several nurses were brought up, suffering from sprained ankles, twisted arms and broken legs.[26]

The incident inspired the Alfred Hitchcock movie *Lifeboat*, with Tallulah Bankhead playing a character loosely based on Margaret Bourke-White.

As *Life*'s representative, Bourke-White went on to take combat photos in Italy and photos of air raids over Germany. She also was on one of the most gruesome and grisly assignments for wartime journalists.

Bourke-White marched with General Patton and his army into Germany and photographed Buchenwald, the first of the Nazi concentration camps to be liberated in April 1945. She described the task as one of the more challenging she had faced and even lost her journalistic detachment when a few of the sights she witnessed made her cry. "I saw and photographed the piles of naked, lifeless bodies," she said, "the human skeletons in furnaces, the living skeletons who would die the next day. . . . Using the camera was almost a relief. It interposed a slight barrier between myself and the horror in front of me."[27] She also photographed the citizens from the nearby town of Weimar whom an enraged General Patton had forced to come out and view the more than 1,200 dead and often charred bodies, not yet buried, piled on top of each other, that were lingering in the camp near their homes.

Two weeks later, Bourke-White and Lee Carson, former White House correspondent for the International News Service who was reporting overseas, stumbled on a work camp that the Nazis had only recently abandoned. Before leaving, the Nazis had locked the prisoners inside the wooden barracks and set it on fire. Bourke-White, Carson, and two male reporters approached the fenced-in compound when they were out looking for an airplane parts factory in Erla, a suburb of Leipzig. All they saw was a locked barbed wire fence surrounding an area containing only a flagpole with a white flag on it. But the main thing that caught their attention was the abominable smell. As they drew closer and their soldier escort used a hand grenade to open the gate, they began to realize what they had come upon.

Along the barbed wire fence were the charred remains of some of those who had managed to fight their way out of the barracks. But their positions facedown on the ground along the fence indicated they had been trying to escape when they got caught up in the barbed wire and died. About eighteen of the prisoners had escaped and when they saw the American jeeps, they came out to tell their story to the stunned and horrified reporters. Bourke-White began taking pictures. One of the male reporters started vomiting. Her photographs of concentration camp victims remain an undeniable testament to the unspeakable terror of the Nazi regime.[28]

Another eminent female photographer, who worked to document the American concentration camps holding Japanese descendants, was Dorothea Lange. She had gained a reputation for showing the suffering of Americans during the Depression years, so it was an interesting choice when the War Relocation Administration hired her to document Japanese internment in the West. Lange began with the initial reaction within the Japanese communities on the West Coast, and then photographed the farewells and travel to the internment camps, as well as life inside the camps.

"On the surface," Lange said, "it looked like a narrow job. . . . Actually, though, it wasn't narrow at all. The deeper I got into it, the bigger it became." Lange was troubled by what she was photographing and later spoke of internment as "a hell of a mistake." Echoing the reaction that most of the Allied nations had to the German concentration camps, Lange called Japanese internment "an example of what happens to us if we lose our heads. . . . What was of course horrifying was to do this thing completely on the basis of what blood may be coursing through a person's veins, nothing else."[29]

Next, Lange worked for the Office of War Information, documenting immigrant communities on the West Coast for propaganda that would be distributed in Europe and North Africa to show American life and how it contrasted with the totalitarian regimes of Germany and Italy. Photographer Ansel Adams also worked on the project for the OWI. The two of them collaborated to produce photographic representations of the four freedoms America was fighting the war to protect, the ones that President Roosevelt had outlined when America joined the fighting. Much of Lange's work was not considered journalistic at the time since she was employed by government agencies, but it remains as some of the best documentation of the subjects she photographed.

Lange seemed to know that she was using the access she gained to the internment camps, for instance, to make photographs that would last beyond the war. "Everything is propaganda for what you believe in, isn't it?" she asked. "The harder and more deeply you believe in anything, the more in a sense you're a propagandist." But she also did some journalistic photography during the war years. In 1944, Lange and Adams also were commissioned by *Fortune* magazine to work in tandem photographing twenty-four hours in the life of workers at the Kaiser shipyard in Richmond, California, on San Francisco Bay.[30]

Dorothy Thompson was a veteran journalist by the time World War II came. She had worked in Berlin during the 1930s and interviewed Hitler. In 1933, she was expelled from Germany by the German secret police after an article she wrote for *Harper's* magazine in which she criticized the Nazis. The reason reported in the American press for her expulsion was that she had written too many anti-German articles. But Thompson described it more pointedly.

> My offense was to think that Hitler is just an ordinary man. That is a crime against the reigning cult in Germany, which says that Mr. Hitler is a Messiah sent of God to save the German people. . . . To question this mystic mission is so heinous that if you are German you can be sent to jail. I, fortunately, am an American, so I merely was sent to Paris. Worse things can happen to one.

When she arrived back in America she reportedly framed the expulsion order and hung it for all to see in her home.[31]

Thompson was well known for her column in *Ladies' Home Journal* and writing for other magazines and for her radio appearances. She was married to writer Sinclair Lewis, who had won the Nobel Prize for Literature. Thompson had become a celebrity journalist. She was known by name across the country and once said to be one of the most popular women in America. She was also well known in Germany, since her anti-Nazi stance had garnered her so much attention.

It was the combination of all these elements that made Thompson a strong advocate for using the power of the written word and especially of radio for propaganda purposes in the war effort. Contrary to many others in the profession, she felt journalists were an important tool in that mission. She used her experiences living in Germany to advise both the OWI and the OSS how to devise effective propaganda. But she was frustrated by what she saw as weak efforts by the government in that area. In a letter to President Roosevelt she said, "All the government does is call us occasionally to ask us to write an article on War Bonds, or back a Scrap Drive; instead of being powerful instruments for the promotion of major policies, we are errand boys. We are sent masses of unconscionably dull and dead releases from all sorts of agencies—stuff that nobody has time to read, prepared by hacks."

Thompson advocated for the president to implement a shortwave radio propaganda campaign. "We could, with plenty of money, organize the most brilliant war of nerves ever seen (or heard). Can't you get the means of setting up a thoroughly hard-boiled, really organized bureau, to drive Mr. Hitler into an insane asylum? It is the dream of my life."

Her dream came true when she was asked by CBS to put together broadcasts to be sent by shortwave into Germany. One feature was an address each week to a fictional friend in Berlin named "Hans."

> I do not hold the German people responsible for this war. I believe they were as much the victims . . . as all the other people on this suffering globe. . . . Their sin is that they did not take the responsibility for the fate of their own nation—that they followed blindly and obediently a leader whom millions in their hearts despised. . . .
>
> Hans, Hans! Think and act before it is too late. Act for Germany and for Europe and for our common cause.

Thompson gave all the arguments her fine mind could conceive against Hitler and the Nazis and added a spirit to it that seemed to strike a chord in Germany. She was so successful that German propagandist Joseph Goebbels criticized her by name, calling Thompson "the scum of America" in his own German radio broadcasts.[32]

LAWYERS AND DOCTORS

In 1940 there were 4,187 women practicing law in the United States. When some of them tried to offer their skills to help the war effort they were rebuffed. A forty-two-year-old lawyer went to her local U.S. employment office to ask if anyone needed a woman lawyer. "I was told that if I were still in my 20s and a good stenographer I could be used, but that no employer wanted an 'old woman past thirty.' " She then spent several days completing examinations for various government jobs that required knowledge of the law, including deputy U.S. marshal. She passed all the tests, but when she called to set up a job interview she was told that the person who sent her the exams had made a mistake and that they wanted only men in the jobs for which she had tested.[33]

Female doctors faced similar obstacles in trying to practice their profession, much less train for it. Harvard Medical School lifted its 163-year ban on admitting women only in 1945, at the end of the war. Other medical schools had quotas that allowed them to admit only one woman for every ten men. And hospitals were not always too keen on offering internships to female medical school graduates. As *Woman's Home Companion* magazine reported in 1943, "Male doctors, as a rule, have been for generations unfriendly to the whole idea of a woman practicing medicine or being a surgeon." Nonetheless, there were approximately 8,000 female doctors in the United States in 1943. Many of them were obstetricians, gynecologists, and pediatricians. But some had specialties such as anesthesia, eye, ear, and nose, or pathology.

The military was reluctant to employ female doctors, preferring to have its medical women serve as nurses instead. Dr. Barbara Stimson, the niece of the secretary of war, had been rejected for service as a doctor in the U.S. military because she was a woman. Instead, she went to Great Britain and served in the British military medical services, attaining the rank of major.

It was estimated that about 3,000 female physicians and surgeons were considered eligible for military service. While President Roosevelt signed a bill giving women doctors equal status with male doctors in the Army and Navy in 1943, there was no clamor for their services. As *Time* magazine reported in 1943, "Neither the Army nor the Navy shows any sign of using many women doctors and none will be used at the front." One obstacle was that women in the Navy were not permitted to go overseas. The only way most in the military could envision using women doctors was to care for female personnel. But the Navy asked for only sixty female doctors to care for the more than 80,000 WAVES. And the Army said they would employ one female doctor for every 500 WACs.[34]

ALL-AMERICAN GIRLS BASEBALL

In the fall of 1942, minor league baseball suspended play because the young male players were needed in the war. Soon the military draft enveloped the major leagues as well. Philip K. Wrigley, the head of the chewing gum company and owner of the Chicago Cubs, had an idea for a replacement league: he would bring in the women. The All-American Girls Professional Baseball League started in 1943. The first teams were all close to Chicago: the Kenosha Comets and the Racine Belles in Wisconsin; the Rockford Peaches in Illinois; and the South Bend Blue Sox in Indiana.

The women not only had to be skilled players, but they had to look good on and off the field too. Wrigley contracted a high-fashion beauty salon to counsel the players at spring training in Chicago. After their daily practice, players had to attend night classes in etiquette, personal hygiene, and how to dress correctly. They were issued a charm school guide with tips on beauty routines, clothes, and rules of behavior. It advised the women that they were representing the league and needed to act with great propriety. "Study your own beauty culture possibilities," it said, "and without overdoing your beauty treatment at the risk of attaining gaudiness, practice the little measure that will reflect well on your appearance and personality as a real All American girl."

Dottie Wiltse Collins began playing for the Fort Wayne Daisies in 1944. "We were not allowed to wear slacks or shorts in public, we weren't allowed to drink or smoke in public, and things like that. . . . It was the greatest thing that ever happened to me—other than my husband and my kids. We were doing what we loved to do."[35]

Each team had fifteen players, a manager, a business manager, and a female chaperone. Salaries ranged from $45 to $85 a week. Former major league players were the managers of the women's teams. At the beginning of each game the two teams formed a V for victory coming out from both sides of home plate while the "The Star-Spangled Banner" played. Players were recruited from local park districts where semipro fast pitch softball leagues had sprung up for women in the 1930s and early 1940s. Some of the players were as young as fifteen years old. The uniforms were designed to be ultra-feminine and modeled after figure skaters' outfits. The women wore satin tights and knee-high baseball socks with a short tunic dress that flared out at the bottom. Wrigley's league gained some popularity in the absence of the male teams. During the South Bend Blue Sox's first season more than 39,000 fans came out to watch the games. The fan total for the 108 games played in the inaugural season was 176,612 in the four cities with women's teams.[36]

South Bend Blue Sox outfielder Betsy Jochum was one of the best hitters in the history of the league. In 1944, her best season, she led the league with a .296 average. She had the most hits (128), the most singles (128), and the most stolen bases in one game (seven), with 127 stolen bases for the year. Her 1944 RBI total was 23. "The same faithful fans would sit behind our dugout every night," said Jochum, "and they would yell, 'Sockum Jochum' when I came up to bat."[37]

After a particularly good hit fans often gave players tokens of their appreciation. In 1944, a Minneapolis newspaper described the reaction to one of Jochum's stellar hits against the Fort Wayne Daisies.

> Other than the amazing antics of the fielders, the feature of the game was Betty Jochum's home run in the seventh. This muscular young lady whaled one of Dottie's best pitches far over Faye Dancer's head in center field and it rolled almost to the flagpole. A fellow named Sweeney, one of South Bend's rootingest rooters, gave her $25 dollars for the smash.[38]

Other women ballplayers received wristwatches, radios, and record players for well-played games. The league went on after the war and finally was disbanded in 1954, soon after the men's major league games began broadcasting on television.

The women who played always had a sense of the great opportunity they had in playing professional team sports, something women would struggle to achieve for many decades to follow. As pitcher Dottie Wiltse Collins said, the league offered women an unparalleled opportunity. "We were young. We were having a good time, and we had money in our pockets. . . . This was the greatest thing that ever happened to us."[39]

PART III

Honolulu
April 18, 1945

The living quarters are in a very lovely convent—the Sacred Heart Convent on Nuunanu and Bates streets. The idea of living in a convent was something of a surprise after our preparation for life overseas among the thousands of men.

Honolulu
Saturday, April 21, 1945

Tonight we found that it's impossible to walk down the streets of Honolulu after about 3 in the afternoon unescorted. Chris, Jean and I wanted to have dinner downtown by ourselves and get home early (meaning about 7 o'clock instead of the usual 9 at the convent or 10—curfew time for the rest of the island) to wash, iron and write letters. Sailors, soldiers, marines stop you every five feet to ask directions or such, and eventually ask you to have dinner or a drink. We stopped on one corner, obeying the traffic rules and a red light, and two soldiers rushed up and asked us to their company dance. They were nice kids and almost pathetic in their eagerness. They were supposed to all take girls they said, and they'd had no luck. Then they got embarrassed and assured us that we weren't the last resort, but they would so much like to take us. One of them, particularly naive and sweet explained earnestly and in rather formal language, "If it's not to your ladies' liking we'll take you home right after dinner." We really wanted to go, but about that time 3 Marines who had stopped us earlier and had been following us ever since (they were just back from Iwo) came along, and we knew we couldn't accept the Army's invitation when we'd turned down the Marines' earlier. So we finally went on, the Marines still following, and eventually, to save time (once you have escorts you aren't bothered any more) we ate dinner with the Marines, took a bus back to the convent and really did get in about 8:15, which was something of an accomplishment.

CHAPTER ELEVEN

The "Wrong Kind" of Woman

PROSTITUTES, UNWED MOTHERS, AND LESBIANS

They don't wear armbands. They are not branded on the forehead. They all look alike, the decent women and the bad ones. You can't tell them apart, until you catch them in an overt act.

COLONEL HOWARD CLARK,
Commanding officer, WAC Training Center,
Fort Oglethorpe, Georgia, 1944[1]

H̲UMAN FEELINGS often have to be pushed aside during wartime. The call of duty demands it. But human emotions are not always so readily denied, and feelings repressed or shunned have a way of coming up again. Most of what is documented about women's sexuality during World War II is either told from a male point of view or from an official government point of view. In both cases it is sometimes hard to discern how the women themselves felt or what they thought. But the undercurrents accompanying the new opportunities women were gaining in the workplace and the military seemed to include a more open attitude toward sexuality among women. Not that it was anything most of them could admit in public without fear of having their character called into question. It was assumed that men, whether married or single, would not be able to remain faithful to one woman during wartime, whereas women, especially single ones, who found ways to fulfill any of their sexual needs were portrayed as enemies.

Throughout the war years, women were implicated as the ones who spread venereal disease, a common condition among enlisted men. Women who strayed outside of marriage, or appeared to do so, were treated as outcasts. And prostitutes were equated with animals and could not expect freedom to exercise rights that any other citizen would take for granted. Unescorted women in public places, especially bars and train stations, were often assumed to be prostitutes and hauled into jail on suspicion only. Women who became pregnant outside of marriage were always to blame, whereas the men who made them pregnant were rarely held accountable for the consequences. And lesbians had to hide their sexuality, because just the suspicion of such tendencies ensured all-out persecution in mainstream society. The double standard for women surrounding sexuality during the war was perhaps the most blatant and ironclad of all the double standards women lived with during World War II.

HOTEL STREET

In the summer of 1942, female protesters set up a picket line in front of the building that housed both the Honolulu police department and the U.S. military police. Every day the striking workers marched carrying signs demanding their rights. Their work stoppage threatened the very heart of Hawaii's most elite society as well as the health and morale of the millions of fighting men who passed through the island on their way to or from the Pacific theater. Yet, the highest levels of government and society in Hawaii ignored the women's complaints. And no newspapers covered their strike. That was because these workers were the prostitutes of Honolulu's Hotel Street.

The elite in Hawaii—the powerful, wealthy, white families—believed they needed the prostitutes to provide a buffer. Without the sex workers, it was feared, the upper-class, white daughters of the island would fall prey to the undeniable urges of the massive influx of sex-starved military men that the Army and Navy brought to the island. The terms of the prostitutes' employment had always been that the rest of society would look the other way. In return, these women were expected to carry on without complaint in the dirtiest, most degrading work of all. The police on the island had rules set up that kept the sex-for-pay business under such tight control that the rest of society was accustomed to taking it for granted. The women were supposed to stay out of sight, so that respectable society would not be inconvenienced by ever having to think of the sex workers' rights or needs. The military accepted their presence too, because prostitution was seen as a way to control the problem of venereal disease, which during the First World War had killed more soldiers than enemy bullets.

The approximately five-block area of the Hotel Street district was a hub of social activity for military men in Honolulu. And Honolulu was a hub of the Pacific theater for Americans. During the war, more than 30,000 people a day visited the Hotel Street district. Bars, tattoo parlors, souvenir stands, cheap restaurants, and places to have a picture taken with a native woman in a hula skirt were everywhere. And so were brothels. About 250,000 men visited the Hotel Street brothels each month, paying $3 for three minutes with a woman. That translated to at least a $9 million per year business. There were approximately 250 prostitutes operating in about fifteen brothels on the street. For some of the youngest men a visit to the brothel was their first sexual experience. For some men who would be shipped off to fight and die in combat, it would be their last.[2]

Most of the prostitutes were white women who had originally worked in San Francisco. When Hawaii madams wanted new workers they contacted San Francisco pimps, who shipped more women over to work on the island for a fee to the madam of $500 to $1,000 per woman. The women were registered as "entertainers" with the local police when they arrived, and paid one dollar a year for an entertainer's license. A member of the vice squad usually met the women upon arrival and apprised them of the rules of working in the sex business on the island, which mainly consisted of living at the brothels and nowhere else on the island and not going to tourist hotels, beaches, and restaurants.

Many women handled up to a hundred men a day, at least three weeks of every month, with time off only during menstruation. There was a curfew in place at night in Honolulu, so the brothels were open from 9:00 A.M. to 2:00 P.M. Men could often be seen lined up around the block waiting to go up the stairs to the second-floor prostitution houses. One common type of work area for the women was called a bull ring or bull pen, with three rooms. In one room a woman took her three minutes with a man, in another room the next man she was to be with got undressed and waited, and in the third room the man she had just been with got dressed. That system kept up a relentless flow of men. The women could not keep up the brutal pace for long. Many lasted only a few months before they had to take time off and so were shipped back to the mainland. Others numbed themselves by using drugs such as morphine, which was available to them through doctors the madams of the brothels contacted. But many women did not do drugs or drink, which was officially prohibited in the brothels.[3]

Technically, prostitution and drug use were both illegal. Hawaii was a territory of the U.S., subject to federal laws. The "regulated brothel" system had existed on the island before Pearl Harbor. Island police allowed prostitution to continue if the prostitutes abided by the rules meant to keep them out of society. Restrictions were placed on where they lived, how they spent their free time, and what they could buy. When martial law was declared and the military took over the island after Pearl Harbor, complicity with the system served well the military's aims of morale building and VD control.[4]

Madams kept one dollar of every three earned by the "sporting girls," as they were sometimes called. But the prostitutes paid many fees, such as room and board, laundry, maids, and even the required weekly checks for VD. The women paid taxes on their income, which could be $30,000 or $40,000 a year. Even with all the fees, the women made big money. A typical female factory worker earned $2,000 to $3,000 a year, at most. The madams, with all the fees they levied from the women, often made upward of $150,000 per year.

Jean O'Hara was a prostitute on Hotel Street and then went on to become a madam. In a typewritten manuscript from 1944 called *My Life as a Honolulu Prostitute,* she spoke frankly about the system set up to regulate the prostitution racket on the island. Her version of the story was not officially published, but she copied and distributed it herself. Although she and other women made lots of money in the business, she never said it was easy money.

> The prostitute pays in many ways. First, she has to pay with her self-respect. She must harden herself against the disrespect, abuse, vulgar insults and disgusting demands of her clientele, some of who are on a level with the lowest form of animal life. The fine ones who display kindness and courtesy, cannot make up for the sexually perverted and intoxicated.
>
> . . . Finally the prostitute pays with broken health and body. The ones that waxed old and fat in the trade during the pre-war days, were always shoved out and younger girls stepped in to take their places. Nowadays, the rush business has put even these old ones back in circulation again.[5]

O'Hara said she started as a prostitute at age seventeen. Even though she said that "Honolulu has always been a veritable gold mine for the prostitutes and the Madames,"[6] by her description, it was also a brutal job.

> I actually loathed the life. . . . Again and again I planned to get away from the life of sex slavery, with all its fearful and revolting experiences. As I think back, I marvel that I withstood the abuses and shameful contacts which were an unavoidable part of the life of a prostitute.

It is not hard to imagine that the grueling pace of managing short, sordid, sexual encounters with so many men, hour after hour, day after day, would take a toll on even the most hardened hearts. And the fact that many of the men were going off to die in war must also have played on these women's sentiments. But human emotions could not be allowed to rise up in the women, or else they would not have been able to carry on. Still, sometimes the women's humanity crept to the surface, even if only briefly. As O'Hara said, in retrospect, "All the money in the world could not compensate for the insults, indignities and lustful abuse of men."

Prostitution offered about the best money a woman could make. The money, however, was a double-edged sword, one that would not necessarily be evident until the woman was already deeply into the trap of the work and the lifestyle. The skills it would take to leave—self-awareness, independence, self-esteem—were the opposite of the skills it would take to survive the business—numbness, subservience, and self-sacrifice. O'Hara pointed out that problem.

> I've known many who tried to quit, but they eventually came back. Their general reaction is one of discouragement. They find that the public gives little help to the efforts of a prostitute who wants to return to normal, decent useful living. No jobs, they are told, are available for such people. The police follow them suspiciously and interfere with their employment. Then they are driven back to the only place they seem welcome: a sporting house. They usually lack the strength to make a second attempt to quit.[7]

As evidence that even the men involved understood the true nature of the work, if only subconsciously, the police and the patrons often referred to the prostitutes as "inmates." In addition, O'Hara said, some of the madams "contrive to keep their girls" by various means of making them dependent and weak, such as getting them into debt or hooked on drugs.

> Some of the madams here in Honolulu are the most hard hearted women I have ever met in my fourteen years experience. They are greedy. They are money hungry, and they drive their girls to the very breaking point.[8]

O'Hara worked as a prostitute for many years before the war and for a while during the war. Then she opened her own brothel and became a madam. She talked of the chief of police in Honolulu, Chief Gabrielson, with special virulence, saying his iron rule made a prostitute into "a football for anyone who chose to throw her around."[9]

According to O'Hara the prewar rules controlling prostitutes said that prostitutes had to live at the brothels and were not allowed to own property on the island, or to own an automobile. They could not visit a golf course, any bars, or "the better class cafes." They were not allowed to have a steady boyfriend, or to be out of the brothel after 10:30 P.M. They were not allowed to attend any public dances or be seen on the streets with a man. And they were not allowed to go to Waikiki beach at any time, since that is where the tourists went.[10] Prostitutes, Jewish people, and black people were all prohibited from staying at Waikiki's most luxurious hotels.[11]

O'Hara became notorious for flouting the rules. She married a local man, although she did not live with him. She had tried to buy property and live outside the district, but the vice squad hounded her wherever she went. She owned a car, a flashy Lincoln Zephyr. She had opened her own brothel in Maui without the chief's approval. Eventually, she moved back to Hotel Street to work in one of the houses again. That, she said, is when she found out most clearly how anyone who had ever defied the authority of Chief Gabrielson was subject to brutal treatment forever more. In early 1940, O'Hara decided she wanted to give up the business and move in with her husband, who lived in Honolulu. One night at about 11:00 P.M., she told her madam, Lillian Martin, of her plans. Martin told her that since it was past 10:30 she would have to clear it with the vice squad, and Martin called the police.

A police captain came out to the Rex Hotel, where O'Hara worked, and told her that she could not leave since it was after ten. She would have to wait until the morning.

> I got up from the table and told him that I was leaving just the same. This was before the war time curfew. Captain Kennedy struck me in the mouth with his fist, and the force of his blow knocked me against the wall. I reeled, stunned with pain, and he hit me several more times . . . I fell to the floor and he kicked me in the ribs. He gave me a brutal, thorough beating.

O'Hara said that two cab drivers who were there to pick her up saw the entire incident, and the madam, Lillian Martin, also stood by, watched, and commented, "I hope that this will be a lesson to the rest of the girls not to break Chief Gabrielson's orders." Then, she said, Captain Kennedy dragged her out by her hair across the sidewalk to the patrol wagon. She was kept in jail for three days before she got any medical treatment. She had two broken ribs, bruises all over, and her bridgework was broken when she was hit in the jaw. Eventually the charges against her were dropped, but she filed a suit against the police. She was persuaded to drop it, but the battle lines were drawn because she had stood up to the police.[12]

When Pearl Harbor was bombed, the prostitutes of Hotel Street had rushed to the hospitals to help nurse the wounded. Their brothels were nearer to the shore than many other Hawaii residents, and the madams opened up the prostitutes' living quarters to be used as temporary hospitals. The women, with nowhere to sleep and a fear that Hotel Street would be too close to the line of fire if a Japanese invasion occurred, started to move into houses and apartments in other parts of the city. For the first few weeks no one took much notice. The women began to believe that the war rules for their lives might be less stringent, that they would be able to live as any other tax-paying, American citizens.[13]

In February 1942, O'Hara, who had gotten back into the business, and two other women rented a room in one of the poshest Waikiki hotels and sunbathed on the beach. One night during their stay, they were having a party in their room and O'Hara was arrested and sentenced to four months in prison for disturbing the peace. She claimed it was her punishment for breaking the chief's rules two years before and continuing to defy him.[14] Despite O'Hara's claims, neither Gabrielson nor Kennedy was ever charged with any wrongdoing in connection with the incidents she described.

When martial law was declared in Hawaii, and the military took over civilian law enforcement after the attack on Pearl Harbor, the military police had a less restrictive attitude toward the women of Hotel Street. They too tolerated the brothels, but their motives were less about morals and threats to respectable women than about practical matters of venereal disease and what the military saw as the uncontrollable urges of men.

By going on strike in August of 1942, the women of Hotel Street took a risk that the power curve had shifted toward them with the war. More and more men were arriving on the island, on their way to or from battle. Both the military and the civilian police felt the women's work was needed more urgently than ever. And with the U.S. military running the island and giving the prostitutes of Hotel Street tacit backing, the women felt they could finally speak out and ask for their basic constitutional rights. After three weeks, a compromise was reached. The women were allowed to live wherever they pleased and go wherever they wanted, but they had to keep their business at the brothel.[15]

Two books included characters who were prostitutes on Hotel Street. One was *The Revolt of Mamie Stover* by William Bradford Huie, and the other was *From Here to Eternity* by James Jones. The men did their best to describe the women's point of view, but the fictional prostitutes were a product of male fantasy more than reflections of real life. Huie's Mamie Stover was believed to have been based upon Jean O'Hara's life. James Jones's prostitute, named Alma, was a waitress from Oregon who was jilted by her blueblood boyfriend to marry a woman of his class. Alma said she became a prostitute only until she could make enough money to go back home and buy her way into the society for which her ex-boyfriend had shunned her. Both books were later made into movies after the war, with Jane Russell as Mamie Stover and Donna Reed as Alma.[16]

A combination of forces closed down the Hotel Street brothels in September of 1944. First of all, martial law was lifted in the summer of 1944 as the threat of another Japanese attack on Hawaii became remote. That meant the civilian police were poised to take control of the district again. Their first order of business was to decree that the prostitutes were no longer allowed to live in residential neighborhoods and had to move back to the brothels. The governor of Hawaii, Ingram M. Stainback, saw the elimination of Hotel Street prostitution as a way to reassert civilian control after the military had protected the brothels throughout the war. Beth Bailey and David Farber described the situation in *The First Strange Place*, a book about race and sex in wartime Hawaii.

> Stainback, a Democrat appointed by Roosevelt, was linking his interests with the progressive elite. He was distancing himself from the old guard, Republicans all, who used the "whores" as a buffer between "respectable" whites and the "disreputable" lower-class white soldiers and sailors with whom they shared the island.
>
> The "sacrifice" of the lower-class white women from the mainland had been a price the old elite had been willing to pay.[17]

The editor of the *Honolulu Star-Bulletin*, the liberal daily paper, articulated the reasons so many were using the lifting of martial law as an opportunity to campaign against the closing of the brothels.

> We have all been remiss, for many years . . . sincerely convinced that
> some catastrophe, some crime wave, some orgy of sex fiends, would
> follow from the closing of the houses. . . . Well we have finally
> waked up. We finally saw conditions become so shameful that in
> moral revolt we said, "this scandalous violation of the law and this
> open invitation to tens of thousands of fine young men is all wrong
> . . . morally indefensible and totally against decent and sound public
> policy." [18]

One of Governor Stainback's first official acts when he retook control of
the Hawaiian government was to order that the Hotel Street brothels be shut
down. The military did not object. In part, their decision not to fight the order
probably came from the fact that penicillin, a cure for VD, had recently become available and so maintaining control of prostitution was not considered
as important. On September 22, 1944, the Hotel Street brothels were officially
shut down after close of business at 2:00 P.M. Contrary to some expectations
there was no increase in sex crimes reported against the elite women of
Hawaii after the closing of the brothels. [19]

VICTORY GIRLS

Since venereal disease was such a threat to the military at home and abroad,
its control became a high priority for public health officials, the military, and
the federal government. The practice most equated with VD was prostitution. So when the U.S. government tried to control VD as the country was
gearing up for war, it cracked down on prostitution. One of the first efforts in
that direction was the May Act, passed by Congress in July 1941, which made
prostitution near military bases a federal offense. Military officials were given
the authority to invoke the May Act and were encouraged to set up zones
around their camps where vice laws could be enforced by federal officials, not
just local law enforcement. [20]

The May Act was invoked only a few times during the war. It mostly
served to motivate local law enforcement officials to work harder at limiting
vice around military bases. Not wanting the federal government coming in
and doing their job, local authorities stepped up their efforts. Areas known for
prostitution in many communities across the U.S. were shut down, with the

government estimating that by 1945, as many as 700 vice districts around the country had been closed by law enforcement.[21]

But another wave of supposed sexual threats to the men came in the form of young women and girls. A term was coined during World War II to describe these females who were not prostitutes but who had sex with young male soldiers: "victory girls." They were described as women and girls as young as twelve to their early twenties, but generally they were thought to be from fourteen to seventeen. They hung around military bases and had sex with men "for free." Their motives were said to be a misplaced patriotism, since, the story went, they would not have sex with civilians, only military men. The characters of the soldiers who had sex, often illegally, with these teenage girls usually were not called into question. These girls, just like the prostitutes, were blamed for the spread of venereal disease.

In the book *No Magic Bullet*, a history of venereal disease in the U.S., author Allan M. Brandt said all of the posters produced to inform soldiers about the dangers of VD during World War II portrayed VD as a woman. One such war poster was a drawing of a woman with a skeleton face in an evening gown representing venereal disease. She walked joyfully with a man on each arm. The caption read, "V.D. Worst of the Three." The man on her right arm was Hitler, the man on her left was Japanese emperor Hirohito. Brandt pointed out that the victory girls, and any women who had sex outside of marriage, were replacing prostitutes in the mind of the public as the main threat to men's health.

> The harlot with the painted face had stepped aside for the girl-next-door. The Army now emphasized in its educational literature for soldiers that these "victory girls" could be just as infectious as the experienced prostitute. The most widely circulated World War II pamphlet was entitled, "She Looked Clean But. . . ." Again, such literature repeated the sorry association of "cleanliness" with chastity, impurity with disease. About these women a federal committee noted: "She is more dangerous to the community than a mad dog. Rabies can be recognized. Gonorrhea and syphilis ordinarily cannot."[22]

The government pamphlet *She Looked Clean But . . .* was published by the Federal Security Agency's Social Protection Division in 1945. Its tone was clearly illustrated by its last page, which summed up its message that women were carriers and men were the innocent targets of VD. In a drawing, two average, wholesome young men, who happened to have had VD, sat in hospital beds comparing notes. The caption of the drawing quoted one man saying, "I can't understand it. That girl sure looked clean." The other man replied, "That's funny—mine did too."

The text next to the picture said: "'She looked clean' is the familiar lament of the victim of venereal disease." The pamphlet concluded:

> We won't use someone else's tooth brush. We would despise anyone for offering us a cud of tobacco out of someone else's mouth. But truthfully, there is far less danger and hazard involved in such detestable practices than in sexual intercourse with a prostitute or a promiscuous woman.[23]

As Allan Brandt pointed out, "a ubiquitous double standard of sexual morality" existed in the standard way in which men were admonished to avoid VD:

> The word "promiscuous" was firmly anchored to "girl"—a promiscuous man was, by definition, an oxymoron. Women in this view, were the keepers of sexual mores—their indiscretions led to a deterioration of morals. "They" infected the soldiers; in this view, venereal disease could only be transmitted in one direction. Therefore, as sexual mores did in fact change, the burden of this transformation came to be placed upon women.[24]

In essence the solution for the moralists and those concerned with controlling disease alike was to repress women's sexual expression, but not men's. An exception to that was a faction that not only expected women to be chaste, but men too. One such voice was Eliot Ness, the law enforcement officer who had arrested Chicago gangster Al Capone before the war. Ness was head of the Social Protection Division of the Federal Security Agency during the war. He wrote a 1943 VD prevention pamphlet entitled *What About the Girls?*, in which he took a hard line with the men who were the targets of its information. After telling them that there was a crackdown all over the country in the "girl racket," he went on to tell the men they had to do their part too.

> The idea is to keep diseased women away from you. Is it too much to ask that you keep away from them?

I ask because I figure the service man in on this objective. First, we have to keep syphilis and gonorrhea from putting you out of action. Second, we want to keep your country "so nice to come home to." This two-part job can't be done unless all of us—every mother's son of us—will pitch in and help.

Some smart alecks and a lot of hysterical fools say that war makes it O.K. for men in uniform to shed all their normal responsibilities and restraints along with their civvies. The wise guys talk about the effects of military discipline and say that it is the soldier's birthright to cut loose when on leave. The sobsisters talk about "lonely hearts" and say that "nothing is too good for our boys." I get fed up with both these points of view, and I expect a lot of service men get fed up, too. Personally, I'd rather be treated like a man who can take the truth, think straight, and act accordingly, than like a mamma's boy who "wants what he wants when he wants it." [25]

Ness emphasized that the men infected with VD got treatment and were saddled with less stigma than the women blamed for giving it to them.

The men may lose some pay; they may not get promoted as fast as they hoped to. But they are getting the best medical care the country can give, in clean, comfortable hospitals. They aren't in jail. They are our nation's heroes.

There are hundreds of jails . . . with hundreds of girls in them. There are not more than thirty hospitals in the entire U.S. where such girls can get good medical care and be treated like human beings.

Yes plenty of them are tough babes, but just as many are fool kids who deserve a lot better in life than sickness, filth, and premature old age. [26]

This hinted at another of the measures Ness implemented in his job of protecting the social fabric of the country. Laws regarding morals and defining prostitution were broadened in many communities with the encouragement and guidance of Ness's Social Protection Division of the Federal Security Agency. The overall goal of revising the laws was to control the ability of women to meet and become sexually involved with soldiers. What resulted was a system in which women were hauled into jail for mere suspicion of promiscuity whenever possible. Once there, they were subjected to mandatory VD testing and held in jail for days at time until test results were returned. A study of such women in Seattle in 1944 showed that of the 2,063 women held by Seattle police that year on suspicion of morals violations, 366 (17.3 percent) were found to have venereal disease. The majority, 1,697 (82.7 percent) women, were not diseased and yet had to spend four or five days in jail waiting for the results of a VD test. Often, they were released and no formal charges were filed against them, but they were referred to social welfare agencies that would counsel them on proper behavior. It was found that many of the women arrested were married.[27]

Some of the women rounded up in Seattle, where it was estimated that the police arrested as many as 300 women a month in 1944, were charged with violating statutes prohibiting women from going to bars too often or without an escort. In Detroit, it was suggested that unescorted women should be banned or at least separated from other patrons in bars. After it became clear there was no legal way to completely ban single women from bars, a rule was instituted that called on bars to refuse to serve unescorted women after 8:00 P.M. Women in Detroit were also detained for disorderly conduct if they were suspected of being immoral. They were held for investigation and VD testing and then released days later without any court action taken against them. The FBI reported that between 1940 and 1944 there was a 95 percent increase in the number of women charged with morals violations in the U.S. Some women around the country were even investigated by police after their names were taken from supposedly confidential information given by men infected with VD who were asked to name their sex partners. The women, who were often branded as "sex delinquents," were not investigated for their own safety as much as for being morally corrupt and disease spreaders. The goal of authorities was often to shame them into getting rehabilitative counseling.[28]

Despite all these apparent violations of so many women's constitutional rights around the country, Roger Baldwin, the founder and director of the American Civil Liberties Union, sent a memo to all the local branches asking them to be sympathetic with law enforcement officials and not pursue these cases. Many of the women detained brought false arrest lawsuits against the authorities. A few had their cases thrown out because arresting officers did not have proper authorization. But most courts ruled in favor of law enforcement, saying jailing the women was acceptable because it was necessary to protect public health. The male partners of these women were almost never arrested and certainly not prosecuted. They were usually not tested for VD or shamed for similar or contributing behavior either, even when the women they were with were underage.[29]

In his *What About the Girls?* pamphlet, Ness spoke of some of these "promiscuous girls" who ended up in jails. In what he knew was soldier jargon, he called them the "free stuff." Ness's descriptions were meant to protect servicemen by scaring them away from these women, not to point out the inequities in the consequences for men and women infected with VD or to question how men were allowed to spread the disease to these underage women.

> Last month I saw a jail-full of free stuff. They were all 17 years old or younger. All had syphilis or gonorrhea. All were service men's pickups. All had infected at least one man. That's why they were in jail. The men they had infected were in hospitals.
>
> I won't forget that jail soon. It stank. It was filthy. The room where the girls were held had two double beds and three single beds, with putrid mattresses and no sheets. The girls slept three in the double beds; two each in the single beds. There were two small barred windows; and a pail of water. These girls were in jail for being the free stuff service men brag about.[30]

Public talk and policy might have blamed women and perpetuated the apparent denial of male responsibility in the spread of VD and increase in sexual relations outside of marriage during the war, but the fact remained that both were indeed issues with consequences beyond what was most publicly acknowledged. During World War II the rate of babies born to unmarried women rose from 7.0 per 1,000 in 1939 to 10.0 in 1945. During World War II approximately 650,000 babies were born to single women. The rate was highest among women aged twenty to thirty. Since abortion was illegal, no records of its occurrence exist, but anecdotes from the military and from the factories tell stories of women, single and married, who had illegal abortions. Often it meant they were able to save their marriages from their own infidelities, or single women were able to save themselves from being branded as immoral women for having a child out of wedlock.[31]

The bottom line was clear. Men's sexual needs came first. Women sacrificed for that. They sacrificed a lot. And even the women who paid attention to their own needs sacrificed, because they compromised their respectability in the process. Social reformers such as birth control pioneer Margaret Sanger saw the inequities early on, and had worked in the first part of the century for more education of women about their sexuality and reproductive health. They had also pushed for more availability of birth control. In fact, Planned Parenthood of America was started during World War II. So women were beginning to find ways to assert their own wills and desires regarding their love lives just as they were with their economic needs. The odds were starting to turn against those dedicated to stopping that tide.

HOMOSEXUALS AND SEX MANIACS

On May 12, 1944, the mother of a WAC from Westby, Wisconsin, wrote a letter to the judge advocate general of the War Department in Washington. She accused the Women's Army Corps—and specifically the training center at Fort Oglethorpe, Georgia—of being rife with lesbianism.

> I am writing to inform you of some of the things at Ft. Oglethorpe that are a disgrace to the U.S. Army. It is no wonder women are afraid to enlist. It is full of homosexuals and sex maniacs.

The Wisconsin mother said she found out about the situation when her twenty-year-old daughter was home on furlough and "received some of the most shocking letters I have ever read in my life from a woman of 30 years." She was not willing to believe that her own daughter could ever have sexual feelings toward another woman. Instead the mother believed her daughter when she told her that this older woman had hypnotized her. The mother said that her daughter was afraid of the older woman, who "has ruined other girls and will continue to use her spell over other innocent girls who join up with the W.A.C., because of their patriotic spirit." The mother said that her daughter "has repented and says she will never make friends with another strange girl again." But she added that her daughter told her of "many others who are practicing this terrible vice." Then the mother ended by naming a handful of other WACs who she said were lesbians.[32]

The Army took this letter very seriously. Recruiting problems because of rumors about the women's morality had been plaguing the WAC. The last thing the leadership wanted was for the Wisconsin mother to take her allegations of widespread lesbianism in the WAC to the public. The inspector gen-

eral's office launched a full-fledged investigation. Two male lieutenant
colonels and two female captains conducted a month-long inquiry in June
and July of 1944, traveling to eleven locales from Pennsylvania to Georgia to
Colorado to Washington, D.C., interviewing witnesses.

In the graphic testimony witnesses were often accused of lesbian acts.
Lead investigator Lieutenant Colonel Birge Holt did most of the questioning.
He often asked extremely personal questions in an attempt to get the women
to admit their actions fully. He often referred to how embarrassing the questioning was for all involved, but he stressed they needed to get the specifics to
see if the basis for the investigation was true. With other officers and a court
reporter in the room, he questioned a twenty-three-year-old private about her
sexual practices with another WAC on a particular night. He asked her to describe in detail what the investigation report called their "oral perversion."

Q: . . . Of course we recognize this is a very embarrassing sort of a matter to you. It is equally to us. It is not a matter of idle curiosity, certainly, that we ask these questions. As I mentioned to you a while ago,
and as I want to stress to you again, this is a confidential inquiry, and it
is designed for determining whether or not the allegations upon
which this investigation is based are true. If such conditions exist
in the Women's Army Corps they should be known and there should
be something done. . . . I would like you to repeat the conversation,
what she said while you were in the room there . . . what she was
planning to do and did subsequently do.
A: Well, she asked me first if I had ever had anyone "go down on me" be-
fore, and I told her I hadn't. Then she told me that was what she was
going to do.
Q: Did you know what she meant by that expression?
A: Yes, sir.
Q: You had at that time heard of or known of other instances of that
sort?
A: Yes, sir.
Q: Did you express any objection or opposition to that occurrence?
A: No, sir.
Q: Did you reciprocate with her?
A: No, sir.
Q: It was not mutual between you?
A: No, sir.
Q: Are you absolutely sure of that?
A: Absolutely, sir. . . .

Q: Did it occur once or more than once?

A: Just once, sir. . . .

Q: Did [she] that night tell you that she been addicted to this practice in civil life?

A: Yes, sir.

Q: Did she state whether she had gone into the Corps with the idea that it would be a place where she could practice such things?

A: No, she didn't, but . . . from the way she talked, I think that is the reason.

Q: Did she say anything about why she had joined the Army?

A: No, sir.[33]

In addition to that private and her partner, three other couples became the primary focus of the investigation and interrogations. The premise of determining lesbianism for the investigation, based on testimony from a WAC psychiatrist who was "treating" most of the women involved, established two types of women who engaged in lesbian behavior. The first group, she said, got into relationships accidentally and were essentially said to be experimenting with lesbianism. The second group were unrepentant and were referred to as "homosexual addicts," especially exemplified by those called "oral perverts."

Lieutenant Colonel Holt asked the psychiatrist who examined the women many questions about the nature of lesbianism. He seemed to be trying to discern the difference between women who were "reclaimable" in the eyes of the Army and those who were not. Those who were reclaimable would go on to get psychological treatment and the others would be discharged or court-martialed. Asking about the sergeant who wrote the letters to the Wisconsin daughter, Holt wanted to know if her lesbianism was treatable.

Q: Is that condition a disease, the condition which causes her to engage in abnormal sex relations with other women?

A: No, it is not a disease.

Q: Is it purely an indication of depraved character?

A: No, it is a trait of character.

Q: Scientifically, how would you characterize it?

A: It is an abnormal bent. It is a personality trait, not necessarily depraved, because she could in any other respect be of the highest order. This particular girl has high moral ideas. . . . She would not steal. She would not kill. She would not take advantage of anybody. She is a generous person. She has never done anything evil. . . . It is a certain bent of character and is part of the personality, but not an illness. Very unfortunate.

Q: Is it not a condition that would respond to treatment of any sort?
A: No.

Lieutenant Colonel Holt, in his thoroughness, returned to the subject of perversion one more time later in his interrogation of the psychiatrist.

Q: It is a fact, is it not, that there are degrees of this relationship, that some of these women are real perverts, that is, that they engage in most abnormal practices, practices which are not even normal between a man and woman, that is, apply their mouths to each other, in a manner which is distinctly abnormal. How do you scientifically classify people such as that? . . . Persons who engage in those practices, the ones I last mentioned, are definitely abnormal, are they not?
A: Yes.
Q: Would you uniformly characterize a person such as that to be detrimental to the Army?
A: Yes.[34]

The Wisconsin daughter, who was a private, and her partner, who was a sergeant, were determined by the investigators to be reclaimable. Instead of discharging them, they were sentenced to Army psychiatric hospitals. (At the time, homosexuality was thought of as a mental disorder.)

A twenty-four-year-old enlisted woman and a thirty-year-old second lieutenant were another couple under investigation. The twenty-four-year-old was interrogated by a man and a woman and her defenses were broken down so that she would admit her lesbianism and implicate her partner. As the questioning got more personal, a female officer, Captain Helen A. Gaynor, took over the interrogation. She asked the corporal if she and her partner (Lieutenant Williams) were "closer than just friends." The corporal replied, "No ma'am, I think a lot of her but we are just close friends." That answer brought forth more forceful questioning.

Q: Are you in love with her?
A: No ma'am.
Q: Is she with you?
A: I don't think so. . . .

Q: Which one of you first made love to the other one?
A: We don't make love to each other ma'am.

At that, Captain Gaynor recited to the corporal the allegations against her and tried to assure her that she knew about "people like her."

Q: Now do we understand each other better . . . ?
A: Yes ma'am.
Q: Has Lt. Williams ever made love to you?
A: Yes ma'am.
Q: How? Describe it to me.

The corporal was then put through a long, torturous grilling about where and how she and Lieutenant Williams touched each other and whether they had orgasms together. The corporal said they did. Once she admitted all that, the male interrogator took over and threatened to tell the corporal's family and her Baptist minister about what she had just confessed.

At that point the corporal named other lesbian couples. Then, the interrogators set out to make this woman admit that what she had done with Lieutenant Williams was wrong and detrimental to the Army.

Q: Do you feel guilty about it?
A: Yes ma'am.
Q: Is the feeling [of guilt] so awfully strong that you don't want your family to know it, and crying as you are now . . . is the feeling so strong that you don't want to break up?
A: I don't want it broken up. . . .
Q: Do you know that the Army wouldn't approve of a friendship that exists between two women like your friendship with Lt. Williams?
A: Yes ma'am. . . .
Q: As much as you don't want [your mother] to find out, do you still say you would rather take a chance at that than give up Lt. Williams?
A: I would hate to give her up.
Q: If you had a choice, which would you take?
A: My family. . . . They mean everything in the world to me.[35]

The last couple investigated was a thirty-one-year-old lawyer who was a second lieutenant and a thirty-six-year-old corporal. These women were a bit more mature and were bolder in admitting their love for each other and in standing up to the interrogators. The investigators had letters the women had written to each other as well as testimony that had been taken by Captain Gaynor and her male cohort. Lieutenant Colonel Holt tried to get the thirty-six-year-old corporal to go into detail about her affair. He even used some of his newly acquired understanding of lesbianism (which he called "well-known facts"), as well as some of the same tactics he had employed before. But he did not get as far this time.

> Q: The testimony in this case, together with these letters, indicate an unnatural sort of love affair between you and [the lieutenant]. I think it is a well-known fact that an affair of this sort would be in degrees, some degrees being more aggravated and more unnatural than others. Would you be willing to describe to us the nature of the affair that existed between the two of you, what you actually did?
> A: I'd rather not sir.
> Q: This is as embarrassing to us as it is to you.
> A: I doubt it sir.

Ultimately the second lieutenant was given the chance to resign and took it. Her partner was declared reclaimable, as were the other women investigated.

Near the end of the month-long investigation, Lieutenant Holt and Captain Ruby Herman, the lead investigators, visited the mother in Wisconsin. When faced with Army officers, she recanted her most explosive charges. The mother said she merely wanted her daughter to live "a normal life" and didn't want her to "associate with people like that," referring to her lesbian partner.

Lieutenant Colonel Birge, another officer conducting additional questioning, said, "Of course . . . these are very serious allegations particularly the broad one to the effect the Army is full of Homosexuals and sex maniacs and based on that general statement we are conducting this investigation into the matter . . . to determine whether or not such an assertion is in fact true."

The mother replied, "I would take back what I wrote about that being full of homosexuals and sex maniacs, I don't know that. . . . I wrote that when I was angry and should have waited." [36]

With that, the investigation ended. After all the hysteria and energy expended during the month, investigators had found that the Women's Army Corps was not full of homosexuals and sex maniacs after all.

Other lesbians managed to hide their sexuality from the military and society as a whole. It seemed the only way to get by. Johnnie Phelps was in the

WAC and worked in General Eisenhower's office in Europe. She began her military life in 1943 by trying to change. She said she considered herself "an American first, a soldier second, a woman third, and whatever else came in line fell in behind." She said that for years she had fought against herself, trying not to be a lesbian because she "knew it was wrong." She said she just wanted to be "like everybody else." But inevitably it turned out to be a futile fight.

There is a legendary story about Phelps after she had worked in Eisenhower's office for a while. Apparently, the general called her in to discuss rumors he had heard about lesbians in his WAC unit. He told her he had gotten reports that there were lesbians in the WAC battalion and he wanted Phelps to look into it and come back with a list of the women she suspected, so he could get rid of them. She said she looked him straight in the eye and told him she would do that, but she added that her name would be at the top of the list. "I think he knew, but I don't think he wanted to know. I think he wanted me to rat on everybody else and then keep quiet about myself, which I wasn't going to do." According to Phelps, Eisenhower then sat back in his chair, looked at her and said, "Forget the order. Forget about it." And they never visited the issue again.[37]

As women became more a part of the world outside the home during World War II, dealing with the issues that surrounded their sexuality became a tricky balancing act for law enforcement, the military, and for the women and men fighting the war or living on the home front as well. Perhaps because so few women, if any, were involved in making policies regarding sexual issues, rules and attitudes often seemed insensitive to women's needs or well-being. And at their worst, policies in the military and civilian life regarding women's sexual lives were downright violations of women's rights and dignity.

CHAPTER TWELVE

A War Within the War

RIGHT-WING, ANTI-SEMITIC MOTHERS' GROUPS AND JEWISH-AMERICAN WOMEN

Just let the Jews come in and the pistol-packing mamas will take care of them. There will be nothing left of them.

AGNES WATERS,
Lobbyist, Washington, D.C., 1944[1]

HATRED, IN MANY FORMS, flourished within the Axis and Allied nations during the war. But few exhibitions of hatred ever rivaled the Nazi concentration camps and the mass extermination of millions of Jewish people, Gypsies, and others whom Adolf Hitler deemed impure and inferior to Aryan Germans. America was not immune to hatred of Jewish people either. Some American women were receptive to it and zealously promoted it among other women. At the same time, American Jewish women actively combated such anti-Semitism, even if not always on a conscious level, by aiding the war effort and making their way as full citizens in American society. America provided them with opportunities to pursue life, liberty, and happiness at the same time fellow Jews in Europe were suffering untold degradation and almost certain murder.

These two groups of American women were on opposite sides of one of the causes that propelled America into World War II. Extreme right-wing women began as allies of the isolationists in this country who opposed American involvement in the war. Many used that sentiment to promote the much broader goal of achieving an all-white, all-Christian society in America. Jewish women in the U.S.—many of them first- and second-generation Americans— were busy appreciating and fighting to maintain the liberties of their country. Oftentimes, they seemed to be sheltered from the extent of the hatred leveled against them by the anti-Semites, but their sense of solidarity against such hatred, if not already in place during the war, was confirmed when the horrors of the Holocaust were revealed.

THE MOTHERS' MOVEMENT

In September 1939, Washington security officials were alarmed when an unidentified, unscheduled airplane flew directly over the White House toward the Capitol, violating what was supposed to be secure airspace. With the onset of war in Europe, special measures had been implemented to protect the White House and other public buildings from attack. Alarm grew when the airplane began dropping huge "bombs" of what turned out to be antiwar leaflets. No one on the ground was hurt and finally the airplane landed. Its pilot, Laura Ingalls, was immediately arrested. Ingalls (not to be confused with the famous writer Laura Ingalls Wilder) was one of the most celebrated pilots in America at the time. A rival of Amelia Earhart, she was famous for her stunt flying as well as for being the first female aviator to complete a transcontinental flight from New York to Los Angeles in 1930.

The leaflets Ingalls dropped over the nation's capital were pro-Nazi messages thinly disguised as "peace" pamphlets. They urged Congress not to support President Roosevelt's move to sell arms to the Allies fighting against Hitler, a move that they pointed out went against the United States's declared neutrality at the beginning of the war in Europe. Ingalls was released within hours and spent the next two years speaking out against impending American participation in the war with Germany. She joined her aviator colleague, Charles Lindbergh, in becoming one of the most popular speakers for the America First Committee, the leading isolationist group in the United States before America joined the war. But she went a few steps further in her pro-German stance than Lindbergh, who had once accepted a medal from Hitler. Before the U.S. joined the war, Ingalls had initiated a secret connection with the German government that led to the Nazis paying her a monthly fee of about $300 to infiltrate isolationist groups spreading the pro-Nazi message in the U.S. America First and its unofficial women's auxiliary, Women United, were two of her most effective platforms.

The New York–born Ingalls was a private-school-educated concert pianist, vaudeville dancer, and nurse who spoke seven languages. In her Nazi work, she reported directly to Baron Ulrich von Gienanth, the head of the German Gestapo in the U.S., whose official title was second secretary of the German embassy in Washington. Gienanth lauded Ingalls for her dedication and effectiveness in promoting their cause, especially the standing-room-only crowds she attracted on her speaking tours. He reportedly compared her crusading to the enthusiastic rallies of Hitler and his closest associates in the early days of Nazism. After France fell to Germany in 1940, Ingalls asked her boss if she could make a solo "peace" flight to Europe and continue the same kind of work there that she had done winning the hearts and minds of average Americans for the Nazis. Gienanth told her to stay put, saying, "The best thing you can do for our cause is to continue to promote the America First committee."

Ingalls scrupulously studied Hitler's *Mein Kampf*, underlining passages in red ink and basing most of her speeches on its principles. She believed Nazi Germany would be victorious in the war, and declared in an April 1941 letter to a German official, "Some day I will shout my triumph to a great leader and a great people . . . Heil Hitler!" When Germany and Italy officially declared war against America on December 11, 1941, Ingalls rushed to Washington to meet with Gienanth and get the names of people with whom she could continue her work in the U.S. Soon after, Ingalls was arrested by the FBI for failing to register with the American government as a paid Nazi agent and was later sentenced to two years and eight months in prison.

The leaflets Ingalls had dropped on Washington were written by her friend Cathrine Curtis, another American woman whose hatred of Communism was rivaled only by her deep hatred of Jewish people, all of whom she equated with Communists. Even before America First was launched, Curtis had started the Women's National Committee to Keep the U.S. Out of War, in September 1939. Curtis enlisted Ingalls and supplied her with money to fly around the country making speeches. Six days later, Ingalls made her flight over Congress. It is unclear whether Curtis was aware of the extent of Ingalls's German connections, but in a letter to Curtis, Ingalls had written, "I have always known that the best way to keep the United States out of war was to pray for or aid a swift German victory."[2]

Cathrine Curtis, a former movie actress and producer and a radio host in New York City, was part of a select, loosely connected network of women who led what was called the Mothers' Movement. Like the America First Committee, their ideas had roots in the isolationist movement. The first "momist" organization was the National Legion of Mothers of America (NLMA), a group that began in California with a broader base than subsequent right-wing, antiwar women's groups. But quickly the NLMA was dominated by Fascist women, including Curtis, who never had any children. Eventually, Curtis spun her women's group away from the NLMA. A myriad of similar groups sprang up with the word "Mother" in their names as well. The appeal was to mothers who did not want to send their sons to war, but the driving force behind the groups was opposition to Roosevelt, Britain, Communism, and Judaism. The groups were designed to disguise their strongest political goals and attract members with the motherhood ploy, members who might not have joined had they understood the deepest intentions of the organizers. One group called Mothers of Pennsylvania had to change its name abruptly when a local newspaper reported that most of its members had no children.[3]

These groups all followed similar patterns, but one organization led the way. Called We, the Mothers, Mobilize for America, the group was based in Chicago and initiated by a woman named Lyrl Clark Van Hyning. Soon after America joined the Allies in the war, she told her inner circle that having many franchises with different names in different neighborhoods across the country would be the most effective plan for their mothers' campaign.

> Instead of having one national organization we want to have thousands of small "block groups." We can send out telegrams and other messages to the person in charge of each group telling them what to do and when to do it.[4]

Indeed, that was what happened. At one point during the war the various Fascist-inspired mothers' groups were thought to have a collective membership of nearly half a million women. Van Hyning was not always able to control all the offshoot organizations, but her organization claimed at least 150,000 members around the country within weeks of its inception, and she was responsible for some of the most visible propaganda techniques of the mothers' groups. She edited and distributed *Women's Voice,* the official publication of We, the Mothers, with a circulation of 20,000.

Brought up on a farm in Ohio, Van Hyning was an ex-schoolteacher, a mother of three and married to a prominent Chicago businessman. She once said of her followers, many of whom were from blue-collar families:

> My women are not intelligent. In fact, they are rather stupid. But they are a group of women who will work hard for me, and that's what is important. Later, perhaps, we will be able to attract a higher type of woman to the cause.[5]

Van Hyning had been raised a Methodist, but did not attend church as an adult. Still, she was quick to take on religious themes in her arguments for the Nazi cause. She thought of herself as a kind of Christian martyr fighting against the Jews. She even compared herself to Jesus, ridiculing Judaism as she said Jesus had. In fact, she said she did not believe that Jesus was really Jewish, nor were any of the apostles, except for the traitorous Judas. She blamed the Jews for starting the Civil War and both world wars, and for plotting the assassination of Abraham Lincoln. She said former President Woodrow Wilson was really a Sephardic Jew named "Wohlson." Dwight D. Eisenhower was a Swedish Jew. Harry S Truman was a Jew and the S in his name stood for "Solomon." She called Franklin D. Roosevelt "Rosenvelt," and said his New Deal was a conspiracy by Jews and Communists to take over the United States. She called FDR a greater threat to America than Hitler. She saw Fascism as pro-Christian and a defense against Communism, which was led by Jewish people. She called Fascism "the only successful means for the protection of the Gentiles from Jewish dictatorship." Speaking of FDR's administration, which she believed was dominated by Jews, Van Hyning said:

> The whole gang are the offspring of the old gang that threw stones at Jesus Christ, wrapped thorns around his head, that flogged him and finally nailed him to the Cross because he spoke the truth, which upset their plans for world domination.[6]

One of Van Hyning's most infamous techniques was to obtain lists of the names of American men from various communities who were killed in the war in Europe. Then, We, the Mothers would send letters to the dead soldiers' mothers, declaring that the president and his war administration were responsible for their sons' deaths, not the Germans. The letters urged the mothers "not to be deceived by propaganda into blaming a foreign power." Van Hyning's We, the Mothers group organized a Women's National Peace Conference, in Chicago in June 1944, attended by 125 women delegates from twenty states. The first conference was held just after D-Day, when the tide of the war was turning against Germany. The women called for a negotiated peace with Germany. They drew up a resolution that said the Allied policy of accepting only unconditional surrender from Germany was "un-Christian."[7]

Van Hyning's views and tactics were not unique among the mothers groups' leaders. But there were American mothers unaffiliated with these groups who spoke out against them, especially mothers of soldiers killed in the war. A Louisiana mother wrote to Van Hyning in 1944, "It is impossible for me to understand how you who call yourselves 'We the Mothers Mobilize for America, Inc.' and express such un-American thoughts, can ask that I, or any American mother, become a party to such plots against our government and our President. I thank God that you are not representative of the mothers of America." The mother sent a copy of the letter to her congressman, who had it read into the *Congressional Record*. Columnist Dorothy Thompson spoke out against the mothers' groups as well. She said they were "black cockroaches, who call themselves American mothers and picket the White House."[8]

Perhaps the most prominent leader of these right-wing women was Elizabeth Dilling. Before America joined the war, she organized antiwar mothers sit-ins outside congressmen's offices. She also led other visible women's demonstrations in Washington, all in protest of FDR's Lend-Lease Act, which would produce weapons for the British to fight the Nazi forces advancing across Europe. Dilling had worked as an ardent anti-Communist through the 1930s, writing a book called *The Red Network,* which she published herself. It detailed what she saw as a huge Communist threat to America, which she said permeated the highest levels of government. She had particular antipathy for President Roosevelt and his "Jew Deal," her name for the New Deal, which she said was a Communist conspiracy. *The Red Network* contained long lists of more than 1,300 people and 460 organizations that she alleged had Communist affiliations, no matter how little evidence of such ties she could provide.

Dilling did not spare women or women's groups in her diatribes. She called the League of Women Voters subversive and dubbed many women "Reds," including social activist Jane Addams, poet Edna St. Vincent Millay, Congresswoman Jeanette Rankin, Secretary of Labor Frances Perkins, and, of course, Eleanor Roosevelt. Dilling had particular hatred for Mrs. Roosevelt, calling her "a disgrace to the nation." She started rumors that FDR had gonorrhea, which he had gotten from Eleanor, who had gotten it from a black man.[9] In 1936 she wrote an expansion of her first book and called it *The Roosevelt Red Record and Its Background,* with even longer lists of supposed Communists. Author Upton Sinclair, who won the 1943 Pulitzer Prize for a novel about Germany's descent into Nazism, was listed in the book as a Communist. He responded by calling Dilling a "pitiful, terror-stricken, hate-consumed candidate for an asylum."[10]

Dilling's third book, *The Octopus,* was so anti-Semitic that she published it under a male pseudonym, the Reverend Frank Woodruff Johnson. She was trying to avoid anyone being able to label her anti-Semitic, especially since she thought such a label might damage her husband's Chicago law practice. In the book she attacked the Anti-Defamation League of B'nai B'rith, saying it was the octopus trying to foster a Communist takeover of America. She went on at painstaking length about all the horrible Jews and ranted that they were all Communists. She called New York City, with its many Russian immigrants, the "Jew Communist" capital of the world. She turned her sights on black people as well, calling them pawns of the Communists. To top it off she said Jews and Communists were promoting interracial sex. "I have never attended a Communist party mass meeting," she said, "without observing the public petting of Negroes and whites." She remembered one such meeting she claimed to have attended in which "three burly Negroes were pawing their white girl companion, a college-type blonde wearing a squirrel coat." [11]

In 1938 Dilling started something called the Patriotic Research Bureau and published a bulletin that detailed her theories on the Red Menace and Jewish and black conspiracies. Dilling remained active through the war but was sidetracked by a nasty divorce proceeding initiated by her husband in 1942. In court, he distanced himself from her work, saying her Patriotic Research Bureau was formed to foment "class and religious hatred." He said her views had alienated his clients and made it hard to practice law in Chicago. He did not admit his own financing and support of her views through the years. The proceedings were raucous, with fistfights and screaming, and Dilling was held in contempt of court four times. Finally, the couple agreed to an uncontested divorce, but the suit was eventually dismissed when the couple reconciled. [12]

Dilling and Van Hyning were the leaders of the Chicago contingent of the Mothers' Movement, which formed its strongest base. But the Mothers' Movement also existed in other parts of the Midwest and Northeast, such as Pennsylvania, Ohio, and New York. In Cincinnati there was the Mothers of Sons Forum. In Detroit were Mothers of the U.S.A. and American Mothers. And in Philadelphia, there was an organization called the National Blue Star Mothers of America, which was deliberately named that so as to confuse people who mistook it for the legitimate and honorable Blue Star Mothers, a national organization with no political ax to grind, of mothers whose sons were serving in the war. [13]

The self-proclaimed Mothers' Movement's operative in Washington, and one of its loudest proponents, was Agnes Waters. Her rhetoric echoed the same themes as the other mothers: hatred of Jews, Communists, the British, black people, and the Roosevelts. Yet Waters was even more strident. She testified before Congress several times before and during the war, always claiming to represent the mothers' groups, but often she was not sanctioned by the groups she claimed to represent. At one women's "peace" rally in Chicago in 1942 she called President Roosevelt a traitor who needed to be impeached and went on to shout, "He ought to be killed." Several women in the crowd reportedly shouted back, "Let's do it!" In 1944, Waters's views were quoted in *Women's Home Companion* magazine:

> If we cannot get these traitors out of office by peaceful legal means
> we can resort to shooting them out! This would be easier than to fool
> with elections. . . . Let us demand that this war be stopped at once.
> Let's keep a clothesline handy in every little back yard to hang the
> traitors, or a gun![14]

Waters, a devout Catholic, had moved to Washington from New York City during World War I, and worked in the Justice and War departments. She also campaigned for women's suffrage and was a secretary to the leading suffragist, Alice Paul of the National Woman's Party. She married a veteran of that war and he died within ten years. Then she moved into real estate and made huge sums of money, including engineering million-dollar land deals in Chevy Chase, Maryland. She eventually retired from real estate and devoted herself to anti-Communist lobbying in Washington and speaking at mothers' rallies around the country. In 1942, she declared herself a candidate for president in the 1944 election. She used that role to give anti-Roosevelt speeches for two years.[15]

One of Waters's campaign promises had been to appoint a cabinet of patriots. "I want only Americans that are real men and women," she said, "not idiots and incompetents and dirty Jews!" She also said she would negotiate peace with the Axis countries and would deport all Russians and English people from the U.S. Waters proposed providing gas masks to every Christian to protect against the Jews, who she believed were plotting to gas all Gentiles. She campaigned to get the nomination of both the Democratic and Republican parties but was surprised when neither party nominated her.[16]

Waters campaigned against a 1939 child refugee bill that would have set up a program through the American Friends Service Committee to allow 20,000 German Jewish children under the age of fourteen into the country to be taken care of until the war was over and they could be returned safely to their parents. She said the children "could never become loyal Americans," and added that they would only be "potential leaders of a revolt against our American form of government." She went on, "Why should we give preference to these potential communists? Already we have too many of their kind in our country now trying to overthrow our government." Members of Congress were against the bill as well and it never passed, leaving at least 20,000 German Jewish children to endure whatever the Nazi government had in store for them.[17]

In 1945, Waters reportedly stole envelopes from congressmen, who received free postage to send mail to their constituents. She used them to send out leaflets and National Blue Star Mothers of America propaganda. One such envelope went by mistake to a Jewish mother in Philadelphia whose son, a soldier, had lost his leg in the war. The leaflet inside read:

> How long are we going to permit our men to be slain to save the Jewish empires all over the world? Did you know that certain Jews are being trained . . . to be the ARMY OF OCCUPATION, with all the prostrated nations under their control? . . . Is that what your boy was fighting for?[18]

The federal government was not exactly tolerant of the groups stirring up anti-government sentiment. FDR was particularly annoyed by these forces working against him. He had enlisted the FBI as early as 1935 to keep tabs on the nationalist groups and especially the leaders who spearheaded attacks, such as Father Charles E. Coughlin, Gerald L. K. Smith, and William Dudley Pelley. Father Coughlin was a Catholic priest with a radio show who had many followers. His simple presentation of complex issues was accessible to most people and always led to an endorsement of the same isolationist, racist, anti-Semitic points of view that the mothers' groups endorsed. Smith, a preacher born in Wisconsin, also had a large following that was broader based than that of any other leader, and published an anti-Semitic magazine called *The Cross and the Flag*. And Pelley was a mystic who openly admired Hitler and organized a paramilitary anti-Semitic group called the Silver Shirts. All three men had ties with leaders of the Mothers' Movement and their members.[19]

FBI director J. Edgar Hoover kept a watch on the groups, but Roosevelt also pressured his attorney general, Francis Biddle, to pursue them. Although reluctant at first because of civil liberties concerns, and fear that it would be hard to win convictions, Biddle eventually appointed a special assistant in early 1941 to investigate the right-wing agitators. That was the beginning of a long series of indictments that led to a large sedition trial in 1944. Two women were among the thirty final defendants indicted: Elizabeth Dilling and Lois de Lafayette Washburn, an ardent Nazi sympathizer who had founded anti-Semitic groups in Chicago and Tacoma, Washington. The indictment that led to the trial charged the defendants had plotted with one another and with the Germans to undermine the U.S. military and overthrow the U.S. government, and had mounted "a systematic campaign of propaganda" designed to "destroy democracy throughout the world." Newspapers like the *Chicago Tribune* that supported the isolationists and some of the mothers' groups railed against the trial, saying, "the mass indictment is itself an offense against liberty." Neither Coughlin nor Smith were among those indicted, but Pelley was.[20]

The two female defendants, along with many of the others, mocked the proceedings. Dilling came into court carrying a false nose and glasses and wearing a badge that said, "I am a spy." Lois de Lafayette Washburn, who was a founder of something called the American Gentile Protective Association, stood on the federal courthouse steps and gave a Nazi salute for photographers as she proudly shouted, "I am a Fascist." After more than a month of delay tactics by the defense during jury selection, the trial began on May 17, 1944. The U.S. prosecutor, O. John Rogge, said he would show that the defendants were in cahoots with Berlin, were trained by the Nazis, and were plotting to overthrow the U.S. government. He said that they were particularly insidious because they were using new techniques of subterfuge so that their intent was "always hidden behind a smoke screen," and that it "flourished under the very democratic system which the defendants sought to destroy."[21]

Elizabeth Dilling's lawyer husband, Albert, gave an opening statement for the defense. He called the government's case "a Jewish conspiracy," and said, "organized Jewish policies appear to conflict with gentile Americanism." Elizabeth Dilling was charged with mailing seditious material and making seditious statements. The charges were brought under the Sedition Act of 1917, which outlawed attempts to undermine the military's morale during wartime. The trial dragged on through the summer and fall. The defense dogged the judge, who tried to maintain order. Between the defendants and the defense attorneys an inordinate number of interruptions were made whenever the prosecution had the floor. *The New York Times* said, "Rising like a nest of disturbed locusts at every attempt of the prosecution to introduce documentary evidence, the defense lawyers kept the court ruling constantly on objections, day after day, week after week. Every document was attacked—and there were hundreds of them—and objection was made to every witness, in endless and redundant speeches by as many lawyers who could get on their feet at the same time."[22]

By the end of November 1944, the judge, Edward C. Eicher, who had tried in vain to handle the rowdy and disorderly atmosphere, died of a heart attack. Francis Biddle, the attorney general, said the trial had killed him. No one was enthusiastic about the idea of continuing with a new judge, who would have to get up to speed on thousands and thousands of pages of testimony and evidence from more than six months of proceedings. The war was winding down and the defendants' activities had been curtailed by the trial. So the case sat around with no one willingly taking it up again. Finally, in late 1946, the case was dismissed on the grounds that the defendants had not gotten the speedy trial that was their constitutional right as American citizens.

The Mothers' Movement also wound down after the war. With the gruesome truth of the Holocaust revealed in all its ugliness, anti-Semitism became less acceptable. In addition, one of the main targets of the movement, Franklin Roosevelt, had died in 1945, so there was not as much political fervor to aid the cause. The main angle of the women, that their sons, if they had any, were fighting an unjust war, was gone. Most of the women who had led the movement were never again in the national spotlight.

AMERICAN JEWISH WOMEN

Thankfully, such blatant anti-Semitism was not something most Jewish people in America had to come in contact with every day. The mothers' groups operated mostly on the fringes of society. And while many Americans were aware of Father Coughlin's radio broadcasts and Gerald L. K. Smith's anti-Semitic diatribes, most Jewish people were able to ignore them and continue with their lives. On the whole, Jewish Americans did all the things other Americans did during the war. Jewish women were sending their sons, husbands, brothers, and boyfriends off to the war, working in the factories, joining the military, and going into the professions, entertainment, and journalism, just like everyone else. Yet there was often lurking a conscious, or unconscious, sense that there was a difference.

Bette Greene, who was a young Jewish teen during World War II, wrote a novel for young adults called *Summer of My German Soldier*. In it, Patty Bergen, a twelve-year-old Jewish girl from Arkansas, fell in love with a German prisoner of war named Anton who escaped from a prison camp near her home. He was not much older than she was. Patty ended up bringing him food and helping him survive in his hiding place near her home. She began to learn that not all non-Jewish Germans, even those who fought for the Nazis, subscribed to Hitler's beliefs. In one exchange Patty asked Anton how he escaped.

> "The actual mechanics of the escape are not important," he said. "The pertinent point is that I was able to create a—a kind of climate that permitted the escape. Specifically, my deception was believed because it was built on a foundation of truth. Hitler taught me that."
> I heard him say it. "Hitler taught you?"
> Anton smiled. "I learned it by analyzing his techniques. Hitler's first layer is an undeniable truth, such as: The German worker is poor. The second layer is divided equally between flattery and truth: The German worker deserves to be prosperous. The third layer is total fabrication: The Jews and the Communists have stolen what is rightfully yours."

He told Patty how he used the fact that he could speak English and had an English governess growing up to create the impression among the guards that he was wealthy. Then, he told one of the guards with financial problems that his father was willing to pay $5,000 to anyone who helped him get out of prison. He showed the guard five glass diamonds and told him they were real. "Five perfect diamonds, each diamond having been appraised in excess of one thousand dollars, will be given to the person who drives me out beyond those gates." Anton said, "So he did it and I paid him with a dollar's worth of glass jewelry."

A few minutes later, Anton asked Patty the question he had been wondering since they met.

> "I'm certain you appreciate the seriousness of what you have done, aiding an escaped prisoner of war. I was wondering why you were taking these risks on my behalf. Because of your German ancestry? Perhaps your father is secretly sympathetic to the Nazi cause?"
> "That's not true! My father's parents came from Russia and my mother's from Luxembourg."

Anton looked alarmed. "I'm sorry. It's just that Bergen is such a good German name."

"It's also a good Jewish name," I said, pleased by the clean symmetry of my response.

His mouth came open. "Jewish?" An index finger pointed toward me. "You're Jewish?"

I thought he knew. I guess I thought everybody knew. Does he think I tricked him? My wonderful Anton was going to change to mean. As I nodded Yes, my breathing came to a halt while my eyes clamped shut.

Suddenly, strong baritone laughter flooded the room. Both eyes popped open and I saw him standing there, shaking his head from side to side.

"It's truly extraordinary," he said. "Who would believe it? 'Jewish girl risks all for German soldier.' Tell me Patty Bergen—" his voice became soft, but with a trace of hoarseness—"why are you doing this for me?"

Being twelve, she did not have the courage to admit to him that she was in love with him, so instead she said that she was doing it because she did not want anything bad to happen to him.[23]

In a book, a young girl such as the fictional Patty Bergen falling in love with a German prisoner of war represents a union that would teach her young readers how to overcome hatred based on what makes people different. In the adult world, such openness and acceptance was rarer.

In the military, white people from different backgrounds mingled together and had to adjust to their differences. The Jewish women who joined the women's services, many of whom were second- and third-generation Americans, found they had to contend with attitudes they had never encountered before.

Ann Kaplowitz Goldberg from Brooklyn, New York, was a sergeant in the WAC. She had a jarring encounter with a woman from the rural South during her first weeks in the Army.

I remember in basic training in the first week, in the barracks . . . I'm in my little cubbyhole, and I'm getting undressed. I could feel somebody staring at me. I turned around, and [it was] a little girl . . . she was from no place, Arkansas. I said to her, "Do you have a problem?"

She said, "No."

I said, "Well, why are you staring at me?"

"My daddy told me that all Jews were born with a money belt, and I'm looking to see what yours is like."

I was absolutely speechless.

Goldberg had another such experience when she was in the hospital after breaking her arm. A male orderly in the hospital found out she was Jewish and came into her room.

He got next to my bed, and he got down on his knees, and he prayed for me that I should be saved.

I kept saying, "Saved from what?" He never answered me. He just kept going on. When he had free time, he would run in and kneel by my bed. I said, "Well, if I've got somebody else praying for me, it can't hurt."

Goldberg said she didn't blame the man personally. "I felt he was very ignorant. A lot of these people are brought up that way. It's not their fault."

After she got out of the hospital, Goldberg remembered going to a Passover seder in Wichita Falls, Texas, where she was stationed, and she found that sometimes even when she was with other Jewish people, military women were still considered second to the male soldiers.

We were invited to participate in this dinner and services at this hotel. . . . And I'm so happy I'm going to be amongst my own kind and get a real good Jewish meal, kosher food. . . .

I was so ignored. The women were hovering over these guys. "Do you need this?" "Can I do that?" Thank God, the guy next to me cut my meat for me, because I couldn't handle it with the cast. They were all invited to homes to meet their daughters, all of them. Nobody had a son at home for me to meet, so I didn't get invited.[24]

That sense of being left out was not uncommon among Jewish women in the military. Often there were few other Jewish people around both at the military base and in the small middle-American and Southern towns were they were stationed. Bernice Sains Freid served in the WAVES and was sent to Stillwater, Oklahoma, for training at Oklahoma A&M College. She had a shock after about two weeks there when she realized that she was the only Jewish woman among hundreds of people on the base. The next day she took a bus to Oklahoma City for a weekend leave.

> Although it was Friday night, it was not a Synagogue or Rabbi that I wanted. I felt literally starved for contact with another Jew. I could not confide in my three bunkmates or any of the other WAVES, who were friendly. There was no anti-Semitism. We ate the same food, wore the same uniforms, slept in the same dormitory. On the outside we all looked alike, but inside I knew I was different. I was a Jew. They could not understand me.

As soon as she arrived in Oklahoma City she rushed to the nearest USO because she knew that it was affiliated with the Jewish Welfare Board, where she would find other Jewish people.

> I entered the building out of breath, surveying the interior frantically. To my left I saw a huge blue velvet banner fringed in yellow bearing the letters "JWB." I felt like a traveler dying of thirst, reaching an oasis. My eyes filled with tears; there was a lump in my throat as I entered the office. On a bench sat a boyish-looking, puny, undersized sailor with horn-rimmed glasses. At any other time I would have ignored him but I knew he was a Jew. That was all that mattered. I sat next to him, and as we spoke, my loneliness evaporated.
> A short while later, a Jewish Welfare Board worker entered the room. "Are there many Jewish servicemen nearby?" I asked hopefully. "There are forty men stationed at Norman Air Base about forty miles from here, but you're the first Jewish servicewoman we've ever seen." [25]

Jewish women made strides into the American mainstream during World War II. In Atlantic City, New Jersey, in 1945, Bess Myerson became the first Miss America who was Jewish. Gertrude Berg had a million-dollar contract to write and star in the popular radio series *The Goldbergs* from 1938 to 1945. Berg played Molly Goldberg, who became the template for the stereotypical Jewish mother. Gertrude Stein and Lillian Hellman were writing throughout the war. Hadassah, the largest Jewish women's organization during World War II, grew from 60,000 members in the 1930s to approximately 120,000 by the end of the war.

Because many Americans of Jewish descent had fled the countries the Nazis invaded, or still had family members who were left behind, their commitment to the war effort was sometimes heightened. As the war ended, and the horror of the concentration camps came into full view, Jewish people in this country were especially grateful to be Americans, yet thoroughly heartbroken by the fate of fellow Jews at the hands of the Nazis.

Loretta Ehrlich graduated from Washington Irving High School in New York City just after the war started. Her boyfriend, Jack Kleiner, joined the Navy and went off to the Pacific war after he graduated from high school the next year in 1943. Loretta signed up for training in electronics and ended up with a job in a factory in Manhattan that produced radar equipment for the military. She loved her job and worked there for the rest of the war. Loretta and Jack had grown up across the street from each other in a mostly Jewish neighborhood in the Bronx. Loretta knew Jack's mother well, and they saw each other every day. Letters were the main means of keeping in touch, and whenever either of them got a letter from Jack they would tell the other. Jack's mother also kept in touch by mail with her parents in Lithuania. "After a while," said Loretta, "she no longer heard from them."

The same thing happened to Loretta's father. His parents and two of his siblings were still in Poland. He and a brother and a sister had gotten out. During the war, the letters stopped coming. "We heard Hitler invaded Poland and that's where his family was," said Loretta. "I was too young to realize, but I think he might have worried more than I thought he did. I think my father kept a lot from us to protect us." Her father and her boyfriend's mother never heard from their parents again. "I don't think anybody knew exactly what was happening," said Loretta, "until the war was over." She particularly remembered her boyfriend's mother being upset after seeing the pictures from the liberation of the concentration camps. That was when, Loretta said, her father and her mother-in-law knew their parents were "no longer alive." Families of concentration camp victims never got the closure that usually came to others who lost someone in the war. "It was never really certified that they died," said Loretta. "They didn't receive a letter to say that your parents were deceased. The records were burned by the Nazis."

A friend of Loretta's from the neighborhood who had served as a soldier came back after the war and told her about liberating a concentration camp. "He told of the horrors. He didn't go into too much detail, but it was horrendous." Loretta was relieved, however, by one thing. Her boyfriend came back and they were able to marry. Both had lost grandparents they never knew to the Nazis. But like many Americans they also knew they had a whole, free life ahead of them.[26]

Phillis Heller Rosenthal said she did not encounter as much anti-Semitism as some Jewish people in America did during World War II. Born in New York City and raised on Long Island, New York, she graduated from Smith College in 1940. Her family had a longer heritage in America than many more recently immigrated Jewish families. Both of her parents' families came over in the 1800s from Bavaria. Three of her grandparents were born in America. Her father had attended Harvard Law School and her brother had a law degree from NYU. Phillis's mother died while she was in college.

When Phillis decided she wanted to go to law school in 1941, she could not follow in her father's footsteps since Harvard Law School did not admit women, so she chose Columbia. She finished law school in 1944 and joined the WAVES. She was sent to Washington to work in administrative law at the Bureau of Naval Personnel. Just as the war ended, Rosenthal embarked on one of the greatest adventures of her life.

Her brother, who had been in the Navy too, told her about an opportunity to work on the Nuremberg trials. The original war crimes trials had begun in October of 1945 with prosecutions against top Nazi officials. Jewish-American women did not get any of the highest profile work on the trials, but they often had important jobs nonetheless. Edith Coliver was a German-born Jew who had fled her homeland with her family in 1936, eventually settling in San Francisco. In September of 1945 she returned to Germany to work as a translator and analyst at the Nuremberg tribunal. The twenty-three-year-old Coliver translated the pretrial testimony of Hermann Göring, the chief of the German air force and a leading official behind the Holocaust. "He was not particularly thrilled to see a woman, a Jewish woman, as his interpreter," Coliver said. Göring was eventually sentenced to be hanged, but committed suicide before his sentence was carried out.[27]

After the international tribunal at Nuremberg, nineteen of Hitler's top officials were found guilty of war crimes. But still left to investigate and put on trial were more former Nazi officials and executives of German companies who were complicit with the Nazis. In 1946, the United States launched what were called "the subsequent proceedings" to bring the remaining Nazis to justice. Phillis was assigned to work on one of the most notorious cases of all.

She researched the German company I. G. Farben, the largest chemical manufacturer in the world. Among other things, Farben had manufactured all of the poison gas Zyklon B that was used to kill inmates in the concentration camps. The company was formed as a conglomerate of many companies, including Bayer, BASF, Agfa, and Hoechst. Farben was the largest single financier of the Nazi Party from 1933 to 1944. And the company built a plant at the Auschwitz concentration camp to produce synthetic rubber, using prisoners from the concentration camps as slave laborers.[28]

Phillis read and classified translated documents that detailed what was done at the Auschwitz plant. She remembered finding contracts between I. G. Farben and the SS in which they laid out just how much food they would have to supply the slave laborers to keep them working for six months before they died. She found more of the most unimaginable details in the documents, which were often printed in triplicate.

> They also conducted weird, painful, unnecessary, really unscientific experiments on the inmates at Auschwitz, most of which resulted in horrible deaths. . . . Some of the directors were scientists. And the company hired scientists. They supervised them or they ordered the experiments. . . . I went through piles and piles of papers. . . . I remember some of the experiments. One was pumping a woman's reproductive organs full of cement. *Why?*
>
> Another was X-raying the breasts until they festered and fell off. Another was injecting typhus and instead of alleviating the symptoms, watching them die a horrible death.
>
> These so-called medical experiments were described and printed in German scientific journals which were widely read by the German medical profession.

Phillis stayed in Nuremberg doing the research for ten months. She was not there when the Farben executives were tried. The subsequent proceedings at Nuremberg ended in 1949 with about 142 convictions. Twenty-four I. G. Farben executives were convicted, but by 1951 all of them had been released from prison and many continued to consult with German companies.

While Phillis witnessed one of the most gut-wrenching aspects of World War II at Nuremberg, she also found the love of her life in Nuremberg. His name was Robert Rosenthal, and he too was an American Jewish lawyer. He was also one of the most celebrated bomber pilots in the U.S. Air Force. By the time the war ended, he was on his third tour of duty with the Eighth Air

Force and had flown fifty-two missions. Among them was the largest bombing mission over Berlin, which he commanded in February 1945.

Phillis Heller met Robert Rosenthal on her first night aboard the ship that took them to Nuremberg. For the ten-day voyage they were inseparable. By the time they reached Germany, he had proposed and she had accepted.

> Then I said to him that I had promised my father that I would ask his permission. He thought, "Oh, a real old-fashioned girl. That's great." So he wrote my father a lovely letter. And my father wrote back a very formal letter saying I think you should wait until you get home and we can discuss it.

At that, Robert Rosenthal thought they would not be able to marry. But Phillis disagreed, on a very lawyerly technicality. "I promised to ask," she told him. "I didn't promise anything but to ask." They married within a few weeks. The groom's mother had to send them rings from America because there was no gold in Germany after the war. They had a reception at the Grand Hotel in Nuremberg. On their honeymoon they stayed in a German hotel that had silverware and tablecloths with Nazi swastikas on them. "We didn't like it," said Phillis, "but we were glad we were using them and there weren't any Nazis around."

On their honeymoon, her husband finally told Phillis the extent of his Air Force career, giving her newfound admiration of him. Fellow soldiers had given Rosenthal the nickname "Rosie." And when it came time for the twenty-five-year-old pilot to pick a name for his plane—the pilot's privilege—he dubbed his B-17 *Rosie's Riveters*. Every time he took his B-17 on the famous daylight bombing raids over Germany, the name on its nose heralded through European skies the women on the American home front doing work vital to him and his fellow soldiers overseas.

Phillis Rosenthal became pregnant and the couple went back to America in May of 1947. She said the gruesomeness of the documents she read at Nuremberg has stuck with her all through her life.[29]

Saipan
Saturday, August 11, 1945

Everyone was so amazed at the atomic bomb. And then at Russia's entry into the war. And it was only then that the pessimists out here actually began to believe the war wouldn't last another 3 years. Up to now, all the other outfits on the island have maintained a more or less amused tolerance at the unbounded optimism of the boys at the B-29 base. Ever since I got here I've been hearing about the bets you could make with the B-29 boys—they were giving 3 to 1 it would be over by August 15. . . . Everyone else seemed to think any of these bets were strictly sure things and regarded the "fly-fly boys" as wildly optimistic. But with the atomic bomb (no one knew about that—including the vast majority of the B-29 boys) and then with Russia's entry into the war everyone joined in the air corps optimism.

CHAPTER THIRTEEN

Inside the Secret City

WIVES AND WACS IN LOS ALAMOS

I . . . realized that when my husband joined the Manhattan Project it would be as if we shut a great door behind us. The world I had known of friends and family would no longer be real to me. . . . The only bridge between us would be the shadowy one of censored letters. . . . Now we were part of the top secret of the war.

RUTH MARSHAK,
Los Alamos, New Mexico, 1946[1]

Los Alamos National Laboratory

IN THE FALL OF 1944, Phyllis Fisher was just starting to settle into her new life in Albuquerque, New Mexico, where she and her husband, Leon, and son, Bobby, had moved a few months before. Leon had recently completed his Ph.D. in physics at the University of California—Berkeley, and was in a new job at the University of New Mexico. Phyllis had finished her graduate program in social work at Berkeley recently too, and was working part-time at a local adoption agency. But in mid-October, Leon, then twenty-six, came home to say they were moving again. That morning, he had received a letter and a phone call from one of his former Berkeley professors, telling him the family must report to an undisclosed location to work on a top secret government project. Leon did not feel he could say no. Phyllis, then twenty-five, wrote to her parents about the move on October 4, 1944. She was not able to tell them much, partly because of the secrecy surrounding her husband's new assignment and partly because she did not know much about it herself.

> Here's what I *can* tell you. We'll be going "there" next week (less than a day's trip from Albuquerque) to select our living quarters, and we will move "there" sometime between the 26th and 30th of this month. We have been directed to drive to a certain city and report to an inconspicuous address where we will be given further instructions. It's alright with me, so long as we're not met by a bearded mystic, given a piece of thread and instructed to follow it to its end. At this point, nothing would surprise me.[2]

That was how it started for most of the scientists who helped create and build the atomic bomb. There was a letter or a phone call or a visit from a colleague (or all three) asking them to join a highly secretive scientific mission, in a remote place, for an indeterminate amount of time. Most of the scientists were men. Many had wives, and some had children. They were given very little chance to adjust to the idea, and only a vague idea of what they would be doing. Unlike being drafted into the Army, the men were allowed to bring their families along. But there was a catch. The scientists could not discuss their work with anyone, not even their wives. So the women were left to follow along on faith, and on the strength of their devotion to their husband's work.

It was not without some trepidation that they went. As Phyllis said in her memoir, *Los Alamos Experience*:

> I had felt a sudden sense of isolation and anger when I discovered that Leon either wouldn't or couldn't answer my questions. . . . I was dumbfounded! Why was it necessary to go there? Why couldn't I be trusted? Trusted with what? We were going off to live in isolation and "we" meant both of us! Why couldn't I know why? I was no physicist and I wouldn't understand a detailed and technical explanation, nor was I asking for specifics. In the past, Leon had always patiently described his scientific projects or research to me. But this time he made it absolutely clear that I wasn't to ask and, if I did, he wasn't about to answer. I didn't like the implications, not at all! I felt uncomfortable, sensing a new distance between us, one that might grow larger with the passage of time.[3]

RECRUITING

By the time the Fishers arrived, Los Alamos had been operating as a scientific outpost for more than a year. The first arrivals had come in early 1943. Before that, the site had been a private boys school called Los Alamos Boys Ranch School. In fall of 1942, the government had gone looking for a remote location to build an atomic bomb. They wanted a site far enough from both coasts to be safe from enemy attack, and secluded enough to remain secret within the U.S. They settled on the school site, and the War Department notified the owners. The boys had to leave, and the school was closed on February 8, 1943. The population of Los Alamos went from fewer than 300 in 1942 to 5,700 by 1945. Two thirds of those residents were civilians, including the scientists and their families, and one third were military personnel.[4]

A landmark moment on the road to America's development of the atomic bomb came when Italian physicist Enrico Fermi, who had won the Nobel Prize in Physics in 1938, conducted experiments in Chicago that led to the first controlled nuclear chain reaction. Another pivotal moment came in the fall of 1939, when Albert Einstein wrote a letter to President Roosevelt warning that the discovery of nuclear fission could lead to the development of "extremely powerful bombs." He told the president that America should beware of Germany developing an atomic bomb before America. By that time, both Einstein and Fermi had left their native lands of Germany and Italy and were working in the United States. Einstein suggested that the president set up a task force to keep track of research in the area and fund new American research. He also recommended that the United States try to get large quantities of uranium, thought to be an important ingredient in a nuclear bomb.

The president took Einstein's advice, and by early 1942 Roosevelt had approved a project to develop an atomic bomb. He appointed General Leslie R. Groves to head up what was called the Manhattan Engineer District. Groves also oversaw the building of the Pentagon and was known as a man who could get things done in government. Groves picked a site in Oak Ridge, Tennessee, where uranium could be processed and enriched to make it usable in a bomb. Then Groves set about finding a site where the bomb could be designed and built, as well as a director for that site.

He picked J. Robert Oppenheimer, a theoretical physicist and professor at the University of California at Berkeley. Together, Groves and Oppenheimer settled on Los Alamos as the perfect place to do the work. Oppenheimer had visited the school as a young man and knew the surrounding area well. In the meantime, at the University of Chicago, Enrico Fermi was working on how to split the nucleus of uranium several times in a chain reaction and control the massive amounts of energy released, the first step in making a nuclear bomb possible. He succeeded at the end of 1942.[5] In addition, a variety of research into nuclear energy was being conducted at other universities around the country. In that climate, Oppenheimer set out to bring all the top academic researchers together in one place and coordinate their work with the goal of producing a bomb.[6]

The secret project, in a remote place, was not always an easy sell to established physicists with wives and children, comfortable heading up their own research teams at major universities. But Oppenheimer managed to sign on top scientists from Princeton, Cornell, MIT, Harvard, the University of Chicago, the University of California at Berkeley, and other schools. Also, two dozen British scientists joined the group in the spring of 1943.[7]

As the project came together, the social structure of the place began to form in a sort of caste system that dictated housing and other perks. The elite were the scientists. They were paid the most, got the best housing, and were able to bring their families along. The next on the totem pole were the Army officers. And close behind came the men in the Special Engineer Detachment, who were young scientists taken from universities and drafted into the Army to work with the senior scientists. But no one in the Army was allowed to bring his family to the site. Then came the WACs assigned to the Manhattan Project to do mostly clerical work. And there were the MPs sent to Los Alamos to guard everyone. Finally, the construction and maintenance crews were last in the order of things. They had the least desirable housing. And because there was not enough of that kind of labor, day workers came in from surrounding Native American and Spanish-American pueblos. That group also included maids, local women whom the government hired to work in the houses of the scientists' families.[8]

Several quickly constructed buildings were erected around the boys school's older stone structures to serve as housing, dining halls, a school, and other public buildings for the community. Included were a store, a hospital, and a movie theater. In a separate part of the site was the tech area, where the scientists did their work. An official white badge was required to enter that area, so most wives could not go to that part of the site. Building on the remote terrain was a challenge, with only a narrow, mountainous road leading to and from the site, a location far away from railroads and supply centers. Even with the fast rate at which new housing went up, builders were not able to keep up with the influx of residents.[9]

URANIUM FISHER

Among the scientists there was a hierarchy. The very senior scientists lived in the older, most attractive houses that had been built for the school. Other elite scientists lived in specially built apartments. Still other scientists lived in newer, more hastily constructed housing. The housing was allotted according to the size of the family. A family with one child was assigned a two-bedroom apartment or house. A couple with no children got a one-bedroom place. The rent was based on a percentage of the family's salary, not the size of the home. The maid service was also allotted according to how many children were in the house and if the mother worked.

The Fishers were assigned a two-bedroom house in a newly constructed part of the site. Phyllis Fisher got a government-supplied maid one half-day a week because she had one child and did not work.

The day to day living was an adventure or disaster, depending on how you wanted to look at it. Our houses were paper-thin. Sand sifted through the windows whenever the wind blew. Sudden downpours of rain turned our hill into a sea of mud. Our single, centrally placed oil heater was temperamental. More than once, we spent a winter night in sub-zero temperatures *inside* our little cottage. Our "quiet" was punctuated from time to time by explosions down in the canyons. These explosions were often enough to shake our flimsy houses and set all the pictures on the walls askew. We would straighten the pictures and then, BANG, another explosion and once again, pictures to straighten.

Admittedly, these inconveniences were nothing compared to the work of the project close at hand, and certainly nothing compared to the wars raging overseas. . . . I simply tried not to hear the sounds of war in those explosions. Instead, I did my best to master the art of cooking on a primitive stove, and to adapt successfully to the "hardships" of mud, cold, shortages, the isolation from normal society, and accept my ignorance of the work being done on our mesa and in the canyons surrounding it.[10]

That task of moving forward no matter what happened was compounded as the work went on, and Phyllis's husband was around less and less.

Leon seemed to be working longer and longer hours and under more and more pressure. On Monday nights he hurried home for a quick dinner and raced back to a meeting of his group. On Tuesday nights he attended the colloquium for all those white badges. Now, so often, on the other nights as well he would hurry back to the tech area and take an Army car out to the site where he worked.[11]

Days occupied with housework and child care and nights alone with her son while her husband worked could be trying. Phyllis appreciated the help she got one morning a week from her maid, Apolonia, who lived in a nearby village. Still, Phyllis was a little troubled by the setup.

Curious, wasn't it, that our project had to be kept secret from the Caucasian population of Santa Fe and yet the Indians and Spanish-Americans were bused daily to the project? A secret community was being infiltrated daily, and no one was concerned. Was it because these people could be trusted more than the white population? I don't think so. Was it because they were considered too unimportant to be a security threat? Was it because we hadn't thought about them as people, as individuals? We needed their services to stoke our coal, clean our houses, collect our garbage, and twist wires in the tech area.[12]

With free hospital services and schools and a population with an average age of twenty-five, it is not surprising that a bit of a baby boom erupted at Los Alamos. Eighty babies were born in the first year, and about ten a month after that. A nursery school was among the first community services set up.[13] In spring of 1945, just as the Manhattan Project was about to come to fruition, Phyllis and Leon joined the ranks of those expecting babies. Many of the babies born at Los Alamos were first children, but the Fishers already had young Bobby, so this child would be their second. But the odd circumstances of their lives meant emotions ran high with the mix of intense work and a pregnancy in the family.

> The approaching climax to the work of the Los Alamos scientists was . . . felt by all. Yet, the super-secrecy . . . made this period almost unbearable for those of us who were ignorant of the purpose of the project. We could sense the hopes and fears that charged the air on the hill, and yet we were unable to share with our husbands the sense of mixed elation and horror that they felt. Snugly content in my pregnancy, I nevertheless felt twinges of apprehension as I wondered what monstrous thing the scientists on the mesa were about to give birth to.[14]

Still, the families tried to maintain their humor. When Leon was home for dinner, he and Phyllis sometimes toyed with names for their baby on the way. Often they would come up with a silly first name, and put it with their last name, so they might say something like "Apple Fisher." One silly name Phyllis innocently pulled out of the hat provoked her husband in a way she had not seen before.

> At dinner one evening, I asked in bantering tone, "Well, how about Uranium Fish . . . ? I never finished "Fisher" because a red-faced, furious Leon was roaring at me, demanding that I *never* use that word again.

"What's wrong?" I asked, startled. "I only said, Ur—," and, blam, his hand was over my mouth.

"Stop that!" he shouted, "You never know when someone is right near this paper house! Someone might hear you. *Never* say that! You've *got* to listen to me!" [15]

After Leon went back to work that evening and Phyllis had put her son to bed, she decided to do a little research herself. She found one of her husband's textbooks written for first-year physics students and looked up references to uranium.

> For the first time, I had some real idea of what was going on in the isolation of Los Alamos. . . . What monstrous horror was being created here? Could it end the war? Could it be the end of us? [16]

POST OFFICE BOX 1663

In government terminology Los Alamos was called "Site Y." It was the only Army base in the Manhattan Project. The few other sites that were part of the project were in Tennessee, Washington state, and on a few university campuses. To those who corresponded with the residents of Los Alamos, the place was known only as Post Office Box 1663. For babies born in Los Alamos during the war, their birthplace was listed merely as P.O. Box 1663. The settlement and laboratory at Los Alamos was not on any wartime map and the residents could not vote in New Mexico. They did pay New Mexico taxes, but without using their names on the tax forms, only a number assigned to them. Their cars were not registered in New Mexico, but remained registered in their home states. Technically, Los Alamos did not exist.

Ruth Marshak went with her husband, just like all the other wives, when he was summoned from Montreal, where he was teaching physics, to Los Alamos. "I can tell you nothing about it," her husband told her. "We're going away, that's all," he said. "I felt akin to the pioneer women," Ruth Marshak remembered, "accompanying their husbands across the uncharted plains westward, alert to danger, resigned to the fact that they journeyed, for weal or for woe, into the Unknown." She soon learned that she would be living on top of a mesa thirty-five miles northwest of Santa Fe.

The most direct road to it was a treacherous washboard running through the Indian pueblo of San Ildefonso, over the muddy Rio Grande, and then up a series of narrow switchbacks. As we neared the top of the mesa, the view was breathtaking. Behind us lay the Sangre de Cristo Mountains, at sunset bathed in changing waves of color—scarlets and lavenders. . . . Ahead was Los Alamos, and beyond the flat plateau on which it sat was its backdrop, the Jemez Mountain Range. Whenever things went wrong at Los Alamos, and there was never a day when they didn't, we had this one consolation—we had a view.[17]

Security was high. Like all visitors, and residents throughout their stay there, Marshak and her husband had to pass through a guarded gate and show badges every time they came or went. And the whole place was enclosed.

The fence penning Los Alamos was erected and guarded to keep out the treasonable, the malicious, and the curious. This fence had a real effect on the psychology of the people behind it. It was a tangible barrier, a symbol of our isolated lives. Within it lay the most secret part of the atomic bomb project. Los Alamos was a world unto itself, an island in the sky.[18]

Because the town was built so quickly, it did not have the most logical layout. Finding things was difficult.

The sprawling town had grown rapidly and haphazardly, without order or plan. Roughly in the center of town was Ashley Pond, a shallow little pool, with the laboratories on the one side and the hospital on the other. To the west stretched a section of four- and eight-family dwellings, identical in appearance, hunter green in hue. This section terminated in tight rows of barracks, housing for the enlisted military personnel, which overlooked the horse pasture. East of the pond was the oldest housing, consisting of green duplexes for childless couples, four family houses for larger families, and Bathtub Row.

The few stone houses that had been built with the school were the only ones in town equipped with bathtubs, so that area was dubbed Bathtub Row. Marshak and her husband did not live in that area.

Adjacent to these relatively luxurious dwellings was the most meager housing on the Hill, a new section known as Morganville. When we finally found the Housing Office, it was to discover with sinking hearts that we were slated to live in one of the white frame Morgan buildings. . . . Morganville houses were set in neat parallel rows. There were no trees in our section of the mesa, and the unpaved roads were muddy during wet seasons and dusty during dry ones. Eventually we moved to one of the older green duplexes; compared to our Morganville residence, it was luxurious.[19]

The laboratories were called the Technical Area. Marshak taught at the school and worked at the housing office for a while, but she was never allowed in the scientists' fenced-off work area.

The Tech Area was a great pit which swallowed our scientist husbands out of sight, almost out of our lives. The men were drawn to their work not only by curiosity and zeal, but also by an inspiring patriotism. They worked as they had never worked before. They worked at night and often came home at three or four in the morning. Sometimes, they set up Army cots in the laboratories and did not come home at all. Other times, they did not sleep well at all. Few women understood what the men were seeking there or comprehended the magnitude of the search. The loneliness and heartache of some scientists' wives during the years before the atomic bomb was born were very real.[20]

Jane Wilson taught English at Los Alamos High School. Her husband, Robert Wilson, was an eminent scientist who directed many of the experiments at Los Alamos. She was among the first wives to arrive at Site Y in 1943.

We had few of the conveniences which most of us had taken for granted in the past. No mailman, no milkman, no laundryman, no paper boy knocked at our doors. There were no telephones in our homes. We shared unique difficulties of living with our husbands without sharing the recompensing thrill or sometimes even the knowledge of the great scientific experiment which was in progress.
. . . We women realized that we were part of something a great deal bigger than ourselves. . . . We were a secret project, probably the most secret project which has ever existed in the United States. That one fact dominated our existence.[21]

But even with the consolation of having other wives around to share in the isolation, the women were never sure what freedom of movement might be taken away next, and never knew how long they would have to endure that way. If they left Los Alamos or when they came back, they had to go through guard gates, and show badges that identified their level of security clearance. And that same badge determined their clearance to enter certain parts of the Los Alamos grounds. The constants they lived with were uncertainty and secrecy.

> We lived night and day, year after year, behind a guarded fence. We had joined the Project with the understanding that eventually the gates were going to close behind us, and we would not even be able to go to Santa Fe for necessary shopping. We were ready for that contingency, although its psychological repercussions would have been enormous. I know that I thought of it with a sinking heart—no escape from the mesa, not even for a day! Fortunately, this threat never materialized, and after a time even the travel restrictions were relaxed.[22]

The fact that there was a high concentration of nuclear scientists in Los Alamos had to be disguised as much as possible. So security officials made rules restricting any possibility of someone figuring that out. Residents were not allowed to bank in Santa Fe. Instead they kept accounts in the place where they had been before coming to Los Alamos and did their transactions by mail. Residents did not have their names on driver's licenses either.[23] Security officials issued pamphlets to guide people on how to keep the secrets of the project, but they were often confusing or vague. One pamphlet warned residents not to mention any of the "typographical details which are essential to the Project." But as Wilson said, not knowing what the project was made it hard for many of the nonscientists to know how to follow those guidelines.

> Were the sunsets essential to the Project? Were the mountains? The canyons? The result of Security's noncommittal policy was that for fear of saying the wrong thing, one said as little as possible. Letters home were inclined to be terse and in my case, anyhow, painfully self-conscious. I couldn't write a letter without seeing a censor poring over it. I couldn't go to Santa Fe without being aware of hidden eyes upon me, watching, waiting to pounce on that inevitable misstep. It wasn't a pleasant feeling.[24]

Once, by chance, I met an acquaintance from my college days on the streets of Santa Fe. It had been more than a year since I had talked to anyone I knew other than the people who lived on the Hill. It was wonderfully exhilarating to see someone from the outside world, someone whose life wasn't all mixed up with supersecret matters. But even this encounter was against the rules.[25]

When her friend asked Wilson to go have a Coke with her, Wilson accepted but was not able to be her natural self. She said she felt her responses were wooden for fear of revealing any secrets.

A moment's slip and I, by nature blabbermouthed, felt that I would find myself hurtling into the gaping entrance to hell. It was a relief to say goodbye. Then, like a child confessing that she had been naughty, I reported my social engagement to the Security Officer. Living at Los Alamos was something like living in jail.

Another security measure meant the scientists were no longer referred to as physicists after they became a part of the Los Alamos project. They became "engineers." The most famous of the scientists had to use false names and have bodyguards when they traveled outside Los Alamos. Enrico Fermi became "Mr. Farmer." Niels Bohr, the Danish scientist, was "Nicholas Baker." Wilson remembered a story that went around "about the time the film 'Madame Curie' was being shown at the Los Alamos theaters." It may even have been true.

The story went that Mr. Farmer approached Mr. Baker, and said, "I've just seen a grand picture."

"Oh? What was it called?" asked Mr. Farmer.

To which Mr. Baker replied smugly, "Madame Cooper."[26]

Another huge challenge to the wives trying to run a household at Los Alamos was the cooking and the heating facilities in the apartments and houses. They were mostly powered by coal, which meant coal dust was everywhere. Wilson said the heat came out of transoms in the walls and left behind "a black and sticky trail of soot. The grime fell like gentle rain from heaven upon our walls, draperies, and furniture." She said the hasty construction of the community made for the problems. "Too many trees had been chopped down by the Army," said Wilson. "Construction was always in progress and this, in league with the region's natural aridness, created a dust situation the like of which I had not experienced before."

As for the appliances, each kitchen had a modern electric refrigerator, but the stoves the military supplied Wilson described as "a hideous, curvaceous, very bleak wood- and coal-burning range." When she first saw her stove she burst into tears. The wives began referring to their stoves as "The Black Beauty." "To supplement this monster," Wilson said, "we were issued hot plates. I did all my cooking on two hot plates plus my own electric broiler and electric roaster. With such implements, I would nonchalantly whip up dinner, occasionally for as many as thirty-five. This was difficult but not impossible, except when the power was shut off." That was another frequent problem on the mesa. Residents would go for hours at a time without electricity. "If dinner happened to be ready," said Wilson, "we ate by candlelight. If our meal was not yet cooked, occasionally we did not eat at all." [27]

The worst hardship was the shortage of water in Los Alamos. The area was not endowed with many good or plentiful water sources. Related Wilson, "As more and more people arrived to work on the Project, the water shortage grew acute to the point of hysteria. Soldiers leaped out of jeeps to present the latest bulletins on the water crisis to anxious householders."

The bulletins gave residents tips on water conservation. They were asked to report leaky faucets immediately, refrain from watering lawns or gardens, and to soap up before entering the shower. As Wilson said, that "could be disastrous if the water didn't come on." And, said Wilson, they were told that "toilet bowls should not be flushed in play." Sometimes water was shut off completely because of the shortages. "The rudest thing one could do," said Wilson, "was to use the bathroom in another house. Diapers went unwashed, and the town plunged into a grim and gray period of mourning." Then notices went around telling everyone that water was available in trucks outside the hospital. Residents had to find their own way of carrying it and bathing was prohibited. Sometimes water would come through the pipes during these shutoffs for about an hour each day. Wilson said:

> This was the time frantically to fill pails and basins of all description with the brown liquid, heavy with sediment. Upon at least two occasions, I found vermilion worms swimming in my treasured supply. The water was ice cold and I wouldn't sit in it myself. In fact, per-

sonal cleanliness by now was in such a state that I avoided social gatherings.[28]

With water in short supply, disease became a worry. The school had to close for a week when a polio scare erupted. And dogs were confined at times when rabies was suspected. Both proved to be false alarms. Yet, Wilson said, they were always aware that in some ways they were very lucky not to be facing the kinds of deprivations that others endured during the war.[29]

> We were constantly annoyed by inefficiency and stupidity. There was nothing simple or easy about running a household on that secret mesa. But we could face it, aware of the drama of our situation, supported by the friends who lived so near to us, and finally buoyed by the fact that here at Los Alamos, an event of magnitude was being wrought.[30]

To lighten the pressure and take advantage of the unique collection of talent and brainpower, the social life on the mesa was often quite lively. Jean Bacher was the wife of Robert Bacher, who headed the Bomb Physics Division of the project. They had two children and she did clerical work in the Theoretical Physics Division. She remembered that the isolation meant people came up with their own forms of entertainment.

> Saturday nights, the mesa rocked with a number of other dances and parties. Fenced in as we were, our social life was a pipeline through which we let off steam—steam with a collegiate flavor. Large dances, which often turned into binges, were popular. They were rowdy and wet parties, but always pretty innocent fun. . . . We were isolated from theaters and nightclubs and all other metropolitan delights. When a party came along, we attacked it with an abandon equal to our fantasies of what we would be doing if we were in New York. That ninety percent of us would have been in some quiet campus town, leading a faculty-tea kind of social existence, was a point we all discreetly forgot.[31]

Women worked at all the Manhattan Project sites. At Los Alamos, by 1944, about 30 percent of the labor force (approximately 200 workers) in the Tech Area, the school, and the hospital were women. About fifty were technicians, more than a hundred were nurses, teachers, secretaries, or clerks. And about twenty women were scientists on the project. Women scientists included physicists, chemists, mathematicians, and biologists.[32]

One of the most eminent was Leona Woods, a physicist who had worked with Enrico Fermi in Chicago during the first nuclear chain reaction. She first worked at Hanford, Washington.[33] A few WACs with scientific qualifications also served at Los Alamos. Most were chemists, including Mary Lucy Miller, who had a Ph.D. from Columbia University. She became the head of one of the chemistry labs at Los Alamos.[34]

Charlotte Serber was the wife of one of Dr. Oppenheimer's main associates, Robert Serber. Charlotte Serber was also one of the few wives who held a skilled position in the Tech Area. She was the scientific librarian and handled reference materials as well as top secret documents, but, true to the era, she still thought of herself as a wife first.

> For the potential working wife, there was one chief worry. Could she manage her home here on the mesa and work too? Would her home life suffer? Would her husband be neglected? Would her children become delinquents? Would it be any more difficult than working a forty-eight-hour week in a city?[35]

Serber said that having a maid relieved some of that worry. The system for determining which women got maids had been started for the working women. Then, Charlotte Serber said, it changed as more women demanded help.

> The Housing Office inaugurated a priority system. Illness and pregnancy were the highest caste, full-time working wives came next, then part-time working wives with children, non-working wives with children, part-time working wives without children, and lastly, non-working childless wives.[36]

But the women who worked in jobs outside their home, just like the women who raised children at Los Alamos, were expected to be in charge of running the house. Serber concluded that while the expectations of women were the same inside and outside Los Alamos, the limits on them sometimes had positive aspects.

> Shopping, for instance, was, in one sense at least, less complicated. There was only one Commissary. If it didn't have chicken, you

couldn't waste time by going to another store. You simply forgot about chicken that night and ate pork or veal. If the laundry wasn't taking clothes one week, you were a little less fastidious or you did the washing yourself at night. If there was no gasoline in the local tank, you walked to work. If the PX had no cigarettes, you rolled your own. Everything that did exist on the Hill was close by: Commissary, PX, trading post, dry cleaners, and beauty shop. And if what you needed could only be gotten in Santa Fe, you had a friend get it for you, or you waited until you could take a day off and get it yourself.

A trip to Santa Fe was a major event for working wives. Over a period of weeks, your list grew and grew. For some, the date for the trek was finally set by the state of their liquor supply; for others, by their supply of baby oil.[37]

The residents of Santa Fe were perhaps the most privy to as well as curious about what was happening in Los Alamos, which they referred to as "The Hill." Rumors abounded and jokes too. Because Los Alamos residents were obviously doing secret war work and were so circumspect on their trips to Santa Fe, people in town started speculating on what was really going on there. A favorite joke was that they were all there to make windshield wipers for submarines. As time went on the rumors got wilder. The director of Los Alamos was concerned that eventually the guesses might become more accurate, so a plan was hatched to spread a rumor of their own that was closer to the truth and would quell further inquiry so that the real truth stayed hidden.

Charlotte Serber became a part of the plot. Dr. Oppenheimer called her into his office one day along with a male colleague, physicist John Manley. The two were asked to go into Santa Fe and spread a new rumor. "It had to account for all the civilian scientists," said Serber, "for the supersecrecy, and for the loud booms that Santa Feans were beginning to hear on fine mornings." So Oppenheimer told the two to talk up the idea that they were part of a project that was making an electric rocket. Serber said Oppenheimer's directions on how to create the false impression were explicit. He told the two to go to Santa Fe as often as possible.

> Talk. Talk too much. Talk as if you had too many drinks. Get people to eavesdrop. Say a number of things about us that you are not supposed to. Say the place is growing. Finally, and I don't care how you manage it, say we are building an electric rocket. No one is to be told

of this assignment. If you are successful, you will be reported on [by military intelligence] in Santa Fe and by other Los Alamosites who overhear you. You will be protected if you get into trouble, but for the moment it is a secret mission.

Serber was a little concerned about how she would pull it off without telling her husband what she was doing. Since she was a part of the project, the two did not have the secrecy in their marriage that was required of other scientists and their wives. Serber was not sure she was going to be able to explain to him her many trips to Santa Fe with Manley. Oppenheimer agreed that Manley and Serber could include their spouses in the plan. The four of them ventured into town a few times, but did not find the interest that they had counted on in their "gossip." They went to nice restaurants as well as to more down-and-dirty bars. But no one they encountered anywhere seemed interested in their stories of life at Los Alamos. The foursome concluded they were a "miserable failure at counterespionage," and went back to their appointed work on the atomic bomb.[38]

WACS AT LOS ALAMOS

More than 400 WACs served on the Manhattan Project in Oak Ridge, Tennessee; Hanford, Washington; New York City; and Los Alamos. Most worked as clerks and drivers, but some were also scientists and took on responsibilities in the labs.

Eleanor Stone Roensch joined the WAC in 1944 and was sent to Los Alamos. She was twenty-four years old and anxious to do her part for the war effort. She lived in a barracks that was similar to any other WAC barracks. But what not many people knew was that the WAC barracks at Los Alamos had two bathtubs, the only bathtubs in town besides the famous ones in the houses on Bathtub Row. The male soldiers were in barracks across the street from the WACs. "The street was a natural divider between male and female domains," said Roensch.

Her job was to work in the PX in the Tech Area, a café where workers came for coffee, ice cream, and cigarettes, with a jukebox that played constantly. Later Roensch was assigned to work as a telephone operator. There were not many phone lines to and from Los Alamos, since none of the homes had phones, but the scientific offices did and the military used the few phone lines as well. The capacity of the lines was not great, so phone time was limited for everyone. "My understanding of the function of Los Alamos grew," said Roensch, "after I started work . . . as a telephone operator." Her office was just inside the pass gate to the Tech Area and shared the building with the distribution center for all the mail addressed to P.O. Box 1663. "One of the first peculiarities of the telephone office that I noticed," Roensch said, "was that there were no directories. It was necessary for a new operator to scan typewritten sheets or learn by memory the names and phone numbers of the personnel. Partly this was due to secrecy and partly because no directory could keep up to date with the daily additions and changes."

Roensch met her husband at Los Alamos. He was a soldier named Arno Roensch, who played trumpet in an Army band that held informal jam sessions on Saturday nights. "After I met him," said Eleanor, "music became extremely important in my life. He played trumpet with feeling and flair. The next week he left the bandstand to dance with me, and I knew that for me no other man existed."

Arno played trumpet for church services, which were held in a theater at Los Alamos. Roensch said the theater "was the center for all large group activities. On Saturday nights, dances were held there and almost everyone went. You could buy beer or Cokes. After the dance, someone would clean up the place and the next morning church services were held there. Even though the room was clean and the chairs were put down and the windows were opened, you could still smell the cigarette smoke and the stale beer."

In early summer of 1945, Roensch started to hear rumors about a test that would be taking place in the remote desert. A soldier friend of her boyfriend's talked of his fear that a chain reaction might take place during the test that could not be controlled and would destroy huge parts of the area and kill the people in it. "This was the first I had heard about this mysterious weapon," said Roensch. But the idea gave her nightmares.[39]

TRINITY, HIROSHIMA, NAGASAKI

The scientists' wives, who had abided the unknown for two or three years, were finally let in on a bit of the secret in the summer of 1945. That is when the scientists of Los Alamos tested the first atomic bomb. It was assembled

and detonated at a remote desert area in southern New Mexico near Ala-
mogordo.

Phyllis Fisher remembered when the test drew near.

> Carried along by the challenge of their work and by sheer momen-
> tum, their thoughts were focused on the job at hand. As I recall,
> there was little talk among the scientists one way or the other about
> the ethics or morality of their endeavor. The sheer size and challenge
> of the scientific effort occupied their thoughts completely.
>
> I had gained some fragmentary knowledge of this endeavor on the
> evening that I had enraged Lee by jokingly suggesting "Uranium
> Fisher" as a name for our baby. But that knowledge only added to my
> own anxiety. Constant nausea plagued my early pregnancy. I'm sure
> it was at least partly due to the apprehension I was feeling.[40]

The Trinity test was conducted on July 16, 1945. Some of the Los Alamos
scientists went to set up the bomb and witness its detonation. Others camped
at nearby mountains to see the explosion. But the Fishers went as far away as
they could.

> Leon had no desire to watch the spectacle. The night of the "Trinity"
> explosion . . . he took Bobby and me camping in the opposite direc-
> tion from the anticipated detonation. We found a lovely spot near a
> stream in the Sangre de Cristo range, spread out our sleeping bags,
> enjoyed a chicken dinner, and settled down for the night. That is, two
> of us did. But a restless Leon, awake most of the night, was so tired
> the next morning that he didn't want to get out of his sleeping bag.
>
> . . . Leon had been given the opportunity to travel to Alamogordo
> for the detonation, but had declined. His partial, but completely il-
> logical, solution was not only to keep me in ignorance of the dan-
> gers, but to drive us north in our car in the opposite direction from
> the detonation. Leon told me later that, as he went to sleep, he won-
> dered if the device would fail completely or if, on the other hand, it
> might be so successful that we wouldn't wake up at all. Little wonder
> he had had trouble sleeping![41]

Later that day the Fishers heard from people who had gone to or near Alam-
ogordo and had witnessed the explosion.

It was as though a dam had burst. Fever-pitch excitement held sway on our hill, as people went wild with the release of long-suppressed emotions. Suddenly, everyone was talking to everyone. In our thrilled, hysterical town there were hugs, congratulations, tears, and laughter.

. . . It seemed almost immediately the jubilation was mixed with profound concern. Sober thoughts circulated on the hill. The monster had been unleashed and there was no way to put it back in its casing, no way to undo the deed perpetrated in the New Mexico desert. The "gadget" developed at our laboratories had power beyond our imagination.

. . . The significance of the detonation began to permeate the hill, and depression and anxiety replaced much of the initially thrilled reaction. Somber thoughts surfaced through the joyous predictions of an early end to the war. Many tried to contemplate the future of a world in which atomic bombs would be a reality.[42]

Less than a month later, when Hiroshima was bombed on Monday, August 6, 1945, Phyllis wrote her parents. It was the first letter in which she was able to admit where they were.

Well, today's news makes everything else seem pretty unimportant! You can't possibly imagine how strange it is to turn on the radio and hear the outside world talking about *us* today! After all the extreme secrecy, it seems positively unreal.

. . . President Truman was quoted as follows: "It is an atomic bomb. It is a harnessing of the basic power of the universe. The force from which the sun draws its power has been loosed against those who brought war to the Far East." . . . The President also disclosed that 6,000 persons had been working at our site in secrecy on the development of the bomb. "We have spent," he continued, "$2,000,000,000 on the greatest scientific gamble in history—and won!"

A few days later, after Nagasaki was bombed on August 9, 1945, Fisher wrote her parents again, saying she "could only interpret the second bombing as a new dimension in cruelty. We were beginning to hear about lingering radiation from the nuclear bombs and of deaths occurring and anticipated from radiation. Our world would never be the same again."[43]

Fisher and her husband felt the physical effects. He was not able to sleep. She had lost four pounds, which is not a good thing for a woman in her fourth month of pregnancy.

> After three days of nausea, I struggled to the hospital. The facility was mobbed. Dr. Stout . . . told me that there had been such a tremendous demand for headache pills, sleeping pills, and medicine for nausea that all supplies already had been dispensed. . . . Until new supplies arrived, there was nothing.[44]

Another wife at Los Alamos whose husband had been at the center of nuclear science for most of his career was deeply affected by the bombs. Laura Fermi, wife of Enrico Fermi, had come over from Italy with him in the late 1930s. They had two children who were teenagers while at Los Alamos. She worked part-time in the Tech Area and was aware of her husband's work, although, like everyone else, she and her husband did not discuss much of what he did at Los Alamos until after the bomb had been dropped on Hiroshima.

> As if caused by reverberation of the atomic bomb, an explosion of feelings and of words was set off in Los Alamos. Women wanted to know. Everything. At once. But many things could not be said even then, cannot be said now.
> . . . Their first bewilderment turned into immense pride in their husbands' achievement and, to a lesser degree, in their own share in the project. Los Alamos had caused the war to end abruptly, perhaps six months, perhaps a year sooner than it would otherwise. Los Alamos had saved lives of thousands of American soldiers. The whole world was hailing the great discovery that their husbands had given to America. . . . When among the praising voices some arose that deprecated the bomb, and words like "barbarism," "horror," "the crime of Hiroshima," "the mass murder," were heard from several directions, the wives sobered. They wondered, they probed their consciences, but found no answer to their doubts.

Fermi said the wives noticed how the bomb had transformed their husbands' worries.

> I was not prepared for the change that the explosion at Hiroshima brought about in our husbands at Los Alamos. I had never heard

them mention the atomic bomb, and now they talked of nothing else. . . . And now they assumed for themselves the responsibility for Hiroshima and Nagasaki, for the evils that atomic power might cause anywhere, at any time.

. . . Our husbands were not different from other generations of scientists. Helped by the physical separation of Los Alamos from the world, they worked in a certain isolation. They knew they were striving to make something that would likely shorten the duration of the war. It was their duty to concentrate all their powers upon this single aim.

Perhaps they were not emotionally prepared for the absence of a time interval between scientific completion and the actual use of their discovery. I don't believe they had visualized a destruction whose equivalent in tons of TNT they had calculated with utmost accuracy.[45]

When the war officially ended on August 14 with the Japanese surrender, Phyllis and Leon Fisher could finally talk openly again.

Suddenly, there was no longer any need for a wall of silence between us. Ahead of us stretched hours and hours of trying to sift through our tangled feelings of hope for peace and of despair for the world.

Night after night we talked. We explored the silence between us that had affected our lives for a year. We spoke of the additional loneliness that silence had caused. We recalled his fury as well as mine on that terrible night when I had jokingly considered naming our baby "Uranium Fisher." I learned for the first time that list of words the scientists were forbidden to mention outside the labs. "Uranium *fission*" led the list! In fact, the term "uranium" wasn't even mentioned in the tech area or anywhere on the hill, but was always referred to by the code word "tubealloy."

. . . I confessed to Leon my fears for the future of civilization and for the safety of our unborn baby. Leon admitted feeling fearful also, but he tried to allay my anxiety. It was important, he felt, that the power and potential of the bomb be known all over the world. That knowledge might be the best hope for peace. Perhaps nuclear weapons could be turned over to the United Nations.[46]

With the war over, most of the scientists and their families went back to academia. The Fermis returned to the University of Chicago. Phyllis Fisher and her husband and two boys moved to New York, where Leon joined the Physics Department of New York University. The family, which had grown to include two more children for a total of four, later moved to California. In the late 1970s Phyllis and Leon lived and worked in Japan for a few years. There, Phyllis's connection to Hiroshima preyed on her mind. So she visited the memorial in that city to all the people who been killed by the bomb, and began to consider her role in it all. "I wanted to forget the Los Alamos years," said Phyllis, "which I remembered as both thrilling and horrifying. But . . . I hadn't been able to forget." [47]

As she took in the decimating effects in Hiroshima of the wartime work that had gone on around her at Los Alamos, Phyllis Fisher was revisited by the same sense of helplessness she said she felt when the bomb was dropped on Hiroshima in 1945. She had lived and kept the secrets of wartime Los Alamos without knowing what the outcome of the work was meant to be. In retrospect, it troubled her to face the consequences of her complicity. She felt the guilt that can plague survivors of a trauma in which so many died. The best information she had at the time affirmed her belief that she was acting out of patriotism, love for her husband, and love for her family when she moved to Los Alamos and accepted the terms of life there. In a pattern that was repeated by millions of women in all nations, Phyllis Fisher had done what she could to go on living life in the midst of a world caught up in the destructive momentum of war. It was almost a defiant act, except that it stemmed from such a basic and utterly universal human instinct to endure. "Clearly, I was no heroine," Phyllis Fisher said, "but just a young wife who wanted only to be a nest-builder and keep my little family together." [48]

Their Legacy

OUR MOTHERS' WAR YEARS RESOUNDING THROUGH OUR LIVES

At TIMES WHEN I WAS RESEARCHING and writing this book I found myself feeling an odd sense that I was being sacrilegious somehow about World War II. I was not paying much attention to the men who planned and fought the war on the battlefields, or theaters as they were called during World War II, of Europe and the Pacific. I even felt a little guilty for that. Those men risked their lives and many died in a fight against tyranny and oppression that was noble and true. They defended our values of freedom and equality so that I could take those things for granted. My father, who was in the Army for four years and served in Burma, was one of those men.

Focusing on the women seemed trivial compared to the men's work of fighting and dying in battle. Women's struggles with shortages of butter and their breakthroughs in being granted the right to do military paperwork, rivet together warplanes, or serve coffee and doughnuts to the men at the front could not compare to the bloody warfare with which their male counterparts were contending. I was aware, as were most of the women with whom I talked or about whom I read, that I should be careful never to claim that the women's part during the war was as significant as the men's. Of course, no one objected to the women being given their due. But it usually seemed like an afterthought. Once all the men's sacrifices were acknowledged, then we as a country could afford to give the women's role in World War II a tip of the hat as well. I understood that mission as I set out, accepted the parameters, and felt honored to be able to pursue it.

As I got further into the task at hand, my perspective began to change. I spoke to so many women with such deep feelings. I found much great source material and many fine scholarly books about different aspects of women's experiences during the war. In their own right, the women with whom I spoke and the women in these books were fascinating to me. I was trying to understand women's lives at a time before I was born. But in much of what I saw and heard the stories were told through a filter of comparison, either direct or implied, to the men's experience and their war. I noticed that anyone considering women's roles in the war usually had to take some time to justify the subject's importance. I started to feel the need to do the same. There were excellent works, but some had almost defensive titles like *They Also Served* and *A Woman's War Too*. Women of World War II were helpers and supporters, but were rarely if ever the most valued players in the most important roles.

My mother had spurred the beginning of this quest when I sat in my attic reading her war letters. Naturally, I returned to her familiar voice again as I began to feel thrown by what I was finding. I searched for some perspective from her to put all I was learning into context. I wanted to know how she had looked back on the war and how it had shaped her life. If only I could hear her attitudes about being a woman of her generation, I knew it would help me better understand how that era fit into history. And I might even gain a selfish insight into what effect her life then had on me, her only daughter. Once again, I struck gold.

I came across an audiotape of a speech my mother had given in 1971 to a church group in Memphis, Tennessee, where we lived. It was entitled "The Humanization of Emily: Some Thoughts on Women's Liberation and My Daughter." I was nine years old at the time and I was in the audience during the speech, though I do not remember it at all. Still, the message of the speech must have somehow permeated to my subconscious self. Her voice on that tape made me feel she had been subliminally working on this book with me back before I even hit puberty. In fact, I got an overwhelming sense of validation when I began to feel, as I listened to my mother's words, that my grandmother, and her mother and grandmother, might even have had a hand in leading me to this subject.

My mother started the talk that day by apologizing for not being better organized.

> I think perhaps this speech should be retitled "Some Thoughts While
> Defrosting the Freezer, and Taking Care of My Daughter Who Had a
> Cold, and Getting My Boys Off to a Baseball Game, and Keeping the
> House Quiet so My Husband Could Work . . . and Making Mine-
> strone for Dinner on the Habachi on the Back Terrace Because the
> Kitchen was Cluttered with Everything Defrosting from the Freezer."
> . . . This is what I was busy doing at the time I had planned to make
> careful notes on what I was going to say to you this morning.

She explained how all those tasks got her thinking about "how women's work
is never done." She thought back to her mother's mother, and realized that
the best way she could talk about the women's liberation movement sweeping the country at the time was to relate family history about her female ancestors.

> The history of women is much like the history of black people in
> this country. It has never been recorded. . . . All of our history has
> been written by men, for men and about men. And women were
> simply the auxiliaries, the ladies' auxiliary. . . . The only kind of his-
> tory that we have of the part women have played in the building of
> this country and of the world for that matter is family history.

Then, she went on to tell a story she had heard as a young girl about her
mother's mother, her grandmother, my great-grandmother, Nina Rogers,
out on the Kansas prairie in the 1880s. One day Nina was home taking care of
her two children while her husband, a lawyer, was "off traveling the circuit
pleading in the local law courts, as was man's work." And there was a prairie
fire. It started spontaneously and by the time Nina saw it, it was threatening
her home and children.

> Here she is alone in the house with two small children, one six-
> month-old baby and one year-and-a-half-old baby. And her husband
> is away, and the nearest farm is a mile away. And there are no tele-
> phones. Somehow, she and the woman from the next farmhouse
> started a crossfire and then beat it out, and burned a barrier before
> the prairie fire reached them and they saved their farmhouses. Well
> this was woman's work. These women had great strength.
>   It is not written in the history books anywhere, but part of the
> building of the West was the women staying home and building

their own crossfires to save their homes and children. We read a great
deal about men defending their homes from Indians. We read a great
deal about the building of the West was man's work. But was it?

My mother pointed out in her speech that day how hard it was to prove
that women had any primary role in the shaping of the country. Even though
she had heard such stories growing up, they were rarely documented. She
spoke of yet another great-grandmother, who had been the first woman
schoolteacher in Pennsylvania. "Nowhere is it written down," my mother
said, "who the first woman schoolteacher was, but it has been handed down
through the women in my family that this is one of my women ancestors. . . .
Clara Barton, Dolley Madison, Martha Washington, you name it. It was the
women in their supportive roles that made the history books. But the first
woman schoolteacher did not make the history books. The history that is
written is not this."

As I met and talked with other women of my mother's generation it usually
took a while to coax these women to tell me about their lives and feelings and
memories of the war years. They often started by saying that what they did was
not as important as what the men did. Then they would tell me amazing stories
of gracefully pushing beyond accepted notions of what a woman could accomplish. And when I mentioned to people of my own generation that I was working on a book about women during World War II, the reaction usually included
some reference to the women "left behind," women "keeping the home fires
burning," or women "building the machinery for the men to use."

Although familiar, that did not seem to be the full picture. In fact, it
started to feel like a slight to the significance I was finding in these women's
stories. In light of my mother's speech that day, I did some further family research and found yet another heroic story about a female ancestor, my great-
great-grandmother, Nina Rogers's mother, Mary Lynn Stivers. When she was
eighteen years old in 1861 (one hundred years before I was born), she was the
only woman working in a printing shop in Sullivan, Illinois. Soon, all the men
left to fight in the Civil War. The story goes that Mary, the sole worker left,
decided that the paper must still go out. So she gathered the news, set the
type by hand, and published the entire paper on her own. I thought of all the
challenges that women had taken up during wars doing work that no one believed they could or should do. It did not start in World War II, but such
female pioneering became so widespread then that it was harder to ignore.

Next, I looked back at an article about my mother in the Memphis paper a year or two before she died. She spoke of her first job out of college as an editor at *Reader's Digest* during World War II, before she joined the Red Cross at the end of the war. "I was an editorial Rosie the Riveter, I think you could say. For the first time in the memory of woman, *Reader's Digest* and other national magazines were hiring women as editors." Before that, she said, women had been allowed to work only as researchers or answering the mail. And I remembered how she always credited my father for supporting her and her career goals. Before they married and began to have children in the 1950s, she told the audience that day, he urged her to continue working.

> He said I insist upon it in fact, because I don't want you saying to our children in years to come, look what I gave up for you. I think that my life would have been unbearable had I not been married to a man who shared my problems and my aspirations and my joys and allowed me to do the same with him. The women who I know who had a terrible problem are women who had similar aspirations and ways of life and tried to work it in combination with a man who they truly loved who was not able to share this feeling with them.

Through my mother, and all the women in this book, I came to see that the small things, the less dramatic changes in the world, were sometimes the most revolutionary. And often those were the kinds of changes women effected. In 1971, for instance, my mother spoke of how a simple issue like a name was still a symbol of the deeper tides in society.

> I have a little private thing that I'm trying to get the Memphis Public Library to issue library cards to women by their first names. I would like my library card to read "Carol Lynn Yellin" instead of "Mrs. David Yellin." This seems like a small and ridiculous thing. But I am more than Mrs. David Yellin. And my husband agrees.
>
> Throughout history, women have yielded and diffused their own personal identities. . . . I think this is changing and let's not be frightened of it. Would it be so terrible if we had a new structure of society that allowed all of us to remain individuals and didn't require as a matter of course for one half of the human beings to yield to the other half? . . . Couldn't there be some awfully good things about it?
>
> I feel that we have so divided human beings, that we have so overemphasized gender that we have limited both the male and the

female. We have cost so much emotional energy to be wasted in worries about which is which, and what is what. And this is where the tremendous new surge of energy will come, when we not only release one half of the human talent pool . . . to achieve what it can on its own, but we release a side of man's nature that has been there all the time and has been equally as suppressed as the ambition and strength of women.

One of the things that often annoyed me about my mother as I was coming into adulthood was what I saw as her Pollyannaish view of the world. Her optimism went way beyond the question of whether the glass was half full or half empty. What did it matter? She always seemed to answer that kind of question with the assurance that there were pitchers enough for many refills just waiting in the refrigerator, not to mention a whole faucet of water at the kitchen sink. My brothers and I had a joke that if mom had been on the *Titanic* as it was going down, she would have turned to her shipmates and said cheerily, "I think we might be a little late for dinner this evening."

About three weeks before my mom passed away, I asked her if she wanted to see any kind of counselor to help her cope with the fact that she was dying of cancer. She looked at me clear-eyed and smiling and said, "No. The way I deal with it is I am in denial." There was a time when that answer would have irked me. I would have seen it as a weakness, a sign that she was not being strong enough to face the truth. But I accepted it gladly that night. I saw that it was a transcendent attitude. I started to see that her fierce denial of anything in her way coupled with her defiant optimism were in fact some of her strongest weapons in life. They were the source of her grace, like the blinders on a horse that make her run her own race instead of being distracted by others. Armed with them, my mother was able to muster the courage she needed to meet whatever came up head-on, even her own death. And in the process, she was showing me the way to live.

As I spoke to other women in her generation, I saw that same kind of fierce optimism and denial not as their weakness but as the armor with which they faced the world. I thought of the kind of courage to survive the internment camps that Japanese-American women like Akiko Mabuchi Toba displayed, making the best of it and biding their time. I thought of the outrage I had felt as I heard about some of the ways women were treated in the military. But then I thought of Lillian Goodman, the WASP. When I asked her how she felt about the fact that people had sabotaged two planes of her fellow women pilots by putting sugar in their gas tanks, causing them to crash and die, she spoke of her obstinate optimism. She said she had never known about that incident until years later. She always believed everyone was so proud of them. And if she ever heard that anyone did not like her, she simply thought, "What's not to like?" Then I remembered the women in Los Alamos and all they had to suppress to abide their secret lives. Instead of seeing all these women as not having any power, I saw them as using their power creatively to adapt courageously and move forward in spite of the obstacles, making small profound strides along the way, if only by their endurance. My mother pointed this out in her speech too.

> In an increasingly technological world . . . to take your gun and to move West and to kill Buffalo and Indians and everything . . . is no longer appropriate. The whole buildup of aggression as a lovely and manly reaction is no longer appropriate. . . . The technological society demands far more cooperativeness than competition. And the machine may finally force us to what we have sometimes denigrated as the feminine—the idea of nonaggression, nonviolence, of yielding. The whole picture may make what we have thought of as the feminine values suddenly more important for all of us and we'll all be gainers in the end.
>
> This rigid classification of jobs according to gender I believe is just on the way out. It has to be. . . . I don't want to stop doing the cooking. I just don't want to have to do it. I don't want it to be assumed that because I am a woman that I have to do it. . . . I think this is changing so fast and this is one of the optimistic things I see.

But it was the anecdote my mother used to end her speech that gave me the almost spooky sense that I might have been destined to write this book all along. It was as if, whether I knew it or not, invisible forces were pushing me to expand my thinking and take a long, serious look at the women's point of view during World War II. That day when I was nine, my mother, the former Red Cross girl, told a story that summed up the mission in my quest, even though it would be some thirty years before I realized it.

> I was driving the carpool as I do often. This is one part of women's work I would not give up. And in the back seat Emily and some of her friends were chattering. And I was thinking of the grocery list as I do between other tasks. But suddenly I heard some very interesting

talk going on. This was several weeks ago. I heard them saying "daughter of a first-aid kit," "daughter of a first-aid kit." And I said, "Emily, what's that?" And Emily said, "Well, you know, we play the land of opposites at school. And there is this boy there who keeps saying 'son of a gun, son of a gun.' So we just say, 'daughter of a first-aid kit.' "

Well, I thought . . . here is the descendant of all the women in my family, the ongoing continuum. Here is this young female person. Maybe she will get the chance. Maybe she will know a day when the daughter of the first-aid kit will be as valued in our society and our culture as the son of a gun.

NOTES

Chapter 1: To Bring Him Home Safely

1. Home Services Staff of General Mills, Inc., *Your Share: How to Prepare Appetizing, Healthful Meals with Foods Available Today* (Minneapolis: General Mills, Inc., 1943), Foreword.

2. Randolph Ray, *Marriage Is a Serious Business* (New York: Whittlesey House, McGraw-Hill, 1944), 39.

3. "I Married My Soldier Anyway," *Good Housekeeping*, June 1942, 74.

4. Ray, *Marriage Is a Serious Business*, 114.

5. Genevieve Eppens, *Waiting for My Sailor* (Lincoln, NE: Infusion Media Publishing, 2000), 8–9.

6. Ibid., 10–13.

7. Roy Hoopes, *Americans Remember the Home Front—An Oral Narrative of the World War II Years in America* (New York: Berkley, 2002), 217.

8. Judy Barrett Litoff and David C. Smith, *Since You Went Away: World War II Letters from American Women on the Home Front* (Lawrence: University of Kansas Press, 1991), 93–100.

9. Maxine Davis, "Women Without Men," *Good Housekeeping*, March 1942, 181.

10. Ethel Gorham, *So Your Husband's Gone to War!* (Garden City, N.Y.: Doubleday, Doran, 1942), 3–4.

11. Ibid., 3–4.

12. Ibid., 9–11.

13. Patricia Davidson Guinan, "Back Home to Mother," *House Beautiful*, August 1943, 17.

14. Michael Stevens, ed., *Women Remember the War, 1941–1945* (Madison: Wisconsin State Historical Society, 1993), 81–86.

15. Janet E. Malley, "Life on the Home Front: Housewives' Experiences of World War II," in *Women's Untold Stories: Breaking Silence, Talking Back, Voicing*

Complexity, ed. M. Romero and A. J. Stewart (Florence, KY: Routledge, 1999), 53–70.

16. *Time,* August 30, 1943, 65.

17. Helen B. Sweedy, "I'm Following You," *New York Times.*

18. *Time,* August 30, 1943, 65.

19. Barbara Klaw, *Camp Follower: The Story of a Soldier's Wife* (New York: Random House, 1943), 13–17.

20. *Time,* August 30, 1943.

21. Stevens, ed., *Women Remember the War,* 86–88.

22. Litoff and Smith, *Since You Went Away,* 84.

23. Amy Bentley, *Eating for Victory: Food Rationing and the Politics of Domesticity* (Urbana: University of Illinois Press, 1998), 24–26.

24. Ibid.

25. Ibid.

26. Richard R. Lingeman, *Don't You Know There's a War On?* (New York: G. P. Putnam's Sons, 1970), 285–286.

27. Doris Kearns Goodwin, *No Ordinary Time* (New York: Simon & Schuster, 1994), 255–256.

28. Ibid., Lingeman, *Don't You Know There's A War On?,* 285–286; Litoff and Smith, *Since You Went Away; BusinessWeek,* October 17, 1942, 104; *Newsweek,* November 2, 1942, 36.

29. Bentley, *Eating for Victory;* Lingeman, *Don't You Know There's a War On?; BusinessWeek,* October 17, 1942, 104; *Newsweek,* November 2, 1942, 36.

30. Litoff and Smith, *Since You Went Away,* 84–85.

31. Ibid., 188.

32. AdAge.com, Crain Communications, Inc.

33. Home Services Staff of General Mills, Inc., *Your Share,* Foreword.

34. Ibid., 27.

35. M. F. K. Fisher, *How to Cook a Wolf* (New York: Duell, Sloan and Pearce, 1942), 28, 195.

36. Nancy A. Walker, *Shaping Our Mothers' World: American Women's Magazines* (Jackson: University Press of Mississippi, 2000), 85.

37. Ibid., 78; Marie F. Valgos, "Selling Rosie the Riveter: How Advertisements in Ladies' Home Journal Sold American Women Their Role During World War II," *The Berkeley McNair Journal,* 2 (Summer 1994).

38. Doris Weatherford, *American Women and World War II* (New York: Facts on File, 1990), 234–235; "You're the WINS: Women in National Service, *Ladies' Home Journal,* March 1943.

39. *Ladies' Home Journal,* May 1944, 100.

40. Ibid., 146.

41. Ruth Faulds Taylor, interview by author, February 2003. Ruth Faulds is my

mother Carol Lynn's cousin, and Almira Faulds was my mother's aunt, my grand-mother's sister.

42. Ibid.

43. *Ladies' Home Journal,* May 1944.

44. Ibid.

45. Ruth Faulds Taylor interview.

46. Melisse Faulds Meeth, "How Dear to My Heart, A Personal Recollection of My Parents and My Family" (unpublished, 1982), 120–123 (another cousin of my mother's).

47. Ibid.

48. Donald L. Miller, *The Story of World War II* (New York: Simon & Schuster, 2001), 361; Paul D. Casdorph, *Let the Good Times Roll* (New York: Paragon House, 1991), 145–146.

49. Hoopes, *Americans Remember the Home Front,* 227.

50. Ibid.

51. Ibid., 297–98.

52. Litoff and Smith, *Since You Went Away,* 244–248.

53. Alleta Sullivan, "I Lost Five Sons," *The American Magazine,* March 1944, 17.

Chapter 2: Soldiers Without Guns

1. U.S. War Department, "You're Going to Employ Women" pamphlet (Washington, D.C.: Government Printing Office), 27, Women in Industry, National Archives, Washington, D.C.

2. Sherna Berger Gluck, *Rosie the Riveter Revisited* (New York: New American Library, 1988), 8, from a poll in *Public Opinion 1935–1946,* Princeton University Press, 1951.

3. Ibid., 10.

4. Donald L. Miller, *The Story of World War II* (New York: Simon & Schuster, 2001), 19–25.

5. President Franklin D. Roosevelt, radio address, December 29, 1940.

6. Miller, *The Story of World War II,* 48–49.

7. Gluck, *Rosie the Riveter Revisited,* 7–8.

8. Judith Sealander, *Records of the Women's Bureau of the US Department of Labor, 1918–1965* (University Publications of America, LexisNexis, 1997).

9. Bessie Stokes, interview by the author, August 2000, Sun City, AZ; Bessie Stokes, interview by the author, May 29, 2001, Sun City, AZ.

10. Gluck, *Rosie the Riveter Revisited,* 11.

11. Ibid.

12. "Rosie the Riveter," lyrics and music by Redd Evans and John Jacob Loeb, 1942.

13. Stokes, interview, August 2000.

14. "The Margin Now Is Womanpower," *Fortune,* February 1943, 100.

15. "More Women Must Go to Work as 3,200,000 New Jobs Beckon," *Newsweek,* September 6, 1943, 74.

16. "The Margin Now Is Womanpower," *Fortune,* February 1943, 102.

17. Maureen Honey, *Creating Rosie the Riveter: Class, Gender, and Propaganda During World War II* (Amherst: University of Massachusetts Press, 1984), 46–47.

18. John W. Jeffries, *Wartime America* (Chicago: Ivan R. Dee, Inc., 1996), 25; National Archives Overview of War Manpower Commission records.

19. John W. Jeffries, *Wartime America* (Chicago: Ivan R. Dee, Inc., 1996), 25; National Archives Overview of War Manpower Commission records; Richard R. Lingeman, *Don't You Know There's a War On?* (New York: G. P. Putnam's Sons, 1970), 123.

20. Doris Weatherford, *American Women and World War II* (New York: Facts on File, Inc., 1990), 128.

21. "The Margin Now Is Womanpower," *Fortune,* February 1943, 101.

22. Susan M. Hartmann, *The Home Front and Beyond: American Women in the 1940s* (Boston: Twayne Publishers, 1982), 82.

23. Gluck, *Rosie the Riveter Revisited,* 13.

24. Elizabeth Stern, "America's Pampered Husbands," *The Nation,* July 10, 1943, 40, cited by Weatherford, Doris, *American Women and World War II* (New York: Facts on File, Inc., 1990).

25. "The Margin Now Is Womanpower," *Fortune,* February 1943, 100.

26. http://www.library.csi.cuny.edu/dept/history/lavender/redstone.html.

27. http://www.carnegielibrary.org/locations/pennsylvania/ww2/ww26.html.

28. Judy Barrett Litoff and David E. Smith, *Since You Went Away: World War II Letters from American Women on the Home Front* (Lawrence: University of Kansas Press, 1991), 147.

29. Hartmann, *The Home Front and Beyond,* 77–78; "Manpower—Fade-out of the Women," *Time,* September 4, 1944, 78.

30. Gluck, *Rosie the Riveter Revisited,* 13.

31. Lee Turner Foringer, interview by the author, August 2000, Sun City, Ariz.; Lee Turner Foringer, interview by the author, May 22, 2001.

32. Joel Davidson, "Building for World War II: The Aerospace Industry," *Blueprints Magazine,* Fall 1993, 2–8.

33. Lee Turner Foringer, interview.

34. "Leave for Mothers," *Business Week,* October 30, 1943, 100.

35. LoRay Tewalt, interview by the author, August 2000, Sun City, Ariz.

36. William H. Chafe, *The American Woman: Her Changing Social, Economic and Political Roles, 1920–1970* (Oxford: Oxford University Press, 1972), 140.

37. Lois Wolfe, interview by the author, August 2000, Sun City, Ariz.

38. Barbara Walls, interview by the author, August 2000, Sun City, Ariz.

39. Richard R. Lingeman, *Don't You Know There's a War On?* (New York: G. P. Putnam's Sons, 1970), 184.

40. Norma Jeane Dougherty, letter to Grace McKee, June 15, 1944, as quoted in Donald Spoto, *Marilyn Monroe: The Biography* (New York: HarperCollins Publishers, 1993) 87–88.

41. Norma Jeane Dougherty, letter to Grace McKee, June 4, 1944, as quoted in Spoto, *Marilyn Monroe*, 91.

42. Spoto, *Marilyn Monroe;* Norman Mailer, *Marilyn* (New York: Grosset & Dunlap, 1973).

43. Department of Labor, Women's Bureau, "Negro Women War Workers," *Bulletin*, no. 205, 1.

44. *Tampa Tribune*, 1943; cited in Lewis N. Wynne and Carolyn J. Baines, "A Story of Gulf Coast Maritime History," *Gulf Coast Review* 5 (Spring 1990).

45. Susan B. Anthony II, *Out of the Kitchen—Into the War: Women's Winning Role in the Nation's Drama* (New York: Stephen Daye, 1943), 79.

46. Ibid.

47. http://www.liberty-ship.com/html/yards/kaiserperm2.html.

48. http://www.rosietheriveter.org/memory.htm.

49. *The Saturday Evening Post,* February 3, 1945.

50. Nancy Baker Wise and Christy Wise, *A Mouthful of Rivets: Women at Work in World War II* (San Francisco: Jossey-Bass Publishers, 1994), 153.

51. Ibid., 54.

52. Augusta H. Clawson, *Shipyard Diary of a Woman Welder* (New York: Penguin Books, 1944); as cited in Judy B. Litoff and David C. Smith, *American Women in a World at War* (Wilmington, Del: Scholarly Resources, Inc, 1997), 192–193.

53. Wise and Wise, *A Mouthful of Rivets,* 25.

54. Karen Anderson, *Wartime Women: Sex Roles, Family Relations, and the Status of Women During World War II* (Westport, Conn.: Greenpoint Press, 1981), 60–61.

55. "Women War Workers: A Case History," *New York Times Magazine,* December 26, 1943, 21.

56. Anderson, *Wartime Women,* 122–53.

57. Ibid.

58. Ibid., 146.

59. "The Margin Now Is Woman Power," *Fortune,* February 1943, 224.

60. Weatherford, *American Women and World War II,* 172–173.

61. Wise and Wise, *A Mouthful of Rivets,* 203.

62. Susan M. Hartmann, *The Home Front and Beyond: American Women in the 1940s* (Boston: Twayne Publishers, 1982), 62.

63. Weatherford, *American Women and World War II,* 234.

64. Ibid., 16.

65. Susan B. Anthony II, *Out of the Kitchen—Into the War: Women's Winning Role in the Nation's Drama* (New York: Stephen Daye, 1943), 77.

66. Wise and Wise, *A Mouthful of Rivets*, 201.

67. *The Huntsville Times*, August 1945, as quoted in Kaylene Hughes, *Women at War: Redstone's WWII Female Production Soldiers* at wwwredstonearmymil/history/women/welcomehtml and wwwlibrarycsicunyedu/dept/history/lavender/redstonehtml.

68. Stokes, interview, August 2000; Stokes, interview, May 29, 2001.

69. Judith Sealander, *Records of the Women's Bureau of the US Department of Labor, 1918–1965* (University Publications of America, LexisNexis, 1997).

70. D'Ann Campbell, *Women at War with America: Private Lives in a Patriotic Era* (Boston: Harvard University Press, 1984), 142–148; www.librarycsicunyedu/dept/history/lavender/redstonehtml.

71. John W. Jeffries, *Wartime America* (Chicago: Ivan R. Dee, 1996), 96.

72. Campbell, *Women at War with America*, 142–148.

73. William H. Chafe, *The American Woman: Her Changing Social, Economic and Political Roles, 1920–1970* (Oxford: Oxford University Press, 1972), 151.

74. Ibid., 141.

75. Department of Labor, Women's Bureau, "Women as Workers, A Statistical Guide" (Washington, D.C., 1953), 15–17; as cited in Campbell, *Women at War With America*, 239.

76. Dorothy Parker, "Are We Women or Are We Mice?" *Mademoiselle*, May 1943.

77. "The Margin Now Is Womanpower," *Fortune*, February 1943, 100.

78. Wise and Wise, *A Mouthful of Rivets*, 128.

79. Ibid., 165–167.

80. Penny Colman, *Rosie the Riveter: Working Women on the Home Front in World War II* (New York: Crown Publishers, 1995), 19.

81. Chafe, *The American Woman*, 148.

82. Colman, *Rosie the Riveter*, 97.

83. Gluck, *Rosie the Riveter Revisited*, 169–170.

84. Ottilie Juliet Gattuso to President Harry S. Truman, September 6, 1945, Records of the Women's Bureau, National Archives, Washington, D.C.

85. *New York Times*, "Weighs Job Hopes of Women in Peace," August 16, 1943, 12.

86. *Saturday Evening Post*, February 20, 1943; as cited by Gluck, *Rosie the Riveter Revisited*, 15.

87. Aileen Keenan, "Learning to Live Together in Good Times and Bad," 1995, transcript, Oral History of Rhode Island Women During WWII, Brown University, Providence, R.I.

88. Colman, *Rosie the Riveter*, 21.

89. Katherine O'Grady, "What Did You Do in the War, Grandma?" 1995, transcript, Oral History of Rhode Island Women During WWII, Brown University, Providence, R.I.

90. Walls, interview, August 2000.

91. Judy Barrett Litoff and David E. Smith, *Since You Went Away: World War II Letters from American Women on the Home Front* (Lawrence: University of Kansas Press, 1991), 157.

Chapter 3: Putting Up a Good Front

1. Betty Grable quoted in Doug Warren, *Betty Grable: The Reluctant Movie Queen* (New York: St. Martin's Press, 1981), 80.

2. *Time*, January 5, 1942; Jean Ruth Hay, interview by the author, September 2002.

3. Roy Hoopes, *When the Stars Went to War: Hollywood and World War II* (New York: Random House, 1994), 81–84; Otto Friedrich, *City of Nets: A Portrait of Hollywood in the 1940s* (New York: Perennial Library, Harper & Row, 1987), 106–107.

4. Jean Ruth Hay, interview by the author, September 2002.

5. Letter to Jean Ruth Hay, from Jean Ruth Hay's personal papers.

6. Jean Ruth Hay, G.I. jive recordings, http://reveillewithbeverly.com/the_music.htm.

7. Jean Ruth Hay, interview by the author, September 2002.

8. Gerald Nachman, *Raised on Radio* (New York: Pantheon Books, 1998), 175.

9. William C. Ackerman, "Dimensions of American Broadcasting," *Public Opinion Quarterly 9* (Spring 1945), 3, 11; *Fortune*, January 1938, *Fortune*, November 1939, and National Association of Broadcasters all cited in Ackerman.

10. Ackerman, "Dimensions of American Broadcasting," 15.

11. Richard R. Lingeman, *Don't You Know There's a War On?* (New York: G. P. Putnam's Sons, 1970), 277.

12. Friedrich, *City of Nets*, 106.

13. Warren, *Betty Grable*, 96.

14. Friedrich, *City of Nets*, 106.

15. *Modern Screen* magazine, February 1943.

16. Hoopes, *When the Stars Went to War*, 112.

17. Ibid., 206.

18. Ibid., 7.

19. Marlene Dietrich, *Marlene* (New York: Grove Press, 1989), 188.

20. Dietrich, *Marlene*, 189.

21. Hoopes, *When the Stars Went to War*, 112.

22. Gerald Nachman, *Raised on Radio* (New York: Pantheon Books, 1998), 142.

23. Hoopes, *When the Stars Went to War*, 132.

24. Ibid., 121.

25. Hoopes, *When the Stars Went to War,* 110, 122; Lingeman, *Don't You Know There's a War On?,* 211.

26. Hoopes, *When the Stars Went to War,* 122.

27. *Modern Screen* magazine, February 1943.

28. Joseph Gustaitis, "Antoinette Perry: The Woman Behind the Tony Awards," *American History Magazine,* April 1997.

29. Lauren Bacall, *By Myself* (New York: Ballantine Books, 1980), 47–48.

30. Gustaitis, "Antoinette Perry," April 1997.

31. Maxene Andrews and Bill Gilbert, *Over Here, Over There: The Andrews Sisters and the USO Stars in World War II* (New York: Zebra Books, 1993), 84.

32. Ibid., 84.

33. Ibid., 85.

34. Hoopes, *When the Stars Went to War,* 169.

35. *Modern Screen* magazine, February 1943.

36. Hoopes, *When the Stars Went to War,* 179–181.

37. Ibid., 172.

38. *Daily Variety,* October 29, 1944, as cited in Lingeman, *Don't You Know There's a War On?,* 210.

39. Roy Hoopes, *Americans Remember the Home Front* (New York: Berkley, 2002), 155–156.

40. Frank Coffey, *Always Home: 50 Years of the USO* (McLean, VA: Brassey's US, 1991), 2–4.

41. Coffey, *Always Home,* 25; Sherrie Tucker, *Swing Shift: "All-Girl" Bands of the 1940s* (Durham, N.C.: Duke University Press, 2000), 237.

42. Coffey, *Always Home,* 26.

43. Modern Screen magazine, February 1943.

44. Andrews and Gilbert, *Over Here, Over There,* 91–92.

45. Ibid., 34–35.

46. Maxene Andrews as quoted in Studs Terkel, *The Good War: An Oral History of World War II* (New York: The New Press, 1984), 296.

47. Andrews and Gilbert, *Over Here, Over There,* 125–126.

48. Hoopes, *When the Stars Went to War,* 199.

49. David G. Yellin, Sergeant, Special Services, Burma, interview with the author, 2001.

50. Julia M. H. Carson, *Home Away from Home: The Story of the USO* (New York: Harper & Brothers Publishers, 1946), 126–130.

51. Ibid., 112–113.

52. Ibid., 115.

53. Tucker, *Swing Shift,* 230.

54. Carole Landis, *Four Jills in a Jeep* (New York: Random House, 1944), 164–165.

55. Hoopes, *When the Stars Went to War,* 206.

56. Dietrich, *Marlene,* 198.

57. Coffey, *Always Home,* 26.

58. Tucker, *Swing Shift,* 49.

59. Ibid., 33.

60. William Peri, "Who Said Girl Musicians Could Play?" *Down Beat,* March 1, 1942, as cited in Tucker, *Swing Shift,* 45.

61. Robert Toney, "That Fem Question, Again!" *Down Beat,* May 1, 1942, as cited in Tucker, *Swing Shift,* 47.

62. Tucker, *Swing Shift,* 49.

63. Ibid., 59–61.

64. D. Antoinette Handy, *The International Sweethearts of Rhythm* (Lanham, Md.: Scarecrow Press, 1998), 162.

65. Maurine Longstreth, interview with the author, September 2000, Sun City, Ariz.

66. Shirley Christian, "But Is It Art? Well, Yes," *New York Times,* November 25, 1998.

67. Jean Preer, "Esquire vs. Walker: The Postmaster General and The Magazine for Men," *Prologue*—The National Archives, Vol. 23, No. 1, Spring 1990; Joanne Meyerowitz, "Women, Cheesecake and Borderline Material: Responses to Girlie Pictures in the Mid-Twentieth Century US," *Journal of Women's History* 8 (Fall 1996).

68. Preer, "Esquire vs. Walker."

69. Cecilia Rasmussen, "Vargas' Pinups Inspired GIs, Became Icons of US Culture," *Los Angeles Times,* June 25, 2000, Metro Section B.

70. Preer, "Esquire vs. Walker."

71. Collins, Max Allan, "Painted Ladies," card set, Kitchen Sink Press, 1993.

72. Hoopes, *Americans Remember the Home Front,* 155; Hoopes, *When the Stars Went to War,* 94.

73. Warren, *Betty Grable,* 77–79.

74. Robert B. Westbrook, " 'I Want a Girl, Just Like the Girl That Married Harry James': American Women and the Problem of Political Obligation in World War II," *American Quarterly* 42 (December 1990), 600.

75. Clayton R. Koppes and Gregory D. Black, "What to Show the World: The Office of War Information and Hollywood, 1942–1945," *The Journal of American History* 64 (June 1977), 88.

76. Hoopes, *When the Stars Went to War,* 99–102.

77. Katharine Hepburn, letters to Robert McKnight, 1943.

78. *Motion Picture* magazine, June 1943.

79. Sherna Berger Gluck, *Rosie the Riveter Revisited: Women, the War and Social Change* (New York: New American Library, 1987), 5.

80. Museum of Television and Radio Web site, http://www.mtrorg/exhibit/wwe/wwe5htm.

81. Nachman, *Raised on Radio*, 366.

82. Gluck, *Rosie the Riveter Revisited*, 5.

83. Nachman, *Raised on Radio*, 369; Gluck, *Rosie the Riveter Revisited*, 14; Museum of Television and Radio Web site, www.mtrorg/exhibit/wwe/wwe5htm.

84. Digitally reproduced versions of *Male Call* are available at the Authentic History Center website, www.authentichistorycom; included is a preface to a book of the comic strips from Milton Caniff. Digital reproduction of *Male Call* are also available at www.mutoworldcom/MaleCall.htm.

85. Vic Herman, *Winnie the WAC* (Encinitas, Calif.: Virginia Herman, 2002).

86. Les Daniels, *Wonder Woman: The Complete History, the Life and Times of the Amazon Princess* (San Francisco: Chronicle Books, 2000), 30–37.

Chapter 4: This Man's Army

1. Colonel Bettie Morden, USA (Ret.), *Women's Army Corps: WAAC and WAC*, article in Major General Jeanne M. Holm, USAF (Ret.), editor, *In Defense of a Nation: Servicewomen in World War II* (Arlington, VA: Vandamere Press, 1998), 47.

2. Encyclopaedia Britannica, "Molly Pitcher."

3. Mattie E. Treadwell, *United States Army in World War II, Special Studies: The Women's Army Corps* (Washington, D.C.: U.S. Government Printing Office, 1954), 8.

4. Treadwell, *United States Army in World War II, Special Studies*, 8–10; Doris Weatherford, *American Women and World War II* (New York: Facts on File, Inc., 1990), 29.

5. Janann Sherman, "'They either need these women or they do not': Margaret Chase Smith and the Fight for Regular Status for Women in the Military," *The Journal of Military History*, January 1990, 59.

6. Treadwell, *United States Army in World War II, Special Studies*, 17.

7. Ibid., 18.

8. Holm, *In Defense of a Nation*, 2.

9. Treadwell, *United States Army in World War II, Special Studies*, 20.

10. Ibid., 22.

11. Ibid., 24.

12. Treadwell, *United States Army in World War II, Special Studies*, 25; Leisa D. Meyer, *Creating GI Jane: Sexuality and Power in the Women's Army Corps During WWII* (New York: Columbia University Press, 1996), 20.

13. Treadwell, *United States Army in World War II, Special Studies*, 29.

14. Ibid., 45.

15. Ibid., 50.

16. Ibid., 48.

17. "Catholics v. WAACs," *Time*, June 15, 1942, 39.

18. Colonel Mary T. Sarnecky USA (Ret.), RN, DNSc, *Army Nurse Corps*, and Susan H. Godson, Ph.D., *Navy Nurse Corps*, in Holm, USAF (Ret.), *In Defense of a Nation*, 27, 32.

19. Judith A. Bellafaire, "The Women's Army Corps: A Commemoration of World War II Service" (Washington, D.C.: U.S. Army Center of Military History Publication 72-15, 1993).

20. Treadwell, *United States Army in World War II, Special Studies*, 66.

21. Margaret Porter Polsky, interview with the author, August 18, 2003.

22. Dorothy Wain Thompson, letters home 1942–1945 (Brian Mead/Hardscrabble Farm, www.hardscrabble farm.com, 2003).

23. Treadwell, *United States Army in World War II, Special Studies*, 301; D'Ann Campbell, *Women at War with America: Private Lives in a Patriotic Era* (Cambridge, Mass.: Harvard University Press, 1984), 38.

24. Elna Hilliard Grahn, *In the Company of Wacs* (Manhattan, Kansas: Sunflower University Press, 1993), 48.

25. Memo from War Department General Staff Organization and Training Division to Organization-Mobilization Branch, May 11, 1943, George C. Marshall Research Library, Lexington, Va., National Archives Xerox 2782.

26. Treadwell, *United States Army in World War II, Special Studies*, 302.

27. Memo from Brigadier General M. G. White to Assistant Chief of Staff, G-3, War Department, June 3, 1943, George C. Marshall Research Library, Lexington, Va., National Archives Xerox 2782; Campbell, *Women at War with America*, 39.

28. Judith Lawrence Bellafaire, Ph.D., "We Also Served," an article in Holm, *In Defense of a Nation*, 133.

29. Donald L. Miller, *The Story of World War II* (New York: Simon & Schuster, 2001), 160–162.

30. Colonel Bettie Morden, "Women's Army Corps: WAAC and WAC," in Holm, *In Defense of a Nation*, 43.

31. General George Catlett Marshall, draft of memo to Military Committee, House of Representatives, December 3, 1942, Box 65, Folder 46, George C. Marshall Research Library, Lexington, Va.

32. Treadwell, *United States Army in World War II, Special Studies*, 361.

33. Alma Lutz, editor, *With Love, Jane: Letters from American Women on the War Fronts* (New York: John Day Company, 1945), 80.

34. Grace Porter Miller, *Call of Duty: A Montana Girl in World War II* (Baton Rouge: Louisiana State University Press, 1999), 68–69.

35. Ibid., 69.

36. Lutz, *With Love, Jane*, 103–104.

37. Lutz, *With Love, Jane*, 123–124.

38. Olga Gruhzit-Hoyt, *They Also Served: American Women in World War II* (New York: Birch Lane Press, 1995), 97.

39. Miller, *Call of Duty*, 114–116.

40. Treadwell, *United States Army in World War II, Special Studies*, 441–444.

41. Irene J. Brion, *Lady GI: A Woman's War in the South Pacific: The Memoir of Irene Brion* (Novato, Calif.: Presidio Press, 1997), 91–98.

42. Lutz, *With Love, Jane*, 144–147.

43. Treadwell, *United States Army in World War II, Special Studies* (Washington, D.C.: U.S. Government Printing Office, 1954), 421–426, 450.

44. Lutz, *With Love, Jane*, 137.

45. H. I. Phillips, *All-out Arlene: The Story of the Girls Behind the Boys Behind the Guns* (New York: Doubleday, Doran and Company, 1943), 81–82.

46. Treadwell, *United States Army in World War II, Special Studies*, 449.

47. Judy Barrett Litoff and David C. Smith, *We're in This War, Too: World War II Letters from American Women in Uniform* (New York: Oxford University Press, 1994), 192.

48. *Washington Times-Herald*, June 8, 1943, as quoted in Treadwell, *United States Army in World War II, Special Studies*, 203.

49. Treadwell, *United States Army in World War II, Special Studies*, 201.

50. Meyer, *Creating GI Jane*, 36–37.

51. Treadwell, *United States Army in World War II, Special Studies*, 204.

52. Ibid., 193.

53. Ibid., 372.

54. *Washington Post*, June 11, 1943, as cited in Treadwell, *United States Army in World War II, Special Studies*, 205.

55. Records of censor reports cited in Treadwell, *United States Army in World War II, Special Studies*, 212–213.

56. Treadwell, *United States Army in World War II, Special Studies*, 218.

57. Seventy-seven nurses were held prisoner in the Philippines, five had been taken prisoner on Guam and held in Japan for about a year, and one had been taken prisoner in Germany.

58. Colonel Mary T. Sarnecky USA (Ret.), RN, DNSc, *Army Nurse Corps*, and Susan H. Godson, Ph.D., *Navy Nurse Corps*, articles in Holm, *In Defense of a Nation*, 54–55.

59. Mary A. Hallaren, Senate, Hearings on S.1641, 9, 15 July 1947, 10, 43 quoted in Sherman, " 'They either need these women or they do not': Margaret Chase Smith and the Fight for Regular Status for Women in the Military," 68.

60. Treadwell, *United States Army in World War II, Special Studies*, ix.

Chapter 5: On Duty at Home

1. Mildred McAfee Horton, "Women in the United States Navy," *American Journal of Sociology,* Volume 51, issue 5, Human Behavior in Military Society, March 1946, 449.

2. Jean Ebbert and Marie-Beth Hall, *Navy Women's Reserve: WAVES,* article in Major General Jeanne M. Holm, USAF (Ret.), editor, *In Defense of a Nation: Servicewomen in World War II* (Arlington, Va.: Vandamere Press, 1998), 59.

3. Mildred McAfee, as quoted in Ebbert and Hall, *Navy Women's Reserve: WAVES,* 59.

4. Ebbert and Hall, *Navy Women's Reserve: WAVES,* 61, 64.

5. *Time,* "Women—Miss Mac," March 12, 1945, 20–23.

6. Ibid.

7. Ruby Messer Barber, interview with the author, August 9, 2003.

8. Dorothy Cole Libby, http://womenofthewaves.com/profiles/index.htm.

9. Margaret Lindeen Routon, interview with the author, August 16, 2003, Memphis, Tenn.

10. Nancy Wilson Ross, *The WAVES: The Story of the Girls in Blue* (New York: Henry Holt, 1943).

11. Marie Cody, letter March 14, 1945, Marie Cody Collection, Women Veterans Historical Collection, the University of North Carolina, Greensboro.

12. Lillian M. Pimlott, letter to mother, July 5, 1945, Lillian M. Pimlott collection, Women Veterans Historical Collection, the University of North Carolina, Greensboro.

13. *Time,* "Women—Miss Mac," March 12, 1945, 21.

14. Captain Mary E. McWilliams, USCGR (Ret.), "Women in the Coast Guard: SPARs," in Holm, USAF (Ret.), editor, *In Defense of a Nation: Servicewomen in World War II* (Arlington, Va.: Vandamere Press, 1998), 97.

15. Mary C. Lyne and Kay Arthur, *Three Years Behind the Mast: The Story of the United States Coast Guard SPARs* (Washington, D.C.: unpublished, 1946), 77–83, as cited in Judy Barrett Litoff and David C. Smith, *American Women in a World at War* (Wilmington, Del.: Scholarly Resources, 1997), 57–65.

16. John A. Tiley, "A History of Women in the Coast Guard," U.S. Coast Guard Web site: www.uscg.mil.

17. McWilliams, "Women in the Coast Guard: SPARs," 104.

18. Olga Gruhzit-Hoyt, *They Also Served: American Women in World War II* (New York: Carol Publishing Group, 1995), 147.

19. Robin J. Thomson, USCG, "SPARs: The Coast Guard and the Women's Reserve in World War II," U.S. Coast Guard website, www.uscg.mil.

20. Tim Wood, "Chatham, the SPARs and Loran: All-Female Unit Played Historic Role in World War II," *Cape Cod Chronicle,* July 25, 2002.

21. Thomson, "SPARs."

22. McWilliams, "Women in the Coast Guard: SPARs," 109.

23. Colonel Mary V. Stremlow, USMCR (Ret.), "Marine Corps Women's Reserve: Free a Man to Fight," in Holm, *In Defense of a Nation,* 77–78.

24. Women in Military Service for America website, www.womensmemorial. org.

25. Stremlow, "Marine Corps Women's Reserve: Free a Man to Fight," 80–81.

26. Ibid., 83.

27. "Toughening up the Women Marines," *New York Times Magazine,* June 20, 1943, 12–13.

28. Mary Amanda Sabouin, interview, June 25, 1999, Oral History Project, Women Veterans Historical Collection, the University of North Carolina, Greensboro.

29. Stremlow, "Marine Corps Women's Reserve: Free a Man to Fight," 82.

30. Mary McLeod Rogers, interview, December 20, 1999, Oral History Project, Women Veterans Historical Collection, the University of North Carolina, Greensboro.

31. Lillian Epsberg Goodman, interview with the author, August 17, 2003, Memphis, Tenn.

32. Jacqueline Cochran, *Finfinella Gazette,* March 1, 1943.

33. Sally Van Wagenen Keil, *Those Wonderful Women in Their Flying Machines: The Unknown Heroines of World War II* (New York: Rawson, Wade Publishers, 1979), 100–103.

34. Eleanor Roosevelt, *My Day,* September 1, 1942.

35. Cochran, *Finfinella Gazette,* March 1, 1943.

36. Jacqueline Cochran, status report on WASP to Commanding General H. H. Arnold, Army Air Forces, August 1, 1944, Texas Women's University Archives.

37. Helan (Kelly) Drake, letter, August 1989.

38. Adaline Blank, *Correspondence July 1943–Dec. 1943,* Denton, Tex., Texas Woman's Collection, Texas Woman's University, 2002, 6–9, 16.

39. Lieutenant Colonel Yvonne C. Pateman, USAF (Ret.), "Women Air Force Service Pilots: WASP," Holm, *In Defense of a Nation,* 116–117.

40. Gruhzit-Hoyt, *They Also Served,* 168.

41. Iris Cummings Critchell, interview with the author, August 18, 2003; David R. Francis, "A Pilot Who's Kept to Her Flight Plan," *Christian Science Monitor,* June 21, 2001.

42. Van Wagenen Keil, *Those Wonderful Women in Their Flying Machines,* 257.

43. Dora Dougherty Strother, "Women of the WASP," in Anne Noggle, *For God, Country, and the Thrill of It* (College Station, Tex.: Texas A&M University Press, 1990), Introduction.

44. Negar Tekeei, "Fly Girl," *Northwestern Magazine*, Spring 2000.

45. Strother, "Women of the WASP," Introduction.

46. Cornelia Fort, "At the Twilight's Last Gleaming," *Woman's Home Companion*, June, 1943.

47. Cornelia Fort, letter to her mother, January 28, 1942, as quoted in Rob Simbeck, *Daughter of the Air: The Brief Soaring Life of Cornelia Fort* (New York: Atlantic Monthly Press, 1999), 238.

48. Van Wagenen Keil, *Those Wonderful Women in Their Flying Machines*, 192–212.

49. Ann Darr, "The Long Flight Home," *U.S. News & World Report*, November 17, 1997, 66.

50. *Los Angeles Times*, March 6, 1994, by Sandra Skowron, Associated Press.

51. Lillian Epsberg Goodman, interview with the author, August 17, 2003, Memphis, Tenn.

52. Sally Van Wagehen Keil, *Those Wonderful Women in Their Flying Machines*, 265–285.

53. Ibid., 290–291.

54. Lillian Epsberg Goodman, interview with the author, August 17, 2003, Memphis, Tenn.

55. Darr, "The Long Flight Home," 66.

56. Doris Brinker Tanner, "We Also Served," *American History Illustrated*, November 1985, 21.

57. Cochran, status report on WASP.

58. Iris Cummings Critchell, interview with the author, August 18, 2003.

Chapter 6: Save His Life and Find Your Own

1. Eleanor Roosevelt as quoted at http://womenshistory.about.com.

2. Judith Lawrence Bellafaire, Ph.D., "We Also Served," an article in Major General Jeanne M. Holm, USAF (Ret.), editor, *In Defense of a Nation: Servicewomen in World War II* (Arlington, Va.: Vandamere Press, 1998), 133.

3. Judy Barrett Litoff and David C. Smith, *We're in This War, Too: World War II Letters from American Women in Uniform* (New York: Oxford University Press, 1994), 83.

4. Bellafaire, "We Also Served," 137–138.

5. Ibid.

6. Billie Banks Doan Ballou, interview with the author, Memphis, Tenn., April 2002.

7. Doris Weatherford, *American Women and World War II* (New York: Facts on File, 1990), 245.

8. Keith Ayling, *Calling All Women* (New York: Harper & Brothers, 1942), 113.

9. Nancy Potter, *What Did You Do in the War, Grandma?* (Providence, R.I.: Rhode Island Historical Society, 1995).

10. Louise Aukerman, *What Did You Do in the War, Grandma?* (Providence, R.I.: Rhode Island Historical Society, 1995).

11. Mary Steele Ross, *American Women in Uniform* (Garden City, N.Y.: Garden City Publishing Company, 1943), 18–23; Ayling, *Calling All Women,* 32–70.

12. "Civilian Defense," *Time,* January 26, 1942, 61.

13. Doris Weatherford, *American Women and World War II* (New York: Facts on File, 1990), 233; Ayling, *Calling All Women,* 88–108; Ross, *American Women in Uniform,* 24–26.

14. Weatherford, *American Women and World War II,* 220–221.

15. "Our Land Army Is Different," *Saturday Evening Post,* July 25, 1942, 25.

16. Weatherford, *American Women and World War II,* 221.

17. "The Women's Land Army Works for Victory," U.S. Department of Agriculture Pamphlet, April 1945; "Pitch In and Help!: The Women's Land Army Calls 800,000 Women to the Farm in 1944," U.S. Department of Agriculture Pamphlet, May 1944; Weatherford, *American Women and World War II,* 222–223.

18. "The Women's Land Army Works for Victory," U.S. Department of Agriculture Pamphlet.

19. Lucy Greenbaum, "At the Front with Our Land Army," *New York Times Magazine,* July 4, 1943, 12.

20. Ibid.

21. "The Women's Land Army Works for Victory," U.S. Department of Agriculture Pamphlet, April 1945.

22. Ibid.

23. Ibid.

24. Bellafaire, "We Also Served," 133–137; Gruhzit-Hoyt, *They Also Served,* 219–221.

25. Jean Archer Rothermel, letter home from Guam, May 23, 1945.

26. Ibid.

27. Michael E. Stevens, editor, *Women Remember the War 1941–1945: Voices of the Wisconsin Past* (Madison, Wis.: State Historical Society of Wisconsin, 1993), 70–72.

28. Ibid., 74.

29. Alice Pennington, memoirs, unpublished, 1999.

30. George Korson, *At His Side: The Story of the American Red Cross Overseas in World War II* (New York: Coward-McCann, 1945), 279–280.

31. Bellafaire, "We Also Served," 137.

32. Oscar Whitelaw Rexford, *Battlestars and Doughnuts: World War II Clubmobile Experiences of Mary Metcalfe Rexford* (St. Louis, Mo.: The Patrice Press, 1989), 38–45.

33. Mary Haynsworth Mathews, interview, Women Veterans Historical Col-

lection, Oral History Project, the University of North Carolina at Greensboro, November 9, 1999.

34. Elizabeth Richardson, letters as quoted in Gordon Brown, "A Life Cut Short, A Life Remembered," Lawrence University website, http://www.lawrence.edu/about/trads/liz.shtml.

35. Mathews interview.

36. Litoff and Smith, *We're in This War, Too,* 257.

37. Holm, *In Defense of a Nation,* 1–7.

38. Colonel Mary T. Sarnecky USA (Ret.), RN, DNSc, *Army Nurse Corps,* and Susan H. Godson, Ph.D., *Navy Nurse Corps,* in Holm, *In Defense of a Nation,* 27, 32.

39. Godson, *Navy Nurse Corps,* 32–33.

40. Bellafaire, "We Also Served," in Holm, *In Defense of a Nation,* 140–142.

41. Doris Wofford Armenaki, interview, May 19, 1999, Women's Veterans Historical Collection, Oral History Project, the University of North Carolina, Greensboro.

42. Page Cooper, *Navy Nurse* (New York: Whittlesey House, McGraw-Hill Book Company, 1946), 6–9.

43. Godson, Ph.D., *Navy Nurse Corps,* 29.

44. Diane Burke Fessler, *No Time for Fear: Voices of American Military Nurses in World War II* (East Lansing: Michigan State University Press, 1996), 16.

45. Judith A. Bellafaire, *Army Nurse Corps: A Commemoration of World War II Service* (Washington, D.C.: Center of Military History, 1994), CMH Pub. 72–14.

46. Dorothea Daley Engel, "I Was Married in Battle," *American Magazine,* October 1942, 27.

47. Bellafaire, *Army Nurse Corps;* Elizabeth M. Norman, *We Band of Angels: The Untold Story of American Nurses Trapped on Bataan by the Japanese* (New York: Random House, 1999), 273–277.

48. Fessler, *No Time For Fear,* 89–92.

49. Mary Harrington Nelson, "World War II Experiences of a POW Navy Nurse," in Paula Nassen Poulos, editor, *A Woman's War Too: U.S. Women in the Military in World War II* (Washington, D.C.: National Archives and Records Administration, 1996), 147–148.

50. Fessler, *No Time For Fear,* 89–92.

51. Bellafaire, *Army Nurse Corps.*

52. Godson, *Navy Nurse Corps,* 35; Bellafaire, *Army Nurse Corps.*

53. Godson, *Navy Nurse Corps,* 35–36.

54. Bellafaire, *Army Nurse Corps.*

55. Ibid.

56. LaVonne Telshaw Camp, *Lingering Fever: A World War II Nurse's Memoir* (Jefferson, N.C.: McFarland & Company, 1997), 79–80.

57. Ibid., 108–109.

58. 2nd Lt. Ruth G. Haskell, A.N.C., *Helmets and Lipstick* (New York: G. P. Putnam's Sons, 1944), 111–113.

59. Bellafaire, *Army Nurse Corps.*

60. Major General Norman T. Kirk, Surgeon General, U.S. Army, "Girls in the Foxholes," *American Magazine*, May 1944, 17, 94.

61. Alma Lutz, editor, *With Love, Jane: Letters from American Women on the War Fronts* (New York: John Day Company, 1945), 61–62.

62. Ibid.

63. Fessler, *No Time For Fear,* 189–190.

64. Lutz, editor, *With Love, Jane,* 52–54.

65. Carolyn M. Feller, Lieutenant Colonel, AN, USAR and Debora R. Cox, Major, AN, editors, *Highlights in the History of the Army Nurse Corps* (Washington, D.C.: U.S. Army Center of Military History, 2001).

Chapter 7: Jane Crow

1. From *Opportunity,* as quoted in Maureen Honey, editor, *Bitter Fruit: African American Women in World War II* (Columbia: University of Missouri Press, 1999), 289.

2. Kenneth D. Durr, *Behind the Backlash: White Working-Class Politics in Baltimore, 1940–1980* (Chapel Hill: University of North Carolina Press, 2003); John A. Davis, "Educational Programs for the Improvement of Race Relations: Organized Labor and Industrial Organizations," *The Journal of Negro Education,* Vol. 13, No. 3, Summer 1944, 345–346; D'Ann Campbell, *Women at War with America: Private Lives in a Patriotic Era* (Cambridge, Mass.: Harvard University Press, 1984), 128–129; Eileen Boris, " 'You Wouldn't Want One of 'Em Dancing with Your Wife': Racialized Bodies on the Job in World War II," *American Quarterly,* 50.1, 1998, 94–96.

3. Pauli Murray, "A Blueprint for First Class Citizenship," *The Crisis,* November 1944 as quoted in Honey, editor, *Bitter Fruit,* 273–279; Lynne Olson, *Freedom's Daughters: The Unsung Heroines of the Civil Rights Movement from 1830 to 1970* (New York: Scribner, 2001), 19–21, 63–64, 286.

4. William L. O'Neill, *A Democracy at War* (New York: Macmillan, 1993), as quoted at "What Did You Do in the War, Grandma?" website: http://www.stg.brown.edu/projects/WWII_Women/; Penny Colman, *Rosie the Riveter: Women on the Home Front in World War II* (New York: Crown Publishers, 1995), 27–31.

5. Colman, *Rosie the Riveter,* 27–31; Sherna Berger Gluck, *Rosie the Riveter Revisited: Women, the War and Social Change* (New York: New American Library, 1987), 23.

6. Karen Tucker Anderson, "Last Hired, First Fired: Black Women Workers During World War II," *Journal of American History* 69, no. 1, June 1982, 83.

7. Ibid.

8. Colman, *Rosie the Riveter,* 27–31; Women's Bureau, U.S. Department of Labor, "Negro Women War Workers," *Bulletin* No. 205, Washington, D.C., 1945.

9. Shirley Graham, *Negro Story,* March–April 1945, as quoted in Honey, *Bitter Fruit,* 49–54.

10. George E. Demar, "Negro Women Are American Workers, Too," *Opportunity,* April 1943, as quoted in Honey, *Bitter Fruit,* 105.

11. Gluck, *Rosie the Riveter Revisited,* 42–43.

12. Lise Funderling, "A Conversation with Maya Angelou and Eleanor Holmes Norton," *Essence,* August 1998.

13. D'Ann Campbell, *Women at War with America: Private Lives in a Patriotic Era* (Cambridge, Mass.: Harvard University Press, 1984), 74–76.

14. Hortense Johnson, "What My Job Means to Me," *Opportunity,* April 1943, as quoted in Honey, *Bitter Fruit,* 74–75.

15. May Miller, "One Blue Star," *Opportunity,* Summer, 1945 as quoted in Honey, *Bitter Fruit,* 294–295.

16. Anna Arnold Hedgeman, "The Role of the Negro Woman," *Journal of Educational Sociology* 17, no. 8, April 1944, 471.

17. "The Negro Woman Serves America," *Aframerican Woman's Journal,* Summer 1943, in Judy Barrett Litoff and David C. Smith, editors, *American Women in a World at War* (Wilmington, Del.: Scholarly Resources, 1997), 160.

18. Marjorie Randolph Suggs Edwards, Oral History Interview, June 26, 2000, Women Veterans Historical Collection, the University of North Carolina, Greensboro.

19. Mattie Treadwell, *The Women's Army Corps* (Washington, D.C.: U.S. Government Printing Office, 1953), 592.

20. Janet Sims-Wood, "Service Life in the Women's Army Corps and Afro-American Wacs," in Paula Naasen Poulos, *A Woman's War Too: U.S. Women in the Military in World War II* (Washington, D.C.: National Archives and Records Administration, 1996), 132.

21. Richard Goldstein, Obituary of Harriet M. [West] Waddy, *New York Times,* March 8, 1999.

22. Brenda L. Moore, *To Serve My Country, To Serve My Race: The Story of the Only African American WACs Stationed Overseas During World War II* (New York: New York University Press, 1996), 56.

23. Moore, *To Serve My Country, To Serve My Race,* 51–54; Treadwell, *The Women's Army Corps,* 392.

24. Brenda L. Moore, "Serving with a Dual Mission: African American Women in World War II," *National Journal of Sociology,* Volume 7.1, Summer 1993, 16.

25. Sims-Wood, "Service Life in the Women's Army Corps and Afro-American Wacs," 137.

26. Charity Adams Earley, *One Woman's Army: A Black Officer Remembers the WAC* (College Station: Texas A&M University Press, 1989), 151.

27. Ibid., 183.

28. Lacy McCrary, "The Enemy Was Discrimination," *Buffalo News*, January 17, 1998, 7C.

29. Maggi M. Morehouse, *Fighting in the Jim Crow Army: Black Men and Women Remember World War II* (Lanham, MD: Rowman & Littlefield, 2000), 34–35.

30. John W. Davis, "The Negro in the United States Navy, Marine Corps and Coast Guard," *Journal of Negro Education*, Volume 12, Issue 3, Summer 1943, 349.

31. Janet Harmon Bragg, interview, May 15, 1989, University of Arizona-Tucson, African Americans in Aviation in Arizona.

32. Leslie Haynsworth and David Toomey, *Amelia Earhart's Daughters* (New York: Perennial, 1998), 110.

33. Lena Horne and Richard Schickel, *Lena* (New York: Signet Books, 1965), 131–32.

34. Ibid., 132–36.

35. Clayton R. Koppes and Gregory D. Black, "Blacks, Loyalty, and Motion-Picture Propaganda in World War II," *Journal of American History*, Volume 73, Issue 2, September 1986, 392–393.

36. Ibid., 399.

37. Ibid., 400.

38. Ibid., 400, 404.

39. Monica L. Haynes, "Hats Off to Hattie," *Pittsburgh Post-Gazette*, August 5, 2001; Kay McFadden, "Hattie McDaniel, rediscovered Hollywood Heroine," *Seattle Times*, August 6, 2001.

40. Elsa Maxwell, "Glamour vs. Prejudice," *Negro Digest*, January 1944, as quoted in Honey, *Bitter Fruit*, 336–337.

41. William F. Yurasco, "The Pittsburgh Courier During World War II, An Advocate for Freedom," www.yurasko.net/vv/

42. From "What's on Your Mind," *Redbook*, as quoted in Honey, *Bitter Fruit*, 289.

Chapter 8: Behind Enemy Lines

1. Oliver Caldwell, *A Secret War: Americans in China, 1944–1945* (Carbondale, IL: Southern Illinois University Press, 1972).

2. Nora Slatkin, Executive Director of the Central Intelligence Agency, "Women in the CIA," Speech to the Chicago Council on Foreign Relations, May 15, 1996.

3. Elizabeth P. McIntosh, *Sisterhood of Spies* (New York: Dell, 1998), 147–156; Jerilyn Watson, "Women Spies," *This Is America*, Voice of America Special English

Program script, June 24, 2002, as posted on www.manythings.org/voa/02/020624ta_t.htm.

4. McIntosh, *Sisterhood of Spies*, 157–159.

5. National Archives and Record Administration, RG 226, Entry 190, Box 347, Folder 240, as quoted in McIntosh, *Sisterhood of Spies*, 157.

6. McIntosh, *Sisterhood of Spies*, 157–159.

7. Ibid., 158–159.

8. Slatkin, "Women in the CIA."

9. Slatkin, "Women in the CIA"; Mary S. Lovell, *Cast No Shadow: The Life of the American Spy Who Changed the Course of World War II* (New York: Pantheon Books, 1992), 128; McIntosh, *Sisterhood of Spies*, 151–152.

10. McIntosh, *Sisterhood of Spies*, 153, 161.

11. Donald L. Miller, *The Story of World War II* (New York: Simon & Schuster, 2001), 160–161.

12. Lovell, *Cast No Shadow*, 233–266.

13. H. Montgomery Hyde, *Cynthia: The Most Seductive Secret Weapon in the Arsenal of a Man Called Intrepid* (New York: Ballantine, 1965), 2.

14. McIntosh, *Sisterhood of Spies*, 13.

15. Julia Child, interview with the author, September 19, 2003.

16. Noël Riley Fitch, *Appetite for Life: the Biography of Julia Child* (New York: Anchor Books, 1999), 89–120; McIntosh, *Sisterhood of Spies*, 268–308.

17. Child, interview.

18. Ibid.

19. Fitch, *Appetite for Life*, 89–120; McIntosh, *Sisterhood of Spies*, 268–308.

20. Child, interview.

21. McIntosh, *Sisterhood of Spies*, 13–15; Michael Warner, "The Office of Strategic Services: America's First Intelligence Agency," Central Intelligence Agency History Staff in the Center for the Study of Intelligence, 2000.

22. McIntosh, *Sisterhood of Spies*, 254–262.

23. Ibid., 71–73.

24. Ibid., 63, 69–70.

25. John A. Pollard, "Words Are Cheaper than Blood," *Public Opinion Quarterly* 9, No. 3, Fall 1945, 300.

26. Leonard W. Doob, "The Utilization of Social Scientists in the Overseas Branch of the Office of War Information," *American Political Science Review* XLI, No. 4, August, 1947, 655.

27. Margaret Mead, *An Anthropologist at Work: Writings of Ruth Benedict* (New York: Avon, 1959), 352–353.

28. Mead, *An Anthropologist at Work*, 352–353; Margaret Mead, letter to Leo Rosten, Manuscripts Division 238a, Library of Congress, August 14, 1942.

29. Margaret Mead, *And Keep Your Powder Dry!* (New York: William Morrow and Company, 1965), 262 [originally published in 1942].

30. Ruth Benedict, *The Chrysanthemum and the Sword* (Tokyo: Charles E. Tuttle Company, 25th printing, 1973), 1–5 [originally published by Houghton Mifflin, 1946].

31. Ibid., 279.

32. Supreme Headquarters Allied Expeditionary Force—Psychological Warfare Division, "Leaflet Operations in the Western European Theatre 1944–1945," report from 1945 as reproduced at www.psywar.org.

33. McIntosh, *Sisterhood of Spies,* 71.

34. Stephen Budiansky, *Battle of Wits: The Complete Story of Codebreaking in World War II* (New York: Free Press, 2000), 304.

35. Jim DeBrosse, "Waves Rolled in to Work on Top-secret Project," *Dayton Daily News,* March 2, 2001; James Cummings, "A Salute to the WAVES: Reunion Reunites the Women Who Secretly Helped Win the War," *Dayton Daily News,* September 10, 1995; James Cummings, "Waves of Silence," *Dayton Daily News,* April 9, 1994.

36. Ibid.

37. Ibid.

38. Alice Marble with Dale Leatherman, *Courting Danger: My Adventures in World-Class Tennis, Golden-Age Hollywood, and High-Stakes Spying* (New York: St. Martin's Press, 1991), 178–236.

39. Rudi Williams, "WIMSA Honors Clandestine Women: Untold Stories of Women in Espionage," *American Forces Press Service,* May 2, 2001.

40. Shareen Blair Brysac, *Resisting Hitler: Mildred Harnack and the Red Orchestra* (New York: Oxford University Press, 2000), 193, 320, 357–360.

41. Ibid., 361.

42. Dorothy Gallagher, " 'Red Spy Queen:' The Witness," *New York Times,* November 3, 2002; Kathryn S. Olmstead, *Red Spy Queen* (Chapel Hill: The University of North Carolina Press, 2002); Lauren Kessler, *Clever Girl: The Spy Who Ushered in the McCarthy Era* (New York: HarperCollins, 2003).

43. Dale P. Harper, "American-born Axis Sally Made Propaganda Broadcasts for Radio Berlin in Hitler's Germany," *World War II Magazine,* November 1995; Susan Heller Anderson, "Mildred Gillars, 87, of Nazi Radio, Axis Sally to an Allied Audience," *New York Times,* July 2, 1988; Gene Amole, "GIs Had the Last Laugh on Germans and 'Sally,' " *Denver Rocky Mountain News,* June 5, 1994.

Chapter 9: A Question of Loyalty

1. Iva Toguri, letter to her family, October 13, 1941, Tokyo Rose Home Page, http://www.dyarstraights.com/orphan_ann/notice.html.

2. Iva Toguri d'Aquino, signed statement to FBI, Tokyo, Japan, April 30, 1946.

3. Scripts for *Zero Hour*, from trial record July through October 1946.

4. Office of War Information, August 1945.

5. J. Kingston Pierce, "They Called Her Traitor," *American History Magazine*, October 2002.

6. Ibid.

7. " 'Axis Sally' faces trial for treason," Paramount Newsreel, August 28, 1948.

8. Ronald E. Yates, "Tokyo Rose Prisoner of Name," *Chicago Tribune*, 1991.

9. Ronald Takaki, *Double Victory: A Multicultural History of America in World War II* (New York: Little Brown and Company, 2000), 145.

10. Chiye Tomihiro in John Tateishi, ed., *And Justice for All: An Oral History of the Japanese American Detention Camps* (Seattle: University of Washington Press, 1984), 239–241.

11. Takaki, *Double Victory*, 141–142; Tateishi, *And Justice for All*, xiii–xiv.

12. Tateishi, *And Justice for All*, xiii.

13. Chiye Tomihiro in Tateishi, *And Justice for All*, 239–241.

14. Stetson Conn, "The Decision to Evacuate the Japanese from the Pacific Coast" (Washington, D.C.: U.S. Army Center of History, 1990), 125–149; Jeffrey F. Burton, Mary M. Farrell, Florence B. Lord, Richard W. Lord, *Confinement and Ethnicity: An Overview of World War II Japanese American Relocation Sites* (Tucson, Ariz.: Western Archeological and Conservation Center, National Park Service, Report Number 74, 1999), Chapter 3, http://www.cr.nps.gov/history/online_books/anthropology74/ce0.html.

15. Takaki, *Double Victory*, 145–147.

16. Takaki, *Double Victory*, 146.

17. Tetsuden Kashima, editor, *Personal Justice Denied*, Report of the Commission on Wartime Relocation and Internment of Civilians, 1982 (Seattle: University of Washington Press, 1997).

18. Takaki, *Double Victory*, 148–149.

19. Akiko Mabuchi Toba, interview with author, September 26, 2003.

20. "Goodby! Write Soon! Alien Exodus Like an Outing," *San Francisco News*, April 7, 1942.

21. Toba, interview.

22. "Their Best Way to Show Loyalty," *San Francisco News*, March 6, 1942.

23. Toba, interview.

24. Yoshiko Uchida, *Desert Exile: The Uprooting of a Japanese-American Family* (Seattle: University of Washington Press, 1982), 106–109.

25. Emi Somekawa, in Tateishi, *And Justice for All*, 146–151.

26. Toba, interview.

27. Yoshiko Uchida, *Desert Exile*.

28. Brenda L. Moore, *Serving Our Country: Japanese American Women in the Military During World War II* (New Brunswick, N.J.: Rutgers University Press, 2003), 77–78.

29. Uchida, *Desert Exile,* 135–136; Burton, Farrell, Lord, Lord, *Confinement and Ethnicity,* Chapter 3.

30. Takaki, *Double Victory,* 157.

31. Toba, interview.

32. Kashima, *Personal Justice Denied*; Burton, Farrell, Lord, Lord, *Confinement and Ethnicity,* Chapter 3.

33. Toba, interview.

34. Harold L. Ickes, letter to President Roosevelt, June 2, 1944, as quoted in Michi Weglen, *Years of Infamy* (New York: Morrow Quill, 1976).

35. Harold L. Ickes, *Washington Star,* September 23, 1946.

36. Dillon S. Meyer, WRA Statement, March 1943, as quoted in Dillon S. Meyer, *Uprooted Americans* (Tucson: University of Arizona Press, 1971).

37. Toba, interview.

Chapter 10: Qualified Successes

1. Hannah Josephson, *Jeanette Rankin: First Lady in Congress* (Indianapolis, Ind.: Bobbs-Merrill, 1974), Chapter 3.

2. Colman McCarthy, "Rankin: Courage Finally Honored," *Washington Post,* May 18, 1985, A19.

3. Jeanette Rankin, *Jeanette Rankin,* Regional Oral History Office, University of California, Berkeley, 1974, available online: http://ark.cdlib.org/ark:/13030/kt758005dx/.

4. Biographical Directory of the United States Congress, Office of the Clerk, U.S. Congress, available online, http://clerk.house.gov.

5. Edith Nourse Rogers, "The Time Is Now," *Woman's Home Companion,* August 1943, 25.

6. Janann Sherman, *No Place for a Woman: A Life of Senator Margaret Chase Smith* (New Brunswick, N.J.: Rutgers University Press, 2000), 68–69.

7. Frances Perkins, *The Roosevelt I Knew* (New York: Viking Press, 1946), 152.

8. Sherman, *No Place for a Woman,* 65–66; additional information on the ERA available at: www.equalrightsamendment.com.

9. Edith Nourse Rogers, "The Time Is Now," 25.

10. Sherman, *No Place for a Woman,* 65–66.

11. Clare Boothe Luce, "Victory Is a Woman," *Woman's Home Companion,* November 1943, 34, 121–122.

12. Madame Chiang Kai-shek, Address to the Joint Session of Congress, *Congressional Record,* February 18, 1943, 1080–1081.

13. Doris Kearns Goodwin, *No Ordinary Time: Franklin and Eleanor Roosevelt: The Home Front in World War II* (New York: Simon & Schuster, 1994), 628–630.

14. Eleanor Roosevelt, "How to Take Criticism," *Ladies' Home Journal*, November 1944, 155, 171.

15. Joseph P. Lash, *Eleanor and Franklin* (New York: W. W. Norton & Company, 1971), 654.

16. Goodwin, *No Ordinary Time*, 629; Lash, *Eleanor and Franklin*, 654.

17. Public Broadcasting Service, "Lady Bird," produced by MacNeil/Lehrer Productions and KLRU, Austin, 2000.

18. Sally Reston, "Girls' Town—Washington," *New York Times Magazine*, November 23, 1941.

19. David Brinkley, *Washington Goes to War: The Story of the Transformation of a City and a Nation* (New York: Alfred A. Knopf, 1988), 244–245.

20. Reston, "Girls' Town—Washington," 8.

21. *Newsweek*, "Ladies of Washington's Working Press: They Get Their Copy—and Their Rights," March 1, 1943, 64; *Time*, "Skirted," March 13, 1944, 83.

22. *Time*, "Skirted," 83; Library of Congress exhibit, *Women Come to the Front: Journalists, Photographers, and Broadcasters During World War II*, available online: www.loc.gov/exhibits/wcf.

23. *Time*, "Skirted," 83.

24. *Newsweek*, "Ladies of Washington's Working Press," 64.

25. Margaret Bourke-White, *Portrait of Myself* (New York: Simon & Schuster, 1963).

26. Margaret Bourke-White, "Women in Lifeboats," *Life*, February 22, 1943.

27. Nancy Caldwell Sorel, *The Women Who Wrote the War* (New York: Perennial, 1999).

28. Sorel, *The Women Who Wrote the War*, 347–354.

29. Milton Metzer, *Dorothea Lange: A Photographer's Life* (New York: Farrar Straus Giroux, 1978), 242–243.

30. Ibid., 245–247.

31. Sorel, *The Women Who Wrote the War*, 8.

32. Peter Kurth, *American Cassandra: The Life of Dorothy Thompson* (Boston: Little Brown and Company, 1990), 358–363.

33. Doris Weatherford, *American Women and World War II* (New York: Facts on File, Inc., 1990), 180–181.

34. *Time*, "Daughters for Harvard," October 9, 1944, 90; *Time*, "Equality for Women Doctors," April 26, 1943, 46; *Woman's Home Companion*, "Women Doctors at War," June 1943, 4.

35. Nancy Baker Wise and Christy Wise, *A Mouthful of Rivets: Women at Work in World War II* (San Francisco: Jossey-Bass, 1994), 224–225.

36. Jeneane Lesko, "League History," All-American Girls Professional Baseball League website, www.aagpbl.org/history/History_1.html; "All-American Girls Professional Baseball League," Northern Indiana Center for History, Northern Indiana Historical Society, www.centerforhistory.org/aagpbl.html.

37. Jim Sargent, "Betsy Jochum, All-American," AAGPBL website.

38. Ibid.

39. Jim Sargent, "Dottie Collins," AAGPBL website.

Chapter 11: The "Wrong Kind" of Woman

1. Col. Howard Clark, testimony, Fort Oglethorpe Investigation, 3d WAC Training Center, June 29, 1944 (College Park, Md.: National Archives and Records Administration, Record Group 159, Box 17, File 333.9), 285.

2. Beth Bailey and David Farber, *The First Strange Place: Race and Sex in World War II Hawaii* (Baltimore: Johns Hopkins University Press, 1994), 97–98 [hardcover published by The Free Press, 1992].

3. Ibid., 97–115; Jean O'Hara, *My Life as a Honolulu Prostitute* (Honolulu: University of Hawaii at Manoa, Hamilton Library, unpublished manuscript, 1944).

4. Bailey and Farber, *My First Strange Place*, 97–115.

5. O'Hara, *My Life as a Honolulu Prostitute*, 11–12.

6. Ibid., 47.

7. Ibid., 2–3.

8. Ibid., 25.

9. Ibid., 13–14.

10. Ibid.

11. Bailey and Farber, *The First Strange Place*.

12. O'Hara, *My Life as a Honolulu Prostitute*, 33–35.

13. Bailey and Farber, *The First Strange Place*.

14. O'Hara, *My Life as a Honolulu Prostitute*, 41.

O'Hara's account has been described as "self-serving" in *The First Strange Place: Race and Sex in World War II Hawaii*, but the authors of that book note that her story is in accord with other sources. Although retired officers interviewed by the authors stood by Gabrielson and Kennedy, Frank Steer, head of the military police at the time, believed the department was corrupt, though he had no proof of wrongdoing.

15. Bailey and Farber, *The First Strange Place*.

16. James Jones, *From Here to Eternity* (New York: Charles Scribner's Sons, 1951); William Bradford Huie, *The Revolt of Mamie Stover* (reprint ed.) (Mattituck, N.Y.: Amereon Ltd., 1984).

17. Bailey and Farber, *The First Strange Place*, 129–130.

18. Ibid., 129.

19. Ibid., 130–132.

20. Allan M. Brandt, *No Magic Bullet: A Social History of Venereal Disease in the United States Since 1880* (New York: Oxford University Press, 1987), 162; John Costello, *Virtue Under Fire* (Boston: Little, Brown and Company, 1985), 213.

21. Bailey and Farber, *The First Strange Place*, 98–99; Costello, *Virtue Under Fire*, 213.

22. Brandt, *No Magic Bullet*, 168.

23. Eliot Ness, "She Looked Clean . . . But" (Washington, D.C.: U.S. Government Printing Office, Federal Security Agency, Social Protection Division, 1945), 16.

24. Brandt, *No Magic Bullet*, 168.

25. Eliot Ness, "What About the Girls?" (New York: Public Affairs Committee of the USO, 1943), 6.

26. Ibid., 24.

27. Karen Anderson, *Wartime Women: Sex Roles, Family Relations, and the Status of Women During World War II* (Westport, Conn.: Greenwood Press, 1981), 106–107.

28. Anderson, *Wartime Women*, 106–107; Cynthia Enlace, *Does Khaki Become You?: The Militarization of Women's Lives* (London: Pandora Press, 1988), 30.

29. Anderson, *Wartime Women*, 109.

30. Ness, "What About the Girls?," 24.

31. Costello, *Virtue Under Fire*, 203; Sherna Berger Gluck, *Rosie the Riveter Revisited* (New York: New American Library, 1987), 251.

32. Report, Fort Oglethorpe Investigation, 3d WAC Training Center, June 29, 1944 (College Park, Md.: National Archives and Records Administration, Record Group 159, Box 17, File 333.9), 1–2.

33. Testimony, Fort Oglethorpe Investigation, 3d WAC Training Center, June 29, 1944 (College Park, Md.: National Archives and Records Administration, Record Group 159, Box 17, File 333.9), 135–136.

34. Ibid., Exhibit B, 107.

35. Ibid., Exhibit B-1, 41–46. "Lt. Williams" is not a real name. This portion of the testimony was quoted in Allan Berube, *Coming Out Under Fire: The History of Gay Men and Women in World War II* (New York: Free Press, 1990), 205–208.

36. Ibid., Exhibit B, 350.

37. Johnnie Phelps, from Mary Ann Humphrey, *My Country, My Right to Serve: Experiences of Gay Men and Women in the Military, World War II to Present* (New York: HarperCollins, 1990), 39–40.

Chapter 12: A War Within the War

1. Glen Jeansonne, *Women of the Far Right: The Mothers' Movement and World War II* (Chicago: University of Chicago Press, 1996), 147.

2. Michael Sawyers and Albert E. Kahn, *Sabotage: The Secret War Against America* (New York: Harper & Brothers, 1942), 209–215; Jeansonne, *Women of the Far Right,* 61–62.

3. E. A. Piller, *Time Bomb* (New York: Arco Publishing Company, 1945), 114.

4. Michael Sawyers and Albert E. Kahn, *The Plot Against the Peace: A Warning to the Nation* (New York: Dial Press, 1945), 208.

5. Jeansonne, *Women of the Far Right,* 88–89.

6. Ibid., 88–89, 96.

7. Sawyers and Kahn, *The Plot Against the Peace,* 207–208.

8. Jeansonne, *Women of the Far Right,* 96.

9. Ibid., 20–24.

10. Ibid., 22–23.

11. Ibid., 25–27.

12. Ibid., 80–81.

13. Piller, *Time Bomb,* 114–119.

14. Sawyers and Kahn, *The Plot Against the Peace,* 206.

15. Jeansonne, *Women of the Far Right,* 138–140, 148.

16. Ibid., 148.

17. Ibid., 143–144.

18. Piller, *Time Bomb,* 111–112.

19. Jeansonne, *Women of the Far Right,* 32–37.

20. Ibid., 152.

21. Sawyers and Kahn, *The Plot Against the Peace,* 218–219; Jeansonne, *Women of the Far Right,* 153–155.

22. Francis Biddle, *In Brief Authority* (Garden City, N.Y.: Doubleday & Company, 1962), 242.

23. Bette Greene, *Summer of My German Soldier* (New York: Puffin Books, 1973), 93–96.

24. Ann Kaplowitz Goldberg, interview, November 16, 2000, Oral History Project, Women Veterans Historical Collection, The University of North Carolina, Greensboro.

25. Bernice Sains Freid, Jewish Women's Archive, "JWA—Navy—Bernice Sains Freid," http://www.jwa.org/discover/inthepast/infocus/military/navy/freid.html.

26. Loretta Ehrlich Kleiner, interview with author, October 26, 2003.

27. Phillis Heller Rosenthal, interview with author, October 27, 2003; Alexandra J. Wall, Edith Coliver obituary, *Jewish Bulletin of Northern California,* January 4, 2002.

28. British Broadcasting Corporation, "I. G Farben to be dissolved," Monday, September 17, 2001.

29. Rosenthal, interview; Robert Rosenthal, interview with author, January 5, 2001.

Chapter 13: Inside the Secret City

1. Ruth Marshak, "Secret City," chapter in Jane S. Wilson and Charlotte Serber, editors, *Standing By and Making Do: Women of Wartime Los Alamos* (Los Alamos, N.M.: Los Alamos Historical Society, 1997), 3.

2. Phyllis K. Fisher, *Los Alamos Experience* (New York: Japan Publications, 1985), 24–25.

3. Ibid., 26.

4. Robert Seidel, "New Laboratory Forged 'The Army Way,'" Los Alamos National Laboratory website, 50th Anniversary History, www.lanl.gov/world view; Fisher, *Los Alamos Experience*, 119.

5. Los Alamos National Laboratory website, 50th Anniversary History, www.lanl.gov/worldview.

6. Los Alamos National Laboratory, *Dateline Los Alamos*, Special Issue 1995, 6.

7. Los Alamos National Laboratory website, 50th Anniversary History, www.lanl.gov/worldview; Los Alamos National Laboratory, *Dateline Los Alamos*, Special Issue 1995, 8.

8. Fisher, *Los Alamos Experience*, 42–44; Marshak, "Secret City," 9–10.

9. Los Alamos National Laboratory website, 50th Anniversary History, www.lanl.gov/worldview.

10. Fisher, *Los Alamos Experience*, 59–60.

11. Ibid., 78.

12. Ibid., 91.

13. Shirley B. Barnett, "Operation Los Alamos," in Wilson and Serber, *Standing By and Making Do*, 92.

14. Fisher, *Los Alamos Experience*, 95–97.

15. Ibid., 99.

16. Ibid., 99–100.

17. Marshak, "Secret City," 4.

18. Ibid., 5.

19. Ibid., 6–8.

20. Ibid., 10–11.

21. Jane S. Wilson, "Not Quite Eden," in Wilson and Serber, *Standing By and Making Do*, 43.

22. Ibid., 44.

23. Ibid., 45.

24. Ibid., 44.

25. Ibid., 44.

26. Ibid., 54.

27. Ibid., 48.

28. Ibid., 50.

29. Ibid., 51–52.

30. Ibid., 55.

31. Jean Bacher, "Fresh Air and Alcohol," chapter in Wilson and Serber, *Standing By and Making Do*, 112–113.

32. Ruth H. Howes and Caroline L. Herzenberg, *Their Day in the Sun: Women of the Manhattan Project* (Philadelphia: Temple University Press, 1999), 13–14.

33. Ibid., 38–39, 41–42.

34. Ibid., 149.

35. Charlotte Serber, "Labor Pains," in Wilson and Serber, editors, *Standing By and Making Do*, 66–67.

36. Ibid., 69.

37. Ibid., 67.

38. Ibid., 62–64.

39. Eleanor Stone Roensch, *Life Within Limits* (Los Alamos, N.M.: Los Alamos Historical Society, 1993).

40. Fisher, *Los Alamos Experience*, 111.

41. Ibid., 112–113.

42. Ibid., 113–114.

43. Ibid., 121.

44. Ibid., 122–123.

45. Laura Fermi, *Atoms in the Family: My Life with Enrico Fermi* (Chicago: University of Chicago Press, paperback 1961, hardcover 1954), 240–42.

46. Fisher, *Los Alamos Experience*, 127–29.

47. Ibid., 235–236, 239–240.

48. Ibid., 16.

BIBLIOGRAPHY

Ackerman, William C. "Dimensions of American Broadcasting." *Public Opinion Quarterly*, no. 9 (Spring 1945).

Amole, Gene. "GIs Had the Last Laugh on Germans and 'Sally.'" *Denver Rocky Mountain News*, June 5, 1994.

Anderson, Karen Tucker. *Wartime Women: Sex Roles, Family Relations, and the Status of Women During World War II*. Westport, Conn.: Greenwood Press, 1981.

———. "Last Hired, First Fired: Black Women Workers During World War II." *The Journal of American History* 69, no. 1 (June 1982).

Anderson, Susan Heller. "Mildred Gillars, 87, of Nazi Radio, Axis Sally to an Allied Audience." *New York Times*, July 2, 1988.

Andrews, Maxene, and Bill Gilbert. *Over Here, Over There: The Andrews Sisters and the USO Stars in World War II*. New York: Zebra Books, 1993.

Anthony II, Susan B. *Out of the Kitchen—Into the War: Women's Winning Role in the Nation's Drama*. New York: Stephen Daye, 1943.

Armenski, Doris Wofford. Interview, May 19, 1999. Oral History Project, Women Veterans Historical Collection. The University of North Carolina, Greensboro.

Ayling, Keith. *Calling All Women*. New York: Harper & Brothers Publishers, 1942.

Bacall, Lauren. *By Myself*. New York: Ballantine Books, 1980.

Bacher, Jean. "Fresh Air and Alcohol." In *Standing By and Making Do: Women of Wartime Los Alamos*.

Bailey, Beth, and David Farber. *The First Strange Place: Race and Sex in World War II Hawaii*. Baltimore: Johns Hopkins University Press, 1994.

Barnett, Shirley B. "Operation Los Alamos." In *Standing By and Making Do: Women of Wartime Los Alamos*.

Bellafaire, Judith A. *The Women's Army Corps: A Commemoration of World War II Service*. Washington, D.C.: U.S. Army Center of Military History: CMH Publication 72–15.

———. *Army Nurse Corps: A Commemoration of World War II Service*. Washington, D.C.: U.S. Army Center of Military History CMH Publication 72–14.

Bellafaire, Judith Lawrence. "We Also Served." In Holm, *In Defense of a Nation*.

Benedict, Ruth. *The Chrysanthemum and the Sword*. 1946. Reprint, Tokyo: Charles E. Tuttle Company, 1973.

Bentley, Amy. *Eating for Victory: Food Rationing and the Politics of Domesticity*. Urbana: University of Illinois Press, 1998.

Biddle, Francis. *In Brief Authority*. Garden City, N.Y.: Doubleday & Company, Inc., 1962.

Blank, Adaline. *Correspondence July 1943–December 1943*. Denton: Texas Women's Collection. Texas Women's University.

Boris, Eileen. " 'You Wouldn't Want One of 'Em Dancing with Your Wife': Racialized Bodies on the Job in World War II." *American Quarterly* 50.1 (1998).

Bourke-White, Margaret. *Portrait of Myself*. New York: Simon & Schuster, 1963.

———. "Women in Lifeboats." *Life*. February 22, 1943.

Brandt, Allan M. *No Magic Bullet: A History of Venereal Disease in the United States Since 1880*. New York: Oxford University Press, 1987.

Brinkley, David. *Washington Goes to War: The Story of the Transformation of a City and a Nation*. New York: Alfred A. Knopf, 1988.

Brion, Irene J. *Lady GI: A Woman's War in the South Pacific: The Memoir of Irene Brion*. Novato, Calif.: Presidio Press, 1997.

British Broadcasting Corporation. "I. G. Farben to be Dissolved." September 17, 2001.

Brysac, Shareen Blair. *Resisting Hitler: Mildred Harnack and the Red Orchestra*. New York: Oxford University Press, 2000.

Budiansky, Stephen. *Battle of Wits: The Complete Story of Codebreaking in World War II*. New York: The Free Press, 2000.

Burton, Jeffrey F., et al. *Confinement and Ethnicity: An Overview of World War II Japanese American Relocation Sites*. Tucson, Ariz.: Western Archeological and Conservation Center, National Park Service, Report No. 74, 1999.

BusinessWeek. October 17, 1942.

Caldwell, Oliver. *A Secret War: Americans in China, 1944–1945*. Carbondale: Southern Illinois University Press, 1972.

Camp, LaVonne Telshaw. *Lingering Fever—A World War II Nurse's Memoir*. Jefferson, N.C.: McFarland & Company, Inc. Publishers, 1997.

Campbell, D'Ann. *Women at War with America: Private Lives in a Patriotic Era*. Cambridge: Harvard University Press, 1984.

Carson, Julia M. H. *Home Away From Home: The Story of the USO*. New York: Harper & Brothers Publishing, 1946.

Casdorph, Paul D. *Let the Good Times Roll*. New York: Paragon House, 1991.

Chafe, William H. *The American Woman: Her Changing Social, Economic, and Political Roles, 1920–1970*. Oxford: Oxford University Press, 1972.

Chang Kai-shek, Madame. Address to Joint Session of Congress, *Congressional Record*. February 18, 1943.

Christian, Shirley. "But Is It Art . . . ? Well, Yes." *New York Times*. November 25, 1998.

Clark, Howard. Testimony from Fort Oglethorpe Investigation, Third WAC Training Center, June 29, 1944. College Park, Md.: National Archives and Records Administration, Record Group 159, Box 17, File 333.9.

Clawson, Augusta H. *Shipyard Diary of a Woman Welder.* New York: Penguin Books, 1944. Cited in Judy Barrett Litoff and David C. Smith. *American Women in a World at War.* Wilmington, Del.: Scholarly Resources, Inc., 1997.

Cochran, Jacqueline. *Finfinella Gazette,* March 1, 1943.

———. Status Report on WASP to Commanding General H. H. Arnold, Army Air Forces, August 1, 1944. Texas Women's University Archives.

Cody, Marie. Letter. March 14, 1945. Marie Cody Collection. Women Veterans Historical Collection. The University of North Carolina, Greensboro.

Coffey, Frank. *Always Home: 50 Years of the USO.* McLean, Va.: Brassey's US, Inc., 1991.

Colman, Penny. *Rosie the Riveter: Women on the Home Front in World War II.* New York: Crown Publishers, Inc., 1995.

Conn, Stetson. "The Decision to Evacuate the Japanese from the Pacific Coast." Washington, D.C.: U.S. Army Center of Military History, 1990.

Cooper, Page. *Navy Nurse.* New York: Whittlesey House, McGraw-Hill Book Company, Inc., 1946.

Costello, John. *Virtue Under Fire.* Boston: Little, Brown, and Company, 1985.

Cummings, James. "A Salute to the Waves: Reunion Reunites the Women Who Secretly Helped Win the War." *Dayton (Ohio) Daily News,* September 10, 1995.

———. "Waves of Silence." *Dayton (Ohio) Daily News,* April 9, 1994.

Daniels, Les. *Wonder Woman: The Complete History: The Life and Times of the Amazon Princess.* San Francisco: Chronicle Books, 2000.

Darr, Ann. "The Long Flight Home." *U.S. News and World Report,* November 17, 1997.

d'Aquino, Iva Toguri. Signed statement to the FBI. Tokyo, April 30, 1946.

Davidson, Joel. "Building for World War II: The Aerospace Industry." *Blueprints Magazine,* Fall 1993.

Davis, John A. "Educational Programs for the Improvement of Race Relations: Organized Labor and Industrial Organizations," *Journal of Negro Education* 13, no. 3 (Summer 1944).

Davis, John W. "The Negro in the United States Navy, Marine Corps and Coast Guard." *Journal of Negro Education* 12, No. 3 (Summer 1943).

Davis, Maxine. "Women Without Men." *Good Housekeeping,* March 1942.

DeBrosse, Jim. "Waves Rolled in to Work on Top-Secret Project." *Dayton (Ohio) Daily News*, March 2, 2001.

Demar, George E. "Negro Women Are American Workers, Too," *Opportunity* (April 1943). Quoted in Honey, *Bitter Fruit: African-American Women in World War II.*

Department of Labor, Women's Bureau. "Negro Women War Workers." *Bulletin*, no. 205.

———. "Women as Workers, A Statistical Guide." Washington, D.C., 1943. Cited in Campbell, *Women at War with America: Private Lives in a Patriotic Era.*

Dietrich, Marlene. *Marlene*. New York: Grove Press, 1989.

Doob, Leonard W. "The Utilization of Social Scientists in the Overseas Branch of the Office of War Information." *American Political Science Review* 41, no. 4 (August 1947).

Dougherty, Norma Jeane. Letter to Grace McKee, June 15, 1944. Quoted in Spoto, *Marilyn Monroe: The Biography.*

Durr, Kenneth D. *Behind the Backlash: White Working-Class Politics in Baltimore, 1940–1980*. Chapel Hill: University of North Carolina Press, 2003.

Earley, Charity Adams. *One Woman's Army: A Black Officer Remembers the WAC*. College Station: Texas A&M University Press, 1989.

Ebbert, Jean, and Hall, Marie-Beth. "Navy Women's Reserve: WAVES." In Holm, *In Defense of a Nation: Servicewomen in World War II.*

Edwards, Marjorie Randolph Suggs. Interview, June 26, 2000. Oral History Project, Women Veterans Historical Collection. The University of North Carolina, Greensboro.

Engel, Dorothea Daley. "I Was Married in Battle." *American Magazine*, October 1942.

Enloe, Cynthia. *Does Khaki Become You? The Militarization of Women's Lives*. London: Pandora Press, 1988.

Eppens, Genevieve. *Waiting for My Sailor*. Lincoln, Neb.: Infusion Media Publishing, 2000.

Feller, Carolyn M., and Debora R. Cox, eds. *Highlights in the History of the Army Nurse Corps*. Washington, D.C.: U.S. Army Center of Military History, 2001.

Fermi, Laura. *Atoms in the Family: My Life with Enrico Fermi*. Chicago: The University of Chicago Press, 1961.

Fessler, Diane Burke. *No Time for Fear: Voices of American Military Nurses in World War II*. East Lansing: Michigan State University Press, 1996.

Fisher, M. F. K. *How to Cook a Wolf.* New York: Duell, Sloan and Pearce, 1942.

Fisher, Phyllis K. *Los Alamos Experience*. New York: Japan Publications, Inc., 1985.

Fitch, Noël Riley. *Appetite for Life: The Biography of Julia Child*. New York: Anchor Books, 1999.

Fort, Cornelia. "At the Twilight's Last Gleaming." *Women's Home Companion*, June 1943.

————. Letter. January 28, 1942. In Ron Simbeck, *Daughter of the Air: The Brief, Soaring Life of Cornelia Fort.* New York: Atlantic Monthly Press, 1999.

Fortune. "The Margin Now is Womanpower." February 1943.

Francis, David R. "A Pilot Who's Kept to Her Flight Plan." *The Christian Science Monitor,* June 21, 2001.

Friedrich, Otto. *City of Nets: A Portrait of Hollywood in the 1940's.* New York: Perennial Library, Harper & Row, 1987.

Funderberg, Lise. "A Conversation with Maya Angelou and Eleanor Holmes Norton." *Essence,* August 1988.

Gattuso, Ottilie Juliet, to President Harry S. Truman. September 6, 1945. Records of the Women's Bureau, National Archives, Washington, D.C.

Gluck, Sherna Berger. *Rosie the Riveter Revisited: Women, the War and Social Change.* New York: New American Library, 1987.

Godson, Susan H. "Navy Nurse Corps." In *In Defense of a Nation: Servicewomen in World War II.*

Goldberg, Ann Kaplowitz. Interview, November 16, 2000. Oral History Project, Women Veterans Historical Collection. The University of North Carolina, Greensboro.

Goldstein, Richard. "Obituary of Harriet M. Waddy." *New York Times,* March 8, 1999.

Good Housekeeping. "I Married My Soldier Anyway." June 1942.

Goodwin, Doris Kearns. *No Ordinary Time.* New York: Simon & Schuster, 1994.

Graham, Shirley. *Negro Story* (April 1945). In Honey, *Bitter Fruit: African-American Women in World War II.*

Grahn, Elna Hilliard. *In the Company of WACS.* Manhattan, Kans.: Sunflower University Press, 1993.

Greenbaum, Lucy. "At the Front with Our Land Army." *New York Times Magazine,* July 4, 1943.

Greene, Bette. *Summer of My German Soldier.* New York: Puffin Books, 1973.

Gruhzit Hoyt, Olga. *They Also Served: American Women in World War II.* New York: Carol Publishing Group, 1995.

Guinan, Patricia Davidson. "Back Home to Mother." *House Beautiful,* August 1943.

Gustaitis, Joseph. "Antoinette Perry: The Woman Behind the Tony Awards." *American History Magazine,* April 1997.

Hallaren, Mary A. Senate Hearing Testimony, S. 1641, July 15, 1947. " 'They Either Need These Women or They Do Not': Margaret Chase Smith and the Fight for Regular Status for Women in the Military."

Handy, Antoinette D. *The International Sweethearts of Rhythm.* Lanham, Md.: Scarecrow Press, 1998.

Harper, Dale P. "American-born Axis Sally Made Propaganda Broadcasts for Radio Berlin in Hitler's Germany." *World War II Magazine,* November 1995.

Hartman, Susan M. *The Home Front and Beyond: American Women in the 1940s.* Boston: Twayne Publishers, 1982.

Haskell, Ruth G. *Helmets and Lipstick.* New York: G. P. Putnam's Sons, 1944.

Haynes, Monica L. "Hats Off to Hattie." *The Pittsburgh Post-Gazette,* August 5, 2001.

Holm, Jeanne M., ed. *In Defense of a Nation: Servicewomen in World War II.* Arlington, Va.: Vandamere Press, 1998.

Home Services Staff of General Mills, Inc. *Your Share: How to Prepare Appetizing, Healthful Meals with Foods Available Today.* Minneapolis: General Mills, Inc., 1943.

Honey, Maureen. *Creating Rosie the Riveter: Class, Gender, and Propaganda During World War II.* Amherst: University of Massachusetts Press, 1984.

Honey, Maureen, ed. *Bitter Fruit: African-American Women in World War II.* Columbia: University of Missouri Press, 1999.

Hoopes, Roy. *Americans Remember the Home Front: An Oral Narrative of the World War II Years in America.* New York: Berkley Publishing Group, 2002.

———. *When the Stars Went to War: Hollywood and World War II.* New York: Random House, 1994.

Horne, Lena, and Richard Schickel. *Lena.* New York: Signet Books, 1965.

Howes, Ruth H., and Caroline L. Herzenberg. *Their Day in the Sun: Women of the Manhattan Project.* Philadelphia: Temple University Press, 1999.

Huie, William Bradford. *The Revolt of Mamie Stover.* New York: Duell, Sloan and Pearce, 1951.

The Huntsville Times. August 1945. Quoted in Kaylene Hughes. *Women at War: Redstone's WWII Female Production Soldiers.* www.redstonearmy.mil/history/ eomen/welcome.html and www.library.csi.cuny.edu/dept/history/lavender/ redstone.html.

Hyde, Montgomery, H. *Cynthia: The Most Seductive Secret Weapon in the Arsenal of a Man Called Intrepid.* New York: Ballantine Books, 1965.

Ickes, Harold L. Letter to President Roosevelt, June 2, 1944. Quoted in Michi Weglen, *Years of Infamy.* New York: Morrow Quill Paperbacks, 1976.

———. *The Washington Star,* September 23, 1946.

Jeansonne, Glen. *Women of the Far Right: The Mothers' Movement and World War II.* Chicago: The University of Chicago Press, 1996.

Jeffries, John W. *Wartime America.* Chicago: Ivan R. Dee, Inc., 1996.

Johnson, Hortense. "What My Job Means to Me," *Opportunity* (April 1943). Quoted in Honey, *Bitter Fruit: African-American Women in World War II.*

Jones, James. *From Here to Eternity.* New York: Charles Scribner's Sons, 1951.

Josephson, Hannah. *Jeannette Rankin: First Lady in Congress.* Indianapolis, Ind.: Bobbs-Merrill Co., 1974.

Kashima, Tetsuden, ed. *Personal Justice Denied. Report of the Commission on War-*

time Relocation and Internment of Civilians, 1982. Seattle: University of Washington Press, 1997.

Keenan, Aileen. "Learning to Live Together in Good Times and Bad." 1995. Oral History of Rhode Island Women During WWI. Brown University, Providence, R.I.

Keil, Sally Van Wagenen. *Those Wonderful Women in Their Flying Machines—The Unknown Women of World War II.* New York: Rawson, Wade Publishers Inc., 1979.

Kirk, Norman T. "Girls in the Foxholes," *American Magazine,* May 1944.

Klaw, Barbara. *Camp Follower: The Story of a Soldier's Wife.* New York: Random House, 1943.

Koppes, Clayton R., and Gregory D. Black. "Blacks, Loyalty, and Motion-Picture Propaganda in World War II." *The Journal of American History* 73, no. 2 (September 1986).

———. "What to Show the World: The Office of War Information and Hollywood, 1942–1945." *The Journal of American History* 64 (June 1977).

Korson, George. *At His Side: The Story of the American Red Cross Overseas in World War II.* New York: Coward-McCann, Inc., 1945.

Kurth, Peter. *American Cassandra: The Life of Dorothy Thompson.* Boston: Little, Brown and Company, 1990.

Ladies' Home Journal. "You're the WINS: Women in National Service." March 1943.

Ladies' Home Journal. May 1944.

Landis, Carole. *Four Jills in a Jeep.* New York: Random House, 1944.

Lash, Joseph P. *Eleanor and Franklin.* New York: W. W. Norton & Company, 1971.

Lingeman, Richard R. *Don't You Know There's a War On?* New York: G. P. Putnam's Sons, 1970.

Litoff, Judy Barrett, and David C. Smith. *Since You Went Away: World War II Letters from American Women on the Home Front.* Lawrence: University of Kansas Press, 1991.

———. *We're in This War, Too: World War II Letters from American Women in Uniform.* New York: Oxford University Press, 1994.

Los Alamos National Laboratory. *Dateline Los Alamos,* Special Issue (1995).

Lovell, Mary S. *Cast No Shadow: The Life of the American Spy Who Changed the Course of World War II.* New York: Pantheon Books, 1992.

Luce, Clare Boothe. "Victory Is a Woman." *Woman's Home Companion,* November 1943.

Lutz, Alma, ed., *With Love, Jane: Letters from American Women on the War Fronts.* New York: The John Day Company, 1945.

Lyne, Mary C., and Kay Arthur. *Three Years Behind the Mast: The Story of the United States Coast Guard SPARs.* Washington, D.C.: n.p., 1946. Cited in Judy Barrett

Litoff and David C. Smith, *American Women in a World at War*. Wilmington, Del.: Scholarly Resources, Inc., 1997.

Mailer, Norman. *Marilyn*. New York: Grosset & Dunlap, 1973.

Marble, Alice, with Dale Leatherman. *Courting Danger: My Adventures in World-Class Tennis, Golden Age Hollywood, and High-Stakes Spying*. New York: St. Martin's Press, 1991.

Marshak, Ruth. "Secret City." In *Standing By and Making Do: Women of Wartime Los Alamos*.

Marshall, George Catlett. Draft memo to Military Committee, House of Representatives, December 3, 1942. George C. Marshall Research Library. Lexington, Va.: Box 65, Folder 46.

Mathews, Mary Haynsworth. Interview. November 9, 1999. Oral History Project, Women Veterans Historical Collection, The University of North Carolina, Greensboro.

McCarthy, Colman. "Ranking: Courage Finally Honored." *The Washington Post*, May 18, 1985.

McCrary, Lacy. "The Enemy Was Discrimination." *The Buffalo (N.Y.) News*, January 17, 1998.

McFadden, Kay. "Hattie McDaniel, Rediscovered Hollywood Heroine." *Seattle Times*, August 6, 2001.

McIntosh, Elizabeth P. *Sisterhood of Spies*. New York: Dell Publishing, 1998.

———. Quoting National Archives. RG 226, Entry 190, Box 347, Folder 240.

McWilliams, Mary E. "Women in the Coast Guard: SPARs." In Holm, *In Defense of a Nation—Servicewomen in World War II*. Arlington, Va.: Vandamere Press, 1998.

Mead, Margaret. *An Anthropologist at Work—Writings of Ruth Benedict*. New York: Avon Books, 1959.

———. *And Keep Your Powder Dry!* 1942. Reprint, New York: William Morrow and Co., 1965.

———. to Leo Rosten, August 13, 1942. Library of Congress, Manuscripts Division 238a.

Meeth, Melisse Faulds. "How Dear to My Heart: A Personal Recollection of My Parents and My Family." (Unpublished, 1982.)

Metzer, Milton. *Dorothea Lange: A Photographer's Life*. New York: Farrar Straus Giroux, 1978.

Meyer, Dillon S. *Uprooted Americans*. Tucson, Ariz.: The University of Arizona Press, 1971.

Meyer, Leisa D. *Creating GI Jane: Sexuality and Power in the Women's Army Corps During WWII*. New York: Columbia University Press, 1996.

Meyerowitz, Joanne. "Women, Cheesecake and Borderline Material: Responses to Girlie Pictures in the Mid-Twentieth Century U.S." *Journal of Women's History* 8 (Fall 1996).

Miller, Donald L. *The Story of World War II*. New York: Simon & Schuster, 2001.

Miller, Grace Porter. *Call of Duty: A Montana Girl in World War II*. Baton Rouge: Louisiana State University Press, 1999.

Miller, May. "One Blue Star," *Opportunity* (Summer 1945). Quoted in Honey, *Bitter Fruit: African-American Women in World War II*.

Moore, Brenda L. *Serving Our Country: Japanese American Women in the Military During World War II*. New Brunswick, N.J.: Rutgers University Press, 2003.

———. "Serving with a Dual Mission: African-American Women in World War II." *National Journal of Sociology* 7.1 (Summer 1993).

———. *To Serve My Country, To Serve My Race: The Story of the Only African American WACs Stationed Overseas During World War II*. New York: New York University Press, 1996.

Morden, Bettie. "Women's Army Corps: WAAC and WAC." In Holm, *In Defense of a Nation—Servicewomen in World War II*.

Morehouse, Maggi M. *Fighting in the Jim Crow Army: Black Men and Women Remember World War II*. Lanham, MD: Rowman & Littlefield, 2000.

Murray, Pauli, "A Blueprint for First Class Citizenship." *The Crisis* (November 1944). Quoted in Honey, *Bitter Fruit: African-American Women in World War II*.

Nachman, Gerald. *Raised on Radio*. New York: Pantheon Books, 1998.

"The Negro Woman Serves America," *Aframerican Woman's Journal* (Summer 1943). From Judy Barrett Litoff and David C. Smith, eds., *American Women in a World at War*. Wilmington, Del.: Scholarly Resources, Inc., 1997.

Nelson, Mary Harrington. "World War II Experiences of a POW Navy Nurse." In Paula Nassen Poulos, *A Woman's War Too: U.S. Military in World War II*. Washington, D.C.: National Archives and Records Administration, 1996.

Ness, Eliot. "She Looked Clean . . . But." Washington, D.C.: U.S. Government Printing Office, Federal Security Agency, Social Protection Division. 1945.

———. "What About the Girls?" New York: The Public Affairs Committee, 1943.

Newsweek, "Ladies of Washington's Working Press: They Get Their Copy—and Their Rights." March 1, 1943.

Newsweek. November 2, 1942.

New York Times. "Weighs Job Hopes of Women in Peace." August 16, 1943.

New York Times Magazine. "Women War Workers: A Case History." December 1943.

Norman, Elizabeth M. *We Band of Angels—The Untold Story of American Nurses Trapped on Bataan by the Japanese*. New York: Random House, 1999.

O'Grady, Kathy. "What Did You Do in the War, Grandma?" 1995. Oral History of Rhode Island Women During WW I. Brown University, Providence, R.I.

O'Hara, Jean. "My Life as a Honolulu Prostitute" (unpublished). Honolulu: University of Hawaii at Manoa, Hamilton Library, 1944.

Olmstead, Kathryn S. *Red Spy Queen*. Chapel Hill: The University of North Carolina Press, 2002.

Olson, Lynne. *Freedom's Daughters: The Unsung Heroines of the Civil Rights Movement from 1830 to 1970*. New York: Scribner, 2001.

O'Neill, William L. *A Democracy at War*. New York: Macmillan, 1933. Quoted in O'Grady, "What Did You Do in the War, Grandma?"

Opportunity. Quoted in Honey, *Bitter Fruit: African-American Women in World War II*.

Paramount Newsreel. " 'Axis Sally' Faces Trial for Treason." August 28, 1948.

Parker, Dorothy. "Are We Women or Are We Mice?" *Mademoiselle*, May 1943.

Pateman, Yvonne C. "Women Air Force Service Pilots: WASP." In Holm, *In Defense of a Nation: Servicewomen in World War II*.

Pennington, Alice. Memoirs. (unpublished). 1999.

Perkins, Frances. *The Roosevelt I Knew*. New York: Viking Press, 1946.

Phelps, Johnnie. From Mary Ann Humphrey, *My Country, My Right To Serve: Experiences of Gay Men and Women in the Military, World War II to Present*. New York: The Free Press, 1990.

Phillips, H. I. *All Out Irene: The Story of the Girls Behind the Boys Behind the Guns*. New York: Doubleday, Doran and Company, Inc., 1943.

Pierce, J. Kingston. "They Called Her Traitor." *American History Magazine*, October 2002.

Pillar, E. A. *Time Bomb*. New York: Arco Publishing Company, 1945.

Pimlott, Lillian M., letter to mother, July 5, 1945. Lillian M. Pimlott Collection, Women Veterans Historical Collection. The University of North Carolina, Greensboro.

Pollard, John A. "Words Are Cheaper Than Blood." *Public Opinion Quarterly 9*, no. 3 (Fall 1945).

Public Broadcasting Service. "Lady Bird." MacNeil/Lehrer Productions and KLRU: Austin (Texas), 2000.

Rankin, Jeanette. *Jeanette Rankin*. Regional Oral History Office, University of California, Berkeley, 1974. http://ark.cdlib.org/ark:/13030/kt758005dx/

Rasmussen, Cecilia. "Vargas' Pinups Inspired GIs, Became Icons of U.S. Culture." *Los Angeles Times*, June 25, 2000.

Ray, Randolph. *Marriage Is a Serious Business*. New York: Whittlesey House, McGraw-Hill, 1944.

Report from Fort Oglethorpe Investigation, 3rd WAC Training Center, June 29, 1944. College Park, Md.: National Archives and Records Administration, Record Group 159, Box 17, File 333.9.

Reston, Sally. "Girls' Town: Washington." *New York Times Magazine*, November 23, 1941.

Rexford, Oscar Whitelaw. *Battlestars and Doughnuts—World War II Clubmobile Experiences of Mary Metcalfe Rexford*. St. Louis: The Patrice Press, 1989.

Richardson, Elizabeth. Letters quoted in Gordon Brown, "A Life Cut Short, A Life Remembered." www.lawrence.edu/about/trads/liz.shtml.

Rogers, Edith Nourse. "The Time Is Now." *Woman's Home Companion,* August 1943.

Rogers, Mary McLeod. Interview. December 20, 1999. Oral History Project, Women Veterans Historical Collection. The University of North Carolina, Greensboro.

Romero, M., and A. J. Stewart, eds. *Women's Untold Stories: Breaking Silence, Talking Back, Voicing Complexity.* Florence, Ken.: Routledge, 1999.

Roosevelt, Eleanor. "How to Take Criticism." *Ladies' Home Journal,* November 1944.

———. "My Day." September 1, 1942.

Ross, Mary Steele. *American Women in Uniform.* Garden City, N.Y.: Garden City Publishing Company, Inc., 1943.

Ross, Nancy Wilson. *The WAVES: The Story of the Girls in Blue.* New York: Henry Holt and Co., 1943.

Rothermel, Jean Archer. Letter home from Guam. May 23, 1945.

———. Letter home from Guam. May 29, 1945.

Sabourin, Mary Amanda. Interview. June 25, 1999. Oral History Project, Women Veterans Historical Collection. The University of North Carolina, Greensboro.

Sains Freid, Bernice. "*JWA—Navy—Bernice Sains Freid.*" Jewish Women's Archive. www.jwa.org/discover/inthepast/infocus/military/navy/ freid.html.

San Francisco News. "Goodby! Write Soon! Alien Exodus Like an Outing." April 7, 1942.

San Francisco News. "Their Best Way to Show Loyalty." March 6, 1942.

Sarnecky, Mary T. "Army Nurse Corps." In Holm, *In Defense of a Nation: Servicewomen in World War II.*

Saturday Evening Post, "Our Land Is Different." July 25, 1942.

Saturday Evening Post. February 3, 1945.

Saturday Evening Post. February 20, 1945. Cited in Gluck, *Rosie the Riveter Revisited: Women, the War and Social Change.*

Sawyers, Michael, and Albert E. Kahn. *Sabotage: The Secret War Against America.* New York: Harper & Brothers Publishers, 1942.

Seidel, Robert. "New Laboratory Forged 'The Army Way.'" Los Alamos National Laboratory website, Fiftieth Anniversary History. www.lanl.gov/ worldview.

Sealander, Judith. *Records of the Women's Bureau of the U.S. Department of Labor, 1918–1965.* University Publications of America, LexisNexis, 1997.

Serber, Charlotte. "Labor Pains." In Wilson and Serber, *Standing By and Making Do: Women of Wartime Los Alamos.*

Sherman, Janann. *No Place for a Woman: A Life of Senator Margaret Chase Smith.* New Brunswick, N.J.: Rutgers University Press, 2000.

———. " 'They Either Need These Women or They Do Not': Margaret Chase Smith and the Fight for Regular Status for Women in the Military." *The Journal of Military History,* January 1990.

Sims-Wood, Janet. "Service Life in the Women's Army Corps and Afro-American WACs." In Paula Naasen Poulos, *A Woman's War, Too: U.S. Women in the Military in World War II.* Washington, D.C.: National Archives, 1996.

Skowron, Sandra. (Associated Press). *Los Angeles Times,* March 6, 1994.

Slatkin, Nora. "Women in the CIA." Speech to the Chicago Council on Foreign Relations, May 15, 1996.

Somekawa, Emi. Quoted in John Tateishi, ed. *And Justice for All: An Oral History of the Japanese American Detention Camps.* Seattle: University of Washington Press, 1984.

Sorel, Nancy Caldwell. *The Women Who Wrote the War.* New York: Perennial, 1999.

Spoto, Donald. *Marilyn Monroe: The Biography.* New York: HarperCollins Publishers, Inc., 1993.

Stern, Elizabeth. "America's Pampered Husbands." *Nation,* July 10, 1943. Cited in Weatherford. *American Women and World War II.*

Stevens, Michael E., ed. *Women Remember the War 1941–1945—Voices of the Wisconsin Past.* Madison: State Historical Society of Wisconsin, 1993.

Stone, Eleanor Roensch. *Life Within Limits.* Los Alamos, N.M.: The Los Alamos Historical Society, 1993.

Stremlow, Mary V. "Marine Corps Women's Reserve: Free a Man to Fight." In Holm, *In Defense of a Nation: Servicewomen in World War II.*

Strother, Dora Dougherty. "Women of the WASP." In Anne Noggle, *For God, Country, and the Thrill of It.* College Station: Texas A&M University Press, 1990.

Sullivan, Aletta F. "I Lost Five Sons." *The American Magazine,* March 1944.

Supreme Headquarters Allied Expeditionary Force, Psychological Warfare Division, "Leaflet Operations in the Western European Theatre 1944–1945," 1945. Reproduced at www.psywar.org.

Takaki, Ronald. *Double Victory: A Multicultural History of America in World War II.* New York: Little Brown and Company, 2000.

Tampa Tribune, 1943. Cited in Lewis N. Wynne and Carolyn J. Baines. "A Story of Gulf Coast Maritime History." *Gulf Coast Review,* no. 5.

Tanner, Doris Brinker. "We Also Served." *American History Illustrated.* November, 1945.

Tekeei, Negar. "Fly Girl." *Northwestern Magazine,* Spring 2000.

Terkel, Studs. *The Good War: An Oral History of World War II.* New York: The New Press, 1984.

Thompson, Dorothy Wain. "Letters to Home 1942–1945." http://www.hard scrabblefarm.com.

Thomson, Robin J. "SPARs: The Coast Guard and the Women's Reserve in World War II," www.uscg.mil.

Tiley, John A. "A History of Women in the Coast Guard," www.uscg.mil.

Time. "Catholics v. WAACs." June 15, 1942.

Time. "Manpower: Fade-out of the Women." September 4, 1944.

Time. January 5, 1942; August 30, 1943.

Time. "Skirted." March 13, 1944.

Time. "Women—Miss Mac." March 12, 1945.

Tomihiro, Chiye. Quoted in John Tateishi, ed. *And Justice for All: An Oral History of the Japanese American Detention Camps.* Seattle: University of Washington Press, 1984.

Treadwell, Mattie E. *United States Army in World War II. Special Studies: The Women's Army Corps.* Washington, D.C.: U.S. Government Printing Office, 1954.

———. *Women's Army Corps.* Washington, D.C.: U.S. Government Printing Office, 1953.

Tucker, Sherrie. *Swing Shift: "All Girl" Bands of the 1940s.* Durham: Duke University Press, 2000.

Uchida, Yoshiko. *Desert Exile: The Uprooting of a Japanese American Family.* Seattle: University of Washington Press, 1982.

U.S. Department of Agriculture. "Pitch In and Help!: The Women's Land Army Calls 800,000 Women to the Farm in 1944." Pamphlet. May 1944.

———. "The Women's Land Army Works for Victory." Pamphlet. April 1945.

Valgos, Marie F. "Selling Rosie the Riveter: How Advertisements in Ladies' Home Journal Sold American Women Their Role During World War II." *Berkeley McNair Journal,* no. 2, Summer 1994.

Walker, Nancy A. *Shaping Our Mother's World: American Women's Magazines.* Jackson: University Press of Mississippi, 2000.

Wall, Alexandra J. "Edith Coliver Obituary." *Jewish Bulletin of Northern California,* January 4, 2002.

War Department General Staff Organization and Training Division. Memo to Organization-Mobilization Branch, May 11, 1943. George C. Marshall Research Library. Lexington, Va., National Archives Xerox 2782.

Warner, Michael. "The Office of Strategic Services: America's First Intelligence Agency." Central Intelligence Agency History Staff in the Center for the Study of Intelligence, 2000.

Warren, Doug. *Betty Grable: The Reluctant Movie Queen.* New York: St. Martin's Press, 1981.

Watson, Jerilyn. "Women Spies." *This Is America.* Voice of America Special English Program script, www.manythings.org/voa/02/020624ta_t.htm. June 24, 2002.

Weatherford, Doris. *American Women and World War II*. New York: Facts on File, Inc., 1990.

Westbrook, Robert B. " 'I Want a Girl, Just Like the Girl That Married Harry James': American Women and the Problems of Political Obligation in World War II." *American Quarterly* 42 (December 1990).

White, M. G., Memo to Assistant Chief of Staff, G-3, War Department, June 3, 1943. George C. Marshall Research Library. Lexington, Va., National Archives Xerox 2782.

Williams, Rudi. "WIMSA Honors Clandestine Women: Untold Stories of Women in Espionage." American Forces Press Service, May 2, 2001.

Wilson, Jane S. "Not Quite Eden." In *Standing By and Making Do: Women of Wartime Los Alamos*. The Los Alamos Historical Society, 1997.

Wilson, Jane S., and Charlotte Serber, eds. *Standing By and Making Do: Women of Wartime Los Alamos*. Los Alamos, N.M.: The Los Alamos Historical Society, 1997.

Wise, Nancy Baker, and Christy Wise. *A Mouthful of Rivets: Women at Work in World War II*. San Francisco: Jossey-Bass Publishers, 1994.

Women Come to the Front: Journalists, Photographers, and Broadcasters During World War II. Library of Congress Exhibit. www.loc.gov/exhibits/wcf.

Women in Military Service for America. www.womensmemorial.org.

Women's Bureau, U.S. Department of Labor. "Negro Women War Workers." *Bulletin*, no. 205 (Washington, D.C., 1945).

Wood, Tim. "Chatham, the SPARs, and Loran: All-Female Unit Played Historic Role in World War II." *The Cape Cod (Mass.) Chronicle*, July 25, 2002.

www.aagpbl.org/history/History_1.html

www.carnegielibrary.org/locations/pennsylvania/ww2/ww26.html

www.centerforhistory.org/aagpbl.html

www.liberty-ship.com/html/yards/kaiserperm2.html

www.library.csi.cuny.edu/dept/history/lavender/redstone.html

www.rosietheriveter.org/memory.htm

Yates, Ronald E. "Tokyo Rose Prisoner of Name," *Chicago Tribune*, 1991.

Zero Hour Scripts, Trial Record. July-October 1946.

ACKNOWLEDGMENTS

First and foremost, I thank all the women and men who allowed me to interview them at various stages of this book. Each time they let me pry into their lives, I came away with a deep sense of gratitude for their generosity and admiration for their accomplishments and insights: Jean Hay, Akiko Mabuchi Toba, Phillis Rosenthal, Robert Rosenthal, Loretta Ehrlich Kleiner, Marge Routon, Ruth Taylor, Louise Cason, Billie Banks Doan Ballou, Margaret Porter Polsky, Lillian Goodman, Iris Cummings, Bessie Stokes, Barbara Walls, Lois Tretheway, LoRay Tewalt, Lee Foringer, Cuyler Voorhees, Martha Webb, Jean Rothermel, Maurine Longstreth, Ruby Messer Barber, Phyllis Fisher, and Julia Child. Special thanks to Happy and Don Sargol for opening their home to me and introducing me to so many women who worked in war industries.

I also had amazing luck in finding the right people at the right time to assist me with research, administration, and proofreading for this book. Meredith Cain, Emily Richardson, and Jessica Hoback were essential to the writing of this book and were each a pleasure to have in my life. Pamela Casey, Susan Weber, Jenny Tomes, and Sarah Metcalf played pivotal parts in the process at key moments as well. I am very grateful to each of these people, not just for their impeccable work, but for their enthusiasm and encouragement in the whole effort.

For help in locating or obtaining key elements of research and assistance I thank: Marvin Bensman at the University of Memphis, author John Leggett, Dr. Mary Kay Vaughan and Ingo Trauschweizer at the University of Maryland Department of History, Jane Barnwell at the University of Hawaii, Rebecca L. Collier at the National Archives, Dee Garceau, Cynthia Marshall, and Sandi George Tracy at Rhodes College, Fran Carter, the American Rosie the

Riveter Association, and Betty Carter at The University of North Carolina—
Greensboro's Women Veterans Historical Project.

For the chances I got that led to this book I must thank *The New York
Times*. In my time working with the great staff there I am especially indebted
to three people. First, I thank Marty Gottlieb, who has been my mentor and
friend since we first worked together on a story in 1995. Marty has always
been ready with encouragement, humor, advice, and excellent editorial judg-
ment that helped me through the rigors of daily journalism. Next, I am indebted to Dean Baquet, who gave me opportunities beyond compare and
challenged me to do my best work. His insight, perceptiveness, and kindness
are rare and much appreciated by all who work with him. And I am forever
grateful for Kevin Sack. His support and friendship and his considerable talent have been guiding forces for me. I also want to give special thanks to Mary
Tabor for connecting me with the paper at the start.

Also at *The New York Times* I was fortunate to work with many great edi-
tors, reporters, photographers, and staff people, many of whom also became
friends, including Susan Taylor, David Firestone, Rollin and Tam Riggs, Nick
Fox, Barbara Strauch, John Darnton, Paul Haskins, Jeff Sommer, Jerry Gray,
Suzanne DeChillo, Peter Applebome, Peter Kilborn, Sam Howe Verhovek,
David Halbfinger, Susan Crowley, Steve Barnes, Alix Pelletier, B. Drummond
Ayres, Henry Fountain, Bill Schmidt, Katie Roberts, and David Rae Morris.

Many other colleagues have supported me at key points along the way
with opportunities and encouragement, including Jack Doppelt, Janis Don-
naud, Lou Prato, Pat Dean, John Wright, Rick Bragg, Ken Neill, Tim Samp-
son, Dennis Freeland, Jackson Baker, Arian Campos-Flores, Kate Gooch, Russ
Abernathy, and Mistina Bates.

One of the pleasures of writing acknowledgments is being able to con-
sider and thank all the people who have given support and friendship through
the years. In that category I have been rich. In no particular order I thank: Lisa
Zingale Sisson and Darryl, Anna, and Margot Sisson, Karen Jozefowicz,
Junius Harris, David Lebson, Anne Cumberland, Ruth and Jerry Dickler,
Mary Deininger, Patrice Eastham, Aleece Hiller and Janet Boyer, Vivienne
Jenkins, John Kinney, Nina and Marshal Zaslove, Marion Siwek and Lou
Angelo, Craig, Linda, and MacKenzie Leake, Nina and Grace Weinstein, Jean
and Dan Rothermel, Tony Horne, Amanda Moss Cowan, Vera Walker,
Michelle Willet and Richard Houghton, Sandy DeRome and Tim Ainger, Lou
Williams, Karina Spero, Tom Junod, Robert Gordon and Tara McAdams,

Barrie Pike, Birney and Beth Imes, Jeff DeMark, Ruth Williams, Jerry and Mary King, Steve and Glinda Watts, Merry, Andy, Allie, and Carolyn Mariano, Robert and Alice Davis, Marsha and Richard Bicks, Nathan, Andrea, Alexandra, and Becky Bicks, Frank, Carol, and Caroline Fourmy, David Lusk and Carissa Hussong, Lee Colquit, Peggy McKnight, Dawn Hayes, Marisa Polesky, Marilou Awiakta, Tammy Piper, Margaret Halle, Laura Prudhomme, Betsy Kelly, Bobby Smith, Robert Neimeyer, Kim Meeks, John Zacharias, Mary Horowitz, Val Russell, Melanie Pyron, Pam Parker and Andy Branham, Laura Marsh, Margaret Metz and Bill Stegall, Linda Raiteri, Paula Casey, Janann Sherman, Leanne Kleinmann, Jean and Lackey Rowe, Dick and Marge Routon, Joyce Morrison, Karen Shea, Linda Ross, Betsy Black, David Leonard, the Couch Family, Claudette Payne, Jocelyn Wurzburg and Bobby Bostick, Ben and Frances Hooks, Deborah Clubb, John Beifuss, Lucille Ewing, Karen Lebovitz, Carol DeForest, Peggy Turley, Leigh Ann Ballard, Bill Thomas and Edith Caywood, Jimmy Crosswaith, Peggy and Chuck Branch, Ann and Jim Utterback, Phillip Blaine, Tina Barr, Jacque Patterson, Michael and Libby Dacaetani, Carol Jernigan, Beth Dooley, Andy and Allison Cates, Martin Lane, Steve Cantor, Sean Bloemer, Rosalyn Willis, Devin Kyles, Peyton Prospere, David, Angela, and Emma Less, Babs and Jef Feibelman, Amy Burcham, Katherine Coleman, Lowry Whitehorn, Polly Cooper, Jean and Jed Dreifus, Maxine Smith, Billy and Arelia Kyles, Scott Graves, Anna Catherine Ball, Duke and Clara Waddell, Martha Hunt Huie, Dana Sachs, Lynne Sachs, Kathy Steuer, Laura Goodman and Mark Bryan, Henry and Rosemary Nelson, Deannie Parker, Corey and Cheryl Messler, Christina Welford Scott, Lou Hoyt, Tedra Smothers, Eric Bran, Susan Murrmann, Ellen and Jon Hornyak, Jenny Munn, James Starks, Simon Hanley, Elizabeth and Charles Jetton, Mary Garrison, Shellie Gravitt, Sarah and Brian Toba, Drew and Mike Stevenson, Mary and Tom Beckner, and all the gang at Otherlands.

I was fortunate to have a wealth of particularly supportive friends around me when I lost my father and my closest friend just after I got the contract to write this book. I could not have made it through without: Kim Shaw Brisco, Rebecca Hanks, Annabel Conrad and Iddo, Theo, Dinah, and Jesse Patt, Jenny, Keith, Sydney, Sadie, and Summer Tomes, Sharon Bicks, Ben Wilson, Anna, Shawn, Connie, Maya, and Riley Kelly, Bill, Susan, Erin, and Joey Remijan, Gini and Tim Mitchell, Roy and Pam Haithcock, Susan and David Weber, Elisa Blatteis, Matt and Lily Roberts, Margaret Woodhull and David Hildebrand, Judy Haas and Gordon Bigelow, Trisha Clark and Jeff Lord, Tom

Graves, Ellen and Brig Klyce, Cookie Ewing and John Sanford, Amanda Moss Cowan, and Tony Horne.

I am also grateful for the loving support of the Kelly and Watts families, for so graciously welcoming me into their circles of kindness. I thank: Jennifer Watts Hoff, my faithful friend, and her husband, Jeramie Hoff, for putting up with our long phone calls, Janie Spataro for e-mails, phone calls, read throughs and letting me whine as only a true friend can do, Gail and Dean Watts, Tripp Watts, Heather Watts, Dot Lingerfelt, Emily Card, Judy Watts, Graham Kelly, Arabella Kelly, Paulette and Carl Kelly, Sissy and David Taylor, and Jeanette and Andy Mayo. And special thanks to Shawn Kelly for a friendship that endures all.

And then there is my own family. I am forever grateful to my parents, David Gilmer Yellin and Carol Lynn Gilmer Yellin. And many thanks are due to my dear brothers: Doug Yellin, Tom Yellin, and Chuck Yellin. They are a buffer against the hard stuff and a joy in all the fun stuff of life.

Also I thank the world for my nephew Peyto Yellin and my nieces Chloe L. Yellin and Isabel L. Yellin. I have known them each since they started life, and have grown to love them and marvel at them more and more as they become such wonderful teenagers and adults. And I am thankful for the joy brought by my newest nieces, Lara Yellin and Nicole Yellin, and for their mother, my friend and sister-in-law Shari Finkelstein. I am also grateful for Jean MacDonald, who has made my brother Doug so happy. And my longtime sister-in-law and friend Linda Yellin has been a rock in my life forever.

To my extended family also go great thanks: Tom Gilmer, Richard Evans, Brad and Mariam Gilmer, Dwight and Laurie Evans, Dick, Joan, Louan, Kathy Jo, Roger and Richard Brown Steve Kleiner, Charlotte and Jack Samuels, Jack Yellin, Joye and Stuart Sabel, Carol Berman, Arthur Yellin, Gail Feldman, Fred Lupowitz, Arnold Lupowitz, my grandmother Eulala Rogers Gilmer, my grandfather Thomas Prather Gilmer and my dear aunt, Nina Emily Evans.

At Free Press I want to thank my editor, Elizabeth Stein. She is an expert at what she does, and she does it with such finesse and good cheer that it is a pleasure to work with her through all the pressures of producing a book. I am grateful that the publishing fates brought us together. I am also indebted to Stephen Morrow, who brought me into the publishing world by acquiring this book. For treating me so well, I thank Martha Levin and Dominick Anfuso. For their invaluable assistance I also thank Maris Kreizman, Stephanie

Fairyington, Carisa Hays, Cassie Dendurent, Jennifer Weidman, Leslie Jones, Edith Lewis, and Fred Chase.

Finally, I thank my agent, Jennifer Gates, without whom this book would not exist. Every step of the way, she has been there doing more than I would ever expect her to do and supporting and encouraging me through thick and thin. I am not sure what I did to deserve her, but I will always be grateful that I have her in my corner. I am also indebted to all her colleagues at the Zachary Shuster Harmsworth agency for their belief in this book and support of my career.

And more special thanks to a few other dear friends and family: Marnie Yellin, Lucas Yellin, Hazel Motes, O. V. Bicks, Henry Wilson, Lizzie Williams, Sam Watts, Jake Mariano, Tillie Sisson, Gideon Weber, and most especially, my canine muse, and most constant ally, Sophia Louise Yellin.

INDEX

ABOUT THE AUTHOR

EMILY YELLIN is a longtime contributor to *The New York Times*. Her work has also appeared in *Newsweek* and other publications. She currently lives in Memphis, Tennessee.